COLLECTED PLAYS
Volume Two

Brian Friel

COLLECTED PLAYS

Volume Two

Edited by Peter Fallon

FABER & FABER

Gallery Books

Collected Plays: Volume Two
is first published in paperback and in a clothbound edition
by The Gallery Press and in paperback by Faber and Faber Limited
in 2016. Originated at The Gallery Press.

The Gallery Press
Loughcrew
Oldcastle
County Meath
Ireland

Faber and Faber Limited
Bloomsbury House,
74-77 Great Russell Street,
London, WC1B 3DA
England

ISBN 978 1 85235 672 9 *paperback*
     978 1 85235 673 6 *clothbound*

A CIP catalogue record for this book
is available from the British Library.

Collected Plays: Volume Two receives financial assistance
from the Arts Councils of Ireland.

Contents

THE FREEDOM
OF THE CITY

Characters

PRESS PHOTOGRAPHER
PRIEST
THREE SOLDIERS
JUDGE
POLICE CONSTABLE
DR DODDS, sociologist
MICHAEL
LILY
SKINNER (Adrian Casimir Fitzgerald)
BALLADEER AND FRIENDS
BRIGADIER JOHNSON-HANSBURY
ARMY PRESS OFFICER
DR WINBOURNE, forensic expert
PROFESSOR CUPPLEY, pathologist
LIAM O'KELLY, RTÉ commentator
ACCORDIONIST

MICHAEL is twenty-two. Strong, regular features but not handsome.

SKINNER is twenty-one. Very lean, very tense, very restless. He is described as 'glib' but the adjective is less than just. A quick volatile mind driving a lean body.

LILY is forty-three. She has eleven children and her body has long since settled into its own comfortable contours. But poverty and child-bearing have not completely obliterated the traces of early prettiness.

Time and place

1970. Derry City, Ireland.

Set

The Mayor's parlour takes up almost the entire stage, with the exception of the apron and a small area stage left (left and right throughout are from the point of view of the audience).

The parlour is on the first floor of a neo-gothic building. One arched doorway upstage leads to a dressing room off. Another arched doorway left opens on to a corridor. A stained-glass window right looks out on Guildhall Square.

The doors and walls of the parlour are oak-panelled, and at ceiling height the walls are embattled. The furnishings are solid and dated, the atmosphere heavy and staid. A large conference table with a leather-covered top. A glass display cabinet. An old-fashioned radiogram on top of which sits a vase of artificial flowers. On one side of the door leading into the dressing room stands a Union Jack flag. On the other side a large portrait of a forgotten civic dignitary. A grand baroque chair for the Mayor; several upright carved chairs for his guests.

The Freedom of the City was first produced at the Abbey Theatre, Dublin, on 20 February 1973, with the following cast:

PRIEST	Ronnie Walsh
SOLDIERS	Niall O'Brien
	Dermot Crowley
	Colm Meaney
JUDGE	John Kavanagh
POLICE CONSTABLE	Geoffrey Golden
DR DODDS	Pat Laffan
MICHAEL	Raymond Hardie
LILY	Angela Newman
SKINNER	Eamon Morrissey
BALLADEER	Micheal O hAonghusa
BRIGADIER JOHNSON-HANSBURY	Clive Geraghty
ARMY PRESS OFFICER	Emmet Bergin
DR WINBOURNE	Edward Golden
PROFESSOR CUPPLEY	Derek Young
RTE COMMENTATOR	Bob Carlile
ACCORDIONIST	Dinny O'Brien

Directed by	Tomás Mac Anna
Set and costumes designed by	Alan Barlow

The Freedom of the City was concurrently produced at the Royal Court Theatre, London, on 27 February 1973, with the following cast:

PRIEST	Peter Adair
SOLDIERS	Nick Llewellyn
	David Atkinson
JUDGE	Basil Dignam
JUDGE'S CLERK	Anthony Nash
COURT USHER	Catherine Harding
DR DODDS	Bob Sherman
MICHAEL	Raymond Campbell
LILY	Carmel McSharry
SKINNER	Stephen Rea
BALLADEER	Michael O'Hagan
BRIGADIER JOHNSON-HANSBURY	Louis Haslar
DR WINBOURNE	Alex McCrindle
PROFESSOR CUPPLEY	Matthew Guinness
RTE COMMENTATOR	George Shane

Directed by	Albert Finney
Set designed by	Douglas Heap
Costumes by	Harriet Geddes

for Dan Herr

ACT ONE

The stage is in darkness except for the apron which is lit in cold blue.
Three bodies lie grotesquely across the front of the stage — SKINNER
on the left, LILY *in the middle,* MICHAEL *on the right. After a silence*
has been established we hear in the very far distance the wail of an
ambulance siren.

A PHOTOGRAPHER, *crouching for fear of being shot, runs on from*
the right and very hastily and very nervously photographs the corpses,
taking three or four pictures of each. His flashbulb eerily lights up the
stage each time. When he gets the length of SKINNER *a* PRIEST *enters*
right, crouching like the PHOTOGRAPHER *and holding a white hand-*
kerchief above his head. He gets down on his knees beside MICHAEL,
hastily blesses him and mumbles prayers into his ear. He then moves
on to LILY *and to* SKINNER *and goes through the same ritual with each.*

While the PRIEST *crouches beside* MICHAEL *a spot picks out the*
JUDGE *high up on the battlements. And at the same moment a* POLICE-
MAN *in dark glasses enters from the left, removes his cap and faces the*
JUDGE. *The* POLICEMAN *reads from his notebook; the* JUDGE *takes notes.*
The JUDGE *is English, in his early sixties; a quick, fussy man with a*
testy manner.

POLICEMAN Hegarty, my lord.
    JUDGE Speak up, Constable, please.
POLICEMAN Hegarty, my lord.
    JUDGE Yes.
POLICEMAN Michael Joseph. Unmarried. Unemployed. Lived
            with his parents.
    JUDGE Age?
POLICEMAN Twenty-two years, my lord.
    JUDGE Was the deceased known to you personally, Con-
            stable B?
POLICEMAN No, my lord.
    JUDGE And when you arrived at the body did you discover

15

	any firearms on his person or adjacent to his person?
POLICEMAN	I wasn't the first to get there, my lord.
JUDGE	Would you answer my question?
POLICEMAN	I personally saw no arms, my lord.
JUDGE	Thank you.

> *Three* SOLDIERS *in full combat uniform run on from right. Two of them grab* MICHAEL *by the feet and drag him off right, while a third, tense and scared, covers them with his rifle. The* PHOTOGRAPHER *runs off left. The* PRIEST *moves to* LILY.

POLICEMAN	Doherty. Elizabeth. Married. Aged forty-three years.
JUDGE	Occupation?
POLICEMAN	Housewife. Also a cleaning woman. Deceased lived with her family in a condemned property behind the old railway — a warehouse that was converted into eight flats and . . .
JUDGE	We are not conducting a social survey, Constable. Was the deceased known to you?
POLICEMAN	No, my lord.
JUDGE	And did you discover any firearms on her person or adjacent to her person?
POLICEMAN	I wasn't the first on the scene, my lord.
JUDGE	I am aware of that, Constable.
POLICEMAN	I saw no weapons, my lord.

> *The* PRIEST *moves on to* SKINNER. *The three* SOLDIERS *return and drag* LILY *off.*

	Fitzgerald. Adrian Casimir.
JUDGE	Pardon?
POLICEMAN	Fitzgerald . . .
JUDGE	I've got that.
POLICEMAN	Adrian Casimir.
JUDGE	Yes.
POLICEMAN	Aged twenty-one. Single. No fixed address.
JUDGE	You mean he wasn't native to the city?
POLICEMAN	He was, my lord. But he moved about a lot. And we

haven't been able to trace any relatives.

JUDGE   Had the deceased a profession or a trade?

POLICEMAN   No, my lord.

JUDGE   Was he bearing any firearms — when you got to him?

POLICEMAN   Not when I got to him, my lord.

JUDGE   And was he known to you personally, Constable B?

POLICEMAN   Yes, my lord.

JUDGE   As a terrorist?

POLICEMAN   He had been in trouble many times, my lord. Petty larceny, disorderly behaviour — that sort of thing.

JUDGE   I see. Thank you, Constable.

> *The* PRIEST *goes off left. The* POLICEMAN *follows him. The three* SOLDIERS *enter right and drag* SKINNER *away as before. A ceremonial hat (the Mayor's) is lying beside* SKINNER's *body. One of the* SOLDIERS *takes it off with him.*

I should explain that I have permitted soldiers and policemen to give evidence under pseudonym so that they may not expose themselves to the danger of reprisal. And before we adjourn for lunch may I repeat once more and make abundantly clear once more my words of the first day: that this tribunal of inquiry, appointed by Her Majesty's Government, is in no sense a court of justice. Our only function is to form an objective view of the events which occurred in the City of Londonderry, Northern Ireland, on the 10th day of February 1970 when, after a civil rights meeting, British troops opened fire and three civilians lost their lives. It is essentially a fact-finding exercise; and our concern and our only concern is with that period of time when these three people came together, seized possession of a civic building, and openly defied the security forces. The facts we garner over the coming days may indicate that the deceased were callous terrorists who had planned to seize the Guildhall weeks before the events of February 10th; or the facts may indicate that the misguided scheme occurred to them on that very day while they listened to revolutionary speeches. But whatever conclusion may seem to emerge it must be understood that it is none of our function to make moral judgements, and I would ask the media to bear this in mind. We will resume at 2.30.

He leaves. Light up the full set. Offstage: a civil rights meeting is being held in Guildhall Square and is being addressed by a WOMAN. *The amplification is faulty and we cannot hear what she is saying; but the speech sounds fiery and is punctuated by clapping and cheering. While the meeting is going on offstage* DR DODDS, *an elderly American professor with an informal manner, enters left and addresses the audience.*

DODDS Good evening. My name is Philip Alexander Dodds. I'm a sociologist and my field of study is inherited poverty or the culture of poverty or more accurately the subculture of poverty. And since I'll be using these terms off and on let me explain what I mean by them. I'm talking about those people who are at the very bottom of the socio-economic scale and more specifically about their distinctive way of life — a way of life which is common to ghetto or slum communities all over the Western world and which is transmitted from generation to generation. And the first thing to be said about this culture or way of life is that it has two aspects: it is the way the poor adapt to their marginal position in a society which is capitalistic, stratified into classes, and highly individuated; and it is also their method of reacting against that society. In other words it is the method they have devised to cope with the hopelessness and despair they experience because they know they'll never be successful in terms of the values and goals of the dominant society. And once it comes into existence — this way of life, this culture — it is handed down from parents to children and to their children, and thus its perpetuation is ensured. Because by the time children are six or seven they have usually taken on the basic values and attitudes of their subculture and aren't psychologically geared to take advantage of changing conditions or increased opportunities that may occur in their lifetime.

Suddenly all sounds are drowned by the roar of approaching tanks. Their noise is deafening and fills the whole auditorium. Then stop. Silence for five seconds. Then the WOMAN *who is addressing the meeting:*

WOMAN Stand your ground! Don't move! Don't panic! This is your city! This is your city!

Her voice is drowned by shooting — rubber bullets and CS gas — and immediate pandemonium in the crowd. Panic. Screaming. Shouting. The revving of engines as tanks and water cannon pursue fleeing groups. More rubber bullets and the quick plop of exploding gas canisters. Very slowly the noise fades to background. As it does DODDS *resumes as calmly as before.*

DODDS People with a culture of poverty are provincial and locally orientated and have very little sense of history. They know only their own troubles, their own neighbourhood, their own local conditions, their own way of life; but they don't have the knowledge or the vision or the ideology to see that their problems are also the problems of the poor in the ghettos of New York and London and Paris and Dublin — in fact all over the Western world. To give you some examples: they share a critical attitude to many of the values and institutions of the dominant class;

they share a suspicion of government, a detestation of the police, and very often a cynicism to the church. But the very moment they acquire an objective view of their condition, once they become aware that their condition has counterparts elsewhere, from that moment they have broken out of their subculture, even though they may still be desperately poor. And any movement — trade union, religious, civil rights, pacifist, revolutionary — any movement which gives them this objectivity, organizes them, gives them real hope, promotes solidarity, such a movement inevitably smashes the rigid caste that encases their minds and bodies.

> DODDS *goes off left. As he leaves, a quick succession of shots — and* MICHAEL *staggers onstage right. He has been blinded by CS gas, can scarcely breathe, and is retching. Before he gets to the centre of the stage he collapses on his hands and knees and his forehead rests on the ground. Just as he drops* LILY *enters right. She, too, is affected by gas, but not as badly as* MICHAEL. *She holds a handkerchief up to her streaming eyes and her free hand is extended in front of her as if she were blind. She, too, is gasping for breath. She bumps into* MICHAEL *on the ground and without a word staggers past him.* SKINNER *races on from right. He has been caught by a water cannon — the upper half of his body is soaked. He is looking about frantically for somewhere to hide. He races past* MICHAEL, *then past* LILY, *and runs upstage. He discovers the door into the parlour and flings it open. He glances inside and then calls to* LILY.

SKINNER Hi! Missus! There's a place up here!
LILY Where?
SKINNER Up here! Come on! Quick! Quick!
LILY Give me a hand, young fella. You'll have to lead me.

He runs down to her, grabs her arm, and drags her roughly upstage.

SKINNER Come on — come on — come on! Move, will you! Move!

LILY No need to pull the arm off me.

SKINNER Did you get a dose of the CS gas?

LILY D'you think I'm playing blind-man's-bluff? God, you're a rough young fella, too.

SKINNER In here. Quick. Watch the step.

LILY My good coat! Mother of God, will you watch my good coat!

SKINNER I should have left you to the soldiers.

LILY They'd be no thicker nor you.

SKINNER D'you want to go back to them, then?

LILY Don't be so damned smart.

SKINNER There's a chair behind you.

LILY I can manage myself.

She drops into a chair and covers her face with both hands.

Oh my God, that's sore on the eyes. There's someone else back there.

SKINNER Where?

LILY Just outside.

SKINNER *rushes out of the room.*

Where's this, young fella? Whose house is this?

SKINNER *finds* MICHAEL *on his hands and knees and gets down beside him.*

SKINNER Come on! Get up! They're going wild out there! (MICHAEL *groans*) Are you hurt? Did you get a rubber bullet?

MICHAEL Gas.

SKINNER You're OK. Come on. You can't lie here. Can you

walk?

MICHAEL Leave me.

> *Sudden burst of rubber bullets, followed by screaming and the revving of armoured vehicles.* SKINNER *lies flat on his face until the burst is over. Then he suddenly grabs* MICHAEL *by the back of his jacket and drags him, face down and limp, up to the door and into the parlour. He drops him in the middle of the room, runs back to the door and locks it. As they enter* LILY *uncovers her eyes momentarily.*

LILY I just thought it was a young fella. Is he hurted bad?

> *After locking the door* SKINNER *moves around the room, examining it with quick, lithe efficiency.*

SKINNER No.

LILY (*To* MICHAEL) Did you get a thump of a baton, young fella?

SKINNER Gas.

LILY Maybe he got a rubber bullet in the stomach.

SKINNER Only gas.

LILY He might be bleeding internal.

SKINNER Gas! Are you deaf?

LILY I like to see the blood. As long as you can see the blood there's always hope.

SKINNER He'll come round.

LILY I seen a polisman split a young fella with a baton one Saturday evening on Shipquay Street. His head opened like an orange and the blood spurted straight up — you know like them pictures you see of whales, only it was red. And at twelve Mass the next day who was sitting on the seat in front of me but your man, fresh as a bap, and the neatest wee plaster from here to here, and him as proud of his-self.

> MICHAEL *gets himself into a sitting position on the floor.*

MICHAEL Aaaaagh.

LILY Are you all right, young fella?

MICHAEL I think so.

LILY (*To* SKINNER) I was afeard by the way he was twisting the kidneys was lacerated.

MICHAEL That's desperate stuff.

LILY It's a help if you cross your legs and breathe shalla.

MICHAEL God — that's awful.

LILY Did you walk into it or what?

MICHAEL A canister burst right at my feet.

LILY You should have threw your jacket over it. They come on us very sudden, didn't they?

MICHAEL I don't know what happened.

LILY What got into them anyway?

SKINNER Did no one tell you the march was banned?

LILY I knew the march was banned.

SKINNER Did you expect them to give you tea at the end of it?

LILY I didn't expect them to drive their tanks through us and shoot gas and rubber bullets into us, young fella. It's a mercy to God if no one's hurted. (*To* MICHAEL) Where were you standing?

MICHAEL Beside the platform. Just below the speakers.

LILY I was at the back of the crowd, beside wee Johnny Duffy — you know — the window cleaner — Johnny the Tumbler — and I'm telling him what the speakers is saying 'cause he hears hardly anything now since he fell off the ladder the last time. And I'm just after telling him, 'The streets is ours and nobody's going to move us,' when I turn round and Jesus, Mary and Joseph there's this big Saracen right behind me. Of course I took to my heels. And when I look back there's Johnny the Tumbler standing there with his fists in the air and him shouting, 'The streets is ours and nobody's going to move us!' And you could hardly see him below the Saracen. Lord, the chairman'll enjoy that.

MICHAEL *gets to his feet and sits on the chair.*

Are you better?
MICHAEL I'm all right.
  LILY Maybe you concussed yourself when you fell. If
       you feel yourself getting drowsy, shout 'Help! Help!'
MICHAEL I'm fine.
  LILY D'you know what they say? That that CS gas is a
       sure cure for stuttering. Would you believe that,
       young fella? That's why Celia Cunningham across
       from us drags her wee Colm Damien into the thick
       of every riot from here to Strabane and him not
       seven till next May.

       MICHAEL *coughs again. She offers him a handker-
       chief.*

       Here.
MICHAEL Thanks.
  LILY Cough hard.
MICHAEL I'm fine.
  LILY If you don't get it up it seeps down through the
       lungs and into the corpuscles.
MICHAEL I'm over the worst of it.
  LILY Every civil rights march Minnie McLaughlin goes on
       — she's the floor above me — she wears a miracu-
       lous medal pinned on her vest. Swears to God it's
       better nor a gas mask.

       MICHAEL *chokes again, almost retches.*

       Good on you, young fella. Keep it rising. Anyways,
       last Wednesday week Minnie got hit on the leg with
       a rubber bullet and now she pretends she has a limp
       and the young fellas call her Che Guevara. If God
       hasn't said it she'll be looking for a pension from
       the Dublin crowd.

       SKINNER's *inspection is now complete — and he
       realizes where he is. He bursts into sudden laughter
       — a mixture of delight and excitement and malice.*

SKINNER Haaaaaaaah!

> *Still laughing, he races right around the room,*
> *pounds on the door with his fists, runs downstage*
> *and does a somersault across the table.*

LILY Jesus, Mary and Joseph!
SKINNER Haaaaaaaah!
LILY The young fella's a patent lunatic!
SKINNER Haaaaaaaah!
LILY Keep away from me, young fella!

> SKINNER *stops suddenly beside her and puts his*
> *face up to hers.*

SKINNER Do you know where you are, Missus?
LILY Just you lay one finger on me!
SKINNER Do you know where you're sitting?
LILY I'm warning you!
SKINNER Look around — look around — look around. (*To*
MICHAEL) Where are you? Where do you find your-
self this Saturday afternoon? (*To both*) Guess — come
on — guess — guess — guess. Ten-to-one you'll
never hit it. Fifty-to-one. A hundred-to-one.
MICHAEL Where?
SKINNER Where, Missus, where?
LILY How would I know?
SKINNER I'll tell you where you are.
LILY Where?
SKINNER You — are — inside — the Guildhall.
LILY We are not!
SKINNER In fact you're in the Mayor's parlour.
LILY You're a liar!
SKINNER The holy of holies itself!
LILY Have a bit of sense, young fella. What would we be
doing in — ?
SKINNER Look around! Look around!
MICHAEL How did we get in?
SKINNER By the side door.

MICHAEL It's always guarded.

SKINNER The soldiers must have moved into the Square to break up the meeting. (*To* LILY) When the trouble started you must have run down Guildhall Street.

LILY How would I know where I run. I followed the crowd.

SKINNER (*To* MICHAEL) You did the same.

MICHAEL After the canister burst I don't know what happened.

LILY So we just walked in?

SKINNER By the side door and along the corridor and in here. Into the private parlour of His Worship, the Lord Mayor of Derry. (*He flings a cushion at the wall*) Yipeeeeeeee!

> LILY *stands up. As does* MICHAEL. *They stare in awe at their surroundings. As they gaze a* SOLDIER *crouches at the very edge of stage right and speaks into his portable radio. His message is received by a* SOLDIER *at the very edge of stage left.*

SOLDIER 1 Blue Star to Eagle. Blue Star to Eagle.

SOLDIER 2 Eagle receiving. Come in, Blue Star.

SOLDIER 1 The fucking yobbos are inside the fucking Guildhall!

SOLDIER 2 Jesus!

SOLDIER 1 What the fuck am I supposed to do?

SOLDIER 2 How did they get in?

SOLDIER 1 On fucking roller skates — how would I know!

SOLDIER 2 How many of them?

SOLDIER 1 No idea. The side door's wide open.

SOLDIER 2 What's your position, Blue Star?

SOLDIER 1 Guildhall Street. At the junction of the quay. What am I to do?

SOLDIER 2 Hold that position.

SOLDIER 1 Fucking great! For how long?

SOLDIER 2 Until you're reinforced.

SOLDIER 1 Thanks, mate!

SOLDIER 2 Do not attempt to enter or engage.

SOLDIER 1 OK.

SOLDIER 2 I'll get back to you in a few minutes.

> *They go off. An RTÉ newsman, LIAM O'KELLY, appears on one of the battlements. Into a microphone:*

O'KELLY I am standing on the walls overlooking Guildhall Square in Derry where only a short time ago a civil rights meeting, estimated at about three thousand strong, was broken up by a large contingent of police and troops. There are no reports of serious casualties but unconfirmed reports are coming in that a group of about fifty armed gunmen have taken possession of the Guildhall here below me and have barricaded themselves in. If the reports are accurate, and if the Guildhall, regarded by the minority as a symbol of Unionist domination, has fallen into the hands of the terrorists, both the security forces and the Stormont government will be acutely embarrassed. Brigadier Johnson Hansbury who was in charge of today's elaborate security operation has, so far, refused to confirm or deny the report. No comment either from the Chief Superintendent of Derry's Royal Ulster Constabulary. But usually reliable spokesmen from the Bogside insist that the story is accurate, and already small groups are gathering at street corners within the ghetto area to celebrate, as one of them put it to me, 'the fall of the Bastille'. This is Liam O'Kelly returning you to our studios in Dublin.

> *As he finishes a man enters left — the BALLADEER. A glass in one hand, a bottle in the other. He is unsteady on his feet but his aggressive jubilance makes him articulate. Dressed in shirt and trousers, the shirt dirty and hanging over the trousers. As he swaggers across the stage he is followed by an ACCORDIONIST and a group of dancing CHILDREN. He sings, to the air of 'John Brown's Body'.*

BALLADEER   'A hundred Irish heroes one February day
Took over Derry's Guildhall, beside old Derry's
quay.
They defied the British army, they defied the
RUC.
They showed the crumbling empire what good
Irishmen could be.'

The CHILDREN *join in the chorus.*

CHILDREN   'Three cheers and then three cheers again for
Ireland one and free,
For civil rights and unity, Tone, Pearse and
Connolly.
The Mayor of Derry City is an Irishman once more.
So let's celebrate our victory and let Irish
whiskey pour.'
BALLADEER   'The British army leader was a gentle English lad;
If he beat those dirty Paddys they might make him
a lord.
So he whispered to his Tommies: "Fix them, chaps;
I'll see you right!"
But the lads inside the Guildhall shouted back,
"Come on and fight!"'
TOGETHER   'Three cheers and then three cheers again for
Ireland one and free,
For civil rights and unity, Tone, Pearse and
Connolly.
The Mayor of Derry City is an Irishman once more.
So let's celebrate our victory and let Irish
whiskey pour.'

They go off right. MICHAEL *begins to move around
the parlour, silently, deferentially.* LILY *stands very
still; only her eyes move.* SKINNER *watches her
closely. Pause.*

MICHAEL   Christ Almighty — the Mayor's parlour!

Silence.

I was here once before. I don't mean in here — in
his public office — the one down the corridor. Three
years ago — that bad winter — they were taking on
extra men to clear away the snow, and my father
said maybe if I went straight to the top and asked
himself . . . That public office, it's nice enough. But
my God this . . .

Silence.

LILY We shouldn't be here.
MICHAEL God, it's very impressive.
LILY No place for us.
MICHAEL God, it's beautiful, isn't it?
SKINNER (*To* LILY) Isn't it beautiful?

> LILY *still has not moved. She points.*

LILY What's that?
SKINNER Record player and radio.
LILY And that?
SKINNER Cocktail cabinet. What'll you have, Missus?
LILY What's in that yoke?

> SKINNER *tries to open the top of the display cabinet.*

SKINNER Locked. But we'll soon fix that.

> *He produces a penknife and deftly forces the lock.*

MICHAEL Feel the walls. And the door handles. Real oak. And
brass. The very best of stuff.

> SKINNER *takes out a ceremonial sword and an
> ancient musket, each with a descriptive label
> attached.*

SKINNER This is a 'Fourteenth-century ceremonial sword with jewelled handle and silver tip'. How are you off for swords, Missus?

MICHAEL Feel the carpet. Like a mattress.

SKINNER And this is a 'Musket used by Williamite garrison besieged by Jacobite army. 1691'.

LILY Who's that?

SKINNER (*Reads*) Sir Joshua Hetherington MBE, VMH, SHIT. Is he a mate of yours?

LILY I was thinking it wasn't the Sacred Heart.

> MICHAEL *reverently examines the desk set on the table.*

MICHAEL Feel the weight of that — pure silver. And look — look — real leather — run your hand over it (*desk top*).

SKINNER We'll have to sign the Distinguished Visitors' Book, Missus. Are you distinguished?

LILY What's in there?

> MICHAEL *opens the dressing-room door and looks in.*

MICHAEL Wardrobes — toilet — wash-hand basin — shower. Pink and black tiles all round. And the taps are gold and made like fishes' heads. (*Closes door*) God, it's very impressive. Isn't it impressive, Missus?

SKINNER Isn't it, Missus?

LILY It's all right.

SKINNER Two pounds deposit against breakages and it's yours for ten bob a week. Or maybe you don't like the locality, Missus?

LILY Mrs Doherty's the name, young fella, Mrs Lily Doherty.

SKINNER Are you not impressed, Lily?

> MICHAEL *reads the inscription below the stained-glass window.*

MICHAEL 'Presented to the citizens of Londonderry by the Hon. The Irish Society to commemorate the visit of King Edward VII. July 1903.'

SKINNER That's our window, Lily. How would it look in your parlour?

MICHAEL I read about the Hon. The Irish Society. They're big London businessmen and big bankers and they own most of the ground in the city.

LILY This room's bigger than my whole place.

SKINNER Have you no gold taps and tiled walls?

LILY There's one tap and one toilet below in the yard — and they're for eight families.

SKINNER By God, you'll sign no Distinguished Visitors' Book, Lily.

LILY And I'll tell you something, glib boy: if this place was mine I'd soon cover them ugly bare boards (*oak walls*) with nice pink gloss paint that you could wash the dirt off, and I'd put decent glass you could see through into them gloomy windows, and I'd shift Joe Stalin there (*Sir Joshua*), and I'd put a nice flight of them brass ducks up along that wall.

SKINNER *and* MICHAEL *both laugh.*

SKINNER You're a woman of taste, Lily Doherty.

LILY And since this is my first time here and since you (SKINNER) seem to be the caretaker, the least you might do is offer a drink to a ratepayer.

She sits — taking possession. MICHAEL *laughs.*

MICHAEL The Mayor's parlour — God Almighty!

LILY (*To* MICHAEL) And will you quit creeping about on your toes, young fella, as if you were doing the Stations of the Cross.

MICHAEL I never thought I'd be in here.

LILY Well now you are. Sit down and stop trembling like Gavigan's greyhound.

SKINNER What'll you have, Lily?

LILY What have you got?

SKINNER Whiskey — gin — rum — sherry — brandy — vodka —

MICHAEL Ah now, hold on.

SKINNER What?

MICHAEL Do you think you should?

SKINNER What?

MICHAEL Touch any of that stuff.

SKINNER Why not?

MICHAEL Well, I mean to say, it's not ours and we weren't invited here and —

LILY Lookat, young fella: since it was the British troops driv me off my own streets and deprived me of my sight and vision for a good quarter of an hour, the least the corporation can do is placate me with one wee drink. (*Grandly to* SKINNER) I think I favour a little port wine, young fella, if you insist.

MICHAEL Honest to God, this is mad, really mad — sitting in the Mayor's parlour on a Saturday afternoon — bloody mad!

He giggles.

LILY What do they call you, young fella?

MICHAEL Michael.

LILY Michael what?

MICHAEL Michael Hegarty.

LILY What Hegarty are you?

MICHAEL I'm from the Brandywell.

LILY Jack Hegarty's son?

MICHAEL Tommy. My father used to be in the slaughterhouse — before it closed down.

LILY Are you working?

MICHAEL I was a clerk with a building contractor but he went bust six months ago. And before that I was an assistant storeman in the distillery but then they were taken over. And now my father's trying to get me into the gasworks. My father and the foreman's mates. And in the meantime I'm going to the Tech four nights a week — you know — to improve myself. I'm doing Economics and Business Administration and Computer Science.

LILY You must be smart, young fella.

MICHAEL I don't know about that. But I'm a lot luckier than my father was. And since that North Sea discovery there's a big future in gas. They can't even guess how big the industry's going to grow.

SKINNER But you'll be ready to meet the challenge; wise man. Are *you* smart, Lily?

LILY Me? I never could do nothing right at school except carry round the roll books. And when the inspector would come they used to lock me in the cloakroom with the Mad Mulligans. Lucky for my weans the chairman's got the brains.

SKINNER Mr Hegarty?

MICHAEL What?

SKINNER A drink?

MICHAEL I don't think I should. I think —

SKINNER Suit yourself.

LILY (*To* MICHAEL) Are you a victim?

MICHAEL What?

LILY To the drink.

MICHAEL No, no, no. It's just that there's no one here and it's not ours and —

LILY Will you take one drink and don't be such an aul' woman! (*To* SKINNER) Give him a drink, young fella.

MICHAEL A very small whiskey, then.

LILY Michael's a nice name. I have a Michael. He's seven. Next to Gloria. She's six. And then Timothy — he's three. And then the baby — he's eleven months — Mark Antony. Every one of them sound of mind and limb, thanks be to God. And that includes our Declan — he's nine — though he's not as forward as the others — you know — not much for mixing; a wee bit quiet — you know — nothing more nor shyness and sure he'll soon grow out of that, won't he? They all say Declan's the pet. And praise be to Almighty God, not one of them has the chairman's chest. D'you see his chest, young fella? Ask him to carry the water or the coal up the three flights from the yard and you'd think Hurricane Debbie was coming at you. And give him just wan whiff of the stuff we got the day and before you'd blink he'd be life everlasting.

MICHAEL Five children?

LILY Five? God look to your wit! Eleven, young fella. Eight boys and three girls. And they come like a pattern on wallpaper: two boys, a girl, two boys, a girl, two boys, a girl, two boys. If I had have made the dozen it would have been a wee girl, wouldn't it?

MICHAEL I — I — it —

LILY And I would have called her Jasmine — that's a gorgeous yalla flower — I seen it once in a wreath up in the cemetery the day they buried Andy Boyle's wife. But after Mark Antony the chairman hadn't a puff left in him.

SKINNER *hands round the drinks.*

SKINNER Compliments of the city.

LILY Hi! What happened to you?

SKINNER Me?

LILY Your hair — your shirt — you're soaked!

SKINNER The water cannon got me.

LILY Will you take that off you, young fella, before you die of internal pneumonia.

SKINNER I'm dry now.

LILY Take off that shirt.

SKINNER I'm telling you — I'm dried out.

LILY Come here to me.

SKINNER I'm dry enough.

LILY I said come here!

She unbuttons his shirt and takes it off — he is wearing nothing underneath — and dries his hair with it.

34

'Wet feet or a wet chemise / The sure way to an early demise.' Lord, there's not a pick on him.

SKINNER Leave me alone. I'm OK.

LILY And you've been running about like that for the past half-hour! What way's your shoes? Are them gutties dry?

SKINNER I'm telling you — I'm all right.

LILY Take them off. Take them off.

He takes off the canvas shoes. He is not wearing socks.

Give them to me.

She hangs the shirt across a chair and puts the shoes on their sides.

D'you see our Kevin? He's like him (SKINNER). Eats like a bishop and nothing to show for it. I be affronted when he goes with his class to the swimming pool.

MICHAEL Well. To civil rights.

LILY Good luck, young fella.

SKINNER Good luck.

MICHAEL To another great turnout today.

LILY Great.

MICHAEL Good luck.

A PRIEST in a surplice appears on the battlements. He addresses a congregation in the parlour.

PRIEST At eleven o'clock tomorrow morning Solemn Requiem Mass will be celebrated in this church for the repose of the souls of the three people whose death has plunged this parish into a deep and numbing grief. As you are probably aware I had the privilege of administering the last rites to them and the knowledge that they didn't go unfortified before their Maker is a consolation to all of us. But it is natural that we should mourn. Blessed are they that mourn, says our Divine Lord. But it is also right and fitting that this tragic happening should make us sit back and take stock and ask ourselves the very pertinent question: why did they die?

I believe the answer to that question is this. They died for their beliefs. They died for their fellow citizens. They died because they could endure no longer the injuries and injustices and indignities that have been their lot for too many years. They sacrificed their lives so that you and I and thousands like us might be rid of that iniquitous yoke and might inherit a decent way of life. And if that is not heroic then the word sanctity has no meaning.

No sacrifice is ever in vain. But its value can be diminished if it doesn't fire our imagination, stiffen our resolution, and make us even more determined to see that the dream they dreamed is realized. May we be worthy of that dream, of their trust. May we have the courage to implement their noble hopes. May we have God's strength to carry on where they left off. In the name of the Father, Son, and Holy Spirit.

When the PRIEST *finishes he goes off, and immediately we hear* VOICES *from behind the battlements call to one another in shocked, awed tones.*

VOICE 1 There's at least a dozen dead.
VOICE 2 Where?
VOICE 1 Inside the Guildhall.
VOICE 3 I heard fifteen or sixteen.
VOICE 1 Maybe twenty.
VOICE 3 And a baby in a pram.
VOICE 1 And an old man. They blew his head off.
VOICE 2 Oh my God.
VOICE 3 They just broke the windows and lobbed in hand-grenades.
VOICE 2 Oh my God.
VOICE 1 Blew most of them to smithereens.

VOICE 2 Fuck them anyway! Fuck them! Fuck them! Fuck them!

An ARMY PRESS OFFICER *appears on the battlements and reads a press release to a few reporters (*O'KELLY, *the* PHOTOGRAPHER *of opening sequence, etc) below.*

OFFICER At approximately 15.20 hours today a band of terrorists took possession of a portion of the Guildhall. They gained access during a civil disturbance by forcing a side door in Guildhall Street. It is estimated that up to forty persons are involved. In the disturbance two soldiers were hit by stones and one by a bottle. There are no reports of civilian injuries. The area is now quiet and the security forces have the situation in hand. No further statement will be issued.

The PRESSMEN *ask their questions with great rapidity.*

O'KELLY What portion of the Guildhall is occupied?

OFFICER The entire first floor.

PRESSMAN 1 Is it true that there are women in there, too?

OFFICER Our information is that women are involved.

PRESSMAN 2 Are they armed?

OFFICER Our information is that they have access to arms.

PRESSMAN 2 They brought the arms with them or the arms are in there?

OFFICER We understand that arms are accessible to them.

O'KELLY What troops and equipment have you brought up?

OFFICER I cannot answer that.

PRESSMAN 1 Have you been in touch with them?

OFFICER No.

PRESSMAN 2 Are you going to get in touch with them?

OFFICER Perhaps.

O'KELLY Are you going to negotiate with them or are you going to go in after them?

OFFICER Sorry. That's all I can say.

O'KELLY	When are you going in after them?
PRESSMAN 1	Is it a police or an army operation?
OFFICER	Sorry.
PRESSMAN 2	Why wasn't the Guildhall guarded?
O'KELLY	Who's in charge of ground forces?
PRESSMAN 1	Do you expect a reaction from the Bogside?
OFFICER	Sorry, gentlemen.

He disappears. The PRESSMEN *hurry off.* MICHAEL *gets to his feet.*

MICHAEL	It was a big turnout, wasn't it?
LILY	Terrible big.
MICHAEL	And the speeches were good, too.
LILY	I don't care much for speeches. Isn't that a shocking thing to say? I can't concentrate — you know?
MICHAEL	They'll never learn, you know; never. All they had to do was sit back nice and quiet; let the speeches be made; let the crowd go home. There wouldn't be no trouble of any kind. But they have to bull in. And d'you know what they're doing? As a matter of fact they're doing two things: they're bringing more and more people out on the streets — that's fine; but they're also giving the hooligan element an excuse to retaliate — and that's where the danger lies.
LILY	(*To* SKINNER) It's a hot whiskey you should be drinking.
MICHAEL	I've been on every civil rights march from the very beginning — right from October 5th. And I can tell you there wasn't the thousands then that there was the day. I've even went on civil rights marches that I was far from satisfied about the people that was running them; for as you know as well as me there's a lot of strange characters knuckled in on the act that didn't give a shite about real civil rights — if you'll excuse me, Missus.
LILY	Port wine's gorgeous.
MICHAEL	But as I say to Norah, the main thing is to keep a united front. The ultimate objectives we're all striving

for is more important than the personalities or the politics of the individuals concerned.

SKINNER At this point in time.

MICHAEL What's that?

SKINNER And taking full cognizance of all relative facts.

MICHAEL What d'you mean?

LILY Who's Norah, young fella?

MICHAEL The girl I'm engaged to.

LILY (*To* SKINNER) Ah! He's engaged.

SKINNER *raises his glass.*

Congratulations.

MICHAEL Thanks.

LILY I wish you health, wealth and every happiness, young fella, and may no burden come your way that you're not fit to carry.

MICHAEL Thank you.

LILY When are you getting married?

MICHAEL Easter.

LILY (*To* SKINNER) Easter! I was married at Easter — April 3rd — my seventeenth birthday. And we spent our honeymoon with the chairman's Auntie Maggie and Uncle Ned in Preston, Lancashire, England, and we seen the docks and everything.

MICHAEL We're getting married on Easter Tuesday.

LILY And where will you live?

MICHAEL We'll live with my people till we get a place of our own.

LILY (*To* SKINNER) A place of their own!

SKINNER Leely, the language I speak a leetle too — yes?

LILY Norah's a nice name. If the chairman had have had his way we'd have had a Norah. But I always favoured a Noelle. She's fourteen now. Between Tom and the twins. Born on a roasting August bank holiday Monday at 3.20 in the afternoon but I called her Noelle all the same.

MICHAEL (*To* SKINNER) How many would you say was there today?

SKINNER No idea.
MICHAEL Six thousand? More?

> SKINNER *shrugs indifferently, rises and goes to the window where he looks out.* LILY *takes off her shoes.*

I'm getting pretty accurate at assessing a crowd and my estimate would be between six and six-and-a-half. When the ones at the front were down at the Brandywell the last of them were leaving the Creggan. I could see both ways 'cause I was in the middle. And the hooligan element kept well out of the way. It was a good, disciplined, responsible march. And that's what we must show them — that we're responsible and respectable; and they'll come to respect what we're campaigning for.

LILY D'you see them shoes? Five pounds in Woolworth's and never a day's content since I got them.
MICHAEL Do you go on all the marches, Lily?
LILY Most of them. It's the only exercise I get.
MICHAEL Do you have the feeling they're not as — I don't know — as dignified as they used to be? Like, d'you remember in the early days, they wouldn't let you carry a placard — wouldn't even let you talk, for God's sake. And that was really impressive — all those people marching along in silence, rich and poor, high and low, doctors, accountants, plumbers, teachers, bricklayers — all shoulder to shoulder — knowing that what they wanted was their rights and knowing that because it was their rights nothing in the world was going to stop them getting them.
SKINNER Shite — if you'll excuse me, Missus. Who's for more municipal booze?

> *He refills his own glass and Lily's.*

MICHAEL What do you mean?
LILY That's enough. Easy — easy.
SKINNER It's coming off a fine broad back. Another whiskey,

Mr Hegarty?
MICHAEL Are you for civil rights at all?
SKINNER Course I am. I'm crazy about them. A little drop?
MICHAEL Not for me.
SKINNER Just a nip?
MICHAEL I'm finished.
SKINNER Have a cigar.
MICHAEL No.
SKINNER A cigarette, then.
MICHAEL No.
SKINNER Or what about a shower under the golden fish?

    LILY *gives a great whoop of laughter.*

LILY Haaaaa! A shower! God but you're a comic, young
    fella.

    SKINNER *lights a cigar and carries his glass to the
    phone.*

MICHAEL I see nothing funny in that.
LILY D'you see if it was a Sunday I'd take a shower
    myself. Sunday's my day. We all have our days for
    bathing over at the granny's — that's the chair-
    man's mother. She has us all up on a timetable on
    the kitchen wall and if you miss your night you lose
    your turn.
SKINNER (*Phone*) Hello? Could you tell me what won the
    3.30?
LILY (*To* MICHAEL) D'you see the granny, young fella?
    Seventy-seven years of age. Lives alone. Supple as
    an aul' cat. Her own teeth, her own eyes. And she
    still does twenty houses a week — you know —
    cleaning them down; and me that could be her
    daughter, I can never manage more nor fifteen.

    SKINNER *hangs up.*

SKINNER Bingo Mistress at eights. Which leaves me slightly

ahead of the millionaire bookie.

LILY   I'd know by the look of you.

SKINNER *dials again.* LILY *continues to* MICHAEL.

Most of them she's been doing for years, and they
think the world of her; you know — dentists and
solicitors and doctors and all. Very swanky. And the
weans in them houses — they visit her and all —
they have a sort of pet name on her — they call her
Auntie Dodie. Wouldn't it make you puke? I'll tell
you something, young fella: them class of people's
a very poor judge of character.

SKINNER   (*Phone*) Jackie? Yes, it's me. No, as a matter of fact
I'm stripped to the waist and drinking brandy in the
Mayor's parlour. (*To* LILY *and* MICHAEL) He's killing
himself laughing! (*Into phone*) Look, Jack, would
you put half-a-note on Bunny Rabbit in the 4.30?
Decent man. See you tonight. 'Bye.

LILY   I'm glad you've a nice cushy career.

SKINNER   It's not all sunshine, Lily.

LILY   D'you bet heavy?

SKINNER   When I have it.

LILY   That'll be often. What do they call you, young fella?

SKINNER   Skinner.

LILY   Mr Skinner or Skinner what?

SKINNER   Just Skinner.

LILY   Would you be anything to Paddy Skinner that used
to keep the goats behind the Mormon chapel?

SKINNER   Both my parents died when I was a baby. I was
reared by an aunt. Next question?

LILY   Lord, I'm sorry, son. (*To* MICHAEL) Both his parents!
Shocking. 'Life is not a bed of roses. Sorrow is our
daily lot.' (*Suddenly bright*) But I'll bet you're musical like all the others.

SKINNER   Who?

LILY   Sure it's well known that all wee orphans is always
musical. Orphans can play instruments before they
can talk. There was the poor wee Mulherns opposite

us — the father and mother both submitted to TB within three days of other — and when you'd pass that house at night — the music coming out of it — honest to God, you'd think it was the Palais de Danse. And sure look at the Nazareth House Céilí Band — thumping away at concerts all over the world — trained armies couldn't stop them. Sure the poor nuns can't get quiet to say their prayers.

> SKINNER *turns on the radio.*

SKINNER I can play the radio, Lily.

> *Waltz music on the radio.*

LILY What's that?

SKINNER Four ways — loud and soft and off and on. Can you?

LILY Oh, you're great.

SKINNER And I play the horses and the dogs.

LILY You're brilliant.

SKINNER Thanks.

LILY Are you working?

SKINNER No.

LILY Did you ever work?

SKINNER For a while when I was at grammar school — before they kicked me out.

LILY What did you ever do since?

SKINNER Three years ago I did some potato picking.

LILY (*To* MICHAEL) He has a long memory.

SKINNER And last August I was a conductor on the buses.

LILY But travel didn't agree with you.

SKINNER Listen, Lily — isn't that the BBC Orphans' Orchestra?

LILY I'll tell you something — you never had to study glibness. Oh, nothing sharpens the wits like idleness. (*To* MICHAEL) You stick to your books, son. That's what I say to our boys.

SKINNER I'll bet you the chairman's glib, Lily.

LILY The chairman never worked on account of his health.

SKINNER *sings with the radio and does a parody-waltz off and into the dressing room.*

SKINNER 1-2-3; 1-2-3; 1-2-3; 1-2-3.

LILY (*Calls*) And he has more brains than you and a dozen like you put together! Brat! Put that thing out!

MICHAEL *switches radio off.*

Cheeky young brat, that Skinner! Easy seen he never had no mother to tan his backside.

MICHAEL Was he on the march at all?

LILY Who?

MICHAEL Skinner.

LILY How would I know?

MICHAEL My suspicion is he just turned up for the meeting.

LILY The chairman worked for a full year after we married. In Thompson's foundry. But the fumes destroyed the tissues of his lungs. D'you think he likes sitting at the fire all day reading the weans' comics?

MICHAEL That Skinner's a troublemaker.

LILY But for all he got no education he's a damn sight smarter nor that buck.

MICHAEL That's what I was talking about earlier, Lily. Characters like that need watching.

LILY Who?

MICHAEL Him.

LILY What about him?

MICHAEL I have a feeling about him. I wouldn't be surprised if he was a revolutionary.

LILY What do they call you again, young fella?

MICHAEL Michael.

LILY Michael's a nice name. I have a Michael. He'll be eight next October. You stick to your books, son.

MICHAEL We'll watch him, Lily. I'm uneasy about that fella.

DODDS *enters.*

DODDS   If you are born into the subculture of poverty what
         do you inherit? Well, you inherit an economic condi-
         tion, and you inherit a social and psychological con-
         dition. The economic characteristics include wretched
         housing, a constant struggle for survival, a chronic
         shortage of cash, persistent unemployment and very
         often real hunger or at least malnutrition. And of
         course the economic environment conditions the
         psychological and social man so that he constantly
         feels inferior, marginal, helpless, dependent. Another
         inheritance is his inability to control impulse: he is
         present-time orientated and seldom defers gratifica-
         tion, never plans for the future, and endures his here
         and now with resignation and frustration. The reason
         for this sense of defeat is the existence of a set of
         values in the dominant class which stresses the
         accumulation of wealth and property, the desirability
         of 'improvement' and explains the low economic
         status of the poor as a result of their personal shift-
         lessness and inadequacy.

> *The* JUDGE *appears on the battlements and*
> BRIGADIER JOHNSON-HANSBURY *enters right.*
> DODDS *does not move.*

JUDGE   Brigadier Johnson-Hansbury, you were in charge of
            security on that day.
BRIGADIER   That is correct, my lord.
JUDGE   Could you tell us what strength was at your dis-
            posal?
BRIGADIER   The 8th Infantry Brigade, 1st Battalion Parachute
            Regiment, 1st Battalion King's Own Border Regi-
            ment, two companies of the 3rd Battalion Royal
            Regiment of Fusiliers.
JUDGE   And equipment?
BRIGADIER   Twelve Saracens, ten Saladins, two dozen Ferrets
            and four water cannons, and a modicum of air
            cover.
JUDGE   And the Royal Ulster Constabulary and the Ulster

Defence Regiment?

BRIGADIER They were present, my lord.

JUDGE Under your command?

BRIGADIER As a civilian authority.

JUDGE Under your command?

BRIGADIER Under my command.

JUDGE I'm an old army man myself, Brigadier, and it does seem a rather formidable array to line up against three terrorists, however well armed they could have been.

BRIGADIER At that point we had no idea how many gunmen were inside the Guildhall. Our first reports indicated forty.

JUDGE But those reports were inaccurate.

BRIGADIER They were, my lord. But I would like to point out that we were in an exposed position between the terrorists inside the Guildhall and the no-go Bogside areas at our flank and back.

JUDGE I see. And you, personally, gave the command over the loudhailer to the terrorists inside to surrender?

BRIGADIER I did, my lord. On two occasions.

JUDGE And approximately ten minutes after the second occasion they emerged?

BRIGADIER That is correct.

JUDGE Brigadier, a persistent suggestion keeps cropping up in the various reports about the events of that day and indeed it was voiced strenuously by counsel for the deceased within these very walls, and I would like to have your reaction to it. The suggestion is that no attempt was made to arrest these people as they emerged, but that they were dealt with 'punitively', as it has been phrased, 'to teach the ghettos a lesson'.

BRIGADIER My lord, they emerged firing from the Guildhall. There was no possibility whatever of effecting an arrest operation. And at that point we understood they were the advance group of a much larger force.

JUDGE So you dismiss the suggestion?

BRIGADIER Completely, my lord.

JUDGE And an arrest was not attempted?

BRIGADIER Because it wasn't possible in the circumstances.

JUDGE And had you known, as you learned later, Brigadier, that there were only three terrorists involved, would you have acted differently?

BRIGADIER My orders would have been the same, my lord.

JUDGE Thank you, Brigadier.

> *The* JUDGE *disappears.* BRIGADIER JOHNSON-
> HANSBURY *goes off right.*

DODDS Middle-class people — with deference, people like you and me — we tend to concentrate on the negative aspects of the culture of poverty. We tend to associate negative values to such traits as present-time orientation, and concrete versus abstract orientation. Now, I don't want to idealize or romanticize the culture of poverty; as someone has said, 'It's easier to praise poverty than live in it.' But there are some positive aspects which we cannot overlook completely. Present-orientated living, for example, may sharpen one's attitude for spontaneity and for excitement, for the appreciation of the sensual, for the indulgence of impulse; and these aptitudes are often blunted or muted in people like us who are middle-class and future-orientated. So that to live in the culture of poverty is, in a sense, to live with the reality of the moment — in other words, to practise a sort of existentialism. The result is that people with a culture of poverty suffer much less from repression than we of the middle-class suffer and indeed, if I may make the suggestion with due qualification, they often have a hell of a lot more fun than we have.

> DODDS *goes off left. The dressing-room door is flung open.* SKINNER *is dressed in a splendid mayoral robe and chain and wears an enormous ceremonial hat jauntily on his head. At the door:*

SKINNER 'You're much deceived; in nothing am I changed /
But in my garments!'

He comes into the parlour carrying robes and head-gear for the other two. LILY *gives one of her whoops.*

LILY Oh Jesus, Mary and Joseph!
SKINNER 'Through tattered clothes small vices do appear; /
Robes and furred gowns hide all.'
LILY Mother of God, would you look at him! And the
hat! What's the rig, Skinner?

SKINNER *distributes the gowns.*

SKINNER Mayor's robes, alderman's robes, councillor's robes.
Put them on and I'll give you both the freedom of
the city.
LILY Skinner, you're an eejit!
SKINNER The ceremony begins in five minutes. The world's
press and television are already gathering outside.
'Social upheaval in Derry. Three gutties become
freemen.' Apologies, Mr Hegarty! 'Two gutties.'
What happened to the Orphans' Orchestra?

*He switches on the radio. A military band. They
have to shout to be heard above it.*

MICHAEL Catch yourself on, Skinner.
LILY Lord, the weight of them! They'd cover my settee
just lovely. (*To* MICHAEL) Put it on for the laugh, young
fella.
SKINNER Don the robes, ladies and gentlemen, and taste real
power.

LILY *puts on her robe and headdress.* MICHAEL
reluctantly puts on the robe only. SKINNER *has the
Union Jack in one hand and the ceremonial sword
in the other.*

LILY Lookat-lookat-lookat me, would you! (*She dances all around the parlour*) Di-do-do-da-di-doorda-da. (*Sings*) 'She is the Lily of Laguna; she's my Lily and my — ' Mother of God, if the weans could see me now!

SKINNER Or the chairman.

LILY Ooooops! Lily, this day I confer on you the freedom of the City of Derry. God bless you, my child. And now, Mr Hegarty, I think we'll make you a life peer. Arise Lord Michael — of Gas.

LILY They make you feel great all the same. You feel you could — you could give benediction!

SKINNER Make way — make way for the Lord and Lady Mayor of Derry Colmcille!

LILY My shoes — my shoes! I can't appear without my shoes!

> MICHAEL *takes off his robe and sits down.* LILY *joins* SKINNER *in a ceremonial parade before imaginary people. They both affect very grand accents, very quickly.*

SKINNER How are you? Delighted you could come.

LILY How do do.

SKINNER My wife — Lady Elizabeth.

LILY (*Blows kiss*) Wonderful people.

SKINNER Nice of you to turn up.

LILY My husband and I.

SKINNER Carry on with the good work.

LILY Thank you. Thank you.

SKINNER Splendid job you're doing.

LILY We're really enjoying ourselves.

> SKINNER *lifts the flowers and hands them to* LILY.

SKINNER From the residents of Tintown.

LILY Oh, my! How sweet! (*Stoops down to kiss a child*) Thank you, darling.

SKINNER *pauses below Sir Joshua. He is now the stern, practical man of affairs. The accent is dropped.*

SKINNER This is the case I was telling you about, Sir Joshua. Eleven children in a two-roomed flat. No toilet, no running water.

LILY Except what's running down the walls. Haaaaa!

SKINNER She believes she has a reasonable case for a corporation house.

LILY It's two houses I need!

SKINNER Two?

LILY Isn't there thirteen of us? How do you fit thirteen into one house?

SKINNER (*To portrait*) I know. I know. They can't be satisfied.

LILY Listen! Listen! I know that one! Do you know it, Skinner?

SKINNER Elizabeth, please.

LILY It's a military two-step. The chairman was powerful at it. Give us your hand! Come on!

SKINNER I think you're concussed.

She drags him into the middle of the parlour and sings as she dances. SKINNER *sings with her.*

LILY 'As I walk along the Bois de Boulogne
       with an independent air,
   You can hear the girls declare,
       "He must be a millionaire".
   You can hear them sigh and hope to die,
       you can see them wink the other eye
   At the man who broke the bank at Monte Carlo.'

LILY drops exhausted into a chair.

Oh my God, I'm punctured!

SKINNER Lovely, Lily. Lovely.

LILY I wasn't a bad dancer once.

SKINNER And now Lord Michael will oblige with a recitation — 'If' — by the inimitable Rudyard Kipling. 'If you can keep your head when all about you / Are losing theirs and blaming it on you . . . ' Ladies and gentlemen, a poem to fit the place and the occasion — Lord Michael of Gas!

SKINNER *switches off the radio and lights a cigar.*

MICHAEL I don't know what you think you're up to. I don't know what sort of a game you think this is. But I happen to be serious about this campaign. I marched three miles today and I attended a peaceful meeting today because every man's entitled to justice and fair play and that's what I'm campaigning for. But this — this — this fooling around, this swaggering about as if you owned the place, this isn't my idea of dignified, peaceful protest.

SKINNER (*To* LILY) I think he deserves to sign the Distinguished Visitors' Book. Doesn't he?

MICHAEL You know what you're campaigning for, Missus. You want a decent home. And you want a better life for your children than the life you had. But I don't know what his game is. I don't know what he wants.

SKINNER Bunny Rabbit to romp home at twenties.

MICHAEL Oh, as you say, he's glib all right. But if you ask me he's more at home with the hooligans, out throwing stones and burning shops!

SKINNER *pours himself a drink and sings quietly. Then very deliberately he stubs out his cigar on the leather-top desk.*

SKINNER (*Sings*) 'Will you come into my parlour, said the spider to the fly. 'Tis the prettiest little parlour that ever you did spy.'

MICHAEL Look, Lily, look! I told you! I told you!

SKINNER 'The way into my parlour is up a winding stair And I have many curious things to show you when you're there.'

MICHAEL He's a vandal! He's a bloody vandal!

SKINNER *pours a drink for* LILY.

SKINNER Lily?
LILY You'll have me on my ear — God bless you. (*To* MICHAEL) Try that port wine, young fella. It's gorgeous.
SKINNER It's sherry. Mr Hegarty?

MICHAEL *turns away and prepares to leave.*

Just the two of us then, Lily. To . . . dignity.
MICHAEL I'm going.
LILY It's time we were all leaving. They'll be waiting for me to make the tea.

SKINNER *sits down and puts his feet up on the table.*

SKINNER Would anyone object if I had another cigar?

He lights one.

LILY What time is it anyway?
MICHAEL Coming on to five.
LILY D'you see my weans? If I'm not there not one of them would lift a finger. Three years ago last May the chairman won the five pound note in the Slate Club raffle and myself and Declan went on a bus run to Bundoran — I took him with me 'cause he doesn't play about on the street with the others, you know — and when we come home at midnight, there they all were, with faces this length, sitting round the bare table, waiting since six o'clock for their tea to appear!
MICHAEL I'm away, Lily. Good luck.
LILY Goodbye, young fella. And keep at them books.
MICHAEL (*To* SKINNER) Thanks for pulling me in.
SKINNER My pleasure. And any time you're this way, don't pass the door.
LILY And good luck on Easter Tuesday.

MICHAEL Thanks. Thanks.
SKINNER (*Before* MICHAEL *reaches the door*) Before you go, take a look out the window.

> MICHAEL *stops, looks at* SKINNER, *then crosses to the window.*

Are they still there?
LILY Is who still there?
SKINNER The army. (*To* MICHAEL) Have they gone yet?
MICHAEL The place is crawling with them. And there's police there, too.
LILY The army's bad enough, but God forgive me I can't stand them polis.
SKINNER If I were you I'd wait till they move.
MICHAEL Why should I?
SKINNER Go ahead then.
MICHAEL Why shouldn't I?
SKINNER Go ahead then.
MICHAEL I've done nothing wrong.
SKINNER How do you talk to a boy scout like that?
MICHAEL I've done nothing I'm ashamed of.
SKINNER You drank municipal whiskey. You masqueraded as a councillor. Theft and deception.
MICHAEL All right, smart alec. (*He tosses coins on the table*) That's for the drink — there — there — there. Now give me one good reason why I can't walk straight out of here and across that Square. One good reason — go on — go on.
SKINNER Because you presumed, boy. Because this is theirs, boy, and your very presence here is a sacrilege.
MICHAEL They don't know we're here.
SKINNER They'll see you coming out, won't they?
MICHAEL So they'll see me coming out and they'll arrest me for trespassing.
SKINNER Have a brandy on me. They'll soon shift.
MICHAEL I certainly don't want to be arrested. But if they want to arrest me for protesting peacefully — that's all right — I'm prepared to be arrested.

SKINNER They could do terrible things to you — break your arms, burn you with cigarettes, give you injections.

MICHAEL Gandhi showed that violence done against peaceful protest helps your cause.

SKINNER Or shoot you.

LILY God forgive you, Skinner. There's no luck in talk like that.

MICHAEL As long as we don't react violently, as long as we don't allow ourselves to be provoked, ultimately we must win.

SKINNER Do you understand Mr Hegarty's theory, Lily?

LILY Yous are both away above me.

MICHAEL I told you my name's Michael.

SKINNER Mr Hegarty is of the belief that if five thousand of us are demonstrating peacefully and they come along and shoot us down, then automatically we . . . we . . . (*To* MICHAEL) Sorry, what's the theory again?

MICHAEL You know damn well the point I'm making and you know damn well it's true.

SKINNER It's not, you know. But we'll discuss it some other time. And, as I said, if you're passing this way don't let them entertain you in the outer office.

MICHAEL *goes back to the window and looks out.*
LILY *giggles.*

LILY D'you see our place? At this minute Mickey Teague, the milkman, is shouting up from the road, 'I know you're there, Lily Doherty. Come down and pay me for the six weeks you owe me.' And the chairman's sitting at the fire like a wee thin saint with his finger in his mouth and the comics up to his nose and hoping to God I'll remember to bring him home five fags. And across from us Celia Cunningham's about half-full now and crying about the Sweepstake ticket she bought and lost when she was fifteen. And above us Dickie Devine's groping under the bed for his trombone and he doesn't know yet that Annie pawned it on Wednesday for the weans' bus fares and he's going to beat the tar out of her when she tells him. And down the passage aul' Andy Boyle's lying in bed because he has no coat. And I'm here in the Mayor's parlour, dressed up like the Duchess of Kent and drinking port wine. I'll tell you something, Skinner: it's a very unfair world.

The JUDGE *appears on the battlements.*

JUDGE One of the most serious issues for our consideration is the conflict between the testimony of the civilian witnesses and the testimony of the security forces on the vital question — who fired first? Or to re-phrase it — did the security forces initiate the shooting or did they merely reply to it? We have heard, for example, the evidence of Father Brosnan who attended the deceased and he insists that none of the three was armed. And I have no doubt that Father Brosnan told us the truth as he knew it. But I must point out that Father Brosnan was not present when the three emerged from the building. We have also the evidence of the photographs taken by Mr Montini, the journalist, and in none of these very lucid pictures can we see any sign whatever of weapons either in the hands of the deceased or ad-jacent to their person. But Mr Montini tells us he didn't take the pictures until at least three minutes after the shooting had stopped. On the other hand we have the sworn testimony of eight soldiers and four policemen who claim not only to have seen these civilian firearms but to have been fired at by them. So at this point I wish to recall Dr Winbourne of the Army Forensic Department.

WINBOURNE *enters left — a Scotsman.*

WINBOURNE My lord.
JUDGE Dr Winbourne, in your earlier testimony you men-tioned paraffin tests you carried out on the deceased.

Could you explain in more detail what these tests involved?

WINBOURNE Certainly, my lord. When a gun is fired the propellant gases scatter minute particles of lead in two directions: through the muzzle and over a distance of thirty feet in front of the gun; and through the breach. In other words, if I fire a revolver or an automatic weapon or a bolt-action rifle (*illustrates with his own hand*) these lead particles will adhere to the back of this hand and between the thumb and forefinger. And a characteristic of this contamination is that there is an even-patterned distribution of these particles over the hand or clothing.

JUDGE And the presence of this deposit is conclusive evidence of firing?

WINBOURNE I'm a scientist, my lord. I don't know what constitutes conclusive evidence.

JUDGE What I mean is, if these lead particles are found on a person, does that mean that that person has fired a gun?

WINBOURNE He may have, my lord. Or he may have been contaminated by being within thirty feet of someone who has fired in his direction. Or he may have been beside someone who has fired. Or he may have been touched or handled by someone who has just fired.

JUDGE I see. And these distinctions are of the utmost importance because on this point we must be scrupulously meticulous. Thank you, Dr Winbourne, for explaining them so succinctly. So that, if we are to decide whether lead on a person's hand or clothing should be attributed to his having fired a weapon, we must be guided by the pattern of deposit. Is that correct?

WINBOURNE Yes, my lord.

JUDGE And now, if I may return to your report — your findings on the three deceased.

WINBOURNE In the case of Fitzgerald — it's on page four, my lord.

JUDGE I have it, thank you.

WINBOURNE In the case of Fitzgerald, a smear on the left hand and on the left shirt sleeve. In the case of the woman Doherty, smear marks on the right cheek and shoulder. In the case of Hegarty an even deposit on the back of the left hand and between the thumb and forefinger.

JUDGE A patterned deposit?

WINBOURNE An even deposit, my lord.

JUDGE So Hegarty certainly did fire a weapon?

WINBOURNE Let me put it this way, my lord: I don't see how he could have had these regular deposits unless he did.

JUDGE And Fitzgerald and the woman Doherty?

WINBOURNE They could have been smeared by Hegarty or they could have been contaminated while they were being carried away by the soldiers who shot them.

JUDGE Or by firing themselves.

WINBOURNE That's possible.

JUDGE But you are certain that Hegarty at least fired?

WINBOURNE That's what the tests indicate.

JUDGE And you are personally convinced he did?

WINBOURNE Yes, I think he did, my lord.

JUDGE Thank you, Dr Winbourne.

The JUDGE *disappears.* WINBOURNE *goes off.*

MICHAEL There's three more tanks coming. And they seem to be putting up searchlights or something.

SKINNER Are you asleep, Lily?

LILY D'you know what I heard a man saying on the telly one night? D'you see them fellas that go up into outer space? Well, they don't get old up there the way we get old down here. Whatever way the clocks work there we age ten times as quick as they do.

SKINNER You're a real mine of information, Lily.

LILY So that if I went up there and stayed up there long enough and then come down again, God I could end up the same age as Mark Antony!

SKINNER No matter how long you'd stay up there your family'd still be waiting for their tea.

LILY I'd give anything to see the chairman's face if that happened.

SKINNER Lily.

LILY What?

SKINNER Why don't you ring somebody?

LILY Who?

SKINNER Anybody.

LILY That young fella's out of his mind! Why in God's name would I ring somebody?

SKINNER To wish them a Happy Christmas. To use the facilities of the hotel. Just for the hell of it. Anyone in the street got a phone?

LILY Surely. We all have phones in every room. Haaaaa!

SKINNER Where do you get your groceries?

LILY Billy Broderick.

SKINNER Ring him.

LILY Sure he's across the road from me.

SKINNER Tell him you're out of tea.

LILY Have you no head, young fella? He'd think I couldn't face him just because I owe him fifteen pounds.

SKINNER You must know someone with a phone.

LILY Dr Sweeney!

SKINNER No doubt. Anyone working in a shop — a factory?

LILY No.

SKINNER A garage — a café — an office — an —

LILY Beejew Betty.

SKINNER Who?

LILY Betty Breen. She's a cousin of the chairman. She's in the cash desk of the Beejew Cinema. We call her Beejew Betty.

SKINNER *looks up the telephone directory.* MICHAEL *turns upstage.*

She used to let our weans into the Saturday matinée for nothing. And then one Saturday our Tom — d'you see our Tom? Sixteen next October 23rd and afeard of no man nor beast — he went up to her after the picture and told her it was the most stupidest picture he ever seen. And d'you know what? She took it personal. Niver let them in for free again. A real snob, Betty.

SKINNER (*Dials*) 7479336.

LILY What are you at? Sure I seen her last Sunday week at the granny's.

SKINNER *hands her the phone.*

What will I say? What in the name of God will I say to — ? (*Her accent and manner become suddenly stilted*) Hello? Is that Miss Betty Breen? This is Mrs Elizabeth Doherty speaking. Yes — yes — Lily. How are you keeping since we last met, Betty? No, no, he's fine, thank you, fine — the chest apart. No, I'm in good health, too, Betty, thank you. It just happened that I chanced to be with some companions near a telephone and your name come up in casual conversation, and I thought I'd say How-do-do. Yes. Yes. Well, Betty, I'll not detain you any longer, Betty. I'm sure you're busy with finance. Goodbye. No, the kiosk's still broken. I'm ringing from the Mayor's parlour.

She suddenly bangs down the receiver and covers her face with her hands.

Jesus, young fella, I think she passed out! Oooooops!

SKINNER That's a great start. Who else is there?

LILY Give us a second to settle myself, will you? I'm not worth tuppence. Look at my hands. (*The bottle stutters against the glass as she pours herself a drink*) Didn't I tell you?

SKINNER I love your posh accent, Lily.

LILY Hold your tongue. Lily's no yokel. Wait till I tell you: one time when the chairman was in the TB hospital I rung him up to tell him that Gloria had fell off the roof — that was eighteen months ago,

	she was four-and-a-half then — and the ward Sister I spoke to asked the chairman who the swank was he was married to!
MICHAEL	I want the two of you to know I object to this carry-on.
LILY	Sure it's only a bit of innocent fun, young fella. Have you no give in you at all? (*Examines bottle*) What d'you call this port wine?
SKINNER	It's sherry.
LILY	I'm going to get a bottle of it next Christmas.
SKINNER	Who else do you know, Lily? Any friends? Relatives?
MICHAEL	You're behaving exactly as they think we behave.
LILY	As who thinks?
SKINNER	Have you any uncles? Any brothers? Any sisters?
LILY	I have one sister — Eileen.
SKINNER	Is she on the phone?
LILY	She is.
SKINNER	Eileen what? What's her second name?
MICHAEL	No wonder they don't trust us. We're not worthy of trust.
LILY	You'll not get her in that book.
SKINNER	From the operator, then.
LILY	No, I'm not going to ring Eileen. She'd think something terrible had happened.
MICHAEL	And even if you have no sense of decency, at least you should know that that's stealing unless you're going to leave the money.
LILY	Lookat, young fella: I don't need you nor nobody else to tell me what's right and what's wrong. (*To* SKINNER) Give me that.

SKINNER *hands her the phone.*

	How do you get the operator?
SKINNER	Dial 100 and give your number.
LILY	I didn't say I wasn't going to leave the money, did I? I'm as well acquainted with my morals as the next. (*Into phone*) Operator, this is 7643225, Derry

City, Northern Ireland. I wish to make a call to Mrs
Eileen O'Donnell, 275 Riverway Drive . . . She's
getting me Enquiries. If you don't mind, I'll take my
glass. Thank you. Enquiries? This is 7643225, Derry
City, Northern Ireland. I wish to make a call to Mrs
Eileen O'Donnell, 275 Riverway Drive — yes —
Riverway — Riverway — (*The accent is dropped*) God,
are you deaf, wee girl? Riverway Drive, Brisbane,
Australia. (*She hangs up*) She'll call me back.

> SKINNER *laughs and slaps the table with delight.*

SKINNER Lily, you're wonderful! The chairman's married to
a queen. Does he deserve you?

> BRIGADIER JOHNSON-HANSBURY *enters right. He*
> *speaks through a loudhailer. He is guarded by three*
> *armed* SOLDIERS.

BRIGADIER Attention, please! Attention!
MICHAEL Listen!
LILY And when I get my breath back I might even give a
tinkle to cousin William in the Philippines.
MICHAEL Shut up! Listen! Listen!
BRIGADIER This is Brigadier Johnson-Hansbury. We know
exactly where you are and we know that you are
armed. I advise you to surrender now before there
is loss of life. So lay down your arms and proceed
to the front entrance with your hands above your
head. Repeat — proceed to the front entrance with
your hands above your head. The Guildhall is completely surrounded. I urge you to follow this advice
before there is loss of life.

> *The* BRIGADIER *goes off. The* SOLDIERS *follow him.*
> *Silence.* LILY *gets to her feet.* SKINNER *gets to his*
> *feet. Pause.*

LILY Arms? What's he blathering about?

SKINNER His accent's almost as posh as yours, Lily.

Pause.

MICHAEL Some bastard must have done something to rattle
them — shouted something, thrown a stone, burned
something — some bloody hooligan! Someone like
you, Skinner! For it's bastards like you, bloody
vandals, that's keeping us all on our bloody knees!

ACT TWO

A short time later. The parlour is almost in darkness. MICHAEL, LILY *and* SKINNER *stand beside the positions they had at the opening of Act One. They do not move. A* BALLADEER *stands at stage right; his* ACCORDIONIST *is behind him. As before, he has a glass in his hand. Before, he was aggressive-drunk; this time he is maudlin-drunk. He is dressed in a dark suit and black tie. He sings (to the air of 'Kevin Barry').*

BALLADEER   'In Guildhall Square one sunny evening three Derry
        volunteers were shot.
     Two were but lads and one a mother; the Saxon
        bullet was their lot.
     They took a stand against oppression, they wanted
        Mother Ireland free.
     Their blood now stains the Guildhall pavements;
        a cross stands there for all to see.

     'We'll not forget that sunny evening, nor the names
        of those bold three
     Who gave their lives for their ideal — Mother
        Ireland, one and free.
     They join the lines of long-gone heroes, England's
        victims, one and all.
     We have their memory still to guide us; we have
        their courage to recall.'

The BALLADEER *goes off. The* JUDGE *appears on the battlements.*

JUDGE   The weight of evidence presented over the past few
     days seems to be directing the current of this in-
     quiry into two distinct areas. The first has to do

with what at first sight might appear to be mere speculation, but it could be a very important element, I suggest, in any understanding of the entire canvas of that Saturday — and I refer to the purpose the three had in using the Guildhall, the municipal nerve-centre of Londonderry, as their platform of defiance. And the second area — more sensible to corroboration or rebuttal, one would think — concerns the arms the deceased were alleged to have used against the army. And I suggest, also, that these two areas could well be different aspects of the same question. Why the Guildhall? Counsel for the deceased pleads persuasively that in the melée following the public meeting the three in their terror sought the nearest possible cover and that cover happened to be the Guildhall — a fortuitous choice. This may be. But I find it difficult to accept that of all the buildings adjacent to them they happened to choose the one building which symbolized for them a system of government they opposed and were in fact at that time illegally demonstrating against. And if the choice was fortuitous, why was the building defaced? Why were its furnishings despoiled? Why were its records defiled? Would they have defaced a private house in the same way? I think the answers to these questions point to one conclusion: that the deceased deliberately chose this building; that their purpose and intent was precise and deliberate. In other words that their action was a carefully contrived act of defiance against, and an incitement to others to defy, the legitimate forces of law and order. No other conclusion is consistent with the facts.

When MICHAEL, LILY *and* SKINNER *speak they speak calmly, without emotion, in neutral accents.*

MICHAEL We came out the front door as we had been ordered and stood on the top step with our hands above our heads. They beamed searchlights on our faces but I could see their outlines as they crouched beside their tanks. I even heard the click of their rifle-bolts. But there was no question of their shooting. I knew they weren't going to shoot. Shooting belonged to a totally different order of things. And then the Guildhall Square exploded and I knew a terrible mistake had been made. And I became very agitated, not because I was dying, but that this terrible mistake be recognized and acknowledged. My mouth kept trying to form the word mistake — mistake — mistake. And that is how I died — in disbelief, in astonishment, in shock. It was a foolish way for a man to die.

LILY   The moment we stepped outside the front door I knew I was going to die, instinctively, the way an animal knows. Jesus, they're going to murder me. A second of panic — no more. Because it was succeeded, overtaken, overwhelmed by a tidal wave of regret, not for myself nor my family, but that life had somehow eluded me. And now it was finished; it had all seeped away; and I had never experienced it. And in the silence before my body disintegrated in a purple convulsion I thought I glimpsed a tiny truth: that life had eluded me because never once in my forty-three years had an experience, an event, even a small unimportant happening been isolated, and assessed, and articulated. And the fact that this, my last experience, was defined by this perception, this was the culmination of sorrow. In a way I died of grief.

SKINNER   A short time after I realized we were in the Mayor's parlour I knew that a price would be exacted. And when they ordered us a second time to lay down our arms I began to suspect what that price would be because they leave nothing to chance and because the poor are always overcharged. And as we stood on the Guildhall steps two thoughts raced through my mind: how seriously they took us and how unpardonably casual we were about them; and that to

65

match their seriousness would demand a total dedication, a solemnity as formal as theirs. And then
everything melted and fused in a great roaring heat.
And my last thought was: if you're going to decide
to take them on, Adrian Casimir, you've got to mend
your ways. So I died, as I lived, in defensive flippancy.

JUDGE We now come to the second area — were the deceased armed? Their counsel insists they were not.
The security forces insist they were. If they opened
fire at the army, their counsel asks with good reason,
why were there no military casualties, and even
more pertinently, what became of their weapons?
To this the army replies that the guns were taken
away by the mob which had gathered. Counsel for
the deceased strongly denies this. They say that no
civilians were allowed into the Guildhall Square
until one hour after the shooting. The security
forces say this is untrue, and point — for example
— to the priest and the newsman who were right
beside the deceased within five minutes of the
shooting. So, in view of this welter of confusion, I
wish to recall the pathologist, Professor Cuppley,
tomorrow morning.

The JUDGE *disappears.* MICHAEL, LILY *and* SKINNER
step briskly back into the parlour. MICHAEL *goes
straight into the dressing room.* SKINNER *fills his
empty cigarette packet from the silver box on the
table.* LILY *moves about the parlour with an air of
business — fixing chairs, emptying ashtrays. She
switches on the light.*

LILY That's better. I'm a great wan for light. The cold I
don't mine but I don't like the dark.

She takes off her robe and examines it.

I'll tell you something, Skinner; it's a shocking sin

having them lovely things lying idle in a wardrobe
and them as fresh as the day they were bought.
Lookat — not an elbow out of them nor nothing.

SKINNER It has the shoulders scratched off me.

LILY What are you wearing it for then? Give it to me, you
clown you! Here's your shirt. And them gutties must
be dry by now.

SKINNER *takes off the robe and puts on the dry shirt.*
He still wears the hat.

D'you know what it would make? A grand warm
dressing gown, wouldn't it? And that's what the
chairman needs for when he be's out in the chest
hospital.

SKINNER Take it with you.

LILY Wouldn't I look a quare sight walking along the
street with this on my back! Like the time the polis
came on the Boxer Brannigan driving off the petrol
lorry. D'you know the Boxer?

SKINNER Th'old one — two — three — one — two — three.

LILY And says the Boxer to them: 'I was only looking for
a refill for my lighter.' Where's the other one (*robe*)?

SKINNER Behind you.

LILY That young fella — what do they call him again?

SKINNER Michael.

LILY That's it. A grand sensible lad that.

SKINNER Admirable.

LILY I have a Michael. Between Declan and Gloria. His
master says he's just throbbing with brains. Like the
chairman.

SKINNER *goes to the window and looks out.* LILY
watches him for a few seconds.

Is the aunt alive or dead, Skinner?

SKINNER Dead. Ten years dead.

LILY May the Lord have mercy on her good soul. And
where do you live?

SKINNER Anywhere — everywhere. As they say — no fixed
address.

LILY And sure if you've no fixed address you can't claim
no dole.

SKINNER Right.

LILY And how do you live?

SKINNER On my wits.

LILY But if anything was to happen to you —

SKINNER If I'm sick the entire wisdom of the health authority
is at my service. And should I die the welfare people
would bury me in style. It's only when I'm alive
and well that I'm a problem.

LILY Isn't that peculiar? All the same, to be put down in
style, that's nice.

SKINNER Great.

LILY And do you just knock about the town all day?

SKINNER Sometimes I move out. To England. Scotland. The life
of Riley.

LILY *continues folding the robes.*

LILY I can't offer you no bed, Skinner, 'cause there's six
in one room and seven in the other. But I could give
you a bite to eat most days of the week.

Pause. Then SKINNER *suddenly picks up the ceremonial sword.*

SKINNER On guard!

He fences with an imaginary opponent.

LILY If you're stuck.

SKINNER OK.

LILY And even if I'm out working the chairman's always
there.

SKINNER Fine.

LILY You know the old station. That's where we live. It's
a converted warehouse. Third floor up.

SKINNER Do you like my technique?
LILY What?
SKINNER My swordsmanship.
LILY Lovely.
SKINNER How do you think I'm doing?
LILY Great.
SKINNER Thanks, Lily.
LILY Who are you fighting?
SKINNER At the moment, the British army.
LILY God help them.

> LILY *goes on with her housekeeping.* SKINNER *continues fencing for a few seconds and then stops.*

SKINNER Lily.
LILY What?
SKINNER Has it anything at all to do with us?
LILY What?
SKINNER This marching — protesting — demonstrating?
LILY What are you talking about, young fella?
SKINNER Has it anything to do with you and me and him —
if he only knew it?
LILY What are you ranting about? It's for us it is. Isn't it?
SKINNER Doctors, plumbers, teachers, accountants, all shoulder
to shoulder — is that us?
LILY Don't ask me nothing, young fella. I've no head. All
I do is march. And if you want to know why you
should be marching you ask the buck inside.
SKINNER Why do you march?
LILY Me?
SKINNER Why did you march today?
LILY Sure everybody was marching the day.
SKINNER Why were you out?
LILY For the same reason as everybody else.
SKINNER Tell me your reasons.
LILY My reasons is no different to anybody else.
SKINNER Tell me yours.
LILY Wan man — wan vote — that's what I want. You
know — wan man — wan vote.

SKINNER   You got that six months ago.

Pause.

LILY   Sure I know that. Sure I know we got it.

SKINNER   That's not what you're marching for, then.

LILY   Gerrymandering — that's another thing — no more gerrymandering — that's what I want — no more gerrymandering. And civil rights for everybody — that's what I want — you know — civil rights — civil rights — that's why I march.

SKINNER   I don't believe a word of it, Lily.

LILY   I'm a liar then?

SKINNER   And neither do you.

LILY   You're calling me a liar, is that it?

SKINNER   I'll tell you why you march.

LILY   He'll be telling me my name isn't Lily Doherty next.

SKINNER   Because you live with eleven kids and a sick husband in two rooms that aren't fit for animals. Because you exist on a state subsistence that's about enough to keep you alive but too small to fire your guts. Because you know your children are caught in the same morass. Because for the first time in your life you grumbled and someone else grumbled and someone else, and you heard each other, and became aware that there were hundreds, thousands, millions of us all over the world, and in a vague groping way you were outraged. That's what it's all about, Lily. It has nothing to do with doctors and accountants and teachers and dignity and boy scout honour. It's about us — the poor — the majority — stirring in our sleep. And if that's not what it's all about, then it has nothing to do with us.

LILY *gazes at him. Pause.*

LILY   I suppose you're right.

He switches to flippancy.

SKINNER And that's why I appeal to you, when you go into that polling station, put an X opposite my name and ensure that your children, too, will enjoy the freedom of the city. And now I think we'll have one for the road, Lily.

He goes to the cabinet.

Let's walk into the future with bloodshot eyes and unsteady step.

Pause.

LILY Did you ever hear tell of a mongol child, Skinner?
SKINNER Where did you hide the brandy?
LILY I told you a lie about our Declan. That's what Declan is. He's not just shy, our Declan. He's a mongol.

She finds the brandy bottle and hands it to him.

And it's for him I go on all the civil rights marches. Isn't that stupid? You and him (MICHAEL) and everybody else marching and protesting about sensible things like politics and stuff and me in the middle of you all, marching for Declan. Isn't that the stupidest thing you ever heard? Sure I could march and protest from here to Dublin and sure what good would it do Declan? Stupid and all as I am I know that much. But I still march — every Saturday. I still march. Isn't that the stupidest thing you ever heard?
SKINNER No.
LILY That's what the chairman said when I — you know — when I tried to tell him what I was thinking. He never talks about him; can't even look at him. And that day that's what he said, 'You're a bone stupid bitch. No wonder the kid's bone stupid, too.' The chairman — that's what he said.

She stops abruptly, as if she had been interrupted.
SKINNER *goes to her and puts his glass into her hand.*

Oh, merciful God.

PRIEST *appears on the battlements.*

PRIEST At eleven o'clock tomorrow morning Solemn
Requiem Mass will be celebrated in this church for
the repose of the souls of the three people whose
death has plunged this parish into a deep and
numbing grief. As you are probably aware I had the
privilege of administering the last rites to them and
the knowledge that they didn't go unfortified to
their Maker is a consolation to all of us. And it is
natural that we should mourn. But it is also right
and fitting that this tragic happening should make
us sit back and take stock and ask ourselves the
very pertinent question: why did they die? That
there are certain imperfections in our society, this I
do not deny. Nor do I deny that opportunities for
gainful employment, for decent housing, for effective
voting were in certain instances less than equal. And
because of these imperfections, honest men and
women, decent men and women came together and
formed the nucleus of a peaceful, dignified movement that commanded the respect not only of this
city and this country but the respect of the world.
But although this movement was initially peaceful
and dignified, as you are well aware certain evil
elements attached themselves to it and contaminated it and ultimately poisoned it, with the result
that it has long ago become an instrument for corruption. Who are they, these evil people? I will speak and
I will speak plainly. They have many titles and they
have many banners, but they have one purpose and
one purpose only — to deliver this Christian country
into the dark dungeons of Godless communism. I

don't suggest for one minute that the three people who died yesterday were part of this conspiracy, were even aware that they were victims of this conspiracy. But victims they were. And to those of you who are flirting with the doctrines of revolution, let me quote to you from that most revolutionary of doctrines — the Sermon on the Mount: 'Blessed are the meek for they shall possess the land.' In the name of the Father, Son, and Holy Spirit.

The PRIEST *disappears as* MICHAEL *bustles in from the dressing room.*

MICHAEL OK — are we all set?
SKINNER How are the nerves now?
MICHAEL You're not going out in that (*hat*)?
SKINNER Why not?
MICHAEL Put that hat away.
SKINNER Would it lead to a breach of the peace?
MICHAEL Put it back where it belongs, Skinner.
SKINNER I'm keeping it. I think it's . . . sympathetic. (*He adjusts the angle*) How about that, Lily?

He begins to sing, grabs LILY *round the waist and turns her round a few times.*

'Where did you get that hat? Where did you get that tile?
Isn't it a nobby one, and just the proper style?
I should like to have one just the same as that . . . '
LILY Oooooops!
SKINNER 'Where'er I go they shout "Hello! Where did you get that hat?"'
LILY You'll have me as silly as yourself, Skinner.
SKINNER Last round before closing. Come on, gentlemen, please. Last call — last call. What's your pleasure, Mr Hegarty?
LILY D'you see our Tom? He found an aul' saucepan on the railway lines one day last summer and put it on

his head for a laugh — just like that (SKINNER). And didn't his head swell up with the heat and as God's my judge he was stuck in it for two days and two nights and had to sleep with the handle down a rat hole in the floor!

MICHAEL The thing to remember is that we took part in a peaceful demonstration and if they're going to charge us they'll have to charge six thousand others.

SKINNER Small Scotch?

MICHAEL Nothing. Now, if they want to be officious, supposing they take our names and addresses, that's all they're entitled to ask for and that's all you're expected to give them. That's the law.

SKINNER (*Toasts*) The law. Personally speaking I'm a great man for the law myself, you know, like, there's nothing like the law.

MICHAEL OK, Lily? And if they try to get you to make a statement you just say you're making no statement unless your solicitor's present.

SKINNER My solicitor's in Bermuda. Who's yours, Lily?

LILY Don't mention them fellas to me. They all have the wan story; you've a great case — you can't be beat. And then when you're in jail they won't let you rest till you appeal.

SKINNER Were you ever in jail, Lily?

LILY No. Were you?

SKINNER Not yet.

MICHAEL Will you listen to me!

LILY What is it, young fella?

MICHAEL Give them no cheek and they'll give you no trouble. We made a peaceful protest and they know that. They're not interested in people like us. It's the troublemakers they're after.

SKINNER They think we're armed.

MICHAEL They know damned well we're not armed.

SKINNER Why is the place surrounded by tanks and armoured cars?

MICHAEL Are you ready, Missus?

SKINNER And why are the walls lined with soldiers and

police?
MICHAEL We'll do exactly as they ask. We've nothing to hide.
I'll go first.

LILY drains her glass.

LILY D'you see that sherry? I'd get very partial to that
stuff.
SKINNER It's brandy.
MICHAEL And if they ask you a straight question give them a
straight answer, and I promise you there'll be no
trouble.
LILY I still think them windows'd be nicer in plain glass.
MICHAEL These (*robes*) were inside, weren't they?

*He takes them into the dressing room. LILY moves
across the room and suddenly grabs the back of a
chair.*

LILY I drunk that glass far too quick. God, I come in reeling and now I'm going out reeling. D'you think
would the equilibrium of my inner ear be inflamed?

MICHAEL returns.

MICHAEL Are we ready?
LILY What time is it, young fella?
MICHAEL Just after five.
LILY That's grand.
MICHAEL (*To SKINNER*) OK?
LILY I'll be back in time to make the tea.
MICHAEL We're going, Skinner.

*SKINNER slowly crosses to the Mayor's seat, sits in
it and spreads himself.*

SKINNER I like it here. I think I'll stay.
MICHAEL For Christ's sake!
SKINNER You go ahead.

MICHAEL We're all going out together.

SKINNER Why?

MICHAEL Because they'll think it's some sort of a trick if we split up.

SKINNER Not if you look them clean in the eye and give them straight, honest answers.

MICHAEL Skinner, are you coming?

> *Pause. Then* SKINNER *suddenly flings open the drawer in the table, pulls out a pile of papers, scatters them around the table, talking very rapidly all the time.*

SKINNER Yes — I'm coming — after we've had a meeting of the corporation — then I'll go. But we can't spend the afternoon drinking civic booze and smoking civic fags and then walk off without attending to pressing civic business —— no, no, no, no. That wouldn't be fair. So. Right. Have we a quorum? We have. Councillor — alderman — how are you? Take a seat. We have a short agenda today, if I remember correctly.

> LILY *sits.*

LILY (*Apologetically to* MICHAEL) God, I need a seat, young fella. Just for five minutes. Till my head settles.

> SKINNER *continues at great speed.*

SKINNER You have before you an account of last week's meeting. I take it to be an accurate account of the proceedings. So may I sign it? Thank you. Thank you. And now to today's agenda. Item 1. Request for annual subscription for the Royal Society for the Prevention of Cruelty to Animals — I suggest we increase our sub to a hundred pounds. Agreed? Agreed. Item 2. Derry and District Floral Society want the use of the main hall for yearly floral

76

display. Granted. Item 3. Tenders for painting all
municipal buildings in the city — in pink gloss? —
why not? Tenders accepted.

LILY Pink gloss! Haaaaa — that's me!

SKINNER Item 4. Invitation to us all to attend the first night of
the Amateur Opera Society's season and buffet supper afterwards. Of course we will. Love to. Item 5.
Municipal grant sought by Derry Rugby Club to
purchase extra acre of land adjacent to their present
pitch. All in favour? Good. Grant granted. Unanimous. Fine. Item 6 —

MICHAEL Are you coming or are you not?

SKINNER Expenses incurred by elected representatives on our
recent trip to Calcutta to study arterial developments.
I think we all benefitted from that visit, didn't we?

MICHAEL You!

SKINNER So I propose those expenses be passed. Seconded?
Good. Good. Item 7 — When you're finished mouth-
ing there! What's wrong, Mr Hegarty? Aren't you
interested? As one of the city's nine thousand unemployed isn't it in your interest that your idleness
is pursued in an environment as pleasant as possible with pets and flowers and music and gaily
painted buildings? What more can you want, Mr
Hegarty?

MICHAEL Nothing that you would want, Skinner. I can tell
you that.

SKINNER No doubt, Mr Hegarty. But now's your opportunity
to speak up, to introduce sweeping legislation, to
change the face of the world. Come on, Mr Hegarty.
The voice of the fourteen per cent unemployed. Speak
up, man, speak up. You may never have a chance
like this again.

LILY I want the chairman to go before me.

SKINNER In a moment, Lily. Lord Michael has the floor. Well,
sir?

MICHAEL *is very angry but controls himself and
speaks precisely.*

MICHAEL   What I want, Skinner, what the vast majority of the people out there want, is something that a bum like you wouldn't understand: a decent job, a decent place to live, a decent town to bring up our children in — that's what we want.

LILY   Good man, young fella.

SKINNER   Go on — go on.

MICHAEL   And we want fair play, too, so that no matter what our religion is, no matter what our politics is, we have the same chances and the same opportunities as the next fella. It's not very much, Skinner, and we'll get it, believe me, we'll get it, because it's something every man's entitled to and nothing can stop us getting what we're entitled to.

LILY   Hear-hear.

MICHAEL   And now, Skinner, you tell us what you want. You're part of the fourteen per cent too. What do you want?

The BRIGADIER *enters right as before. He is guarded by three* SOLDIERS. *He speaks through the loudhailer:*

BRIGADIER   Attention, please! Attention!

LILY   Whisht! Listen!

BRIGADIER   This is Brigadier Johnson-Hansbury. I will give you five minutes more to come out. Repeat — five minutes. You will lay down your arms immediately and proceed to the front entrance with your hands above your head. The Guildhall is completely surrounded. I advise you to attempt nothing foolhardy. This is your last warning. I will wait five more minutes, commencing now.

He goes off. SKINNER *lifts the ceremonial sword, looks for a second at* MICHAEL, *goes to the portrait and sticks the sword into it. Then he turns around and smiles at* MICHAEL.

SKINNER   It's only a picture. And a ceremonial sword.

The Freedom of the City

The JUDGE *appears on the battlements;* PROFESSOR
CUPPLEY *enters left.*

JUDGE Professor Cuppley, you carried out post-mortem examinations on the three deceased.

CUPPLEY Yes, my lord.

JUDGE And your report states that all three were killed by SLR rifle-fire.

CUPPLEY Yes, my lord.

JUDGE Could you tell us something about this type of weapon?

CUPPLEY It's a high-velocity rifle, using 7.62 mm ammunition; and from my point of view it's particularly untidy to work with because if the victim has been hit several times in close proximity it's very difficult to identify the individual injuries.

JUDGE Could you elaborate on that?

CUPPLEY Well, the 7.62 is a high-velocity bullet which makes a small, clean entry into the body. There's no difficulty there. But once it's inside the body its effect is similar to a tiny explosion in that it shatters the bone and flesh tissue. And then, as it passes out of the body — at the point of exit — it makes a gaping wound and as it exits it brings particles of bone and tissue with it which make the wound even bigger.

JUDGE I see. And your report states that the deceased died from a total of thirty-four wounds?

CUPPLEY Forgive me correcting you, my lord, but what I said was — the second paragraph on page two — I think I pointed out that thirty-four was an approximation.

JUDGE I see that.

CUPPLEY Because, as I say, with the SLR it's very difficult to identify individual injuries if they're close together. But in the case of Fitzgerald there were eight distinct bullet wounds; in the case of the woman Doherty — thirteen; and in the case of Hegarty — twelve, thirteen, fourteen; I couldn't be sure.

JUDGE I understand.

CUPPLEY Fitzgerald's wounds were in the legs, lower ab-

domen, the chest and hands. Doherty's were evenly
distributed over the whole body — head, back,
chest, abdomen and legs. Hegarty was struck in the
legs and arms — two wounds in the left leg, one in
each arm; but the majority of the injuries were in
the head and neck and shoulders, and the serious
mutilation in such a concentrated area made precise
identification almost . . . guesswork.

JUDGE I think we have a reasonably clear picture, Professor
Cuppley. Thank you.

CUPPLEY Thank you.

      The JUDGE *disappears.* CUPPLEY *goes off left.* DODDS
      walks on.

DODDS All over the world the gulf between the rich and the
poor is widening; and to give that statement some
definition let me present you with two statistics.
In Latin America one per cent of the population
owns seventy-two per cent of the land and the vast
majority of the farm-labourers receive no wages at
all but are paid in kind. And in my own country of
'magnificent affluence', the richest country in the
history of civilization, twenty per cent of the population live in extreme poverty.

So the question arises: what of the future? What
solutions are the economists and politicians cooking
up? Well, the answer to that is that there are about
as many solutions as there are theorists, ranging from
the theory that the poor are responsible for their
own condition and should pull themselves up by
their own shoestrings to the theory that the entire
free enterprise system should be totally restructured
so that all have equal share of the cake whether they
help to bake it or not.

And until these differences are resolved nothing
significant is being done for the poor. New align-
ments of world powers don't affect them. Changes of
government don't affect them. They go on as before.

They become more numerous. They become more and more estranged from the dominant society. Their position becomes more and more insecure. They have, in fact, no future. They have only today. And if they fail to cope with today, the only certainty they have is death.

> LILY, MICHAEL *and* SKINNER *begin tidying up in silence.* SKINNER *puts on his shoes.* LILY *puts the flowers back into the vase and the glasses back into the cabinet.* MICHAEL *arranges the things on the desk (papers, etc) and attempts to rub off the cigar-burn on the leather. All the exuberance is gone. They move about as if they were deep in contemplation.* MICHAEL *goes to the portrait and catches the sword.*

SKINNER Don't touch that!

> MICHAEL *looks at him, surprised at his intensity; then shrugs and turns away.* SKINNER *smiles.*

Allow me my gesture.

> *The chairs are back in place; the room is as it was when they first entered.*

MICHAEL That's everything. I'm going now.
LILY We're all going, young fella.

> LILY *looks around.*

I never seen a place I went off as quick.
MICHAEL It looks right again.
LILY You can have it.
SKINNER The Distinguished Visitors' Book! We haven't signed it yet! Come on, Lily!
LILY Will we?

SKINNER *opens the book.*

SKINNER Of course we will. Aren't you as distinguished as (*reads*) Admiral Howard Ericson, United States Navy?

LILY Never heard of him. Give us the pen. What do I write?

SKINNER Just your name. There.

LILY Get out of my road. I need space to write. 'Elizabeth M Doherty.'

SKINNER What's the 'M' for?

LILY Marigold. What do I put down over here?

SKINNER Where?

LILY There. That Sunday we went to Bundoran we all signed the visitors' book in the hotel we got our tea in and we all writ — you know — remarks and things, about the food and the nice friendly waiters and all. For the food, honest to God, Skinner, it was the nicest I ever ate. I mind I writ, 'God bless the cook.' Wasn't that good?

MICHAEL Lily.

LILY And d'you see all them people that was staying there? We got terrible friendly with them and we all exchanged addresses and all. And then after me boasting to the chairman about all the letters I was going to get — not as much as a Christmas card from one of them! People let you down.

MICHAEL Lily.

LILY Coming, young fella, coming. (*To* SKINNER) You're smart. Tell me what I'll put down there. You know — something grand.

SKINNER 'Atmosphere Victorian but cellar excellent.'

LILY Whatever that means. Sure they'd know that wouldn't be me.

SKINNER 'Décor could be improved with brass ducks and pink gloss.'

LILY Haaa. He's not going to let me forget that.

MICHAEL Lily, please.

LILY Hold on now — hold on a minute . . . I have it! 'Looking forward to a return visit.' That's it — you know — nice and ladylike.

SKINNER Perfect. Mr Hegarty?

MICHAEL They won't wait any longer.

SKINNER You're really the one should sign.

LILY There! Not a bad fist now, is it?

SKINNER Beautiful.

LILY They'll think I have a quare cheek on me, won't they? What are you putting down?

SKINNER My name.

LILY But over at the side?

SKINNER 'Freeman of the city.'

LILY Sure that means nothing.

SKINNER I suppose you're right, Lily.

MICHAEL Can we go now?

LILY God, would you give me one second, young fella? I've got to —

She dashes into the dressing room.

MICHAEL Will you for God's sake — !

LILY (*Off*) One second, young fella. One second.

MICHAEL He said five minutes. What's the point in crossing them?

SKINNER Do you trust them?

MICHAEL Do you not?

SKINNER No.

MICHAEL Do you trust anybody?

SKINNER I don't trust them.

MICHAEL Do you think they'll beat you up, Skinner?

SKINNER Maybe.

MICHAEL Or shoot you?

SKINNER Maybe.

MICHAEL You really think they'd shoot you! You really do!

SKINNER Yes. They're stupid enough. But as long as they've only got people like you to handle they can afford to be.

LILY *returns.*

LILY That's better. Are we all ready?

MICHAEL Come on.

LILY You know where I live, young fella. Don't forget to bring Norah over to see us.

MICHAEL Promise.

LILY (*To* SKINNER) And you'll call in any time you want a bite to eat.

SKINNER I'll be there on the stroke of one every day.

LILY You needn't bother your head. Just when you're stuck. (*To Sir Joshua*) Goodbye, Mister.

MICHAEL I'll go in front.

LILY Goodbye, young fella.

MICHAEL Good luck, Lily.

SKINNER Shouldn't we go out singing 'We Shall Overcome'?

MICHAEL I'm warning you, Skinner!

SKINNER Do you not trust them?

> MICHAEL *leaves the parlour; his hands are above his head.*

LILY Lord, I enjoyed that. The crack was good. Wasn't the crack good, Skinner? (SKINNER *nods*) Good luck, son.

SKINNER Good luck, Lily.

> *Pause. They are about to shake hands. Then* SKINNER *leans forward and kisses her on the forehead.*

LILY Jesus, not since the chairman was courting me, have I . . .

> *Pause. Then to shatter the moment* SKINNER *puts his hands above his head and sings and dances.*

SKINNER 'As I walk along the Bois de Boulogne
with an independent air — '

MICHAEL For Christ's sake!

LILY Come on! Come on! Get to hell out of this damned

place! I hated it from the first moment I clapped eyes on it!

> LILY *leaves the parlour, her hands above her head.* SKINNER *switches off the light, closes the door, and joins them in the passageway. All three have their hands above their heads. They begin to move very slowly downstage in ritualistic procession. The moment* SKINNER *closes the door the auditorium is filled with thundering, triumphant organ music on open diapason. It is sustained for about fifteen seconds and then fades to background as* LIAM O'KELLY *enters left with microphone in hand. He talks into the microphone in soft, reverential tones.*

O'KELLY I am standing just outside the Long Tower Church. And now the Solemn Requiem Mass, concelebrated by the four Northern bishops, is at an end, and the organ is playing Bach's most beautiful, most triumphant and in a curious way most appropriate 'Prelude and Fugue No. 552'. And the clouds that have overcast this bitterly cold and windswept city of Derry this February morning can contain themselves no longer, and an icy rain is spilling down on all those thousands of mourners who couldn't get into the church and who have been waiting here in silent tribute along these narrow ghetto streets. But, despite the rain, no one is moving. They still stand, as they have stood for the past two hours, their patient, drawn faces towards the church door; and as one watches them, one wonders will this enormous grief ever pass, so deeply has it furrowed the mind of this ancient, noble, suffering city of St Colmcille. And now the church doors are open and the first of the cortège emerges. This is surely the most impressive gathering of church and state dignitaries that this humble parish of the Long Tower has ever seen. There is the Cardinal Primate, his head stooped, looking grave and weary; and indeed he must be weary because he flew in from Rome only this morning in order to be here today. And beside him I see Colonel Foley who is representing the President. And immediately behind them are the members of the hierarchy and the spiritual leaders of every order and community in the country. And now the Taoiseach, bare-headed, gently refusing an umbrella being offered by one of the stewards; and flanking him are the leaders of the two main opposition parties. Indeed I understand that the entire Dáil and Senate are here today. And if one were to search for a word that would best describe the atmosphere here today, the tenor of the proceedings, the attitude of the ordinary people, I think the word would be dignified. And now the first of the coffins. And all around me the men are removing their caps and some are kneeling on the wet pavements. This is the remains of Michael Joseph Hegarty. And immediately behind it the coffin of Elizabeth Doherty, mother of eleven children. And lastly the remains of Adrian Fitzmaurice — I beg your pardon — Adrian Fitzgerald, and this coffin is being carried by the Knights of Malta. And as the cortège passes me the thousands on the footpaths move gently forward on to the road and take their place quietly among the mourners. I now hand you over to our unit in the cemetery.

He goes off. The music stops suddenly. MICHAEL, LILY *and* SKINNER *now stand across the front of the stage, looking straight out. The* JUDGE *appears on the battlements.*

JUDGE In summary my conclusions are as follows:
1. There would have been no deaths in Londonderry on February 10th had the ban on the march and the meeting been respected, and had the speakers on the platform not incited the mob to such a fever that a clash between the security forces and

the demonstrators was almost inevitable.

2. There is no evidence to support the accusation that the security forces acted without restraint or that their arrest force behaved punitively.

3. There is no reason to suppose that the soldiers would have opened fire if they had not been fired on first.

4. I must accept the evidence of eyewitnesses and various technical experts that the three deceased were armed when they emerged from the Guildhall, and that two of them at least — Hegarty and the woman Doherty — used their arms. Consequently it was impossible to effect an arrest operation. The detailed findings of this tribunal I will now pass on to the appropriate authorities.

The entire stage is now black, except for a battery of spotlights beaming on the faces of the three. Pause. Then the air is filled with a fifteen-second burst of automatic fire. It stops. The three stand as before, staring out, their hands above their heads.
Blackout.

VOLUNTEERS

Characters

GEORGE
MR WILSON
KNOX
BUTT
SMILER
KEENEY
PYNE
DESMOND

Time and Place

The present in Ireland, an archaeological site in the centre of the city.

Set

The action takes place in a huge crater or, as Keeney describes it, 'a huge womb' or a 'prison yard'.

The back wall is a fifteen-foot bank shored up by beams. On top of this bank, i.e. at street level, sheets of corrugated iron prevent sightseers from looking down into the pit. Above and beyond this protective fence we can see rooftops, TV aerials, etc. This bank is shelved at a height of seven feet. Along the back wall this shelf is perhaps two feet wide, anyhow wide enough for a man to walk along. Occupying a large portion of stage right (left and right from audience point of view) is the office which is built on this seven foot high shelf; in fact only a cross-section of this office — we have to be able to see inside it. Inside the office is a large drawing table, shelves, wall charts, etc., the usual site works office.

A wooden verandah with a railing runs round this office. And one gets from the site floor to the office level by a wooden stairway. On the verandah is a trestle table.

The floor of the site, i.e. boulder clay level, is littered with planks, plastic bags, wheelbarrows, timbers on which the barrows run, etc. But the two dominant features on the boulder clay / stage-floor level are the remains of a clay-and-wattle house and the skeleton, Leif. The house — about twenty feet by fifteen feet — is really only a rectangular outline. The clay-and-wattle walls have crumbled away and are now only about five inches high. The house is left of stage centre.

The skeleton of Leif is right of stage centre. Although it lies on the flat, feet to the audience, it will have to be banked slightly so that it can be seen fully and clearly. The cesspit is offstage left. We see only the timbers supporting the wooden surround. There are two entrances: one left beside the pit; and one at back, stage right. The entrance left leads past the cesspit (off) and to the tool-house (off) and the street above. The entrance back right leads to another area being excavated.

Note to Director
Throughout the play, especially in Act One, there is a lot of archaeological business and the actors are constantly entering and exiting as they do this work. This will have to be worked into the script during rehearsals. The only business I have indicated and the only exit and entry directions I have scripted are those which are absolutely necessary.

Volunteers was first produced at the Abbey Theatre, Dublin, on 5 March 1975, with the following cast:

GEORGE	Edward Golden
MR WILSON	Peadar Lamb
KNOX	Micheál Ó Bríain
BUTT	Geoffrey Golden
SMILER	Niall O'Brien
KEENEY	Donal Donnelly
PYNE	Raymond Hardie
DESMOND	Bryan Murray
Directed by	Robert Gillespie
Set and costumes by	Wendy Shea

for Seamus Heaney

ACT ONE

Early in September. About 8.00 a.m. GEORGE *enters left. A bachelor of about fifty. Competent at his work and eminently reliable. Precise in manner and humourless in disposition. On a site he prefers to be associated with the academics than with the diggers. Under one arm his lunch tin, under the other a large, brown paper parcel (the jug). He crosses the set, climbs up the stairs, unlocks the office door and enters. He hangs up his raincoat and cap, lights the portable gas stove, takes the wrapping off the jug, carries it outside and leaves it on the trestle table. He returns to the office where he picks up a bucket and disappears behind the office. We hear the bucket being filled from a tap. He reappears and leaves the bucket beside the trestle table, goes into the office again and emerges with two cardboard shoeboxes filled with pot shards, bones, shells, etc. Throughout most of the morning he washes these finds in the water and stores them.*

Just before he begins this washing job someone, off, kicks three times on the corrugated paling.

GEORGE Come on! Come on! It's not locked!

> *After a brief delay, during which* GEORGE *goes on working,* WILSON *enters. A lean, tough, city man in his sixties. Probably served in the British army as a young man. He is now in civilian clothes and looks — and probably feels — dressed up. During the* GEORGE/WILSON *exchange we hear voices, off, occasionally.*

WILSON Good morning, George.
GEORGE Good morning, Mr Wilson.
WILSON Touch of frost this morning.
GEORGE Season of mists and mellow fruitfulness.
WILSON What's that?
GEORGE The summer's gone, Mr Wilson.

WILSON Well, we got our share.

GEORGE True enough and more than our share. (WILSON *yawns*) Tired?

WILSON Thank God it's Friday. The week on the early shift always kills me.

> WILSON *goes slowly up the steps, passing the time, whistling, looking around without interest.*

Funny, you get so used to looking at a place, you almost forget what it was like before you boys started hoking it up. That's where the car park ended there, didn't it?

GEORGE A bit further over.

WILSON And there were houses beyond that?

GEORGE That's right — above the paling.

WILSON Bloody marvellous.

GEORGE That's the way.

WILSON Hard to imagine a bloody big hotel standing here. I suppose that'll be the basement and kitchen and things down there.

GEORGE At the very bottom? I'm told that'll be a swimming pool.

WILSON Hoh! Very swanky.

GEORGE So they say.

WILSON Well, there can't be much left for you boys now, George?

GEORGE We're finished, Mr Wilson.

WILSON Aye, another week'll see you through.

GEORGE This is our last day.

WILSON What?

GEORGE Packing up this evening.

WILSON You're not serious?

GEORGE Orders from the boss: no more digging after today.

WILSON The least he might have done was notify us.

GEORGE He'll be in touch with you this morning. The builders gave him an ultimatum last night — they won't hold off any longer.

WILSON That was bloody sudden.

GEORGE In a way. But the season's as good as over and we've got all we want anyway.

Laughter, off.

WILSON They don't know, do they?
GEORGE Not yet.
WILSON Will you tell them or will we?
GEORGE Might be wiser not to mention it to them at all. They can be told some time over the weekend.

Another burst of laughter, off.

WILSON That'll knock some of the spunk out of them. But to tell you the God's truth, George, I'll not be sorry. I'm sick trotting over and back twice a day.
GEORGE I'm sure you are. But you certainly pulled us out of a hole, Mr Wilson.
WILSON Well, I mean to say —
GEORGE No, no, only for you we couldn't have carried on.
WILSON We did what we could.
GEORGE Dr King and I are most grateful; and I'm sure he's told you that many's the time.
WILSON Oh, he has indeed. Fine man. Fine gentleman. (*Sees the jug on the table*) Hi-hi-hi, what's this?
GEORGE What?
WILSON You have the lad all put together!
GEORGE (*Pretending innocence*) Who?
WILSON The yoke there!
GEORGE Oh.
WILSON By God, that was some job — eh?
GEORGE Aye.
WILSON You must be at him damn near three months.
GEORGE Fourteen weeks and two days — not counting nights.
WILSON I know; sure wasn't I here when the bits were got up in the corner. Butt came on them, didn't he?
GEORGE It was Smiler actually — strange as it may seem.
WILSON And how many pieces was there?
GEORGE Five hundred and ninety-three as a matter of interest.
WILSON (*Lifting the jug*) And you got them all fitted together!
GEORGE A bit of a challenge all right. Easy, Mr Wilson, easy!
WILSON Only I seen it with my own eyes I wouldn't believe it.

GEORGE   A little patience — a little art — and there he is in all
         his pristine dignity.
WILSON   Bloody marvellous! He'll be worth a bob or two, George?
GEORGE   Money couldn't buy that.
WILSON   That's a fact?
GEORGE   Priceless, Mr Wilson. A thing like that's beyond value.
WILSON   My God. And he'll be a fair age, George?
GEORGE   (*Taking jug*) Let's see . . . twelve inches high, green
         glaze, unpatterned except for gently fluted lip, French in
         style obviously . . . I would hazard . . . early thirteenth
         century.
WILSON   My God — thirteenth century!
GEORGE   Early thirteenth.
WILSON   Tch-tch. Bloody shocking.
GEORGE   But don't quote me on that. That's only an educated
         guess. Dr King'll give us a precise dating.
WILSON   Bloody desperate.
GEORGE   Funny thing, the layman always finds it fascinating. To
         us it's just another job of work — you know.

         Another burst of mocking laughter, off.

         They seem in good form.
WILSON   Bloody trash. (GEORGE *laughs*) Amn't I right? How would
         you describe them?
GEORGE   I wouldn't quarrel with that.
WILSON   'Political prisoners' — huh! In my book they're all
         bloody criminals. And now that this job's over, that's
         what they'll miss most — you know — the chance to
         talk. Would you believe it, George, since the day they
         volunteered to work here five months ago — May 3rd,
         am I right?
GEORGE   Correct.
WILSON   Not one of their mates back there has broken breath
         with them.
GEORGE   I know. You've told me.
WILSON   Not one. What about that for solidarity?
GEORGE   Remarkable.
WILSON   And outside it's the same thing — they're a dirty word

with their mates outside, too. Mind you, George, I'm not bleeding for them. Matter of fact it suits us down to the ground: run away from here and their own crowd would get them before we could reach them.

GEORGE They're nicely cornered.

WILSON Cornered's the word. Not a friend inside or out. But to be sent to Coventry for three months — believe me, George, that's bloody tough.

GEORGE They're tough men, Mr Wilson.

WILSON You've got to be hard to survive that.

GEORGE All the same they performed a public service — not that they'll see it that way.

WILSON Damn right, they won't.

GEORGE And maybe we expanded their horizons just a little, too.

WILSON Huh!

GEORGE You never know these things, Mr Wilson.

WILSON Don't fool yourself. No, no, George, speaking from a lifetime of practical experience, you're either born right or you're not. And there's nothing nor nobody can change the way you were born. I'm a firm believer in genetics and in all my years in the service I've never seen —

> *He breaks off because* KNOX *has entered.* KNOX — *a snuffling, shuffling, grubby man of about sixty-five but looks older. Because of his very thick glasses he thrusts his face right up to people when he is speaking to them. Not far removed from the kind of man one sees at night wrapped in newspapers and sleeping in the doorways of banks and cinemas.*
>
> *As he enters* KNOX *is pulling on dungarees and carrying wellingtons — the outfit all the diggers wear. He walks with the slow, sleepy movements of early-morning workmen.*

Well, just take my word for it, George.

GEORGE Morning, Knox.

No answer.

WILSON Didn't you hear George speaking to you?

KNOX *looks up, grunts something inaudible and shuffles across the stage.*

Bloody pig. One of these days I'll expand his backside with my bloody boot.

GEORGE Are you not working today?

WILSON Got a couple of hours off.

Enter BUTT *and* SMILER. BUTT *is a countryman in his late forties. A quiet man who gives an impression of strength and obstinacy and self-knowledge.*
SMILER *is about thirty-five. There is no trace of the man he once was. We see only the imbecile with the perpetual grin. He wears a woollen ski cap with a huge tassel that looks suitably ridiculous in this context. Both men are adjusting their clothes as they enter.*

GEORGE Yes, men.

BUTT Yes, George.

GEORGE How are you, Smiler?

SMILER That's right — that's right.

WILSON Go on, Smiler, go on — get started. (*Lowering his voice; to* GEORGE) As a matter of fact I'm bringing the eldest girl, Dolly, to her music examination.

Mocking laughter, off.

GEORGE Ah.

WILSON Grade Four. Guildhall School of Music, London. Practical.

GEORGE Pianoforte?

WILSON Viola.

GEORGE Viola? Very nice.

WILSON The viola's a nice instrument.

GEORGE Lovely instrument, the viola.

WILSON Nice for a girl. You know — mellow.
GEORGE Lovely for a girl.
WILSON Takes it from her mother's side — sodden with music.
GEORGE There you are — proves your point.
WILSON What's that?
GEORGE It's in the blood. Genetics.
WILSON You see!
GEORGE Well, I hope she does great.
WILSON (*Descending briskly*) Thanks, George. I'll be able to tell you all this evening.

> *He is the prison officer again. Looks offstage where he sees* KEENEY *and* PYNE *approaching.*

Right, then — everybody accounted for? Come on, you two! One — two — three — four — five. All present and correct. Over to you now, George.
GEORGE Over and out, Mr Wilson.

> *The moment* WILSON *leaves* KEENEY *and* PYNE *enter and at the same moment burst into their usual excessively enthusiastic greeting. No one pays the least attention to them.* KEENEY *is in his forties. Quick-witted, quick-tongued, and never for a second unaware. Years of practice have made the public mask of the joker almost perfect.*
>
> PYNE *is more than ten years younger than* KEENEY, *but an eager apprentice. He is now so attuned to* KEENEY *that his harmonies to* KEENEY'S *themes are expert. But unlike* KEENEY *his public mask slips in times of crisis. His is the uncertain breeziness of a sailor. They move about the stage, waving, smiling, pouring out their double-act patter at great speed.*

KEENEY Good morning, George! (*Calls*) Good morning, Leif! Morning, Knox. Morning, Butt. Morning, Smiler. (*Calls*) Hello, Leif!
PYNE (*At the same time as* KEENEY *above*) Hello, George. (*Calls*) Hello Leif! Morning, Butt. Yes, Smiler. Hello, Knoxie.

(*Calls*) Yes, Leif!

KEENEY Morning, George.

PYNE Morning, George.

KEENEY One political limerick coming up, George. Composed in the monastic silence of last night.

PYNE Hear ye! Hear ye!

KEENEY There once was a bird called O'Shea
Who was known as a fabulous lay —

PYNE Yea-yea.

KEENEY Then along came Parnell
Who screwed her to hell
And we feel the results to this day.

PYNE Wheee!

> KEENEY *goes straight into an exaggerated military march.*

KEENEY Hup: one-two-three-four. Hup: one-two-three-four.

> As soon as KEENEY *begins to march* PYNE *falls in behind him. Their wellington boots make the march ridiculous.*

PYNE (*Now marching*) God bless you, men. You're doing a splendid job.

KEENEY (*Marching rhythm*) Your granny was there when you left.

PYNE You're right.

KEENEY With lots of gold hair on her chest.

PYNE You're right.

KEENEY OK, Pyne. Your turn.

PYNE (*Saluting*) One limerick on the way, sir.

> *They stop marching,* KEENEY *claps.*

KEENEY Thank you — thank you — thank you. You're a truly wunnerful people. And now, friends, I give you — Brother Pyne! Alleluia!

PYNE I've forgotten the first line.

KEENEY There once was a Norseman called Leif.

PYNE Got it. There once was a Norseman called Leif
Whose visit to Ireland was brief
He was caught in a war
Between Jesus and Thor
And came to a permanent grief.

KEENEY (*Clapping*) Wunnerful — wunnerful — wunnerful.

PYNE (*Bowing*) Thank you. Thank you.

KEENEY (*Rolling a cigarette*) Morning, George.

PYNE Yes, George.

KEENEY Nothing like beginning the day with a laugh, George, eh?

PYNE He won't answer us, Keeney.

KEENEY Could he be off-colour?

PYNE Are you off-colour, George?

KEENEY No, he's looking fine.

PYNE Handsome, too.

KEENEY D'you think so?

PYNE Very attractive.

KEENEY He thinks you're handsome, George. I'd watch that — never sure with these merchant seamen. (*To* PYNE) I thought you were married?

PYNE That's long over.

KEENEY English, wasn't she?

PYNE Once upon a time.

KEENEY Thought so. And now you fancy him?

PYNE George?

KEENEY He fancies you, George.

PYNE You're embarrassing him.

KEENEY George? Stalwart George? Never embarrass George. All the same I think he's *genuinely* glad to see us.

PYNE He ought to be. We're his trusted team.

KEENEY His researchers.

PYNE His right arm.

KEENEY His muscle and sinew.

PYNE And he's our foreman.

KEENEY George? George's more than a foreman.

PYNE Really?

KEENEY An expert in his own right, George. Worked with Dr

King on every major archaeological site in the country.

PYNE Go on!

KEENEY A craftsman to the soles of his feet, George.

PYNE You'd know by the look of him.

KEENEY Dr King's right-hand man. Dedicated his last book to him.

PYNE Never!

KEENEY 'For George — my confrère.'

PYNE Beautiful.

KEENEY Shows what he thinks of him.

PYNE The world, I'd say.

KEENEY 'Confrère' — nice democratic touch, that.

PYNE God, that's moving.

KEENEY Only one snag, Pyne.

PYNE What's that?

KEENEY King's a quack.

PYNE D'you hear what he's saying?

KEENEY I'm afraid.

PYNE Quack! How could he be a quack! He's a doctor and a university professor!

KEENEY Quack-quack-quack-quack-quack.

PYNE Nothing but disappointments.

KEENEY And to disillusion you still further, friend, the book — like all his others — is shite.

PYNE Professor King's?

KEENEY S-h-i-g-h-t.

PYNE (*Laughs*) What's it about?

KEENEY Establishing the age of an object by radiocarbon tests.

PYNE Has it a title?

KEENEY Tell him what it's called, George.

PYNE I'm telling you — he's huffing.

KEENEY It's called *Radiocarbon Dating in West Cork*.

PYNE Jesus!

KEENEY Put that in your dudeen.

PYNE In West Cork! So it has crept in there, too?

KEENEY The very dogs are at it in their sleep, man.

PYNE Agh, the country's finished.

KEENEY A randy young buck from Kilgarvan
On a girl tried out radiocarbon —

PYNE Yerra schtop, bhoy!

KEENEY Though she screamed as if thrilled —

PYNE gives girlish scream.

The poor lad was chilled
To discover she dated pre-Norman.

PYNE Ha-ha.

KEENEY A *very* good morning to you, George.

KNOX Ground's bloody frozen. Couldn't work with ground like that.

PYNE A truer word was never spoke, Knoxie.

KNOX Give us a drag, Keeney. I'm out till Des comes.

KEENEY gives him the cigarette he is smoking.

Decent man.

He sucks greedily at the cigarette. PYNE goes over to SMILER and shadow-boxes before him.

PYNE OK, Smiler?

SMILER Yes, Pyne.

PYNE I was watching you wolfing down a big bowl of porridge this morning.

SMILER That's right — that's right.

PYNE Great for keeping your mind off women — plenty of porridge and plenty of exercise; so the chaplain told me. (*Boxing*) One-two, one-two, bang, bang, bang.

He goes off. KNOX offers the cigarette back to KEENEY.

KNOX Ta. Here.

KEENEY After you've soaked it? D'you want me to get gangrene?

KNOX Bugger off.

KEENEY Language! Language! A very good morning to *you*, George.

GEORGE (*Dryly*) How are you, Keeney?

KEENEY (*Excessively*) Splendid, George, splendid. Thank you for asking.

> *He bounds up the steps.*

Senses vibrant, faculties alert, mind finely honed. And I've a feeling, George, I'm going to make a discovery of moment today.

> KEENEY *slips past* GEORGE *and into the office. There he quickly gathers up cigarette butts from ashtrays. His eyes dart around for anything else he might forage.* GEORGE *follows him into the office.*

GEORGE Come on, Keeney. Out of there.
KEENEY Just tidying up, George. An instinct you'd applaud.
GEORGE Out! Out!

> KEENEY *puts the butts into a tin box.*

KEENEY Thank God Professor King smokes. Positive lifesaver these. May the giving hand never fail. Pity he isn't an alcoholic — with a harem.
GEORGE Out! Out! Out!
KEENEY True as God, George, at this very minute I'd give an arm for a large, neat whiskey and a large, loose woman. (*Discovery*) And a forgotten biscuit by the hokey! I told you the discoveries would be momentous today.

> *Both* KEENEY *and* GEORGE *are now out on the terrace.*

GEORGE You're here to work, Keeney.
KEENEY Tell me, George, in your considered opinion — an educated guess, as you would put it —
GEORGE What?
KEENEY Was Hamlet really mad?
GEORGE Get down and get at it.

> GEORGE *goes back to his table.* KEENEY *stays on the*

verandah salvaging the tobacco from the butts.

BUTT   Hi, Knox!
KNOX   Wha'?
BUTT   You have my wellingtons.
KNOX   What d'you mean?
BUTT   These are yours.
KNOX   How d'you know?
BUTT   Take them off. Take them off.

> KEENEY *on the verandah wolf-whistles and claps.*

KEENEY   Take them off, Knoxie! Take them off!

> BUTT *holds Knox's boots at arm's length and sniffs.*

BUTT   'How do you know?' he says.
KNOX   Christ, you'd think he owned them.

> BUTT *cautiously runs his hand over the crumbling remains of the Viking house.*

BUTT   Every day another bit crumbles away. And with this frost the ground's getting wetter and the whole damn thing's going to be lost. (*To* GEORGE) Did you ask him to get some scaffolding and a bit of canvas covering?
GEORGE   Hardly worth our while now.
BUTT   There's at least a week's work in this section alone.
GEORGE   The budget's long spent.
BUTT   Then we'll just have to cover the house and all this part with sacking. That might save it a bit.

> PYNE *enters with two buckets.*

PYNE   You're a real dandy in that cap, Smiler.
SMILER   That's right — that's right.
PYNE   A real smasher, isn't he?
SMILER   I got a new cap, George.
PYNE   What d'you think of that for a cap, George?

GEORGE That's a nice cap, Smiler.

SMILER Butt gave it to me. Yes, Butt?

BUTT Yes, Smiler.

SMILER That's right. Butt gave it to me. And I stood up at the meeting and put the proposition to the house and at least half the delegates there were in favour but the crowd at the back began to heckle and —

BUTT (*Quietly, firmly*) That'll do for you.

SMILER — and the chairman called for a vote but no one was listening anymore and . . .

BUTT (*Stern command*) Shut up, Smiler! Just shut up!

> *The others look away — they have witnessed this before.* SMILER's *brief elation dies; the vacuous smile returns. Pause.*

Now let's get some work done about here. The ground's not as hard in there in the shelter of the bank. So you take this section here, Knoxie, inside the house. Start at the door and work slowly up. And be careful close to the walls or they'll come away in your hands. I'll finish off outside the house. Smiler, you carry on along that street — but don't stand on the baulks. Pyne, you can finish that far section. Keeney, you . . . Keeney!

KEENEY My child.

BUTT Come on, Keeney.

KEENEY In nomine Smiler simplissimo et Knoxie stinkissimo et George industrissimo et —

BUTT There's work to be done.

KEENEY I'm on my holidays in Castel Gandolfo. Hi, Pyne!

PYNE What?

KEENEY You know those newsreels you see of the Pope being carried about through the thousands of tourists; well, d'you know what he's saying out of the corner of his mouth as he's making this gesture? (*He illustrates the arm gesture*)

PYNE I give up. What is he saying?

KEENEY 'Getta those wops offa de grass.'

PYNE Ha-ha.

BUTT   Your turn for the cesspit, Keeney. The gloves and leg-
       gings are out at the far wall.

       KEENEY *comes running down the steps.*
KEENEY Come on, Butt; fair's fair. I did the cesspit yesterday.
BUTT   I did the cesspit yesterday. And Smiler did it on Wed-
       nesday. And Knox on Tuesday. And Pyne on Monday.
KEENEY Knoxie — be a sport.
KNOX   Wha'?
KEENEY Do the pit and I'll give you three fags.
KNOX   Bugger off!
KEENEY Five fags — handmade — monogrammed.

       KNOX *gestures with his fingers and shuffles away.*

       And the tragedy is the cesspit's a natural environment
       for a man like you.

       *He looks around for another victim —everyone is now
       working. Only* SMILER *hasn't begun yet.*

       Smiler — Smiler — look, Smiler, look.

       He holds out two closed fists before SMILER'S *face.*

       Chance of a lifetime. Toss you for the cesspit — OK?
SMILER Yes, Keeney.
BUTT   Leave Smiler alone.
KEENEY Now, Smiler, which hand has a biscuit in it?
SMILER Which hand has a biscuit in it.
KEENEY No, no, there's a biscuit in one hand.
SMILER A biscuit.
KEENEY And if you pick the hand that has the biscuit you don't
       have to do the cesspit *and* you get the biscuit to keep!
       You understand?
SMILER Yes, Keeney.
KEENEY Good. Guess. Which hand?
SMILER That's right — that's right.

KEENEY *opens his right hand — it's empty.*

KEENEY No. It's the left. Hard luck, Smiler. A great effort. On with the leggings and away you go. Pull that cap down over your nose and you'll smell nothing. (*As* SMILER *leaves*) And if you find a crock of gold down there I'll go halves with you. That's a promise — hold me to it.

PYNE Ha-ha.

BUTT Bastard!

KEENEY That's right, Buttie; that's right.

BUTT I'll not forget that, Keeney.

KEENEY Don't I know? That old Gaelic head's stocked with a million grudges. God bless it and God bless Ireland. (*Switching to sudden and very real concern*) Hi, boys, where's Leif?

PYNE Leif?

KEENEY Leif's gone.

PYNE Don't be silly.

KEENEY (*Calls*) Leif!

PYNE How could he be gone! He was here a minute ago.

They both begin moving around the stage looking for Leif. Nobody pays the slightest attention to them.

KEENEY I'm telling you — he's gone.

PYNE How can he be gone, for God's sake!

KEENEY (*Calls*) Leeeif!

PYNE He must be here. He gave his word of honour to George, to Wilson, to all of us.

KEENEY He's gone — I'm telling you!

PYNE Good gracious! Don't stand there, men! Look for him! Look for him!

KEENEY Leif! Leif! Give us a hand, Butt. Come on, Knoxie, come on.

PYNE Leeeeeif!

KEENEY *races up the steps. As he passes* GEORGE:

KEENEY You'd better call his embassy. There could be an international incident over this. Leif! Leif!

KEENEY *takes a quick look into the office and runs down the stairs again. As he and* PYNE *pass:*

PYNE Maybe he just nipped out for a jar.
KEENEY Don't be ridiculous — he's been off it for centuries. Leeeif!

PYNE *rushes off calling Leif's name.*

KEENEY (*To* KNOX, *who ignores him*) Give his description to anyone you meet. Small, thin, very thin, leather thong around his neck, pronounced Scandinavian accent. Leeeif! (*To* BUTT, *who also ignores him*) And as Pyne says, he gave us all his word! You can trust no one these days.

He goes to the rectangular square of tarpaulin which is stretched on the ground just right of the house, lifts up a corner and peeps under.

Aha, aha, aha.
PYNE (*Off*) Leif! Leif!
KEENEY (*Calls*) He's here, Pyne.
PYNE (*Off*) Where?
KEENEY (*To Leif*) You rascal.

PYNE *enters.*

PYNE God, that's a relief. Where is he?
KEENEY Here.
PYNE And he was hiding there all the time!
KEENEY (*Wagging his finger*) Naughty — naughty — naughty.
PYNE And wouldn't even answer you! I see no fun in that! Show me.
KEENEY Look — all innocence.
PYNE You divil you, Leif. You put the heart across us.
KEENEY You're a persistent joker, too, aren't you? All right,

men, the panic's over. Back to work. All's well.
PYNE I was thinking he hadn't slipped out for a jar. I just said
that for a laugh.

He crouches down and peers under the tarpaulin.

Hi, Keeney, is he all right?
KEENEY Of course he's all right.
PYNE He's not looking well.
KEENEY I see no change.
PYNE Definitely lost weight.
KEENEY Maybe a pound or two.
PYNE What do you say, Butt?
KEENEY Here — take an end of this. That's it.

*Together they remove the tarpaulin. And now for the
first time we see Leif — a skeleton. The ground around
him has all been scraped away so that he is lying on
top of the boulder clay. A leather rope hangs loosely
round the neck. There is a small round hole in the skull.*

PYNE I'm telling you — I don't like the appearance at all.
He'd just be skin and bone — if he had any skin. OK,
Keeney — you found him — you're on it now. Give us
ten to get away. (*As he runs off*) One — two — three —
four — five — six — seven —

Counting fades, KEENEY *crouches down bedside Leif.*

KEENEY Nice wee hole that in the top of the head. I wonder
what did it? Maybe an aul' pickaxe. Lovely bit of leather
that, too, isn't it? Best of good stuff. And beautifully
plaited. Man, that wouldn't chafe your neck at all. But
the question persists, George — and who knows better
than a metaphysician like yourself — damn it, the
question that haunts me, George, is: what in the name
of God happened to him? D'you think now could
he have done it to himself? Eh? Or maybe a case of un-
requited love, George — what about that? Or maybe

he had a bad day at the dogs? Or was the poor eejit just grabbed out of a crowd one spring morning and a noose tightened round his neck so that obeisance would be made to some silly god. Or — and the alternative is even more fascinating, George — maybe the poor hoor considered it an honour to die — maybe he volunteered: 'Take this neck, this life, for the god or the cause or whatever.' Of course acceptance of either hypothesis would indicate that he was — to coin a phrase — a victim of his society. Now, you're an erudite man, Knoxie — what's your opinion?

KNOX Why don't you shut up, Keeney!

KEENEY Knoxie may well be on to something. Maybe he was a casualty of language. Dammit, George, which of us here isn't? But we're still left with the problem: was Hamlet really mad?

PYNE (*Entering*) Are you playing or are you not?

KEENEY I'm always playing. Right, George? No, George and I were considering the hazards of language (*He picks up a bucket and trowel. To Leif*) Don't stir till I come back.

PYNE And me out in the shed like a fool hiding behind the boss's anorak. (*To* GEORGE) Is he not coming in today?

> KEENEY *looks as if he is about to begin working. He goes into the Viking house where* KNOX *is scraping, surveys the task, and lights a cigarette.*

KEENEY (*To* KNOX) God bless all here. And God bless you, man of the house.

PYNE George!

GEORGE What?

PYNE Is the boss not coming in today?

GEORGE He's at a meeting.

PYNE Great. And us slaving away here. And what the hell's keeping Dessy the Red? Is he not coming either?

GEORGE As far as I know he is.

PYNE These commies are all the same: grand for spouting revolution but not so good at doing an honest day's work.

KEENEY *addresses* KNOX *very softly, very confidentially.*

KEENEY Desmond'll be late this morning.
KNOX Watch.
KEENEY Must be feeling terrible.
KNOX Get out of my road.
KEENEY Imagine having your stomach pumped for forty-five
minutes. God — agony!

PYNE, *sensing a game, joins the* KNOX / KEENEY *huddle.*

PYNE Was it really forty-five minutes?
KEENEY According to Wilson.
PYNE Jesus!
KNOX What are you ranting about now?
PYNE You're really going soft in the head, Knoxie! Didn't you
hear Wilson telling us on the way over?
KEENEY No, Knoxie didn't hear. He was at the back of the van.
PYNE He must have.
KEENEY I'm telling you he didn't. He was at the back with
Smiler.
KNOX Hear what? I didn't hear nothing about —
KEENEY Shhh! George isn't to know.
PYNE He'd tell the boss.
KNOX What about his stomach?
KEENEY Tell you later.
KNOX (*To* PYNE) Is Des sick?
KEENEY Later.
PYNE (*To* KEENEY) Go on — tell him. Knoxie can keep a secret.

KEENEY *looks cautiously around and then moves close
to* KNOX.

KEENEY D'you remember a fortnight ago he got a telegram here
that his Auntie Coco had died in California?
KNOX Aye, I —
PYNE Shhh!
KEENEY Well, they had her cremated out there and sent the

remains back here. And when Des went back to his flat yesterday evening there was the casket.

PYNE Poor old Des.

KEENEY But there was no covering letter. And poor Desmond made a terrible mistake.

KEENEY *lights a cigarette and gives it to* KNOX.

KNOX Ta.

KEENEY He thought it was a swanky jar of American coffee and he made a cup of coffee out of his Auntie Coco.

PYNE (*Anguished*) Oh God!

KNOX You're a . . . !

KEENEY Of course the *moment* he realized he rushed to the hospital and got it pumped out.

PYNE All of it?

KEENEY The very last grain.

PYNE That itself.

KEENEY But the pain of the stomach pump — I'm told it's hell.

PYNE I can imagine.

KNOX You must take me for a bloody eejit!

KEENEY You, Knoxie? Never!

PYNE Shh! Here he is.

KEENEY But the really disquieting thing is this: Wilson says he *loved* the taste. Shh. Not a word.

DES *enters and* KEENEY *gets to his feet.* KNOX *stares at* DES. DES, *a student of archaeology, an earnest young man of about twenty, is carrying a shoulder bag.*

Ah! The coxcomb himself. (*Softly to* KNOX) Look at the bags under his eyes.

DES Morning, morning, morning.

GEORGE
BUTT } (*Simultaneously*) Good morning, Des.

DES God, it's nippy. Hard at it, Keeney?

KEENEY As usual, Desmond.

DES There's a pool of water gathered at that far foundation trench. Needs to be let away. (*To* PYNE) Take these up to the office, Pyne, would you? (*He hands* PYNE *a small parcel*) Thanks. OK, gather round — gather round, gather round — who ordered what?

> *They gather round him as he produces things from his shoulder bag.*

Last night's paper — anybody want it?
KEENEY I'll take it.

> KEENEY *goes over to stage left and reads the paper.*

DES Razor blades — these are yours, Butt, aren't they?
BUTT Mine.
DES And your change.
BUTT Thanks.
DES (*Producing a magazine*) And that's the article you were asking about — establishing dates from the pattern of tree rings.
BUTT Good man.
DES There's another piece in that issue, too — actually we're mentioned in a footnote — about climatic conditions and the shells of *Mollusca*.
KEENEY (*Looking at the paper; almost to himself*) Many's the shell I took off Mollusca in my day.
DES A bit technical but worth persevering with.
KEENEY (*Still privately*) That describes her!
DES What are you muttering about, Keeney?
KEENEY (*Beaming*) Just trying to keep sane, Desmond.
DES Your chewing gum.

> *He throws the packet to* KEENEY.

KEENEY Bless you.
BUTT Can I hold on to this (*magazine*) over the weekend?
DES OK. But I'll want it back by Monday or Tuesday.
BUTT Thanks.
KEENEY (*Eyes still on his paper, again almost to himself*)
An assiduous old digger called Butt

Was disturbed with his life in a rut —

DES Was there anything else?

KNOX Ten fags for me.

DES Ten fags — here you are.

KEENEY I may be a conjunction
But I know it's my function
To inform my poor ignorant nut.
(*He senses* BUTT *staring aggressively at him. With a brilliant smile*) Splendid journal that, Buttie. Very scholarly.

KNOX (*To* DES) That's the wrong kind.

DES That's all they had in tens.

KNOX These are the dear ones.

DES Do you want them or do you not? (*To* PYNE, *who is coming down the steps*) Your writing paper and envelopes.

PYNE Great. Thanks.

DES That's everything. No — you (KNOX) owe me a penny.

KNOX I — ?

DES You gave me 16p.

KNOX I gave you —

DES 16p and the fags cost 17.

KNOX These do!

DES One penny please.

KNOX Christ, he's making a fortune on us all right!

DES I have to earn my fees somehow, don't I? (*Accepts the penny*) Thank you. And what the hell are you staring at?

KNOX Me? I'm not staring.

PYNE Of course you are. Leave poor Des alone. Des's fine now.

DES And if there's any more questioning about the orders you can all get George to do your huckstering for you from now on.

GEORGE For that gang? Huh!

BUTT Des, you'll have to speak to the boss about getting some sort of covering for these last few weeks.

DES Why don't you ask him yourself?

BUTT Look at these posts. (*He points to the clay-and-wattle house*) The frost's playing hell with them. And the ground — another night like last night and you'd need a bloody drill. And if it rains on top of this we'd be up to our knees in mud and we'd wreck all round us.

DES   He'd listen to you quicker than he'd listen to me.

BUTT   I'm a bloody labourer here.

DES   And I'm a bloody student and he's my bloody professor! OK, OK, I'll ask him again. Not that he gives a damn at this stage; he's got all he wants out of here and out of all of us. (*To* PYNE) Give me that spade — I want to clear that water.

PYNE   (*Passing the spade*) I say he's lost a couple of pounds weight, Des. What d'you think?

DES   Who?

PYNE   Leif.

DES   For God's sake, Pyne — it's too early in the morning.

PYNE   Ha-ha.

DES *goes off.* KEENEY *leans over the cesspit.*

KEENEY   Hello, hello, hello — is that you, Smiler? Speak up — the line's bad. Hello? Hello? Press button A, Smiler.

SMILER   (*Off*) Yes, Keeney.

KEENEY   That's better. Chewing gum — catch.

He drops the packet down the pit.

Everything in hand down there?

SMILER   (*Off*) That's right — that's right.

KEENEY   (*To himself*) 'That's right — that's right'. Did you turn left? — 'that's right'. Two and two make five — 'that's right'. One little piggy was left — 'that's right'. Oh my God.

BUTT   Are you going to work or are you not?

KEENEY   (*Charming*) How do you want to use my talents, bwana?

BUTT   Do the street and do it carefully.

KEENEY   Don't I always?

BUTT   And watch where you're bloody-well walking.

KEENEY *gets down on his knees. And now for the first time all four diggers —* BUTT, KNOX, PYNE *and* KEENEY

— are working. PYNE *whistles the opening bar of 'The Bonny Labouring Boy' and then:*

PYNE *(Sings)* 'As I went out one morning fair
All in the bloomin' spring
I overheard a damsel fair
Most grievously did sing:
"Cruel were my parents,
They did me sore annoy,
They would not let me tarry with
My bonny labouring boy."'

He continues whistling.

KNOX Did any of yous hear anything last night?
PYNE Hear what?
KNOX Noises.
PYNE Noises! What sort of noises?
KNOX Sounded like . . . *(dry chuckle)* screaming?

BUTT *stops working.*

PYNE When was this?
KNOX When? How would I know when? Some time in the middle of the night.
PYNE It was in your head, Knox. I knew you'd be the first to crack. You can't stick it any longer.
KNOX It was fierce, Butt. You must have heard it.

GEORGE, *up on the verandah, is listening intently.*
KEENEY *notices this.*

KEENEY Oh, the pranks and rascality we do be up to in the upper sixth dorm, George — you'd never guess.

GEORGE *goes into the office.*

KNOX *(To* BUTT*)* Maybe five or six screams. Then a kind of sobbing.

PYNE   I'd watch that, Knoxie, if I was you.

KNOX   You must have heard it, Butt. It was terrible.

PYNE   It was the big blonde I had. I gave her her money but she kept yelling for an overtime bonus.

BUTT   I heard it.

KNOX   (*To* PYNE) There! There!

BUTT   It was Smiler.

KNOX   You see!

BUTT   It was Smiler.

PYNE   Jesus. Did they — ?

BUTT   No. In his sleep.

Pause.

PYNE   It's almost every night now. Jesus, he must go through agonies.

KNOX   I knew I heard it. I knew. I knew.

PYNE   Jesus, the bastards — the bloody bastards.

A very brief silence. Then suddenly KEENEY *leaps to his feet.*

KEENEY   (*Very rapidly*) Good afternoon, children, and welcome to our dig. Your teacher tells me that none of you has ever seen an excavation before and you could well be excused for thinking that it does look more like a bomb crater — or maybe a huge womb — or, as one of these men has suggested, like a prison yard with the high walls and the watchtower up there and the naughty prisoners trying to tunnel their way out to freedom, ha-ha-ha.

PYNE joins the game as the teacher, addressing a group of imaginary pupils around him.

PYNE   To freedom, ha-ha-ha.

KEENEY   Now, as your teacher will have told you — Miss O'Driscoll, isn't it?

PYNE   Flora O'Driscoll. But the children just call me Tits.

KEENEY As Miss O'D will have told you, archaeology is the
scientific study of people and their culture by analysis
of their artefacts and inscriptions and monuments and
other such remains.

PYNE I've told them a dozen times, Dr King.

KEENEY And our excavations here extend from early Viking
right down to late Georgian — in other words over a
period of approximately a thousand years. So that what
you have around you is encapsulated history, a tangible
precis of the story of Irish man.

PYNE Repeat that — Irish man, Irish man.

> *Throughout* KEENEY's *lecture* PYNE *picks up the last
> two words of each sentence and repeats them* sotto
> voce *two or three times to impress them on 'her'
> pupils' minds. This echo does not interrupt the flow
> of 'King's' speech. And when the convention is estab-
> lished 'Miss O'Driscoll' merely mouths the words.*

KEENEY To give you just one instance: from our diggings we have
established what a man in the year 930, for example, had
for his lunch, what clothes he wore, what games he
liked, what musical instruments he played, what vegetables he planted in his garden. Isn't that marvellous?

PYNE Isn't that marvellous?

KEENEY And of course the more practical our information about
our ancestors the more accurate our deductions about
his attitudes, the way he thought, what his philosophy
was — in other words the more comprehensive our
definition of him. And as I keep insisting to my helpers
here — (*confidential aside*) Incidentally, when we began
this dig we had a full complement of ordinary labourers. But when our budget was exhausted we had to let
them go and now we're reduced to — (*points with elaborate secrecy to the men scraping*) And as the Swan of
Avon says, they are not what they seem.

PYNE (*Repeating the gesture*) These?

KEENEY All volunteers.

PYNE How wonderful!

KEENEY Of a sort. And unpaid of course.

PYNE Why did they volunteer?

KEENEY A good question, Tits — why? Instinct?

PYNE Boredom?

KEENEY Disaffection?

PYNE Anger?

KEENEY Estrangement?

PYNE Necessity?

KEENEY Necessity?

PYNE I want five volunteers — you, you, you, you and you.

KEENEY Oh, that kind of necessity! No, they are all genuine volunteers.

PYNE Marvellous!

KEENEY But men, I'm afraid, of turbulent tendencies. But that's an intriguing story in itself.

PYNE Really?

KEENEY Tell you in bed tonight, Tits.

PYNE Oh, Doctor!

KEENEY (*Loudly again*) And as I keep insisting to my friends here, the more we learn about our ancestors, children, the more we discover about ourselves — isn't that so? So that what we are all engaged in here is really a thrilling voyage in *self*-discovery.

PYNE He makes it all so interesting.

KEENEY But the big question is: how many of us want to make *that* journey? Be that as it may, let's look around, shall we, and get a general picture first.

PYNE Into line, children. Butt, pay attention! Knox, leave yourself alone!

KEENEY Now, up here we have the remains of Georgian cellars. And below that is a bank of debris from Norman times.

PYNE Norman times — Norman times — Norman times.

KEENEY And beside us here . . . Excuse me, Knox, could you let the children through?

KNOX Fuck off.

KEENEY (*Aside*) Fluent Norse speaker; and although he does have the characteristic stature and odour of a Norseman he is in fact much later. And almost certainly the last of the fertility symbols — wouldn't you agree?

PYNE Definitely.

KEENEY (*Loud again*) And here — here we have the remains of three centuries of waste. And where I stand — can you all see, children? — where this man (BUTT) is digging, we have the remains of a Viking house. Any exciting finds today, Butt? (*Aside*) One of our most dedicated men. Married — adept with the trowel — ten kids. A real primitive but passionately interested.

PYNE How primitive?

KEENEY Startling. Tell you in bed tonight.

PYNE You rascal!

KEENEY (*Loud again*) Now this house, as you see, is a teeny-weeny place by our standards — it's really the size of a prison cell, isn't it? — but very compact and very cosy and I'm sure our Viking ancestor was idyllically happy in it. Known as a post-and-wattle house.

PYNE Post-and-wattle, post-and-wattle.

KEENEY Ash or elm uprights with hazel wattling. Clay floor. Fireplace in the centre. And around it at night sat our tenth-century stonemason or farmer or sailor, combing and narding his tresses while his good wife, Mollusca, and her happy brood practised their swordsmanship.

PYNE Ab-so-lutely fascinating. And who is this gentleman?

KEENEY That, Miss O'D, is the gentle of the land.

PYNE Is he . . . dead?

KEENEY Ah, there are two schools of thought about that. (*To* GEORGE, *who has returned to his table*) Wouldn't you agree, George?

GEORGE What about telling the kids the startling history of the diggers, Keeney?

PYNE Who is he, Professor?

KEENEY George — who accompanies me on all my excavations: site manager, foreman, caretaker, and ass-licker of everyone in authority.

PYNE We work for an ass-licking gaff
Who considers his diggers riff-raff — Ha-ha.

DES (*Entering*) Am I the only one's frozen this morning? George!

GEORGE Hello.

DES In that brown parcel there's a new jar of coffee. Make us a cup, will you?

KEENEY (*Gripping* KNOX's *elbow*) My God, he's really hooked on it.

GEORGE Do you want it just now?

DES If you're not too busy.

GEORGE Actually I'm in the middle of —

DES OK, OK, I'll make it myself.

GEORGE No, it's all right. I'll do it.

DES Thank you, George. Anyone else want a cup?

BUTT None for me.

PYNE Nor me.

DES Keeney?

KEENEY Damn it all — why not? A dash of San Francisco in the blood!

DES Knox?

Pause.

KEENEY The man's talking to you, Knoxie.

DES Do you want a cup of coffee?

KNOX Me? Christ, no; no, no, no, no, no.

KNOX *busies himself scraping.*

DES It's all right, Knox — I'm only asking you. What's wrong with that guy?

PYNE (*Going to pit*) Smiler might take a cup.

DES (*To* BUTT) Remember those seeds you found last June?

BUTT What seeds?

PYNE Smiler!

SMILER Baby!

DES Remember — you got them inside a bowl in that lower Viking section.

BUTT Oh, those. Aye.

DES Well, they're . . . (*produces a letter*) Just got the report back from the lab . . .

PYNE Coffee!

DES (*Reads*) 'Chenopodium — goosefoot — pale persicaria.'

124

BUTT What's that?

DES 'Knot grass and black bindweed.'

BUTT Never heard of it.

DES Chenopodium is 'an edible weed with a green flower and includes the family of mangelwurzel and orach' — whatever they are.

KEENEY Quite common.

DES So apparently that was part of their diet.

KEENEY Anywhere the soil's alkaline.

DES Turn it off, Keeney, would you?

KEENEY Chenopodium — goosefoot — footloose — fancy-free — tickle-my-fancy — fancy-meeting-you-here — 'tell me where is fancy bred' — it has a lot of names. My grandmother used to boil it with nettles and give it to us.

DES That a fact?

KEENEY Yes. When we were young turkeys and she wanted to redden our combs.

He goes off with a bucket.

PYNE Ha-ha.

DES (*Calling*) Pity she didn't break your bloody neck!

DES *goes towards the steps.*

KNOX Hi, Butt, what's this?

KNOX *has unearthed a small piece of bone. The find is of routine interest; no excitement.*

BUTT Is it a bit of an antler?

KNOX I got it here.

BUTT It's bone. And there's some sort of a design.

PYNE Let's see.

KNOX Bugger off, you!

PYNE Sorry — sorry.

BUTT Probably a trial piece.

KNOX I knew it was a bone. It felt like a trial piece — you

know — smooth.

BUTT It's an illustration of a ship. (*Increased interest*) Hi, Des, come here till you see this.

KNOX A ship — a ship — I just thought it was a ship.

PYNE I think it's a nuclear sub, Knoxie.

KNOX Is — ?

PYNE Ha-ha-ha.

KNOX Bugger you, Pyne!

BUTT (*To* DES) Look at the illustration.

DES Very clear, isn't it? A warship and one — two — three — four warriors. Who got it?

KNOX Me. I did. I got it.

DES Where?

KNOX Just there. At the corner.

DES Right, OK. I'll record it.

He moves towards the steps.

BUTT Des — is it a warship?

DES Didn't you see the four warriors?

BUTT She's very broad for a warship.

DES So?

BUTT That chart behind the office door — the one of all those ships in that Danish museum — it's the very same ship as the bottom one on that chart.

DES Are you sure?

BUTT I'm sure. And she's listed as a trader.

DES So she's a trader — an armed trader.

BUTT And on that chart she's dated 1150.

DES OK. So she's a twelfth-century trader. Go to the top of the class.

BUTT But we found her here beside this house. And this house is tenth century. So the dating of that museum trader is . . . isn't right.

DES Come off it, Butt.

BUTT The chart's wrong, Des!

DES Don't be absurd.

BUTT Either the chart's wrong or the dating of this house is wrong.

DES Would it not occur to you that this (*trial piece*) mightn't belong to the same period as the house?

BUTT But it must — we're at boulder-clay level. The museum's wrong, Des.

DES OK — OK — no need to get aggressive. We'll check it out calmly. All right — could we settle down now and get a bit of solid work done?

He goes up the steps.

KNOX Christ, what bit him?

BUTT The museum is wrong.

KNOX You're right, Butt. The moment I seen it I knew it was a trader.

KEENEY enters. His speech takes him right across the stage.

KEENEY Let us pray. Beloved St Persicaria, who in thy lifetime among the pagan eskimo didst vouchsafe to make the viola honoured and revered, we now beseech you to smile upon the endeavours of young Dolly Wilson who at this moment is doing her Grade Four Guildhall School of Music London practical. But only if success in her efforts would be in the interests of her immortal soul.

He goes off.

PYNE Amen. Ha-ha. Great aul' instrument, the viola, all the same. Ha-ha.

He goes off. Only BUTT and KNOX are left on the site floor. Pause. KNOX moves closer to BUTT. His speech is a mixture of confidence and a reverie.

KNOX I learned the cello, Butt. Up till I was nine. Christ. (*Pause*) He used to come to the house every Thursday — an Italian fella. And at the end of the lesson my mother and the maid would bring us up tea and cakes on a big posh silver tray. And your man Vitelli — Christ, *that* was his name! How in Christ's name did I remember that? — he'd bow low and kiss my mother's hand and then he'd eat the cakes with his fingers out like this — eat every damned one of them down to the last crumb. And then my father would have the car sent round to drive him home to wherever it was he came from . . . Signor Vitelli . . . Christ, where did that name come out of . . . ?

He begins working again. BUTT, *who stopped to listen to his story, still gazes at him for a few seconds. Then he, too, begins working.* DES *has been looking at the articles on the trestle table, including the jug. He now goes into the office where* GEORGE *is making coffee. He consults the chart behind the door.*

GEORGE   We look at the pictures in a couple of professional journals and suddenly we're experts.
DES   Mm?
GEORGE   Next thing he'll be looking for a site of his own.
DES   What are you talking about?
GEORGE   Butt.
DES   He might well be right.
GEORGE   A thick customer, Butt.
DES   Isn't that a good one — he could very well be right.

DES *leaves the chart and consults a book.*

GEORGE   Your coffee.
DES   In a minute.
GEORGE   I finished the jug last night.
DES   So.
GEORGE   What do you think of it?
DES   Pretty.
GEORGE   Exquisite, isn't it?
DES   Pretty.

Brief pause.

GEORGE Desmond, I'd appreciate it if you didn't order me about before the labourers.

DES Mm?

GEORGE I'm talking to you, Desmond.

DES What's that?

GEORGE The boss wants you to finish the photographing today.

DES Yes.

GEORGE He wants a complete series of the west section, especially the wall junction and the bank of debris.

DES Right.

GEORGE And all the sacks will have to be labelled and recorded before they're left up at the gate.

DES George, could I have time to check this first?

GEORGE As long as we get the whole place cleared up by this evening.

DES Are we expecting visitors?

GEORGE This is our last day.

DES What do you mean — our last day?

GEORGE I thought you knew. The dig's over.

DES The dig's over when the dig's finished.

KEENEY *enters and begins working.*

GEORGE I'm only repeating instructions, Desmond.

DES Whose instructions? What are you talking about?

GEORGE The boss called in yesterday after you left — all the stuff's being carted off on Monday and the builders move in on Tuesday.

DES What are you talking about, George?

GEORGE Dr King's orders.

DES But we're not finished here! There's at least another two weeks' work to be done! We haven't even touched that outer wall!

GEORGE Boss's orders!

DES Bloody marvellous! The speculators whistle once and Professor King says, 'It's all yours, boys. Sorry for holding you up' — a site the like of which this country has never seen before!

GEORGE The money's finished.

DES The money was finished three months ago. Money's not the problem. They're not paid. I'm not paid. For God's sake, the royalties from his worthless books would keep this place going for six years. What do they say?

PYNE *enters and begins working.*

GEORGE They haven't been told yet.

DES I suppose they don't matter?

GEORGE I didn't say that.

DES So the only people in on the secret are you and King and the builders?

GEORGE And the museum board. And there's nothing secret about it. Wilson'll tell them over the weekend.

DES They'll be told now — by me.

GEORGE I don't think that's wise, Desmond.

DES Maybe not. But they did more work here than all of us put together. Is King at the museum?

GEORGE At a board meeting.

DES (*Preparing to leave*) Right. You just don't abandon a site like this because you've looted enough for another coffee-table book or because you've another fat site lined up for next year.

GEORGE Where are you going?

DES To the museum — to lodge a formal protest with the committee.

GEORGE Desmond, don't be hasty, don't do anything you'll —

DES *marches out of the office, stands on the verandah. He is angry, but he is also conscious of the moment.*

DES I want you all to listen to me.

PYNE Quiet, there! Quiet! Quiet! Quiet!

DES I've something very important to tell you — something that affects all of us.

KEENEY A speech, be God, a speech!

PYNE Settle down there!

KEENEY Let the dog see the rabbit!

PYNE Silence!

KEENEY Quiet!

PYNE Quiet!

KEENEY Silence gentlemen, for Dessy the Red!

DES I've just learned from the site manager that —

KEENEY I've been chosen Queen of the May!

PYNE Ha-ha.

DES — the dig ends this evening.

PYNE What's this? What's this?

DES Orders from Professor King.

PYNE The dig's over?

DES This is as big a shock for me as it is for you. And I'm going straight over to the museum now to see Dr King and the board. And I'm going to tell them that if they allow the builders on to this site before our job is finished I personally will write to every newspaper in the country and expose this act for what it is — a rape of irreplaceable materials, a destruction of knowledge that the Irish people have a right to inherit, and a capitulation to moneyed interests.

KEENEY That's good. That's impressive. God but I'm a sucker for that sort of stuff.

DES As for you men, no one knows better than myself how much toil and sweat you have put into this dig and I know that you are as angered by this news as I am. As to what form your anger will take, that is up to you. I appreciate that your circumstances are peculiar. But I also know that you are in the circumstances you are in because you are men of passionate conviction. And I just want you to know that whatever stance you take, whatever protest you think fit, it will be the right one and I will be fully and wholeheartedly behind you.

He runs down the steps and quickly off. BUTT *scarcely moves from his kneeling position.* KNOX *is not quite sure what has happened.* KEENEY *and* PYNE *stare after* DES *with exaggerated incredulity because they recognize that his speech and his exit were that bit too histrionic. Pause.*

PYNE By the Lord Harry.

KEENEY Well-well-well-well-well.

PYNE What was that all about?

KEENEY Good question. I think we've just been sacked.

PYNE Us? Never.

KEENEY Looks like.

PYNE (*Calls*) Hi, George, what's happening?

KEENEY In fact I'm sure of it.

PYNE Sacked?

KEENEY Booted.

PYNE Fired?

KEENEY Just like that.

PYNE God, that's heartbreaking. I mean to say, this is the first time in my life I've ever felt — you know what I mean like — fulfilled in my work.

KEENEY As the actress said to the bishop.

PYNE Ha-ha. Hi, Leif, you're redundant. Go up to the office and George'll give you your cards.

KEENEY All the same it was a great speech.

PYNE Des's? Magnificent.

KEENEY Positively stirring.

PYNE No spittle nor nothing.

KEENEY That's a fact.

PYNE (*Holds face up for inspection*) Look. Dry as a bone. And I was right below him.

KEENEY The clichés were only cascading out of him. 'Whatever stance you take, whatever protest you think fit' — if he ever packs up this job he can walk straight into politics.

PYNE (*Sings*) 'Vote, vote, vote for Comrade Desmond.'

KEENEY He looks that part, too.

PYNE Hi, Keeney, he said something mighty funny.

KEENEY Everything he said was hilarious.

PYNE He said we were angry. Are we angry?

KEENEY Naturally we're furious.

PYNE That's OK. But you never told me your circumstances were peculiar.

KEENEY As for my convictions, by Christ they're so passionate you could grill lamb chops on them.

PYNE Ha-ha.

KNOX Is the job over, Butt?

KEENEY The perceptive Knox. Did you ever notice that about Knoxie? — Straight through the waffle and right to the kernel. Yes, Knoxie, back to the mailbags. But as Desmond says, boys, we ought to take up a stance.

PYNE Are yous mice or are yous men?

KEENEY What about a dignified withdrawal of labour?

PYNE Or a go-slow.

KEENEY Or lobby our TD.

PYNE That's more like it.

KEENEY Did you ever lobby your TD?

PYNE Never.

KEENEY Or his wife?

PYNE Now you're talking. 'Deputy's wife lobbied by irate diggers.'

KEENEY 'But nothing uncovered,' says triumphant Mrs Immaculata Kelly.

PYNE Ha-ha. (*He goes to cesspit*) Hi, Smiler!

KEENEY Have you any suggestions, Butt? We've got Desmond's word that he'll back us.

BUTT I'm going to finish this section.

KEENEY Did you hear that, Pyne?

PYNE What's that?

KEENEY I ask Buttie Boy here for his suggestions and d'you know what he says?

PYNE What?

KEENEY 'I'm going to finish this section.'

PYNE That's our Butt.

KEENEY *Buttie's Aplomb and Other Stories*. I didn't think they bred men like that anymore.

PYNE Never underestimate Butt.

KEENEY I mean to say, he may be a poor peasant crofter but that's real public school — that's what that is. Don't be deceived by that rustic appearance. As good a man as Casabianca any day — that's what our Buttie is.

PYNE The boy stood on the burning deck

And he was playing cricket;
The captain bowled a spinning ball
And hit his middle wicket. Ha-ha-ha.

KEENEY Or Francis Drake — Butt knows that story. D'you know it, Pyne?

PYNE What's that one?

KEENEY 'Sir Francis, Sir Francis, the Armada's within sight of the coast!' 'First I'll finish my game of bowls and then I'll thrash the Spaniards.'

PYNE Frightfully good.

KEENEY Marvellous aul' shite they taught you at school, too, Butt, wasn't it? And I'm sure you remember the one about Thomas More mounting the scaffolding. 'I pray you, Lord Lieutenant, see me safe up and for my coming down let me shift for myself.' D'you think did Leif say something like that when he was being hoisted?

PYNE Come on up, Smiler. We're sacked.

PYNE goes off.

KEENEY Marvellous bloody phoney lines. All the same when you were a kid and the Christian Brothers were beating the tar out of you, be Jaysus you'd have swopped your aul' crags for aplomb like that, wouldn't you, Buttie? Give us one of your crags and I'll give you a bite of a-plomb, eh? What am I talking about? You did, man. You have it.

Slowly and menacingly BUTT *gets to his feet, armed with a trowel.*

BUTT I'm going to close your mouth, Keeney.

PYNE (*Entering*) Hi, boys, where's Smiler? (*Crosses stage calling*) Smiler! Smiler!

He goes off.

BUTT I've stood your taunting day in and day out for the past five months and now I'm going to close your mouth

for good.
KEENEY George, he's going to hit me, George!
PYNE (*Off*) Smiler!
BUTT Come on, Keeney, come on, come on! Give us some of your yap now, Keeney — give us some of your smart chat now. Just once more, Keeney, just once more!
PYNE (*Entering*) Smiler's gone, boys!
KEENEY Don't let him hit me, Pyne!
PYNE D'you hear me — Smiler's gone!

Very brief pause.

KEENEY Yes, we know — he's slipped out to the pub with Leif.
PYNE I'm not joking, Keeney. He's not here.

The reaction is more than surprise — there is an element of panic.

KEENEY He's in the pit.
PYNE He's not. He's not on the site.
KEENEY Are you sure?
PYNE Positive. I'm telling you — he's cleared.
KEENEY Christ Almighty!

Very brief pause. Then KEENEY *rushes off, calling:*

Smiler! Smiler!
BUTT Did you look in the shed?
PYNE Not there.
BUTT (*Up to* GEORGE *who has appeared*) Is Smiler up there?
GEORGE No one up here.
KEENEY (*Off*) Smiler!
BUTT (*To* KNOX) Look out there. Quick! Quick!
KNOX Maybe he's —
BUTT Now!

KNOX *shuffles off.* BUTT *runs up the steps.*

GEORGE You're not allowed into —

BUTT *tosses him aside and goes into the office.* KEENEY *enters and as he runs across the stage he calls:*

KEENEY Smiler! Smiler!

He exits again, BUTT *comes out of the office and goes behind it.*

BUTT OK, Smiler, where are you? This is no time for fooling. Come on, Smiler, where are you?

GEORGE *has come down the steps.*

GEORGE (*To* PYNE) When did you see him last?
KEENEY (*Off*) Smiler!
PYNE I don't know — a while ago — he was standing there, wasn't he? — Jesus, I don't know.

BUTT *on verandah.* KEENEY *enters.*

BUTT He's not here.
KEENEY He's gone.
KNOX (*Enters*) No, he's not out there, Butt.

A long pause as they look at one another. Finally:

GEORGE How long is he gone?
PYNE How would I know — half-an-hour — three-quarters — five minutes —
GEORGE Did he say anything to any of you?
PYNE Not to me he didn't. (*To* BUTT) Did he say anything to you?
BUTT No.
PYNE To you, Knoxie?
KNOX Nor me neither.
GEORGE Where would he head for?
BUTT D'you think he knows that himself?
GEORGE Where's he from?
PYNE Donegal.

GEORGE Would he head for there?
BUTT What for?
GEORGE Family — relations — friends.
BUTT You don't know what you're talking about.
GEORGE He must have some sort of a plan in his head.
PYNE Aul' Smiler? Jesus, sure he hardly knows his own name.

> GEORGE *goes briskly towards the steps.* KEENEY *is standing at the bottom, blocking his way.*

GEORGE I've a phone call to make. (*Pause*) Get out of the road. (*Pause*) I've got to notify the authorities that Smiler has escaped. Move, Keeney!

> *Pause.*

BUTT He's right, Keeney. If it was anyone else but Smiler. Let him phone.
PYNE Butt's right.
BUTT It's for his own good, Keeney. With a man like Smiler it's not squealing.
GEORGE Move!

> *Pause.*

PYNE (*Quickly*) We'll take a vote on it. George phones or he doesn't — which is it? Butt?
BUTT Phones.
PYNE Knoxie?
KNOX I think he should phone.
PYNE So do I.
GEORGE Let me past, Keeney.
BUTT Let him past, Keeney.
PYNE You're only wasting time. The quicker he's found the better.
KEENEY Do me a favour, George, would you? Leave us alone for two minutes. I've something private to say to my friends here.
GEORGE I'm going to —

KEENEY What I have to say is of interest only to the criminal element. Just two minutes. Please. I'm asking a favour, George. Please.

GEORGE *looks around at the others.*

GEORGE Two minutes exactly. Then I'm phoning.

He goes off.

KEENEY (*Beaming*) My God, this is all very serious. Look at all those solemn faces.

BUTT What have you got to say, Keeney?

KEENEY Just a few words — nothing more than a few words — and I promise you, Pyne, there'll be no saliva.

BUTT Are you going to say what you have to say or not?

KEENEY Yes. Well. All I've got to tell you is this. That our fellow internees held a meeting the night before last — no, not really a meeting — a sort of kangaroo court. And they discussed again our defection in volunteering for this job. And they were unanimous that being sent to Coventry wasn't an adequate punishment for us. So the court ruled that a punishment to fit the crime of treason be meted. And the assembled brethren decided that the only fit punishment would be . . . capital.

PYNE Who told you this? When did you hear this?

KEENEY So there is to be a contrived riot in Block C probably next Monday night. And in the course of that riot they're going to take care of us — a fall from a roof — a tumble down a stairs — you know how accidents can happen in a chaotic situation —

KNOX Are they going to do us, Butt?

KEENEY Correct, Knox. They're going to do us — or at least some of us.

KNOX (*To* BUTT) Not the screws?

KEENEY Correct again, Knox.

PYNE Jesus, the man that comes near me will —

KEENEY Exactly. But what chance has Smiler? — None!

BUTT What chance has he out there?

KEENEY Very little, agreed, but still a chance. So the choice we have is to let him have that chance, however slender, or have him brought back to a certain accident. It's up to you, gentlemen; because if you all disagree with me, who am I to oppose the process of democracy? (*Calls*) Right, George, come and join us!

Pause. Then quick blackout.

ACT TWO

Late afternoon on the same day. Already a portion of the site has been cleared — e.g. the trestle table and many of the plastic sacks are gone. BUTT *and* KNOX *enter and exit, carrying off timbers, buckets, etc.* GEORGE *is in the office, taking books from the shelves, charts off the walls, etc. We can hear* PYNE *offstage singing a song.* KEENEY *is on the verandah rinsing cups. He stops and listens to* PYNE's *song. Then he joins with great gusto in the last line and as he sings it he joins* GEORGE *in the office. There he makes tea.* KEENEY *seems to have established a right to be in the office; and he is even more assured, more relaxed, than in Act One.* GEORGE *tries to ignore him.*

PYNE (*Singing, off*) 'Said the mother to the daughter fair,
    "Why did you stoop so low
    To marry a poor labouring boy
    Around the world to go?
    Some noble lord might fancy you,
    Great riches to enjoy . . . "'
KEENEY (*Joining in*) 'So why do you throw yourself away
    On a poor labouring boy?'
    (*Now in office*) Powerful aul' song that, too, isn't it, George? Boys, but there's nothing I like better than to hear men singing at their work. Gives you a wonderful aul' feeling of . . . reassurance, doesn't it? God's in his heavens and the eternal verities are still thumping along. Or maybe I'm being romantic, George, am I? What d'you think? (*Searches*) Milk — milk — (*Finds it*) Ah. Of course I'm not talking about my own croaking. I mean to say I just threw in my couple of aul' bars there just to nettle you — as you well know. But I'll say that for old George: he's not easy riz, by God he's not. (*Reaching across* GEORGE) The professor wouldn't mind if I borrowed his Wedgwood mug, would he? No, he

wouldn't. Aye, the very first day I slapped eyes on you you reminded me of the manager of the first bank I was posted to. At least once a week he'd say to me: 'Mister Keeney' — he was from Belmullet but the poor eejit thought that a Scotch accent was more appropriate for a bank manager — 'Mister Keeney, the client who always withdraws is no man.' And honest to God, George, I was an innocent cub in those days and I thought it was a class of dirty aul' chat he was at. D'you know does Buttie take sugar? Dammit it's good for him. (*Counts cups*) One — two — three — four — that's it. Pity we hadn't a wee cake now and the farewell party'd be complete. Aye, there used to be an aul' hoor in Derry. Spent her nights dodging about the quays. Her name was Vera McLaughlin but she was known as Eternal Verity — wasn't that apt? (*Searching*) A spoon — a spoon — (*Discovers the jug*) Here — what's this? So this is where you have it?

GEORGE Don't you lay a —

KEENEY Smiler's pieces all put together and making a hand-some jug! Oh you're a secretive wee man, too, George.

GEORGE Put that — !

KEENEY Well, isn't that elegant; very elegant indeed. Oh, the boys will have to see this, George. Oh, they've a right to see this. I mean to say, George, aesthetic delights aren't for the elite alone — as Dessy the Red'll tell you. But it's more than an aesthetic delight, this, George. This is an omen. What am I talking about — it's much more than an omen — it's a symbol, George. This is Smiler, George; Smiler restored; Smiler full, free and integrated. Or maybe I'm being romantic again, George, am I?

GEORGE Keeney, if you —

KEENEY Dammit no, I'm not. Not about Smiler. The rest of us now, we're different. I mean to say, we — well, not to put a tooth in it — we deliberately 'offended against the state', or to be strictly accurate, George, they in-terned us because of 'attitudes that might be inimical to public security'. But Smiler — d'you know Smiler's story? A stonemason from the west of Donegal; a quarry employing seven men; and Smiler's the shop steward. And when they interned one of his mates, what d'you think the stupid bugger did but call his men out and set off on a protest march to Dublin! Can you imagine? Six thick quarrymen from the back of nowhere, led by Smiler, thumping across the country behind a tatty banner and a half-drunk mouth organ. Well, of course they got about as far as the Derry border and there they whipped Smiler off to jail in Dublin and beat the tar out of him for twelve consecutive hours — you know, just as a warning. And begod it worked, George, worked like a spell. I mean to say, look at him now — a more civil man you couldn't meet in a day's travel. That's right — that's right. Course they give him the odd bleaching still — you know — just to keep him in trim. But it's kind of superfluous, wouldn't you say so? (*Admiring the jug*) All the same there's a victory there, George. Be Jaysus, George, I know he's going to defeat them.

GEORGE (*With quiet fury*) I'm giving you adequate warning now, Keeney, that when Mr Wilson gets here I'm going to make a formal charge against you. One — that you connived at the escape of a fellow prisoner; and two — that you threatened violence against my person if I reported that escape to the appropriate authorities.

KEENEY (*Confused innocence*) Isn't that two charges, George?

GEORGE And I'll do all in my power to see that the full rigours of the law are applied against you.

KEENEY Believe me, George, even detectives in bad thrillers don't talk like that anymore. (*Lifts tray and exits*) Party time! Party time!

> Only BUTT is onstage as KEENEY descends. We can hear PYNE whistling, off.

Call them in, Butt, for a farewell celebration. (*Calls*) Doctor Pyne, strawberries and cream on the lawn!

PYNE (*Off*) Coming!

KEENEY *puts the tray down close to* BUTT *and speaks quietly, almost gently, but with a passion that is scarcely concealed.*

KEENEY I'm going to let you in on a secret, Buttie: I'm feeling reckless — no, not reckless — wild. You know on a Friday night after you've washed and shaved and put on the good suit and the pay packet's in the pocket and the first half's sitting on the counter before you and you've an almost overwhelming sense of power and control and generosity and liberation — and yet at the same time there's nothing you'd like better than to smash something or go roaring down the street with a woman under each arm. Well, that's how I feel now, Butt — anarchic, is that the word? But sure who am I tellin'? Isn't that what has us all in bother?

BUTT I think we done the wrong thing, Keeney — you know, about Smiler.

KEENEY, *deliberately parodying his previous speech, now takes up a drunken, belligerent stance.*

KEENEY Come on, yous bastards, come on! Yous couldn't bate time with a toy drum!

BUTT We should have let George report him.

KEENEY Where's the father of Calvinism? (*Calls*) Knoxie!

BUTT We made a mistake, Keeney.

KEENEY A religious reformer called Knoxie
Made love to a Papist from Hoxie —

BUTT Any of the rest of us it would have been different.

KEENEY Cried she, 'Something's wrong!
There's a terrible pong!
It's the smell of your unorthodoxy!'

BUTT Smiler's special. You know that yourself.

KEENEY You agreed that he take his chance.

BUTT Only because that's the way you were all voting.

KEENEY He may make it. You never know.

BUTT Make it! How can Smiler make it!

KEENEY He thinks he can.

BUTT　He doesn't know the day of the week it is. And when they catch him they really will kill him this time — you know that.

KEENEY　Yes, they'll kill him. Or his own mates'll kill him — or kill you or me or Pyne or Knox. Yes, one way or the other there's going to be a bloodletting. But at least now he's not going to be a volunteer. And then again, Buttie Boy, you never know, he might escape — remember, fools have a long and impressive history of immunity.

> PYNE *enters.*

PYNE　Great! Where did the tea come from?

KEENEY　The provident George — who else?

PYNE　One decent man. (*Calls up*) God's blessing on you and yours, George. You wouldn't have an aul' loaf of bread or an aul' pair of shoes or an aul' jacket you don't need? Ha-ha.

BUTT　I was just saying to Keeney that —

PYNE　Which (*cup*) is mine?

KEENEY　Any one at all.

PYNE　If I drank out of the boss's mug, d'you think it would make me smart? (*To* KNOX, *who has just entered*) Here you are, boy.

KNOX　It isn't that coffee, is it?

PYNE　You're a suspicious bastard, too, Knoxie. It's tea, man. D'you want it or do you not?

KNOX　Ta.

BUTT　I was saying to Keeney I think we should get George to phone in and say that —

> KEENEY *produces the jug with a flourish.*

KEENEY　Gentlemen, the item you've been waiting for!

PYNE　What's that?

> GEORGE *has discovered that the jug is missing. He comes out on to the verandah.*

144

KEENEY Lot 142 — the unique Burgundy Jug discovered in Ireland in the 1970s by Professor Smiler!

BUTT Is it . . . ?

PYNE It's the lad, by God!

KEENEY Nothing less. And what can I say to connoisseurs like yourselves except that the only other comparable piece is one of the most treasured possessions of the British Museum and that in my long career in the art world never before have I had the privilege of handling an item of this distinction. Gentlemen, what am I offered for Smiler's Jug?

PYNE Ha-ha. (*Calls*) Hi, George, you might pick up a bargain here!

GEORGE *comes slowly down the steps.*

BUTT Show me.

KEENEY Certainly.

KNOX (*Privately to* PYNE) What's he drinking his tea out of that for?

PYNE Jesus, Knox, you can take you nowhere.

KEENEY 'To what green altar, O mysterious priest,
Lead'st thou that heifer lowing at the skies.'
Well, Buttie?

BUTT He made a great job of it.

KEENEY Didn't he?

BUTT Good.

KEENEY Beautiful, isn't it?

BUTT It's good.

KEENEY (*Quietly*) I knew you'd like it.

PYNE Show me it. (KEENEY *gives the jug to* PYNE)

KEENEY Right, gentlemen, make me a bid. What am I offered? Everything must be disposed of today.

GEORGE (*Now beside* PYNE) I'll take that.

GEORGE *and* KEENEY *both reach for the jug.* KEENEY *gets it.*

KEENEY Now, now, now, George, don't be a spoilsport.

GEORGE Give it to me.

KEENEY If you have an offer to make, George, put up your hand like everybody else.

> GEORGE *is now between* PYNE *and* KEENEY *who pretend they are going to throw it over and back across his head.*

PYNE (*Clapping his hands*) Here, Keeney, here, here!

GEORGE Give it to me, Keeney.

KEENEY Sing us a song, George, and I'll give it to you.

GEORGE Hand it over.

KEENEY (*Sings*) 'She was only the sergeant's daughter . . . '

PYNE Over his head, Keeney! Over his head!

KEENEY 'But she let the county inspect-or — '

GEORGE I'm asking you, Keeney.

PYNE Quick, man, quick!

GEORGE I've warned you already!

KEENEY (*To* BUTT) Maybe this is what I should smash — what d'you think?

PYNE Throw — throw — throw!

GEORGE (*Turning to* BUTT) All right — I'm holding you responsible for that jug. Anything happens to that jug, Butt, it's your responsibility. Remember that.

> GEORGE *goes off.*

PYNE (*Calling after him*) Don't you worry, George. I'll keep an eye on it. Ha-ha.

BUTT (*To* KEENEY) Come on. Cut out the fooling. I don't want any accidents with that. Leave it up where it belongs.

KEENEY Now that's a curious phrase — 'where it belongs'. Where does it belong? Is it Smiler's — finders keepers? Or is it the Professor's? Or does it belong to the nation? Or does it belong to — Brother Leif? Dammit, that's a thought! And if it's Leif's, isn't it about time he got it back?

PYNE Bloody good idea!

KEENEY *places the jug at Leif's feet.*

KEENEY And when you think of it, what safer place could it be than in the vaults of a 150-storey hotel?

PYNE Look! He's smiling. He says thanks very much — he was lost without it.

KEENEY Isn't that nice? The courtesy of the older generation.

KEENEY *crouches beside Leif and keeps looking at him throughout the following sequence.*

All the same that's a fair big hole in the top of the skull. A clout like that would knock the thought of women out of your head for a couple of hours, wouldn't it?

PYNE Speak for yourself. I damn near died of a fractured skull in New York. Going back on board and slipped on the bloody gangway. Fourteen weeks I was on my back, but I swear to God — I'm not joking — it was thinking about women all the time that pulled me through.

KEENEY (*Quietly, still staring at Leif*) Talk to me about him, Butt.

PYNE The doctors said it was a bloody miracle.

KEENEY What sort of man was he, Butt?

PYNE Leif? I'll tell you everything about him. What d'you want to know?

KEENEY Was he a Friday-night man? Did he think he was invincible? Did he challenge them all? Or was he a husk, like George, a cliché? Tell me about him, Butt.

PYNE I'll tell you. I read the whole inside story in the Sunday papers.

KEENEY *suddenly leaps to his feet.*

KEENEY (*With excessive enthusiasm*) Right, Pyne! You tell us! We'll start with you! You tell us his story!

PYNE Well, children . . .

KEENEY We're off!

PYNE Once upon a time . . .

KEENEY Tits O'Driscoll!

PYNE Behave yourself, Keeney.

KEENEY Yes, Miss, sorry, Miss.

PYNE Once upon a time . . .

KEENEY 'Once upon a time' — ah sure, thanks be to God, lads, it's only an aul' yarn.

PYNE Once upon a time there were two cousins. One was tall and fair and his name was Ulf; and the other was small and ginger and his name was Leif.

KEENEY 'The one red leaf, the last of its clan.'

PYNE Jesus, d'you want to hear the story or do you not?

KEENEY We're all ears — aren't we, Butt? (*To* PYNE) Go ahead — 'and his name was Leif'.

PYNE And they lived in a modest little settlement at the top of a fjord.

KEENEY Now wasn't that grand entirely.

PYNE And when they were still little boys their families decided to emigrate from Norway and they sailed for Ireland and settled in a colony here and became Christians.

KEENEY Settled where?

PYNE On this very spot.

KEENEY Where we stand?

PYNE Just there.

KEENEY (*With reverence*) The holy ground. (*Suddenly sings*) 'Once more, boys —'

KEENEY ⎱
PYNE   ⎰ (*Together*) 'Once more — the holy ground once more.'

They break off. PYNE *laughs.*

PYNE Now I'm bloody lost. Where was I?

KEENEY Little Ulf and little Leif — Ulfeen and Leifeen — gulpin and elfin —

KNOX Why don't you shut up, Keeney!

KEENEY *turns to him in amused astonishment.*

KEENEY Now there's a compliment for you, Pyne.

PYNE Thank you, Knox.

KEENEY Relax, Knoxie. Your turn's coming. (*Confidentially to* BUTT) Over-eager — that's his problem.

PYNE And as they grew up the two little boys were inseparable. Everything Ulf did, Leif did the same. And when they were both sixteen they signed on the same tanker and sailed together to Greenland and North Africa and the Middle East and up the Baltic . . .

KEENEY 'Once upon a time' — keep up the protection of the myth.

PYNE And then in their twenty-first year they were both crewmen on the first Viking ship to discover America.

KEENEY Hurrah!

PYNE And they never had a time together like the time they had there — between hunting and fighting and Indian women and making expeditions inland together. Leif wanted to settle down there but after a few months Ulf became homesick, and even though it was the month of February nothing would satisfy him but they'd equip a ship and set out for home.

KEENEY For Norway.

PYNE Here — this was their home now.

KEENEY Of course. Merely trying to divert them.

PYNE So Ulf loaded the ship with all the booty he could lay hands on, and Leif — all he took with him was the Indian girl he'd set up with out there. And on their way back they were torn to pieces by the winter gales, and Ulf and his booty were washed overboard, and the only two to make it back were Leif and his woman.

KEENEY (*To* BUTT) Ah, shure I can schmell dishaster comin'.

PYNE And instead of welcoming them the two families stared at Leif and his brown woman and said, 'Where's Ulf? And who is this black pagan?' And although Leif told them about the terrible Atlantic gales, they said, 'No. This black woman is evil. She killed our Ulf. Now you and she must die.'

KEENEY Don't you know!

PYNE And they burned the Indian woman before Leif's eyes. And then they put a rope round his neck and strung him up, and just for good measure opened his skull.

And there he is. Brother Leif. Jesus, I didn't know how that was going to end!

Just as PYNE *finishes* GEORGE *enters. He is taking site photographs.*

KEENEY (*Clapping*) Not bad, Pyne. Fairly trite melody but an interesting sub-theme. Not bad at all.

PYNE Not bad? It was bloody good. Out of the top of my head, too! Wasn't it bloody good, Knoxie?

KEENEY (*Very rapidly*) Why did he come back?

PYNE Who?

KEENEY Leif.

PYNE He had to come back.

KEENEY Why?

PYNE Sure he had to come back with his mate, hadn't he?

KEENEY Why?

PYNE Jesus, Ulf was his mate, wasn't he?

KEENEY Is that why he came back?

PYNE (*Blustering, confused*) Why the hell do you think he came back! He wasn't going to stay out there by himself, was he? 'Why did he come back?' — Such a stupid bloody question. 'Why did he come back?' — Jesus, that's the stupidest question I ever heard!

GEORGE Stand where you are, Pyne. You, too, Keeney.

PYNE (*Irritably*) What for?

GEORGE To give the picture a scale. Go on talking.

PYNE (*To* KEENEY) Oh, Lord, I'm sure I'm a sight! And these old flat shoes, too! Oh heavens!

KEENEY *flashes on a brilliant smile and becomes an American matron while* GEORGE *— the reporter — takes pictures.*

KEENEY Let me tell you: just before we left Baton Rouge, Louisiana, the travel agent warned Ethel and I that we might experience some civil commotion in your country. But I can tell you right now, sir, that we had a simply wunnerful time and we want your Irish readers to know that, too.

PYNE Just fan-tastic.

KEENEY As soon as we landed at Shannon we were frisked by
two of your enormous guards — remember, Ethel?

PYNE Oh my! And were they thorough!

KEENEY And when we got to Dublin we were frisked again.

PYNE Five minutes each!

KEENEY Everywhere we went it was the same — hotels, bars,
cinemas. Sometimes they were regular cops but more
often they were plainclothes men.

PYNE We were frisked right round the Ring of Kerry.

KEENEY And all over Connemara.

PYNE Tell him about the Aran Islands, Katie.

KEENEY Yeah — Special Branch men — they told us themselves.
In wellingtons and cloth caps. It was just frisk, frisk,
frisk, day and night for almost a week.

PYNE Truly wunnerful.

KEENEY And we just want your readers to know how grateful
we are.

PYNE Ha ha.

GEORGE All that stuff's got to be shifted up to the gate — when
you're finished your tea break.

He goes briskly off.

PYNE Hi, George, will you send us copies of the photos?
Fame and fortune at last, Buttle.

Enter DES. *He looks very solemn.*

Look at who's here! Yes, Dessy boy. Well, how did it go?

DES Hi.

He goes straight up the steps.

PYNE Did you lay into them, give them the old one-two-
three, tell them to stick their bloody job — ?

PYNE *breaks off because* KEENEY, *without taking his*

eyes off DES, *puts a restraining hand on* PYNE's *arm.*
They all watch DES *go straight into the office where he*
picks up his shoulder bag and two books. He comes
down the steps again.

PYNE We're having a bit of a party. What'll it be — Scotch or
Irish?

DES *stops beside the group. After a brief pause he*
speaks, choosing his words very carefully.

DES Actually the board meeting was over when I arrived.
But the boss was there and I said what I had to say to
him. He wants you to know that he understands your
. . . frustration. But as he pointed out the building con-
tractors have already given us three extensions. And
as a matter of fact — and this is something I wasn't
aware of — only for their subsidy we'd have had to
close long ago. But apart from that altogether, digging
is only part of the work, and the assessing of the stuff
we actually have in hand is going to occupy all our
time for the next eight months — right up to our next
dig. In fact the boss wants me to start on that right now.
So all in all . . . Good luck, Knox: you were a big help.

KNOX Luck.

DES Good luck, Butt.

BUTT I've a journal of yours.

DES Doesn't matter. Hold on to it. And if you feel like keeping up your interest in the game just get in touch with
me. Pyne — see you. Keeney. Where's Smiler?

BUTT He's —

PYNE He's in the bog.

DES Say goodbye to him for me.

PYNE Sure.

DES That's everybody. I'll be seeing George over the weekend. OK? Thanks. We had a good time.

He moves off uncertainly. After he has gone a short
distance KEENEY *speaks with pretended embarrassment.*

KEENEY The trouble is, Desmond, that you've put us in a sort of an awkward spot now.

DES *stops and turns.*

You see, when you said you'd be behind us in whatever stance we'd take, naturally we thought you meant ... (*To others*) It's not a secret, is it?

PYNE He'll find out anyway, won't he?

DES *watches* KEENEY *very closely, trying to determine if he's serious or joking.*

KEENEY Well, after you left we had a meeting, Desmond — you know — the lads here —

PYNE Be fair to George — George didn't take part.

KEENEY That's true — George wasn't involved ... Anyhow, we considered various suggestions — you know — how best to register our objections to the rape of the site and the destruction of knowledge that the Irish people have a right to inherit and be sustained and enriched by — all that sort of stuff — you know. And after one hell of a lot of to-ing and fro-ing and quite frankly one hell of a lot of soul-searching — (*To* PYNE) Didn't we search our souls?

PYNE With fine-combs and flash lamps.

KEENEY The decision we came to, Desmond, was that the most effective protest we could make would be the one you yourself suggested and —

DES The one I . . . ?

KEENEY We wrote a letter to the papers.

PYNE (*Searching pockets*) I've a copy here somewhere —

KEENEY But you can rest assured, Desmond, we've said nothing in that letter that you yourself haven't said repeatedly over the past months. Right?

PYNE Absolutely. When you read it you'll be proud of it.

KEENEY Damn it, I've forgotten — we surely didn't leave out Desmond's name from the signatures, did we?

PYNE Afraid so.

KEENEY Hell!

PYNE But we quoted him in the last paragraph.

KEENEY That itself.

DES Is this one of their peculiar jokes, Butt?

BUTT deliberately turns away from him and goes to the far end of the stage where he busies himself with sacks.

KEENEY Dear Sir: We, the undersigned — a fairly crude paraphrase but the sentiments are accurate — we think the Irish people should know that the enormously valuable archaeological treasure house — that was Pyne's phrase . . .

PYNE (*Beaming*) Good?

KEENEY . . . it is being shut down because Professor King has been bribed by the speculators to say that the dig is finished, even though it isn't, and because he has looted enough material to make another of his Auntie Coco coffee-table books —

PYNE Knoxie's phrase. Right, Knoxie?

KEENEY Then words to the effect that although the readers might consider *us* less than reliable, the anxiety we felt was shared by an honest and fair-minded young scholar who had toiled unselfishly here with us — by name Dessy the Red.

PYNE He's taking a hand at you — we didn't put in 'the Red' bit.

KEENEY Was there anything else?

PYNE The line about the sit-in.

KEENEY Oh, yes. We said there'd be a series of sit-in protests on the site every day at noon, beginning next Monday; and that strawberries and cream would be provided by George, learned talks by Butt, and authentic atmospheric smells by Knoxie. And then we all put our names at the bottom.

PYNE And Leif's.

KEENEY And Ulf's.

PYNE And Wilson's.

KEENEY And young Dolly's.

PYNE And George's.

KEENEY And de Valera's.

PYNE And Master McGrath's.

KEENEY And King Kong's.

PYNE And Hitler's.

KEENEY And me great uncle Billy McCluskey who had a hare-lip and went down with the Titanic.

PYNE A smashing letter, Des. Full of exclamation marks and things.

KEENEY He'll see it himself tomorrow. Any tea left?

> *Brief pause as* DES *controls his anger and searches for calm words.*

DES Over the past five months, Keeney, I thought I had come to understand you people and maybe even to have a measure of sympathy with you. But by God I think now that hanging's too good for you.

> *As he marches off* PYNE *blows a kiss after him and calls:*

PYNE A student called Dessy the Red —

KEENEY Preferred fellow subversives all dead.
I may quote Karl Marx,
But it's really for larks.
He's much better not done, only said.

PYNE Ha-ha.

KEENEY Indeed — indeed — indeed. Did you ever write to the papers, Knoxie?

PYNE Knoxie? Every week. Dear Auntie May, the girls all shun me. I suffer from smelly feet. What do you advise?

KEENEY Lag your feet and legs with asbestos soaked in rum for three weeks. And if that doesn't work, try washing them.

> *To* GEORGE, *who has just entered:*

You've just missed Desmond, George. He really gave

it to King. And for his honesty he's been kicked out of the faculty. Do you call that fair, George?

GEORGE *ignores him; goes straight up to his office.*

PYNE But he's unrepentant.
KEENEY Beaten but unbowed and sustained by a cast-iron certainty — like Brother Butt here. Isn't he lucky? And he says to tell you he enjoyed working with you —
PYNE Oh, he fancies George.
KEENEY — even though you're a sycophantic aul' bollocks and hanging would be too good for you. (*To* PYNE) I'm not misquoting him, am I?
PYNE His very words.
KEENEY (*To* KNOX, *who is about to exit with a barrow*) Where are you off to, Knoxie? Hold on, man, you were about to tell us Leif's story, weren't you?
PYNE So he was. Good old Knoxie — your turn.
KEENEY Quiet, gentlemen, please.
PYNE Don't be shy, man. Face the company.
KEENEY The Knox version, friends.

KNOX *stands facing upstage.*

PYNE Come on, Knoxie. Once upon a time.
KEENEY Once upon a time there was a raggedy old man called Leif who scraped together a living by painting an odd boat or by running messages for sailors or by getting them back on board when they were drunk. But what nobody knew was that Leif was the only child of a merchant prince and that tutors from all over Europe came to his house to educate his precious son.
PYNE Oo-la-la! Very posh!
KEENEY But one day when the merchant prince was out riding a boar ran across his path — Daddy's horse reared — Daddy was thrown — Daddy's neck was broken —
PYNE Click!
KEENEY — and of course Daddy's empire collapsed with Daddy because Mammy was an idiot and all young Leif could

do was say 'I own a well-trained falcon' in seven
languages.

PYNE And play the viola.

KEENEY Of course. Which he played first in the taverns and then
in the streets. But many's the night young Leif crept into
his viola and slept in doorways and cried with hunger
and loneliness. And then he made a major discovery.

PYNE What was that?

KEENEY He discovered that certain people — let's not be diffident — subversives — they were willing to pay him
for carrying messages from one clandestine group to
another — pay him not only with money and food and
lodgings but with their companionship. And that discovery was more important to Leif than his music or
his logic or his astrology or his rhetoric or his —

> KNOX, *still facing upstage, bursts into tears of anger
> and embarrassment.*

KNOX Fuck you, Keeney! Fuck you! Fuck you! Fuck you!

> KNOX *rushes off.*

KEENEY He's not upset, is he?

PYNE Ah come on, Knoxie. It's only a bit of fun, man. (*To others*)
Jesus, poor aul' Knoxie.

> *He runs off after* KNOX.

Come on back and finish your tea, man.

> KEENEY *looks after* PYNE. *The exhilaration — the 'wild-
> ness' — has died in him.*

KEENEY (*Wearily*) There once was a nanny named Pyne
Who was blessed with a nature divine . . .

> *A weary laugh — he loses interest in his rhyme, then
> turns and looks at* BUTT. *Pause.*

And then suddenly, Butt, for no apparent reason the Friday-night man goes limp. All the wildness and power evaporate and all that's left is a mouth. Of course there is a reason — my overriding limitation — the inability to sustain a passion, even a frivolous passion. Unlike you, Butt. But then your passions are pure — no, not necessarily pure — consistent — the admirable virtue, consistency — a consistent passion fuelled by a confident intellect. Whereas my paltry flirtations are just ... fireworks, fireworks that are sparked occasionally by an antic imagination. And yet here we are, spancelled goats complementing each other, suffering the same consequences. Is it ironic? Is it even amusing?

> BUTT *moves closer to* KEENEY. *The exterior is calm but the eyes are burning.*

BUTT   I can tell you his story.

KEENEY   Yes.

BUTT   I know his story.

KEENEY   I'm sure you do. That Gaelic head.

BUTT   Yes, I know it. But you're wrong — not here (*tapping his head*) but here in my guts. Yes, I can tell you his story.

KEENEY   (*Suddenly alert again*) I know your version, Butt. A poor Viking slave who rowed his masters across the seas on their plundering expeditions, until one morning suddenly all the muscles of his body atrophied with exhaustion and then because he could never row again they disposed of him.

BUTT   Yes.

KEENEY   Or he was a blacksmith who tramped the country shoeing other men's horses and then one day he asked: 'Why can't I have a horse of my own?'

BUTT   Yes, Keeney.

KEENEY   Or he was a carpenter who had built a whole Viking village and then asked to be allowed to keep one house for himself.

BUTT   Yes, Keeney.

KEENEY   Or he was a crofter who sucked a living from a few

acres of soggy hill-farm — a married man with a large family. And then one day a new landlord took over the whole valley and he was evicted because he had no title.

BUTT Yes, Keeney, yes.

KEENEY Maybe yes. But for Christ's sake not with the assurance of your yes!

BUTT Or he was a bank clerk who had courage and who had brains and who was one of the best men in the movement.

KEENEY Once upon a time.

BUTT Yes, Keeney. And you're sure of it in your guts, too.

KEENEY I'm sure of nothing now.

BUTT You were once. You shouted yes louder than any of us.

KEENEY Did I?

BUTT Five — six months ago. Before you volunteered for this job. You knew where you stood then. Are you going soft, Keeney?

> PYNE *and* KNOX *enter. Between them is* SMILER. *They have him by the arms.*

PYNE Ta-ra-ra! Look who's here!

BUTT Good God!

PYNE What about this for a surprise?

BUTT Bloody Smiler!

PYNE Walks in the gate as cool as you like.

KNOX 'Where's Butt?' — that's all he says — 'Where's Butt?'

BUTT Bloody bastard! I thought he'd deserted us. Look at him, will you — the bloody bastard!

> BUTT *goes quickly to* SMILER *and embraces him with undisguised affection and relief.*

KNOX There you are. Safe as houses.

PYNE And the cap as jaunty as ever. (*Calls*) Hi, George, look who's here!

KNOX 'Where's Butt?' — That's all he says.

BUTT Where did you find him?

GEORGE *is watching from the verandah.*

PYNE I'm telling you — just walked in the gate.
BUTT Where had he been? Where had he gone?
PYNE Who cares? He's back, isn't he? D'you see, George?
KNOX 'Where's Butt? Where's Butt?' He-he-he.
PYNE (*Boxing*) OK, Smiler Baby. Put them up.
BUTT Smiler, you bastard, I was worried sick about you.
PYNE Weren't we all?
BUTT Where did you go to, man? Where have you been?

> *Pause. Finally:*

SMILER That's right, Butt. That's right.

> BUTT, KNOX *and* PYNE *explode with laughter as if*
> SMILER *had said something brilliantly witty. Through-*
> *out this whole sequence — from* SMILER*'s entrance*
> *until* KEENEY *speaks further down —* KEENEY *is stand-*
> *ing by himself, rigid, tense, barely able to control*
> *himself.*

PYNE (*Laughing*) That's right — he says! That's right!
BUTT (*Laughing*) Oh my God, Smiler — you bastard!
PYNE That's right.
BUTT Sit down, sit down, sit down, man. Get him tea. Get
      him hot tea.

> *All three lead* SMILER *downstage and sit him down. In*
> *their fussing over him they bump into one another.*

PYNE He can take mine.
BUTT Is it warm enough?
KNOX Mine's warm.
PYNE Show me. (*Feels the cup*) Yes, that's warmer.
BUTT Give me.

> *He puts the cup into* SMILER*'s hands and holds it*
> *there.*

His hands are cold. He's all cold.
PYNE Get him a coat.
BUTT Anyone got a coat?
PYNE I've none.
KNOX Neither have I.
BUTT Give me that sack.
KNOX Is it dry?
PYNE It's fine.
BUTT Give me.

He drapes a very large sack round SMILER*'s shoulders.*
It is so long that it hangs down his sides and looks like
a ritualistic robe, an ecclesiastical cope.

SMILER I walked along the street and —
BUTT You're OK, Smiler. You're OK now. Don't talk, man.
You're fine now.
PYNE What about his feet? Those damn wellingtons aren't
comfortable.
BUTT (*As he takes off the wellingtons*) Where are his boots?
PYNE They're over there, Knoxie. Get them.
BUTT Drink your tea, Smiler. Drink it up, man.
KNOX (*With the boots*) Here.
PYNE His foot are frozen.
BUTT Rub them with your hands.
PYNE (*As he massages one foot*) You do that one, Knoxie.
BUTT He must have sat somewhere for a long time.
PYNE How are the hands?
BUTT Warming up a bit. We'll soon have him perfect, won't
we, Smiler?
KNOX (*Offering packet*) Would you like a fag, Smiler?
PYNE Jesus, Smiler, it must be Christmas!
BUTT Smiler doesn't smoke.
PYNE He'll smoke one of Knoxie's! He'll never get a chance
again! Right, Smiler?

PYNE *puts a cigarette into* SMILER*'s mouth.* KNOX
lights it.

KNOX Good fags, Smiler. Dear ones.

BUTT (*Holding the hands still*) They're warming up.

PYNE OK, boy?

BUTT He's OK. He's back again. He's OK now.

PYNE The colour's coming back to his cheeks, too. Good old Smiler. (*Turns to* KEENEY) Looking great, isn't he?

KEENEY (*After a brief pause*) He's an imbecile! He's a stupid, pig-headed imbecile! He was an imbecile the moment he walked out of his quarry! And that's why he came back here — because he's an imbecile like the rest of us! Go ahead — flutter about him — fatten him up — imbecile acolytes fluttering about a pig-headed imbecile victim. For Christ's sake, is there no end to it?

> KEENEY *goes off. The suddenness and passion of his outburst have stunned the others. They look at one another in shock. Pause.*

PYNE (*Attempting brightness*) What in the name of Jesus was that . . . was that all about?

> *The words die. Brief silence. He attempts another rally — this time shadow-boxing with* SMILER.

OK, Smiler Baby, put them up, man, put them up — boom-boom-boom — one-two-three — he's cold out — bang-bang-bang — right on the chin . . .

> *Again the words wither. He looks at the others with a mixture of panic and anger.*

Imbecile! He's the only imbecile here, for Jesus sake! Am I right, Butt? If anyone's a bloody imbecile, it's bloody Keeney — amn't I right, Butt?

BUTT It's just that he's afraid.

PYNE (*Aggressively*) Who's afraid? I'm not afraid!

BUTT Keeney.

KNOX What's he afraid of, Butt?

BUTT He's the one persuaded us to volunteer for this job —

that's one of the reasons they hate him. He's the one
they'll go for first — that's one of the reasons he's afraid.

KNOX Now that the job's over, Butt, there'll be no trouble?
Now that we're back with them there'll be no trouble.

PYNE (*To* BUTT) Are you afraid?

BUTT I'm . . . I'm not sure anymore.

> GEORGE *comes bustling down the steps. Now that*
> SMILER *is back everything is well.*

GEORGE (*Being pleasant*) Come on, men, come on — Mr Wilson'll
be here any minute, and we don't want him to find us
sitting down on the job and us in the last lap, do we?
Are we going to get the site cleared or are we not? You
wouldn't want to leave the place in a mess like this.

PYNE Bloody housewife, George.

GEORGE Take all the sacks out of the shed and leave them lying
beside the gate. There's a couple lying back there.

PYNE All right, all right, all right.

> *He goes off.*

GEORGE Knoxie, wash out all the wheelbarrows with the hose
and then leave them lying upside down.

> *KNOX goes off*

You give him a hand, Smiler.

BUTT Smiler sits where he is — he's still cold.

GEORGE Is he? Oh in that case certainly — certainly. Would you
like to sit up at the fire for a while, Smiler?

BUTT Leave him where he is.

GEORGE Whatever you say. You look after the planks, will you?
And if you come across any trowels or brushes give
them to me.

> GEORGE *goes off.* BUTT *begins picking up the timbers*
> *that are littered all over the floor.*

SMILER Yes, Butt.
BUTT Yes, Smiler.
SMILER Butt, I . . .

> SMILER *gets to his feet. He is staring straight ahead and his mouth is working as if he were trying to capture some elusive intelligence.* BUTT *goes to him.*

BUTT What is it, Smiler?
SMILER When I went up to the gate I wanted to run away — I knew I had to run away — I knew that — I knew that — I — I —
BUTT Easy, man, easy.
SMILER And then when I was outside, I — I — I — I didn't know anymore — I didn't know anything, Butt — and I had to come back — to come — to —
BUTT Shhh.
SMILER — to come back to you 'cause you'd tell me what to do — what to — what — what —
BUTT Easy — easy — easy.
SMILER Was that right, Butt? Was that right?
BUTT We'll see, Smiler. We'll see. We'll see.
SMILER We'll see?
BUTT Yes, we'll see, Smiler. We'll see.

> *Whatever it was* SMILER *was about to capture has escaped him. His face softens into its usual witless smile.*

OK now, Smiler?
SMILER That's right.
BUTT That's right. Why don't you go and change out of those? You'll be more comfortable in your own clothes.

> *As* SMILER *exits* KNOX *enters quickly, furtively. He is carrying something under his jacket. He looks about to make sure* BUTT *is alone.*

KNOX Psst — psst — psst, Butt. Come here — come here — come here.

BUTT What?

KNOX Come here till you see this.

BUTT *joins him downstage.*

Look, man, look.

He produces a paper bag and opens it.

BUTT What is it?

KNOX Look at that.

BUTT I can't see.

KNOX Some of the things I found myself. Some of them I swiped out of the office.

BUTT What have you got?

KNOX Pieces of brooches, bones, bits of combs, trial pieces, scraps of leather, broken rings —

BUTT What do you want them for?

KNOX What d'you think! Christ, they're worth a fortune!

BUTT Knoxie —

KNOX Antiques, man! There's a small fortune there, man!

BUTT Knoxie, they've no —

KNOX Shh. Too much for me to smuggle out by myself. But if you take half of them we'll make a deal — I'll go fifty-fifty with you. We'll be made for life, Butt.

BUTT I'm telling you — they're not worth —

KNOX I'll put your share into your boots and tonight we'll —

He breaks off because GEORGE *enters. He shuffles off.*

GEORGE I can tell you, Butt, I'm as relieved as you are that Smiler came back to us. I mean, you fellows did a good job here and it would have given me no pleasure to report you. For, as I've said to Mr Wilson, you helped us out of a fix and I would hope that this experience has given you something — you know, new interests, new insights. (*Lowers his voice*) Butt, it's none of my business and you can tell me to shut up if you like, but I'm going to give you a bit of advice.

BUTT   What's that, George?

GEORGE Keep away from Keeney.

BUTT   What's wrong with Keeney?

GEORGE The governor has asked us to submit a report on your
        conduct here and in all honesty I can find nothing good
        to say about him. The rest of you — you did the job to
        the best of your ability, and I'll say that, and it'll be
        taken into consideration. But Keeney — a danger-man,
        Butt, a real danger-man. No loyalty to anyone or any-
        thing — that's his trouble. No loyalty to the job. I doubt
        very much if he's even loyal to what the rest of you
        stand for. But I'm telling you nothing new, Butt. You
        know. He's heading for disaster. Keep away from him.
        All right? (*Aloud again*) Better take my friend up to the
        office for safe keeping.

        BUTT, *who is closer to the jug than* GEORGE, *stoops and
        lifts it.*

        That's an example — you saw the way he was throw-
        ing that about. No appreciation whatever.

BUTT   That's right.

GEORGE I was just saying to Dr King last night: if we'd got noth-
        ing else here the dig would have been worth it for that
        alone. Exquisite, isn't it?

BUTT   Good.

GEORGE Really beautiful. (*Holds out his hand*) Thanks — I'll take
        it up.

        BUTT *has been staring at the jug since he lifted it off
        the ground. Now, without taking his eyes off it, he
        opens his hand and the jug falls on the ground and is
        smashed to pieces.*

        Oh my God — (*He drops on his knees*) Oh my God —
        (*Gathering the pieces together, almost in tears*) Damn you,
        Butt! God damn you to hell! Oh my God, you'll pay for
        this, Butt! By God you'll pay and pay and pay — I'll
        see to it that you pay! There'll be nothing in your life

that you'll regret as much as this! I promise you, Butt
— that's a promise! This'll be the biggest regret of your
life! Oh my God, how you'll regret this!

*He has gathered the pieces together and rushes off with
them up the steps.* BUTT *looks after him with flat eyes.
Then* KEENEY'*s singing diverts him and he returns to
his work.*

KEENEY (*Off*) 'Fare thee well, for I must leave thee;
Do not let this parting grieve thee.

He enters.

'And remember that the best of friends must part,
must part.

PYNE *enters from other side; he and* KEENEY *sing
together.*

'Adieu, adieu, kind friends, adieu, adieu, adieu.
I can no longer stay with you, stay with you.'

PYNE *continues whistling.*

KEENEY Well, there you are, Buttie Boy. We spend months and
months making a bloody big hole and next week a
different crowd of tribesmen'll come along and fill it
all in. If a fella had any head on him at all he'd be able
to extract some kind of wisdom from that. Wouldn't
he, Leif? Where did the jug go?
BUTT George took it up with him.
KEENEY You may be sure.
BUTT He's sending in a report about us to the governor.
KEENEY That'll be thrilling material.
PYNE I know what he'll say about me. 'Pyne is just . . .'

*He closes his eyes, purses his lips, and makes a kissing
sound quickly three times.*

And Jesus, if word of that gets around I'll never get a night's sleep.

SMILER *enters in his street clothes.*

KEENEY What'll he say about Butt?

PYNE Oh, he respects Butt.

KEENEY 'The success of the venture was due in large measure to Butt, whose brilliant wit, ready smile and endless good humour made the sometimes tedious work a constant pleasure.'

PYNE Bloody hell!

KEENEY 'He was an example to all of us. He is survived by a wife and ten children.'

PYNE Ha-ha. What'll he say about you? (*Calls*) Hi, George, are you going to give Keeney a good report?

KEENEY 'I found it difficult at first to get to know Keeney because of his natural reticence and his modest disposition. But when I got past that carefully cultivated armour of a shy man I discovered a very real, a very warm human being. It was a privilege to know him.'

PYNE Ho-ho-ho. What about Knox?

KNOX *enters.*

KNOX What about Knox?

KEENEY 'Knox was our Adonis. His golden locks and blue eyes will haunt me till I die.'

KNOX Wilson's here. He's talking to someone up at the gate.

The announcement has the finality of a sentence. Pause.

PYNE So Wilson's here. Well. There you are — the end of the line. Wilson's here. Well, that's it, lads. Back to porridge.

SMILER Porridge — that's right, Pyne — that's right.

PYNE Bloody right, Smiler. And it'll be a hell of a relief to get peace from Keeney's yapping, won't it? Won't it, Knoxie?

Brief pause. Then he sings:

'Adieu, kind friends, adieu, adieu, adieu . . . '

The words fade. He whistles.

BUTT (*To* KEENEY) About next Monday —

PYNE (*Very quickly, very sharply*) What about it?

BUTT This is our last chance to talk about it.

PYNE What's there to talk about?

BUTT As Knoxie says, maybe now that we're back with them, maybe there'll be no trouble — maybe the whole thing'll be dropped.

PYNE 'As Knoxie says' — Jesus' sake, you're really desperate if you're listening to bloody Knoxie! George is very quiet. (*Calls*) Working on your bloody report, George?

BUTT The question is — if they're going to go ahead — what's the best thing for us to do?

PYNE (*Bitterly, rapidly*) What d'you want us to do? Take Wilson aside when he comes in and say to him, 'Mr Wilson, can you help us with our little problem? We understand that some of us are going to get killed in a riot next Monday night. What advice do you have to offer us, Mr Wilson?' Jesus! You know what he'd say — Wilson — you know what he'd say? 'Fucking wonderful!' That's what he'd say. 'Pity there weren't fucking twenty of you!' That's what he'd say!

BUTT So we do nothing, Keeney — is that it?

PYNE What's your suggestion?

BUTT We could —

PYNE (*On the point of tears*) Fight them? Take them all on? Five of us against two hundred of them? That'd be some contest. Or what about throwing ourselves on the mercies of the authorities — plead for a transfer to the Curragh — there's only seventy of our old companions there. That'd be a more equal fight.

BUTT So we do nothing, Keeney? Is that it? We do nothing?

Pause. Then KEENEY *begins very softly, very soberly, as if he were about to deliver a solution.*

KEENEY Listen to me, boys. Where we are now, this very spot we're standing on, this is going to be the foundation of an enormous glass and steel hotel with a swimming pool in the basement and a restaurant on the roof. And to make that foundation is going to take hundreds and hundreds of tons of hardcore. And all that hardcore is going to come thundering down over the top there —

PYNE So what?

KEENEY — right down here — on top of old Leif. And my suggestion is —

PYNE Your suggestion is?

KEENEY My suggestion is that we should demonstrate our affection and our respect for our friend here by burying him properly now.

PYNE Jesus, Keeney. (*Meaning 'Is there no limit to your fooling?'*)

SMILER That's right, Keeney, that's right.

KEENEY Thank you, Smiler. (*Moving* KNOX *aside*) I beg your pardon, Knox.

KEENEY *opens up the tarpaulin and spreads it over the skeleton. Then he secures the sides and bottom with stones and pieces of timber. The skull is left exposed. While he is doing this job:*

KNOX (*To* BUTT) What does he think he's at?

KEENEY *now stands at the exposed skull.*

KEENEY I'm not a religious man myself. But if some of you would like to . . . ? Pyne? Butt?

KNOX (*Privately to* BUTT) I hid your share in your boots.

KEENEY Knoxie? No? Well . . . (*He clears his throat; in the same sober tones*) The last time I saw him — the first week of last May as a matter of fact — he was talking and laughing and joking as usual — the old Leif we all remember so well. But there was a definite something about him that day — it was a Tuesday, I remember, a warm, breathless day — an unrest, a disquiet — it's difficult to define. And perhaps I'm investing that last meeting with a significance it didn't in fact have. But he said something that day that I think you ought to know.

GEORGE *is now tidying up on the terrace.*

He propped himself up on his elbow — the conversation up to that had been vintage Leif, the usual brilliant persiflage — but he suddenly got up on his elbow and he gazed at me for I'm sure thirty seconds with those extraordinary eyes of his — remember those grey eyes? — and he said, 'Tell me, George — ' 'It's Keeney, Leif,' I said. But he was so intense he didn't hear me. 'Tell me, George,' he said, 'I must know — I *must* know — was Hamlet really mad?'

PYNE Jeouo! Hi, Georgo!

GEORGE *goes into the office.*

KEENEY And then he collapsed. It was all over. (*No longer solemn*) God rest you, me aul' buttie!
PYNE Me darlin' soldier laddie!
KEENEY Isn't he looking like himself, though?
PYNE The spitting image of himself.
KEENEY And content?
PYNE Lovely.
KEENEY And the wee smile on his lips.
PYNE Like a child, God be kind to him.
KEENEY One civil man, Leif.
PYNE Never harmed man nor beast.
KEENEY And generous — give you the shirt off his back.
PYNE The bite out of his mouth.
KEENEY One of nature's gentlemen.
PYNE A great husband — a great father.

KEENEY May the hardcore rest light on him.

PYNE We'll never see his likes again.

KEENEY All the same, boys —

PYNE What?

KEENEY Is there a look of the mother's side of the house about the set of that jaw?

PYNE The Boyces of Ballybeg?

KEENEY They all had that hard, jutting jaw.

PYNE Now that you mention it.

KEENEY Tight crowd, the Boyces.

PYNE He favoured the mother's side all right.

KEENEY Tight and bitter.

PYNE And notionate, too.

KEENEY Man, they held grudges for generations. And in drink!

PYNE Balubas!

KEENEY Be Jaysus, they'd fight with their shadow.

PYNE And did, too.

KEENEY Oh, he's a Boyce all right.

PYNE One bad connection.

KEENEY One hungry connection.

PYNE Hungry's the word.

KEENEY Hungry and vicious.

PYNE Bad seed — bad breed.

KEENEY *briskly covers the skull with the tarpaulin.*

KEENEY All our bad luck go with him.

PYNE Amen to that.

WILSON *enters. He is in the uniform of a prison officer. His manner seems crisper and more officious now that he is in uniform.*

WILSON Right — right — right — the holiday's over. Out you go and get changed. Look smart — make it snappy. Come on, Smiler, put an inch to that step. Get a move on — we haven't all day. Move, Knox, move, move, move. Come on, Butt. Shift, Pyne, shift.

The diggers move off morosely.

Good evening, George.

GEORGE (*Coming down steps*) Good evening, Mr Wilson.
WILSON Touch of frost again this evening.
GEORGE The winter's here, Mr Wilson.
WILSON Would you think so?
GEORGE It's not far away, anyhow.
WILSON Well, we did all right, I suppose. (*Lowering voice*) By the way, George, she did great.
GEORGE Who?
WILSON Dolly.
GEORGE Oh, the exam. And she did well?
WILSON *Very* well.
GEORGE I'm glad of that, Mr Wilson.
WILSON Very well indeed. I'm very satisfied.
GEORGE Naturally.
WILSON Hell of a nice chap — English — you know — no side with him — a man you could talk to.
GEORGE That was a help.
WILSON Said she played 'with grace and discretion'.
GEORGE Very nice.
WILSON I think that's encouraging.
GEORGE Certainly is.
WILSON You know — for a girl there. I mean when an expert like that says she plays with grace and discretion, George, it's no bad recommendation for a young slip of a girl — am I right?
GEORGE Indeed.
WILSON Playing a difficult instrument with grace and discretion, George, you would call that high praise, wouldn't you?
GEORGE It's all that.
WILSON Oh, she has grace all right — I can see that myself and I'm no musician. But what do you make of the discretion part? That doesn't make much sense to me, George.
GEORGE I think that's good, Mr Wilson.
WILSON The wife thinks so, too. I hope you're right. 'With grace

and discretion.' The grace — that's grand — that's all right.

GEORGE She must be a graceful player, Mr Wilson.

WILSON Oh, lovely to look at, just lovely.

GEORGE And he spotted that — there you are.

WILSON He might have got a better bloody word than 'discretion'.

GEORGE I don't know, Mr Wilson. Depends on how he said it.

WILSON 'Discretion' — in the name of God wasn't that a rotten thing to say about a wee girl trying to do her best? English expert my arse! He knows as much about it as I know myself!

Enter KEENEY *and* KNOX *in street clothes.*

KEENEY (*Very demurely*) We're ready when you are, Mr Wilson.

WILSON OK. Fine. Off we go.

GEORGE Mr Wilson —

WILSON Yes, George?

GEORGE I want a word with you.

WILSON Now?

GEORGE No, no, not here; not now.

WILSON Are you sure?

GEORGE No, I'll call you later tonight.

Enter PYNE *and* BUTT.

WILSON OK. (*To others*) All right — are we all set? Where's Smiler?

SMILER *enters.*

Last as usual, Smiler.

SMILER That's right.

WILSON Up to the van then. Have you all your stuff with you?

BUTT It's up at the gate.

WILSON Good. Off we go. I'll be hearing from you, George?

GEORGE About nine o'clock tonight — will that suit?

WILSON Perfect. We're away then. Come on — come on — move — move.

He goes off. GEORGE *looks momentarily at the diggers and then busies himself picking up the tea things.*

BUTT   Goodbye, George.
GEORGE   (*Without looking up*) 'Bye.
BUTT   Coming, Smiler?
SMILER   Yes, Butt.
BUTT   Will we sit at the front or the back?
SMILER   I like the front.
BUTT   That's where we'll sit then and we'll see all the sights.

BUTT *and* SMILER *exit.*

KEENEY   (*To* KNOX) Say goodbye to George, Knoxie.

KNOX *shrugs his shoulders, grunts something and shuffles off.*

Actually he's heartbroken. A real aul' softie, Knox.
WILSON   (*Off*) Come on! Come on!
KEENEY   What does he want?
PYNE   He wants us to go with him.
KEENEY   Why?
PYNE   Because he *likes* us.
KEENEY   Does he?
PYNE   He does — genuinely.
KEENEY   Why couldn't he say that to our faces?
PYNE   He's shy, like George.
KEENEY   Will we go with him?
PYNE   I'm easy. Maybe we should.
KEENEY   OK. Maybe he needs us more than George. (*To* GEORGE) It has been a *great* pleasure, George; and I would like to think that fate will bring us together again some day. (*To* PYNE) Do you think it will?
PYNE   With the help of God.
KEENEY   You know, he really expanded my horizons.
PYNE   Sure that's his trade.
KEENEY   Did he expand your horizons?
PYNE   He tried hard but mine were seized up with the frost.

KEENEY Well, mine he expanded and expanded and expanded until I thought, honest to God, they'd just snap.
PYNE But they didn't.
KEENEY They did not, more power to him.
WILSON (*Off*) Keeney! Pyne!
PYNE Like a spoiled child, isn't he? George, don't move, George, I want to remember you as you are now. (*Blows a kiss*) Au revoir, my love.

He goes. Pause.

KEENEY What can I say, George, that won't sound trite? Friend, good friend, site manager — may God take care of you.

He goes. Now that everyone is gone GEORGE *stops working, straightens up, and looks after them. Pause. Suddenly* KEENEY's *head appears.*

On an archaeological site
Five diggers examined their plight
But a kangaroo court
Gave the final report —
WILSON (*Off*) Keeney!
KEENEY They were only a parcel of . . .

Good night, sweet prince.

He disappears again. Pause. Then GEORGE *goes to Leif's grave, kicks away the stones and timbers, then pulls off the tarpaulin and begins folding it. As he does this bring the lights down slowly.*

LIVING QUARTERS

after Hippolytus

Characters

SIR
COMMANDANT FRANK BUTLER
HELEN KELLY
MIRIAM DONNELLY
BEN
TINA
FATHER TOM CARTY
CHARLIE DONNELLY
ANNA

SIR: Middle-aged. Always in full control of the situation, of the other characters, of himself. His calm is never ruffled. He is endlessly patient and tolerant, but never superior. Always carries his ledger with him. Dressed in a dark lounge suit, dark tie, white shirt, black, highly polished shoes.

COMMANDANT FRANK BUTLER: Tall, lean, military man in his early fifties. Grey hair, military moustache. Has been in the Irish army all his life. Four children by his first marriage.

HELEN KELLY: Twenty-seven, divorced; has been living in London for six years. An attractive woman with style and apparent self-assurance.

MIRIAM DONNELLY: Twenty-five, married to Charlie Donnelly; mother of three children. Plump, practical. Chain-smokes.

BEN: Twenty-four, hesitant, nervous, with a volatile face. Miriam describes him as a 'mother's boy'.

TINA: Eighteen, the youngest, 'the pet of the family', fresh, warm, eager.

FATHER TOM CARTY: Sixty-four, chaplain to the camp, with the rank of Commandant. A self-aware man with a professional, breezy manner. (Preferably overweight)

CHARLIE DONNELLY: Early thirties; Miriam's husband; court clerk; cautious and proper; always with a raincoat across his arm. Views the Butler family with smiling caution.

ANNA: Early twenties; Frank's second wife; mature, intelligent, passionate, direct in speech and manner.

Time and place

The present in Ireland.

Set

Commandant Frank Butler's living quarters — a detached house close to a small military barracks in a remote part of County Donegal, Ireland.

The action takes place in the living room and garden on a warm May evening and night. The living room and garden have acting areas of almost equal size (left and right from the point of view of the audience).

The furnishings of the living room are old and worn. Fireplace in the centre; an armchair on each side. The armchair left of the fireplace is of wicker. Small table, television set, sideboard on which are drinks. Some family photographs on the walls. On the mantelpiece a distinctive glass ornament with pendulous glass lobes. Door left of the fireplace leads to the kitchen, off. Door right of the fireplace (used once in Act Two). A third door right leads to the hallway, which we see. Hall stand, small table, etc. A stairway rises from the hall. Another door (invisible and approximately opposite the fireplace) in the fourth, invisible, wall separating the living room from the garden.

The garden begins at the front door and runs the full length of the side of the house, i.e. right across the front of the stage. In the garden a summer seat and some old deckchairs.

Down left, tucked into the corner, is a small, low footstool used only by Sir.

Living Quarters was first produced at the Abbey Theatre, Dublin, on 24 March 1977, with the following cast:

SIR	Clive Geraghty
COMMANDANT FRANK BUTLER	Ray McAnally
HELEN KELLY	Fedelma Cullen
MIRIAM DONNELLY	Máire Hastings
BEN	Stephen Brennan
TINA	Bernadette Shortt
FATHER TOM CARTY	Micheal O hAonghusa
CHARLIE DONNELLY	Niall O'Brien
ANNA	Dearbhla Molloy
Directed by	Joe Dowling

for Seamus Deane

ACT ONE

SIR sits on his stool down left, his ledger closed on his knee. Nobody else on stage.

SIR   The home, the house, the living quarters of Commandant Frank Butler, OC of B Company of the 37th Battalion of the Permanent Defence Forces. It is here on May 24th some years ago that our story is set, as they say — as if it were a feast laid out for consumption or a trap waiting to spring. And the people who were involved in the events of that day, although they're now scattered all over the world, every so often in sudden moments of privacy, of isolation, of panic, they remember that day, and in their imagination they reconvene here to reconstruct it — what was said, what was not said, what was done, what was not done, what might have been said, what might have been done; endlessly raking over those dead episodes that can't be left at peace.

He rises and moves to centre stage.

But reverie alone isn't adequate for them. And in their imagination, out of some deep psychic necessity, they have conceived this (*ledger*) — a complete and detailed record of everything that was said and done that day, as if its very existence must afford them their justification, as if in some tiny, forgotten detail buried here — a smile, a hesitation, a tentative gesture — if only it could be found and recalled — in it must lie the key to an understanding of *all* that happened. And in their imagination, out of some deep psychic necessity, they have conceived me — the ultimate arbiter, the powerful and impartial referee, the final adjudicator, a kind of human Hansard who knows those tiny little details and interprets them accurately. And yet no sooner do they conceive me with my authority and my knowledge than they begin flirting with the idea of circumventing me, of foxing me, of outwitting me. Curious, isn't it? But to get back to that day.

He moves into the living room which now lights up.

May 24th; Commandant Frank Butler's home just outside the village of Ballybeg; a remote and rundown army camp in the wilds of County Donegal; and a day of celebration because Commandant Butler and his company have returned in triumph after five months' service with the United Nations in the Middle East. And their return is triumphant because in their last week of duty, at an outpost called Hari, (*reads*) 'while under siege and heavily outnumbered by guerrillas they responded gallantly, Commandant Butler behaving with outstanding courage and selflessness, personally exposing himself to heavy and persistent fire to carry nine of his wounded men to safety'. And this evening top army brass and politicians and local dignitaries have gathered here to celebrate the triumphant return and to honour the triumphant Commandant. So much for the occasion. And hovering in the wings, once more reconvened in recollection to take yet another look at the events of that day, is the Butler family.

He now moves around the living room and addresses the family, off.

Are we all set? Good. Now — you've all been over this hundreds, thousands of times before. So on this occasion — with your co-operation, of course — what I would like to do is organize those recollections for you, impose a structure on them, just to give them a form of sorts. Agreed? Excellent! Naturally we'll only get through a tiny portion of all that was said and done that day; but I think we should attempt some kind of chronological order; and I promise you that the selection I make will be as fair and as representative as possible. So I'll call you as I require you and introduce you then. Agreed? Fine! (*Opens ledger*) Let's see. 'Helen arrives' — we'll not go back as far as that. 'Anna takes up her dress skirt. Tina prepares lunch' — we can skip all that. Yes — let's begin here: 'It is late afternoon. Anna is in bed. Tina is sponging her father's dress suit. In the camp Frank Butler is greeting his distinguished guests. Helen is out for a walk. Miriam has gone to the mess for a carton of ice cream. Ben is washing a shirt in his caravan in the sand dunes.' So. We require only Tina at the moment. And remember — it's all here, every single syllable of it. But if you wish to speak your thoughts as well — by all means. Thank you. Thank you.

> SIR *looks around the set and goes to adjust the position of the garden seat.* TOM *enters.*

TOM Sir.

SIR (*Busy*) What is it, Father?

TOM I don't suppose it would be a breach of secrecy or etiquette if I — if you were to let me know how I'm described there, would it? You know — something to hang the cap on — 'good guy', 'funny guy', 'bit of a gossip'. Which of my many fascinating personas should I portray?

SIR (*Still busy*) You'll be yourself, Father.

TOM Of course. Naturally. But you've a description there, haven't you? And an objective view would be a help.

SIR I don't think so.

TOM As chaplain I've a right to — (*Pleasant again*) Please.

SIR I think you shouldn't.

TOM Please.

> SIR *regards him calmly.*

SIR Very well.

TOM (*Breezily*) Soldier — man of God — friend of the boys — you name it.

SIR 'Father Thomas Carty, sixty-four years of age, chaplain, Commandant, close friend of the Butler family.'

TOM (*Saluting*) Yours truly.

> ANNA *enters in her dressing gown. She stands at a distance and watches this scene.*

SIR 'Married Frank and Louise — '

TOM May the Lord have mercy on her.

SIR '— baptized their children and grandchildren: and six months ago married Frank again — to Anna.'

TOM Indeed. A happy day.

SIR 'The children used to call him Uncle — Uncle Tom — '

TOM (*Delighted*) Tina still does — occasionally.

SIR '"Is Uncle Tom coming with us?" they'd say. And he did. Always. Everywhere. Himself and the batman — in attendance.'

TOM That's one way of —

SIR '— and that pathetic dependence on the Butler family, together with his excessive drinking make him a cliché, a stereotype. He knows this himself — '

TOM Cliché? For God's sake — !

SIR '— but he is not a fool. He recognizes that this definition allows him to be witness to their pain but absolves him from experiencing it; appoints him confidant but acquits him of the responsibility of conscience — '

TOM That's not how — ! Oh my God . . .

SIR 'As the tale unfolds they may go to him for advice, not because they respect him, consider him wise — '

TOM (*Sudden revolt*) Because they love me, that's why! They love me!

SIR '— but because he is the outsider who represents the society they'll begin to feel alienated from, slipping away from them.'

TOM (*Beaten*) Outsider?

ANNA *goes to* TOM *and puts her arm around him.*

SIR 'And what he says won't make the slightest difference because at that point — the point of no return — they'll be past listening to anybody. At that point all they'll hear is their own persistent inner voices — ' And so on and so forth.

TOM (*On point of tears*) Oh my God — Oh my God —

SIR It's your role.

TOM No, it's not. No, no, no, it's not.

SIR And to have any role is always something.

ANNA *begins to lead* TOM *away.*

When you've thought about it you'll agree with me.

TOM No, no, no —

SIR And you'll do it.

TOM No, no —

SIR Oh, yes, you'll do it. Now I think everything's in position.

CHARLIE *enters. Almost furtive. Almost ingratiating.*

CHARLIE By the way, Sir —

SIR You're not needed, Charlie.

CHARLIE Because I'm not one of the family?

SIR Because we're beginning in the afternoon.

CHARLIE But I *was* there that night, you know, and —

SIR Early afternoon, Charlie.

CHARLIE But I *did* come — about half-eleven — to pick up Miriam.

SIR I know.

CHARLIE And I would have been here earlier only I had to leave the babysitter home.

SIR I know.

CHARLIE And if I'm nervous, she's late — I mean to say, if I'm late, she's nervous.

SIR I know.

CHARLIE But I did get here before midnight. And doesn't that make me a witness? Relevant material, as we say.

SIR   Charlie, if I need you I'll call you.

CHARLIE   Tell you what: supposing I just sat about, you know, and looked on, I'd —

SIR   There are no spectators, Charlie. Only participants.

CHARLIE   Promise you — wouldn't open my mouth —

SIR   If your turn comes I'll call you.

CHARLIE   Could keep an eye on the ledger for you.

SIR   Charlie.

CHARLIE   Oh, well — see you later — good luck.

He leaves.

SIR   And now to begin. The Butler home. Early evening of May 24th.

He sits on his low stool. Lights change. TINA enters from kitchen. The jacket of her father's dress suit is lying across an ironing board and she is carrying a bowl of water to clean stains. We can hear in the far distance a military band playing. TINA listens to the music for a few seconds and then hums the melody.

'Tina, the youngest of the four Butler children. The pet of the family. Singing because her father is back from the Middle East and because she has never seen such excitement in the camp before. Her life up to this has been protected and generally happy and content. True, her mother died. But that was six years ago. And Tina loves her stepmother, Anna, at least as much as she loved her mother.'

HELEN enters left and crosses slowly to the garden seat right. She is carrying a bunch of May flowers. As she passes the living room TINA sees her and calls out:

TINA   Helen!

HELEN   Hello.

TINA   It's like a carnival, isn't it?

HELEN Yes.

TINA The Number One Army Band — first time ever in Ballybeg!

HELEN I know.

TINA Did you have a swim?

HELEN What?

TINA Did you swim?

HELEN Paddled.

TINA Oh, you're daring!

HELEN I am.

TINA Was it cold?

HELEN Can't hear you. Come on out — it's glorious.

TINA When I finish this.

> HELEN *places the flowers on the seat and picks up the broken ones.* TINA *exits to the kitchen.*

SIR 'The eldest of the family — Helen. Twenty-seven and divorced. When she was nineteen and impetuous and strong-willed she married Private Gerry Kelly, her father's batman, despite her mother's bitter and vicious opposition. The marriage lasted a few months. Private Kelly deserted and vanished. And Helen went to London. This is only her second time home since then. The last time was for her mother's funeral.'

> HELEN *stands still.*

HELEN When I got off the bus and walked in there this morning the room was still stifling with her invalid's smell. Strange, wasn't it? And small things I thought I'd forgotten: her tiny, perfect, white teeth; the skin smooth and shiny over the arthritic knuckles; her walking-stick hooked on the back of the wicker chair. And that glass ornament on the mantelpiece that trembled when she screamed at me — (*Calmly, flatly*) 'You can't marry him, you little vixen! *Noblesse oblige!* D'you hear — *noblesse oblige!*'

SIR She never spoke to you again?

HELEN No.

SIR Nor to him?

HELEN Never to him.

SIR Do you still feel anger?

HELEN No, not a bit, I think. Not a bit.

SIR And him — how real is he?

HELEN Gerry? That's over.

SIR Altogether?

HELEN I'm wary. I'm controlled. I discipline myself.

SIR Then this homecoming was a risk?

HELEN In a way.

SIR A test? A deliberate test?

HELEN Perhaps.

SIR And you're surviving it?

HELEN I'm surviving it.

SIR All right, Helen, you've tested yourself and you've paid your respects to your father. You could leave now.

HELEN No. I'll see it through.

SIR Your discipline may not hold.

HELEN How can I be sure that I want it to?

SIR Only you can answer that.

> *She suddenly busies herself with the flowers.* MIRIAM *comes briskly through the front door, the hall, into the living room.*

MIRIAM Oh my God — that heat!

> *Once in the living room* MIRIAM *gets three plates from the sideboard and begins dividing the carton of ice cream she has brought home.*

SIR 'Miriam — the middle daughter. Married to Charlie Donnelly, clerk of the district court. She has three children. She is thinking of them.'

MIRIAM They should be arriving home from school just about now. I hope they don't feel altogether abandoned.

SIR She hasn't seen them for three hours.

MIRIAM I gave them soup and sandwiches and a bar of chocolate each for lunch; and Mrs Moyne'll have a hot meal ready for them when they get back. And she'll stay with them until Charlie gets home from the court in Glenties. Then he'll leave her home and come back and make them liver and bacon for their tea. And then he'll go and collect her again and she'll get them porridge and bread and jam for supper and put them to bed.

SIR They are not neglected children.

MIRIAM Then he'll come and collect me and we should be home soon after midnight. He doesn't like hanging about here — no more than I do myself.

SIR 'Before she married, Miriam was a nurse.'

MIRIAM All the same it's a big day for Papa and I'm glad I came. God, wouldn't the kids love some of this ice cream!

SIR *looks at the audience and spreads his hands.*

(*Calling*) Who's for ice cream? Anyone for ice cream?

TINA (*From kitchen*) Me!

MIRIAM *carries the tray of dishes out to the garden.*

MIRIAM Ice cream, Helen?

HELEN Lovely.

MIRIAM Did you ever see the likes of that crowd milling about the gates?

HELEN I came up the back way.

MIRIAM TV cameras and reporters and what-not. And Sergeant Burke trying to control the traffic and looking as if he was going to cry. And that mad wife of his with her hair dyed a bright orange, beside herself with excitement and blowing kisses into all the nobs' cars as they pass through the gate. Sweet God — bedlam! And all the buckos from the village — the Morans and the Sharkeys and all that gang — all squinting and gleeking and not missing a bar. Oh, but there'll be tales to be told for years to come.

TINA *has joined them.*

TINA (*To* MIRIAM) Did you get the May flowers?
MIRIAM Not me — her ladyship here.
HELEN Aren't they pretty?
TINA Remember — we used to gather great armfuls of them and put them up on the May altar on the landing.
MIRIAM In jam jars. (*Passes plate*) Here.
TINA And bundles of bluebells that would go limp overnight and hang over the sides.
HELEN The smell of them through the house — a sickly smell, wasn't it?
TINA And us kneeling on the lino for the prayers and easing up one knee and then the other with the pain. Do you remember, Helen?

Very brief pause.

HELEN That meadow beyond the school's full of flowers.
MIRIAM What meadow's that?
TINA Phil the Butcher's field.
HELEN Phil Boyle and Mary! I saw him watching me from behind the byre but I couldn't remember his name.
MIRIAM Baldy Phil and Hairy Mary — I never could enjoy meat from that place.
TINA Did you not speak to him?
HELEN No, he wouldn't remember me now.
TINA Course he would.
MIRIAM God, they must be ancient, that pair.
TINA D'you remember — Mammy used to send us for eggs every Saturday morning —
MIRIAM 'You're to say: "A dozen eggs for *Commandant* Butler, please"' — hoping to get them cheap!
TINA And if Ben came with us Mary'd always give him a huge kiss.
MIRIAM A rub of her beard!
TINA And he always cried and then she'd give him a duck egg for himself and Daddy used to say he cried just to get the duck egg — d'you remember?

MIRIAM Oh, sweet God!
TINA D'you remember, Helen?

As HELEN *passes her she hugs her briefly. Pause.*

HELEN Yes. Yes, I remember.
MIRIAM God bless Mammy and make her healthy again. God
bless Daddy and have him transferred to Dublin.
TINA We all had that bit.
MIRIAM God bless Uncle Tom and make him a good priest.
God bless Helen, Ben and Tina. And God bless me and
give me bigger thighs than Josie McGrenra. And I got
them.
TINA What's this my rhyme was? God bless Mammy, Daddy,
Uncle Tom, Helen, Miriam, Ben and Stinky Bum Blue.
MIRIAM Who?
TINA A rag doll. Still have her. God bless the Irish army and
make it strong and brave.

MIRIAM *and* HELEN *laugh.*

HELEN Tina!
TINA That's true. And look at Daddy! And God bless me
and take me up to heaven before my tenth birthday.
MIRIAM Weren't you lucky you were ignored!
HELEN ⎱ Does he come — ?
TINA ⎰ What did you — ?
TINA Sorry — go ahead.
HELEN I was just going to ask you, do you see Ben often?
TINA You know Ben.
MIRIAM Yes!
TINA Whenever he takes the notion. When Daddy was out
in the Middle East he called in maybe a couple of
times a week. But now that he's back —
MIRIAM Did you know that Charlie got him a job driving the
mobile library? Surely to God that wasn't too taxing
on him. And he stuck it for how long? Four days.
Walked out without as much as a by-your-leave. Left
the bloody library van sitting out in the bogs beyond

Loughcrillan. Oh, that fella!

HELEN   Do they speak at all?

TINA   Daddy and him? When they meet. If they have to.

HELEN   I thought I might have run into him when I was down at the shore. Where has he got his caravan?

TINA   God knows where you'd find him. Sometimes he works on the boats. Or does odd days labouring. And then he disappears for weeks — I don't know where he goes — Scotland — Dublin. But he always comes back. Always.

MIRIAM   Like malaria.

TINA   But if he's around and hears you're here he'll be sure to call.

HELEN   I hope so.

MIRIAM   Listen to me — let there be no romantic aul' chat about brother Ben. He's a wastrel — a spoiled mother's boy. And if he turns up today to ruin the biggest event in Father's life I'll soon send him packing. So. (*Lights a cigarette*) Sure you're not smoking?

HELEN   Positive.

TINA   Three years off — isn't she great?

MIRIAM   Magnificent. Tell us about London.

HELEN   It's all right. The same office job, the same landlady since I went there.

MIRIAM   Digs or flat?

HELEN   Digs.

TINA   Mrs Zimmermann from Zürich.

HELEN   If she thinks I need cheering up she says: 'Come and have a cup of coffee with me, Mrs Kelly. I have a most funny joke to impart to you.'

MIRIAM   (*Finishing ice cream*) That was good. Does she feed you well?

HELEN   Very well.

TINA   And her four cats and her seventeen canaries and her son, a medical student.

MIRIAM   How do you know all that?

TINA   We write occasionally.

MIRIAM   If the Donnellys get a card at Christmas they feel honoured.

HELEN We're finished with cats and canaries and we're into Pekinese dogs now. And the son's a successful young doctor —

TINA Jean.

HELEN Jean — with a large practice. And the confidential stories she insists on telling me about him and his private life and his patients — I can't stop her.

TINA Is he handsome?

HELEN In a way.

MIRIAM Well?

HELEN And married.

MIRIAM Bugger him — that's him scrubbed. Oh, isn't that just perfect.

> TINA *and* MIRIAM *stretch out in the sun.* HELEN *sits upright.*

TINA It's almost too hot for me.

MIRIAM Don't know when I sunbathed last.

TINA Glorious.

MIRIAM We'll come out in blisters.

TINA Yes, nurse.

MIRIAM Any olive oil in the house?

TINA Kitchen.

MIRIAM Where?

TINA Bottom press.

MIRIAM I suppose you wouldn't go for it?

TINA Too lazy.

MIRIAM Me, too. God, the big snout'll be like a beacon. (TINA *laughs*) We get one hot day every five years and it goes to our heads. Oh, perfect — perfect —

> HELEN *looks at them for a few seconds. Then, very suddenly, she goes down to* SIR *and addresses him in urgent undertones.*

HELEN It's not right! It's not right!

SIR Yes, it is.

HELEN No, it's not. It's distorted — inaccurate.

SIR I would tell you. Trust me.

HELEN The whole atmosphere — three sisters, relaxed, happy, chatting in their father's garden on a sunny afternoon. There was unease — I *remember* — there were shadows — we've got to acknowledge them!

SIR Why?

HELEN Because they were part of it.

SIR Don't you think they're aware of them? They're thinking the very same thing themselves. (HELEN *looks up at her sisters*) Believe me — it's exactly right. (*Pause*) Go on — join them again.

HELEN goes back. She stands looking at them.

TINA (*Her eyes closed*) Do you have to go back tomorrow?

HELEN Afraid so.

TINA Hardly worth your while for one night, was it?

HELEN I've paid my respects to the Commandant.

TINA When you phoned you were coming he was really thrilled.

HELEN And I saw you two, didn't I?

MIRIAM A sight that has driven strong men to distraction. (*She sits up*) God, that's too much for me. And you met our new stepmother.

TINA (*Sitting up*) And she liked her — didn't you, Helen? So there!

MIRIAM So what?

TINA So she thinks she's beautiful — that's what. And so do I.

MIRIAM All I ever said —

HELEN Shhh!

MIRIAM Damn the hair I care if she hears me or not. I just think she's far too young for him and that the quiet of this backwater'll drive her bonkers. You and her and a batman running this house — I mean what the hell do you *do* all day?

TINA She loves Ballybeg — she told me.

MIRIAM As for himself, you'd hardly describe him as a court jester, would you? I mean he's set in his ways and

damned selfish and bossy and —
TINA　Selfish? After the way he nursed Mammy for years?
MIRIAM　So well he might.
TINA　What does that mean?
HELEN　Will you both keep your voices down!
TINA　(*To* HELEN) What does she mean by that?
MIRIAM　That this bloody wet hole ruined her health and that he wouldn't accept a transfer — always waiting for the big promotion that would be worthy of him and that never came. Clonmel, Templemore, Mullingar, Kilkenny — they all came up at different times and he wangled his way out of them — not important enough for Commandant Butler. Well, he'll probably get what he wants as a result of this ballyhoo and I wish him luck — I really do — himself and his child bride. I'd strip in a minute only those Sharkey stallions would be sure to be peeping over that hedge.
TINA　What any of us thinks isn't important. What is important is that he loves her and she loves him.
MIRIAM　Mother of God! Would you grow up, child.
TINA　And they're perfectly happy together.
MIRIAM　Married for five months and out of that they've been together all of what — ten days?
TINA　Amn't I right, Helen?
MIRIAM　Unless the daily love letters count — do they?
TINA　Amn't I right, Helen?
MIRIAM　How would she know? She's a stranger here.

Suddenly sorry, she jumps up and kisses HELEN.

Sorry, sorry sweetie — I didn't mean that. Really. I'm a coarse bitch. Always was. You know that. Sorry.

She sits down again.

As mother used to say — (*Grand accent*) 'Miriam, you're neither a Butler nor a Hogan. I'm afraid you're just — pure Ballybeg.' (HELEN *and* TINA *laugh.* MIRIAM *closes eyes again*) Not a day passes but I thank God for that eejit, Charlie Donnelly. (*Military music in the distance — the same piece as before*) She always called him 'Charles'. But I think she liked him.

TINA Of course she did.

MIRIAM But how could she? Maybe because his Uncle Mickey was land steward to the Duke of Abercorn.

They listen to the music. MIRIAM *hums with it.*

TINA I suppose you never hear from your Gerald, Helen?

HELEN 'My' Gerald?

TINA Gerald, then.

HELEN No.

MIRIAM *sits up.*

MIRIAM I hope to God the kids have the sense to have on their sun hats.

TINA And no idea where he is?

HELEN None.

HELEN *rises and gathers her flowers.*

MIRIAM Wouldn't you think that aul' band would have a second tune!

TINA Daddy said someone saw him recently in Liverpool.

HELEN Really.

MIRIAM Should be called the Only One Army Band.

TINA Whoever it was said he had a beard.

HELEN They (*flowers*) go so limp in the sun, don't they?

TINA Do you ever think of him at all, Helen?

HELEN *passes* TINA *on her way into the living room; as before, she hugs her briefly, only this time almost shaking her. As she hugs her:*

HELEN For God's sake, Tina darling, will you —

MIRIAM Oh, smart, smart, smart!

TINA I thought she might like to —

MIRIAM You thought! (*Calmer*) Come on — we'd better get Pop's duds laid out for him.

She sings the military music loudly as she gathers the plates. She and TINA *go into the living room.* HELEN *is putting the flowers in water.*

Be marvellous, wouldn't it, if you turned a nice golden colour like those women in the travel brochures? God, aul' Charlie'd go off the head altogether! (*To* TINA) Are his black shoes ready?

TINA Not yet.

MIRIAM I'll do them and you do the suit — OK? (*To* HELEN) The years may have passed but we're still Daddy's little beavers!

TINA (*To* HELEN — *in apology*) Helen, I — I'm —

MIRIAM (*Catching her arm*) Get me the shoe polish, duckie, will you? You keep changing where you keep things in this damned house.

MIRIAM *polishes the shoes.* TINA *presses the suit.* HELEN *goes out to the garden.* FRANK *enters by the front door, dressed in commandant's UN uniform, carrying two bottles. He pauses in the hall, looks up the stairs, calls gently:*

FRANK Anna?

SIR 'Commandant Frank Butler.'

FRANK Anna?

SIR 'Twelve months ago a widower, commandant of a remote barracks, surrendering hope. Today a young wife, the Hero of Hari, and certain promotion.' (*To* FRANK) 'Outstanding courage and selflessness' — is that accurate?

FRANK *shrugs.*

SIR You're nervous.

FRANK Yes.

SIR Of what?

FRANK I don't know.

SIR Can it be to do with Anna?

FRANK Yes. Maybe. I don't know. With myself. I'm jittery for some reason.

SIR That's understandable.

FRANK And unhappy. Suddenly unhappy. Profoundly unhappy.

SIR It's the tension.

FRANK Yes?

SIR And all the fuss. All those people.

FRANK I suppose so.

SIR But remember — they're here to honour you.

FRANK I know that.

SIR So keep calm. Keep cool.

FRANK Yes.

SIR Everything's running smoothly. Everything's in hand.

FRANK Yes, yes. Everything's in hand.

He goes quickly into the living room.

Anna must be asleep. We'll give her another quarter-of-an-hour — it's going to be a tiring evening for her. (*Hands the bottles to* TINA) These are for later, in case we have some people back. Leave them on the sideboard. Did the cufflinks turn up?

TINA In the jacket pocket.

FRANK I thought you said you looked there. (*To* MIRIAM) Are those ready?

MIRIAM Another minute, Commandant, sir.

FRANK (*To* TINA) And Anna's stuff — her dress and all that — that's all arranged?

TINA Lying on the bed in Ben's old room. Everything's perfect. Stop fussing, Daddy.

FRANK No, I'll tell you what you can do: give her another ten minutes and then bring her a cup of tea.

TINA What about yourself?

FRANK I think I'll take a drink instead — no, maybe I shouldn't. Yes, I'll take a cup of tea, too.

MIRIAM What are they all at over there?
FRANK Standing around, talking, drinking.
MIRIAM Isn't it time you changed?
FRANK I know. And I've still to get a speech ready.
TINA Helen'll help you.
MIRIAM (*Offering the shoes*) There you are.
FRANK I don't want them just now, do I?

MIRIAM *makes a face.*

(*To* TINA) Where is Helen?
TINA In the garden. (*Calls*) Helen! Daddy wants — !
FRANK Shhh — Anna. I can go out, can't I?

He goes out to the garden. MIRIAM *looks up at the ceiling.*

MIRIAM God, isn't he a charmer! Sooner you nor me, daughter.

MIRIAM *goes into the kitchen. After a time* TINA *joins her.*

HELEN 'See the conquering hero comes;
Sound the trumpets, beat the drums.'
FRANK Hah!
HELEN (*Offering a flower*) For the Hero of Hari.
FRANK Thank you.

As he accepts it he leans over her as if he is about to kiss her forehead, hesitates, then quickly:

Did you see the heading in today's *Donegal Enquirer*?
HELEN No.
FRANK It's above the photograph taken at the airport yesterday — 'President Greets Humble Hannibal'. (*They both laugh. He sits beside her*) God, I feel so ancient, Helen.
HELEN It'll soon be over.
FRANK Walking over here from the camp, d'you know what I was thinking: what has a lifetime in the army done to

me? Wondering have I carried over into this life the too rigid military discipline that — that the domestic life must have been bruised, damaged, by the stern attitudes that are necessary in the — I suppose what I'm saying is that I'm not unaware of certain short-comings in my relationships with your mother and with Ben, and indeed with you when you and Gerald decided to —

HELEN The past's over, Father. And forgotten.

FRANK That's true. Over and forgotten. (*Then briskly — to their mutual relief*) Any good at writing after-dinner speeches?

HELEN Expert. What kind?

FRANK Short and brilliant. And modest.

HELEN Let's see. 'Gentlemen, I want to welcome you most sin-cerely, and even more sincerely to congratulate you on finding your way here.'

FRANK Ah-ha!

HELEN 'I will not dwell on the modest part I played in the event which the world now calls the Siege of Hari — '

FRANK I certainly will.

HELEN '— and which brought fame and honour not only to United Nations troops everywhere — '

FRANK But also —

HELEN '— to this country and to our own illustrious army.'

FRANK Hear, hear; hear, hear.

HELEN 'As for my own paltry part — '

FRANK Silence! Silence!

HELEN '— as I carried each of those nine men back to safety — '

FRANK '— across those burning desert wastes — '

HELEN '— my one sustaining thought was — '

FRANK (*Quickly*) Do you know what it was?

HELEN '— that you'd make me Chief of Staff as from this moment.'

FRANK And why not?

HELEN There you are — nothing to it.

FRANK I knew you'd be good.

HELEN Pleasure.

Pause.

FRANK When's your flight tomorrow?

HELEN Eleven.

FRANK I'll get someone to drive you to Derry.

HELEN I enjoy the bus.

FRANK I'm delighted you came, Helen. And very, very grateful.

HELEN A big occasion. A national hero.

FRANK For a day.

HELEN And some time before I go you must tell me exactly what happened. All I know is what I've read in the papers.

FRANK I'll post you a copy of the reports I've got to make out for GHQ.

HELEN Will you?

FRANK Promise.

> *Again a silence. And as before he stretches across instinctively to catch her hand. She looks at him. A moment of embarrassment. He pats her hand briskly instead.*

Well, at least they're seeing the place at its best.

HELEN That's true.

FRANK In weather like this you forget how grim it can be. When you heard about Anna and me —

HELEN Yes?

FRANK Were you hurt?

HELEN Why would I be hurt?

FRANK That I hadn't told you about it in advance.

HELEN No, not at all.

FRANK We told nobody. It was all very — at my time of day I thought — just Anna and myself, and Tom. I suppose I should have told Tina, being in the house and all, but I knew Tina wouldn't mind. And I was on the point of phoning you one night but we decided — I felt — it would be better to present you all with the *fait accompli*. Very impressive little ceremony it was, too; quiet, you know, simple, very — that little Franciscan church in Dublin — the one along the quay. Full of atmosphere; lovely. And we came straight back here intending to take a honeymoon later. And then, as you know, no sooner am I back than I'm off for five months. So in a way we still haven't had a honeymoon — you're sure you didn't mind?

HELEN Positive.

FRANK As soon as the fuss dies down we'll head off somewhere.

HELEN So you should.

FRANK France, maybe.

HELEN You deserve a holiday.

FRANK Or Italy. Somewhere. (*Pause*) Have you and she had a chance to talk yet?

HELEN For half-an-hour or so.

FRANK Oh, good, good — yes?

HELEN We had lunch together.

FRANK Yes?

HELEN Then I set her hair for her.

FRANK Yes?

HELEN Haven't you seen it?

FRANK (*Sudden rush*) Isn't she beautiful, Helen? Isn't she beautiful?

HELEN Yes.

FRANK Yes, and warm and open and refreshing. And so direct — so direct — so uncomplicated. Anything she thinks — whatever comes into her head — straight out — it must come straight out — just like that. So unlike us: measured, watching, circling one another, peeping out, shying back.

HELEN Is that us?

FRANK Oh, yes, that's us — you, me, your mother —

HELEN Tina?

FRANK Tina's special, you know that, Tina's a baby.

HELEN Is she? And Miriam?

FRANK All right — maybe not Miriam.

HELEN And Ben?

FRANK I know nothing about him. But my mascot — I call her

my mascot. A good name for her, isn't it? — whatever she is, it's there before you. And from the moment I met her — and I can say this to you, Helen: you're the only person I could say this to without embarrassment . . . There! You see! Typical! You're withdrawing!

HELEN I'm not! — I'm not!

FRANK Yes, you are. And now I'm embarrassed. It's a family —

HELEN Go on. Say what you were going to say.

FRANK I can't now.

HELEN Say it, Father.

Pause.

FRANK (*Simply*) What I was going to say is that for the first time in my life I am profoundly happy. (*Pause*) And now you're thinking there's no fool like an old fool.

HELEN No.

FRANK (*Quickly*) Infinitely happier than I ever was with your mother. Is that a despicable thing to say? No, it's not. It's the truth. During all those years of illness she was patient and courageous and admirable. And I responded to that as best I could. Despite what Ben thinks, I did my best. But it had all withered into duty, Helen. There was no joy — the joy had gone. And that's what Anna did — she restored joy to me — she animated me again. If I'm a hero today — whatever that silly word means — it is because of her.

HELEN I'm sure that's true, Father.

FRANK And nothing would give me more pleasure than to bestow some of that joy on you.

HELEN Me?

FRANK If I could.

HELEN Why me?

FRANK Because I have a super-abundance and because I sense a melancholy about my first child.

TINA *enters the living room with a tray.*

TINA (*Calls*) Tea, everybody!

FRANK   If that's not too arrogant of me — is it? (*He looks at her. Pause*) And now you're convinced I'm an old fool, aren't you?

HELEN   You keep looking for reassurance, hero.

FRANK   (*Rising briskly*) Do I? — It must be — because I need it. God, look at the time — and I've still to get dressed.

> FRANK *goes quickly into the living room.* TINA *is about to bring a cup of tea upstairs.*

Did you wake her up yet?

TINA   On my way.

FRANK   Take the suit with you, too.

> *He sits and changes his shoes.* TOM *enters the hall carrying a camera.*

TOM   Hannibal!

FRANK   I can see that's going to stick.

TOM   (*Breezy, confident to* SIR) You were right — I'll do it.

SIR   I knew you would.

TOM   But maybe not as you think. You just can't label a man a cliché and write him off.

SIR   The assessment isn't mine.

TOM   Just watch and you'll see. You may be surprised.

SIR   I'm watching.

> TINA *goes into the hall.*

TOM   Tina, my love, are they ready?

TINA   Almost. You're looking great, Uncle Tom.

TOM   Feeling terrific, thank the Lord, terrific.

> TINA *goes upstairs.* TOM *goes into the living room.* MIRIAM *enters from the kitchen.*

Is this all the length you are?

FRANK   Aren't you dressing?

TOM   I'm not one of the big shots. And how are you, Miriam?

MIRIAM Great, thanks, Father.

FRANK Are they getting restless over there?

TOM Just waiting breathlessly in the ante-room to get a glimpse of you.

FRANK Go to hell.

TOM (*To* MIRIAM) Hoping to touch his sleeve as he passes.

FRANK (*Leaving*) Give him a drink, Miriam.

TOM The way he said that you'd think my tongue was hanging out. Nothing for me, thanks.

MIRIAM It's a thirsty day.

TOM Honestly. How's Charlie?

MIRIAM Great.

TOM Pity you didn't bring the kids — they'd have enjoyed the band.

MIRIAM Isn't there chaos enough? Have you seen Helen yet?

TOM Where?

MIRIAM Here.

TOM She's not!

MIRIAM Arrived this morning.

TOM Well, good Lord! Why did nobody tell me?

He goes out to the garden.

(*To* HELEN) I've only just heard.

HELEN Father Tom! It's good to see you!

He embraces her.

TOM It's great to see you, Helen. How *are* you? Show me — you've lost weight.

HELEN I don't think so — have I?

TOM The answer I want is: as a matter of fact I have, Uncle Tom, and so have you.

They both move into the living room.

HELEN Well, as a matter of fact, Father —

TOM Don't tell me. I know. I know.

MIRIAM Looking powerful, isn't he?

HELEN   You are.

TOM   I'm grotesque. Food, drink and sloth — they're killing me. The question is: will I survive until next November?

HELEN   Why then?

TOM   That's when I retire. And even if I last six months more, what's to become of me then? Kicked out of the only world I've known for forty years — I'll be lost. D'you know who I met the other day? Jackie Sheridan — Daddy knows him — chaplain down at Athlone all his life. Retired last year; living with a widowed sister in Waterford. And d'you know what he does to pass the time? Studies all the death notices in the morning paper and spends the rest of the day writing letters of condolence to the relatives. Black strangers! Honestly. Terrifying, isn't it? What d'you think of Anna?

HELEN   That was always an old trick of yours.

TOM   Trick? Trick? What trick?

HELEN   The disarming chatter and then the sudden, probing question.

MIRIAM   She's wise to you, Father Tom.

TOM   (*To* MIRIAM, *who is laughing*) Is that fair? D'you think that's fair? (*To* HELEN) Well, I think she's terrific. And sure the world knows Frank's terrific.

HELEN   So they'll make a terrific couple.

TOM   (*To* MIRIAM) Lord, hasn't she got sharp!

MIRIAM   England smartens them up all right.

TOM   I didn't mean that at all.

HELEN   Yes, you did.

TOM   Tell me, girls, I want your advice. The powers that be have some kind of a notion that on a night like this I always get plastered.

MIRIAM   Tch-tch-tch.

TOM   Wait — wait — wait! Now — should I confirm that notion for them? Or should I stay sober and confound them? I could, you know.

HELEN   Confirm them?

TOM   Confound them!

MIRIAM   Do that then, Father.

TOM   Should I?

MIRIAM Anything to confound them.
TOM That's it then. Settled. (*To* HELEN) What are you looking sceptical about?
HELEN Not a thing — not a thing.

FRANK *enters in his dress uniform.* TINA *behind him.*

FRANK Anna'll be down in a minute.

The following lines — MIRIAM's, TOM's, HELEN's, TINA's — *all overlap.*

MIRIAM (*Clapping*) Well — well — well — well!
TOM Ah, the prince himself!
HELEN Very smart — very smart indeed!
TINA Three cheers for the hero!
TOM (*Sings*) 'For he's a jolly good fellow — '
FRANK Stop — stop — stop — stop — stop!
ALL } 'For he's a jolly good fellow;
     For he's a jolly good fellow;
     And so say all of us.'
TOM Everybody outside for a picture!
TINA A photo — hurrah — hurrah — hurrah — a photo!

They move to the garden — talking — still singing/ humming 'Jolly Good Fellow'. Comments like: 'My God, look at my dress', 'Anybody got a comb?', 'You're fine', 'Where do you want us to stand?' etc, etc.

TOM Over here, please, everybody. You in the middle, Frank. Miriam, you and Tina on one side.
FRANK Where? Here?
TOM A bit to the left.
FRANK Here?
TOM That's the right.
FRANK It's *my* left.
TOM No wonder you could never march!
TINA What about me?
TOM Fine where you are.

MIRIAM Not a word — the cap's still over the lens.

HELEN It's not!

TOM You're quite right — so it is! (*Takes it off*) That'll be a help.

MIRIAM Maybe — maybe.

TOM A little tighter in, Helen, please. Good, good. At ease, Frank.

FRANK I am at ease.

TOM Are you? Look at me. Big smile, everybody.

The group is facing almost straight out. ANNA *in a long dressing gown comes downstairs and into the living room. She looks around.*

ANNA (*Softly*) Frank?

She looks out, sees the photographing, stands watching.

TINA Cheese — isn't that what you say?

HELEN *Noblesse oblige.*

MIRIAM Oh, very posh. Is that a London one?

ANNA (*More loudly*) Frank!

FRANK Come on, Tom. Get a move on.

SIR 'She calls Frank twice. But Frank does not hear her. And she goes back to her room and cries.'

TOM Little tighter in, love.

TINA Me?

TOM No, Miriam. Tight in — perfect!

ANNA Look at them — tight — tight — tight — arms around one another — smiling. No, I won't go back to my room and cry. I'll tell them now!

SIR *gets quickly to his feet and goes to* ANNA.

SIR They won't hear you now.

ANNA They will! They will!

SIR Anna, believe me —

She rushes away from him and out to the garden

where she stands facing the group. SIR *looks on patiently. She is almost hysterical.*

TOM Frank.

FRANK What?

TOM This way.

FRANK I'm glaring at you, for God's sake!

TOM That's what I'm saying. Will you stop it! Now — terrific — Commandant Butler and his beautiful family.

MIRIAM He really means me.

ANNA (*Trying to control herself*) Listen to me, all of you. You, too, Chaplain.

MIRIAM No film in the camera.

TINA I'm going to laugh.

ANNA When you were away, all those months I was left alone here —

TOM Great — don't move — terrific. And another.

ANNA Listen to me, Frank!

FRANK (*To* TOM) No, no, no, no.

TOM One more — just one more — that's all.

ANNA I had an affair with your son, Ben — with your brother, Ben! An affair — an affair — d'you hear!

TOM Even closer together.

MIRIAM Thanks be to God Charlie isn't watching this caper.

ANNA An affair, d'you hear — out of loneliness, out of despair, out of hate! And everybody in the camp knows — everybody except the Butlers!

TINA *can control her laughter no longer — she explodes.*

TOM Terrific, Tina! Everybody join in!

The laughter is infectious. They laugh so much we can hardly hear what they are saying.

MIRIAM *Noblesse oblige!*

TOM Lovely, Frank.

HELEN Is there really no film in it?

TINA Hold me up! Hold me up!

TOM (*Clicking, clicking*) Terrific, terrific! Stay where you are!

> ANNA *is staring at the others as if she had come out of a dream.* SIR *goes to her and takes her arm, leading her off.*

SIR I told you, didn't I? 'Frank does not hear her and she goes back to her room and cries.'

ANNA (*Crying*) It wasn't despair.

SIR I know.

ANNA And it wasn't hate — no, not hate for him.

SIR You'll tell us later.

ANNA It wasn't even loneliness —

SIR Later — later — you'll do it *later* exactly as it's here. Now go back to your room.

ANNA I'm sorry.

SIR No harm done.

ANNA Did I mess it all up?

SIR You shuffled the pages a bit — that's all. But nothing's changed.

> *Throughout this* ANNA/SIR *exchange, the others have stood with frozen smiles. Now that* ANNA *has gone off they are released again.*

TOM There! Thank you — thank you — thank you.

FRANK Right — off we go, Tom. Let's move — let's move.

> FRANK *goes into the house and hall. The others drift into the living room.*

TOM Can I leave this (*camera*) here?

TINA I'll look after it.

HELEN When will we get copies?

MIRIAM Have you never seen his pictures?

FRANK (*Calling upstairs*) Anna! We're all set.

MIRIAM If you get a word with the Taoiseach, Father, tell him we're still waiting for the sewage out at Kilclooney.

TOM The very first thing I'll say to him.

MIRIAM Just to give him an appetite.

> ANNA *comes downstairs.* FRANK *stands at the bottom with his hands outstretched.*

FRANK Beautiful.

ANNA I'm nervous, Frank.

FRANK You are beautiful. (*Calls*) Look! Everybody look! Look what I'm bringing to the reception!

> *The others move out to the hallway.*

TOM Terrific, Anna, terrific!

HELEN ⎫ Lovely, Anna. It's a beautiful dress.

MIRIAM ⎬ You did the hair very well. Those are lovely shoes.

TINA ⎭ Lovely. Lovely.

FRANK And look — look — (*jewellery*). And this, isn't this elegant (*dress*)?

ANNA Frank, I —

FRANK And what about that (*hair*)? Your handiwork, isn't it, Helen?

HELEN You're going to be late, Father.

FRANK Let them wait.

ANNA Please, Frank.

FRANK All in all   beautiful!

ANNA Please —

FRANK And she says she's nervous! My darling, they'll never have seen a sight like it in the mess — in any mess — in all their puny lives. (*Briskly*) We're away. Don't wait up for me.

> BEN *enters left. Very diffident, very hesitant, as if he might turn and run away. He looks into the living room — but the others have now moved out to the front of the house.*

TOM We're off. God bless.

HELEN ⎫ Have a good time. Confound them, Father Tom.
MIRIAM ⎬ Enjoy yourselves. Make a good speech, Daddy.
TINA ⎭ Don't eat too much, Anna.

> *They are all offstage now — except* HELEN, *who is standing at the front door.*

FRANK Are we taking my car or yours?
TOM It doesn't matter — either.
TINA Take your own, Daddy.

> *The car moves off. We hear* TINA *and* MIRIAM *calling goodbyes.* HELEN *waves from the door.* BEN *moves closer to the house.* HELEN *turns and comes into the living room.*

SIR 'Benedict Butler — Ben — twenty-four years of age. Only son of Frank and Louise. His father wanted him to go for a commission, but his mother wanted him to be a doctor. Was a first-year medical student at University College, Dublin, when his mother died.'
BEN (*Softly*) Helen.

> HELEN *is standing looking at the photographs on the mantelpiece. She has her back to him.*

SIR 'Shortly after her death his health broke down and he never went back to college. Now fully recovered, the only after-effect being a stammer which afflicts him occasionally when he is tense.'
BEN Helen.
SIR 'As he looks into the living room he imagines for a second that the figure at the mantelpiece is his mother.'
BEN She had her back to me. She didn't hear me. And I stood outside in the garden and just watched her. Everything — her hair, her neck, her shoulders, the way she moved her arms — precisely as I remembered. (HELEN *is now fingering the glass ornament*) Not a sound except the tap-tap-tap of her stick as she

216

moved about. And for a second my heart expanded with an immense remembered love for her, and then at once shrank in terror of her. And then suddenly she turned and came towards the open door, and I saw it wasn't — it w-w-w-wasn't —

> HELEN *has turned and has moved to the open door. She is startled to see a man staring in at her.*

HELEN Who — ? (*Loud*) Ben!

> *He responds as if someone — a stranger — had called him.*

BEN (*Quickly, confused*) Yes? Yes?

> HELEN *runs out and throws her arms around him.*

HELEN⎱ Oh — Ben, Ben, Ben, Ben, Ben!
BEN ⎰ Yes? Yes? Yes? Yes? Yes?
SIR (*Rising*) Thank you. (*Claps his hands twice to interrupt the action*) That's fine — that's fine. We're moving along very nicely. (*Sees that* BEN *and* HELEN *are still locked in an embrace*) Thank you.

> *They separate.*

Yes, very nicely indeed.

> *As soon as he claps his hands,* TINA, ANNA, FRANK *and* TOM *appear.*

Now, we'll leave it there, I think, and move straight on to the point when —

ANNA 'The point of no return.'

SIR The — ?

ANNA It's your phrase; you used it to Father Tom.

SIR 'The point of no return' — you're quite right; so I did. Wasn't that very histrionic of me! Oh, no; heavens, no.

We're nowhere near that — that decisive point yet.

ANNA Then let's skip all the rest and go straight to it.

SIR You've already been naughty and attempted that, Anna!

ANNA Because it's the essence of it all, isn't it?

SIR Well, of course we can do that. But if we do, then we're bypassing all that period when different decisions *might* have been made. Because at the point we've arrived at now, many different conclusions would have been possible if certain things had been said or done or left unsaid and undone. And at this point it did occur to many of you to say certain things or to omit saying certain things. And it is the memory of those lost possibilities that has exercised you endlessly since and has kept bringing you back here, isn't that so?

TOM I'm sure he's right.

SIR For example, Helen, you did think of spending the night with Charlie and Miriam.

HELEN We've already been over all that.

SIR We have indeed. And what you said was, 'No, I'll see it through.'

HELEN Yes, I stayed, and I saw it through, and I didn't survive the test. And I've cracked up three times since. Now are you content?

SIR It's your content we're talking about. And Ben, at this point you still had time to join your friends on the salmon boat.

BEN Am I complaining? Am I?

SIR But the thought did occur to you. And they didn't set out for — what? — another hour at least. So if you would like to explore that area of —

BEN Just stick to the f-f-f-facts.

SIR But that is a fact. And every time you get drunk it's the one thing you keep talking about.

BEN What happened happened. Leave it at that.

SIR As you wish. As for yourself, Anna, you could have resolved — sitting up at that top table in the mess — bored by the talk around you — you could still have resolved to live with your secret —

ANNA   'Live with my secret'! For God's sake!

SIR   Be fair, Anna. You did think of it. In which case Frank's life would have stayed reasonably intact. Oh, there were many, many options still open at this stage.

TOM   I agree completely. (*He is ignored*)

TINA   For me, too?

SIR   Not for you, Tina, I'm afraid. You had no choice. That night you were faced with the inevitability of growing up. But that's all — well, almost all.

TOM   He's absolutely right — about the rest of us, I mean. (*No one listens to him, either here or later when he preaches*)

SIR   As for yourself, Frank —

    FRANK *holds up his hands.*

FRANK   You're in command, Sir.

SIR   At this point, indeed at any point, you could well have —

FRANK   Please — please. I did what I had to do. There was no alternative for me. None. What I had to do was absolutely clear cut. There was never any doubt in my mind.

SIR   I'm afraid that's true, Frank.

FRANK   So carry on as you think best, Sir. I'm in your hands.

SIR   Very well. Let's proceed. Let's leap ahead to — yes, several hours later.

TOM   Our options are still open — he's perfectly right.

SIR   And for this episode I think I need only Helen and Ben and Tina.

TOM   I'm not a sermonizing kind of fellow — good Lord, you know me better than that —

    The others begin to drift away, each encased in his privacy.

    — but I've got to speak what I know to be true, and that is that grace is available to each and every one of us if we just ask God for it —

SIR   Yes — here we are.

TOM — which is really the Christian way of saying that our options are *always* open. Because that is the enormous gift that Christ purchased for us — the availability of choice and our freedom to choose.

He stops and looks around. SIR *is poised with his finger on his ledger — he has all the time in the world.* ANNA *and* FRANK *have gone.* HELEN, BEN *and* TINA *have not heard a word he has said. His rally falters.*

So that what I'm saying is — is that at this point there isn't necessarily an incompatability between your attitude, Sir, and my own —

SIR Good. 'It is 1.45 a.m. and — '

TOM And, Sir.

SIR *looks at him.*

(*Forced roguishness*) Keep watching — you're going to be surprised.

TOM *leaves.*

SIR 'It is 1.45 a.m. and Miriam and Charlie are at home, in bed. Charlie is sleeping. Miriam is staring at the ceiling. In the camp the reception is just over. Frank Butler and the Minister of Defence and the Chief of Staff are standing in a corner conversing privately. Father Tom is in the car park searching his pockets for car keys. Anna is standing alone at the mess waiting for Frank. In the Butler living room — '

He breaks off because his eye catches CHARLIE, *dressed as usual, tiptoeing across the stage.* CHARLIE *senses the silence, smiles at* SIR, *touches his forehead with his index finger.*

CHARLIE (*Confidentially*) Carry on — pay no attention to me — I'll just nip over here — look on from that corner.

He begins walking again.

SIR I'm sorry.

CHARLIE Fascinating to watch people — observe them, you know — just like in the courts — as long as you're not involved yourself — how the other half lives sort of thing.

SIR It is 1.45 a.m. You arrived at 11.30 and left with Miriam.

CHARLIE Honest to God, you won't hear a cheep out of —

SIR You're at home in bed. You're asleep and Miriam's awake.

CHARLIE I know the reason for that! If she's sleeping she can't think. (*Pause*) I mean to say — if she's thinking she can't sleep. (*Begins moving*) Just for this next piece —

SIR Goodnight, Charlie.

CHARLIE *stops.*

Goodnight.

CHARLIE *looks at him, sees he is adamant, and leaves.*

'In the Butler living room the doors and windows are wide open because the night is sultry. Helen and Ben have a few drinks together.' I'll leave it to yourselves.

He retires to his stool. The lights change. The lights from the living room spill out to the garden. BEN *and* HELEN *are slightly intoxicated and completely relaxed. This must not be played as a drunk scene, but lightly, full of laughter.* BEN *is striding about with a glass in his hand, a cigarette in his mouth. The diffident, uncertain* BEN *is suddenly voluble. The scene is played in almost constant movement — around the living room, out in the garden, around the garden. Wherever* BEN *and* HELEN *go* TINA *follows. But their accord, their intimacy, excludes her.*

BEN Follow behind me, keep me in sight, and I'll lead you there.

HELEN I'm on your heels.

BEN Right. Do you happen to remember a place by the name of Carrickfad?

HELEN Carrickfad! Do I remember Carrickfad!

BEN Good. So you pass Carrickfad. Turn right at the old coastguard station. Pass the old limekiln. Pass the old rectory.

HELEN Ruins — ruins — ruins!

BEN Cross the wooden bridge and straight down that track until you come to the ringfort —

HELEN On your left when you're facing the sea.

BEN Turn left there, carry on for three-quarters of a mile until you come to the sand dunes —

HELEN In Culhame.

BEN Culhame is correct. But you have still to find my hermitage. Now, when you get to the foot of the sand hills, you stop, face north-north-west and look straight ahead; and if you've very good eyesight you'll see rising out of the bent the roof of a little blue caravan.

HELEN (*To* TINA) 'A secret place', he says!

BEN And there I can be consulted any morning between the hours of nine and eleven, except on those occasions when I'm off lecturing.

He goes out to the garden. HELEN *follows. Then* TINA.

HELEN Secret! I could make my way there now — in the dark!

TINA I was never there.

HELEN Didn't we spend every Sunday in the summer sliding down those same dunes!

TINA Had you great fun?

BEN And when I'm travelling abroad I can usually be contacted at the nearest Salvation Army hostel. You know, we old army types — a great freemasonry. (*Calls in the direction of camp*) My greetings, Chief of Staff, Adjutant General and Quartermaster General! God bless you, Number One Army Band!

HELEN They've left hours ago, clown!

BEN And warmest wishes to you, magazine, parade square

222

and flagpole!

HELEN D'you remember the day the two of us climbed up onto the roof of the old coastguard station?

BEN A mad, mad pair!

TINA Was Miriam with you?

BEN Mad!

HELEN She went to the top of the walls but didn't go up onto the roof.

TINA And what happened?

HELEN (*To* BEN) Tell her what happened!

BEN What happened was that we were stuck up there for six hours.

HELEN Right!

BEN The pair of us clinging to two charred rafters.

HELEN Remember them groaning!

BEN Rigid with fright — couldn't move either forward or back in case they'd snap.

HELEN Mother calling up, 'Don't wriggle, Ben. Don't wriggle!'

BEN I was shaking with *cold*. And if I opened my eyes I could see Father directly below me. And cute enough, I remember thinking: if the rafter does snap, he'll break my fall.

HELEN Oh my God.

TINA How did you get down?

BEN It took a full detachment of engineers — scaffolding, generators, arc lights — the biggest peacetime operation ever mounted by Western Command. And an ambulance —

HELEN Two ambulances!

BEN And that old MO — Colonel — ?

HELEN Hayes.

BEN That's him. 'Where the hell are the blankets?'

HELEN What a day — what a day!

TINA You must have had a lot of fun.

HELEN I don't know what I'm laughing at. I thought I was finished.

BEN I pointed it out to Anna about a month ago — one day we were out at the caravan — and told her the whole escapade; but somehow there was none of the terror, none of the delight. (*Goes inside*) Now I have a feeling that if my commandant father knew I was here he'd rush home and throw his arms around me and say, 'Welcome, son. Help yourself to a drink.'

HELEN *goes inside.* TINA *follows.*

HELEN Part of him probably wants to.
BEN Offer me a drink?
HELEN You know very well.
BEN 'A large whiskey, Sir? Thank you very much, Sir. You're altogether too kind.'
HELEN And if he did?

Pause as BEN *pours a drink.*

BEN Too late — too late.
HELEN But if he did?
BEN We're long beyond that.
HELEN What if he did?
BEN What if he did? After all that's been said?
HELEN Despite all that.
BEN The day she died I called him a murderer.
HELEN Six years have passed.
BEN And he hit me — don't you remember? — he hit me!
HELEN That's all over.
BEN Years, years of hostility.
HELEN That fades.
BEN Does it?
HELEN You know it does.
BEN You can preserve it.

He goes outside again. HELEN *follows. As before,* TINA *tags along.*

HELEN Why would you want to?
BEN In case you'd forget.
HELEN No!
BEN Out of a sense of loyalty.

HELEN To whom?

BEN You can embalm it consciously, deliberately —

HELEN That would be wrong.

BEN — in acts of terrible perfidy —

HELEN You wouldn't do that, Ben.

BEN — which you do in a state of confusion, out of some vague residual passion that no longer fires you; hitting out, smashing back, not at what's there but at what you think you remember, and which you regret instantly — oh, yes, yes, yes, never underestimate the regret. But then it's too late, too late — the thing's preserved in perpetuity — as Charlie would say.

HELEN You shouldn't drink.

BEN So, as we used to say — put that in your pipe and smoke it.

HELEN (*To* TINA) Going off his head in that hermitage of his.

BEN Helen.

HELEN You *are* drunk.

BEN Sister Helen.

HELEN Sit down on that seat.

BEN Helen Sarah Fidelma.

HELEN HSF — yes, I remember

TINA What was that?

HELEN Horrible Smelly Feet.

TINA I never heard that before!

HELEN He used to drive me mad with that.

TINA I'm going to remember that — HSF!

BEN I want to tell you something.

HELEN You're getting silly.

BEN I am not. And I want to tell you something.

HELEN (*To* BEN) Give me a cigarette.

TINA No, Helen, no!

HELEN Just one.

BEN Honourable Sincere Friend.

TINA Don't, Helen, please.

BEN We'll both have one.

TINA You'll regret it, Helen.

BEN I've something to say to you.

HELEN Is it important?

BEN Very important — vitally important — and you'll know it's important.

HELEN How?

BEN Because I'll probably start stammering in the middle of it!

They all laugh at this.

HELEN Give me a light.

TINA I'm disappointed in you, Helen.

HELEN (*Mocking*) She's disappointed in me! Now I'm really upset. (*To* BEN) D'you remember — out in the turf shed — passing the cigarette from one to the other and it hot with sucking!

BEN What I'm going to tell you is a big secret.

HELEN I hate secrets.

BEN No, not really a secret.

HELEN Make up your mind.

BEN More a confidence than a s-s-s-secret.

They all laugh.

HELEN You faked that!

BEN I did not!

HELEN You did — to hook me!

TINA Tell us your secret.

BEN May I confide my confidence?

HELEN You may not.

BEN I'm going to tell you.

HELEN I don't want to hear it.

BEN Helen —

HELEN Everybody tells me their confidences.

BEN Please —

HELEN I'm sick of their confidences.

BEN It's about —

HELEN (*Covering her ears*) No, no, no, no!

TINA (*Laughing*) Tell me, Ben! Tell me!

BEN It has to do with my embalming job.

HELEN Can't hear a word you're saying!

BEN (*Shouts*) And with my profound regrets.
HELEN We all have our regrets. Look after your own.
BEN I'll shock you, Helen.

> HELEN *takes her hands away from her ears. The atmos-phere suddenly changes: the laughing is finished.*

HELEN (*Imperious*) I want a cup of coffee! He needs a cup of coffee! Go and make it for me, Tina!
BEN Mother's voice — exactly!
TINA I want to hear what Ben's —
HELEN (*Calmer*) Would you, darling, please?

> *She looks firmly at* TINA *until* TINA *finally gives way and goes into the living room. She is about to go into the kitchen but hesitates to listen.*

On a night like this you can hear the sea breaking on the Tor Mór.
BEN (*Quiet, urgent*) I've got to tell you, Helen.
HELEN You've got to nothing.
BEN When you wanted to talk about your Gerry I listened to you.
HELEN Years ago. For God's sake, you're a man now!
BEN I was the one carried your messages.
HELEN Stop bleating! Stop snivelling!
BEN Stood watching outside the gym hall when you and he were inside. Warned you that night the two of you took the jeep and went to the dance in Omagh —
HELEN And stood there at Mother's side — and held her hand — held her hand as if you were her husband, while he stood at the door with his cap in his hand, trembling, the fool, trembling because the Commandant's wife was quizzing him in her quiet and most reasonable voice about his 'educational background' and his father's 'profession' and his 'prospects in his chosen career' — Private Gerald Kelly, batman — my Gerry — *my* Gerry. And all the time you stood beside her in that wicker chair, facing him, stroking her hand. *You*

did, Ben; yes, you. And d'you know what he did when he came outside? Gerald Kelly — the defiant, reckless, the daredevil Gerry Kelly? He cried, Ben. Yes; like a child. Gerry Kelly cried. Yes. He cried. Yes.

She goes to the other end of the garden. She cries quietly. BEN *goes to her.*

BEN I'm sorry, Helen.

HELEN (*Simply*) Sorry? What's sorry? 'Never underestimate the regret.' Is that what you said? I've lost him. She killed him. He's gone. Do I love Gerry Kelly still? I thought I'd squeezed every drop of him out of me. But now I know I haven't forgotten a second of him.

BEN Helen —

Pause. Then SIR *rises and moves forward.*

SIR Thank you. We've got quite a bit done. I'd say the back's broken. (*To audience*) We'll resume again in approximately — what? — fifteen minutes.

Quick black.

ACT TWO

Only MIRIAM *is onstage, sitting in the wicker chair, reading the* Donegal Enquirer, *eating a slice of cake, an empty coffee mug beside her. Great bursts of laughter come from the kitchen. And as the other characters come on they carry with them an air of good humour — a gaiety or, as* SIR *calls it, a 'giddiness' that permeates the beginning of this sequence, right up until the arrival of* SIR. *They are dressed as we saw them at the end of Act One, except* FRANK, *who is in desert uniform.* TINA, *laughing, opens the kitchen door.*

TINA There's a few cream cakes left. Do you want one?

MIRIAM Don't tempt me.

TINA Or a doughnut?

MIRIAM Please. I'm up to here. What are they laughing at?

TINA Father Tom's telling stories about when he was a curate in Yorkshire.

MIRIAM God, weren't we reared on them!

TINA Daddy says he makes them up as he goes along.

MIRIAM Listen to this — from the *Enquirer* — 'Commandant Butler's eldest daughter, Christina, is in London — '

TINA Me!

MIRIAM 'His youngest daughter, Helen, lives at home.'

TINA Sure they never get anything right, that crowd.

MIRIAM But wait till you hear this. 'And another daughter is married to Mr Charles Donnelly who is popular in the legal and sporting life of Donegal. As a young man he was a well-known amateur high-jumper and is the father of three children!'

TINA (*Laughing*) I'm away back to London.

She returns to the kitchen.

MIRIAM High-jumper — sweet God. Amateur — my foot!

She continues reading. BEN *enters left, singing, and meets* ANNA, *who enters from upstage — throughout this sequence none of the characters obeys the conventions of the set. They meet in the garden area.*

BEN We're not late, are we?

ANNA I don't think so.

BEN I suppose he'd be out clapping his hands for us. Come along, children, come along, come along.

ANNA *sits on the garden seat.*

You're eager to get it over with, aren't you?

ANNA At the beginning I was. Now I don't care. Are you?

BEN I don't give a damn about anyone or anything. I feel . . . flushed, giddy . . . I feel euphoric. (ANNA *laughs*)

ANNA 'Euphoric'!

BEN I do. I haven't felt like this since — (*Stops*)

ANNA When?

BEN I can tell you exactly — six years ago, October 19th — the day of my mother's funeral. That's when. That afternoon. After we had come back from the cemetery. Shocking, isn't it?

ANNA Tell me about it.

BEN Nothing much to tell. We were all in there (*living room*) — it was pouring with rain — there were some visitors — the girls were crying — everybody was whispering. And suddenly I had to rush out of the room because I was afraid I'd burst out singing or cheer or leap into the air. Honestly. Walked across the sand hills for maybe a couple of hours — I don't remember. Anyhow, until that madness passed.

ANNA Was it madness?

Pause. He looks at her quickly, then resumes as before.

BEN And then I came back. Guilty as hell and soaked to the skin. (*Smiling*) And assumed the grief again — a greater grief, a guilty grief. All very strange.

ANNA Are you going to sing for us now?

BEN Sing, dance, anything you like.

*He does a few extravagant leaps around the stage,
singing a few lines of 'Singing in the Rain' at the same
time. In the middle of his performance* MIRIAM *shouts
out:*

MIRIAM Ben, will you — for the love of God!

ANNA (*When he finishes*) Very good. Very impressive.

He flops down beside her.

BEN I really am giddy now!

ANNA I think you should stick to the fishing all the same.

BEN What are you going to do — when it's all over?

ANNA An aunt of mine has a café in New Jersey. She always
wanted me over. So I'll stay with her for six months
— until I've saved some money. Then I'll move on to
San Francisco or Los Angeles; more likely San Francisco.

BEN Just like that?

ANNA Yes.

BEN Have you any relatives in California?

ANNA No.

BEN Do you know anybody there?

ANNA No one.

BEN God, I wish I could be as decisive as that.

ANNA What'll you do?

BEN When this is all over? Oh, I'll — I suppose I'll head off,
too.

ANNA To America?

BEN Not America. America's too — too foreign for me.
Scotland. England, maybe. Somewhere. Who knows?

ANNA But you'll keep coming back here, won't you?

Great laughter from the kitchen.

BEN Are you laughing at me, too?
ANNA But that's what you'll do, isn't it?

> BEN *leaps up.*

BEN Let's go and see what's so funny.
ANNA Oh, Ben, there's one thing I'd like you to do for me —
BEN Yes?
ANNA If you would.
BEN What's that?
ANNA You look startled.
BEN Why should I look startled? What is it?
ANNA I left a pair of old flat shoes in the caravan — I think they're in that press under the sink. And a blue and white scarf — it's hanging behind the door.
BEN I'll get them for you.
ANNA That's all.
BEN Fine.

> *She goes up to him and kisses him lightly on the forehead.*

ANNA Dismiss.
BEN (*Uneasy laugh*) What's that for?
ANNA Our attempt at a love affair.

> *Laughter from kitchen.*

BEN What do you mean — attempt?
ANNA That's what it was, wasn't it?

> *She takes his arm and leads him into the living room.*

Come on — we're missing the fun.

> *As they enter, the others —* FRANK, TOM, TINA, HELEN *— emerge from the kitchen. Now that they are all together the euphoric atmosphere is heightened.*

FRANK I don't believe a word of it, Tom!

TOM Would I tell a lie, Helen?

HELEN I keep telling you — I believe you.

FRANK He now suddenly remembers that Canon Bradshaw had a wooden leg!

MIRIAM God forgive you, Father Tom!

TOM May I be called before my Maker.

ANNA Who's Canon Bradshaw?

> FRANK *is standing beside* ANNA, *his arm casually around her shoulders.*

FRANK An eccentric parish priest he had when he was a curate in Hull.

TOM A terrific yoke made from Parana pine and treated with linseed oil. And he had two types of ferrule that he could screw into the bottom: one was brass that he used to polish every Friday night when he was doing the candlesticks —

HELEN He's remembering more details.

MIRIAM More lies.

BEN Let him tell the story.

FRANK (*To* ANNA) This was his first post.

TOM — and the other ferrule was wooden and covered with black astrakhan —

> *Great laughter.*

BEN Astrakhan?

TOM Just like a drumstick.

MIRIAM This is all new! Canon Bradshaw used to be a cripple in a wheelchair!

TOM God's my judge. And he'd use the wooden one when he'd be saying Mass upstairs in the oratory. And when he'd come to the Sanctus he'd suddenly kick out back-ways, just like a donkey, and bang the bell three times with the astrakhan head.

BEN Boom-boom-boom.

Laughter.

FRANK Tom! Tom!

TINA When did he use the brass one?

HELEN You're encouraging him.

MIRIAM Try to stop him.

TOM He used the brass one —

MIRIAM This is definitely a lie.

TOM No. He used the brass one for walking, of course. And for beating carpets.

Again they all laugh.

I know — I know — no one ever believes me.

HELEN All that laughing — my sides are sore.

FRANK We're all sore. What has made all of us so frivolous?

MIRIAM Listen — listen — listen — have you all seen this (*paper*)?

BEN What is it?

FRANK Yes, study that. I look very distinguished in that.

TINA I think so too, Daddy.

FRANK (*To* ANNA) Have you seen it?

ANNA It's very good.

BEN Let me see.

MIRIAM Make up captions for the two of them as they shake hands. What's the President thinking? What's Father thinking?

TOM Hannibal's old eyes; and the way he's leaning slightly backwards. You're thinking: The cute hawk smells the brandy off my breath!

HELEN Very good. Anna?

ANNA Show me.

FRANK You be careful now.

ANNA The President's saying to himself: My God, I've forgotten! Footman, Batman, Butler — what's the man's *name*?

FRANK If you want to know he called me Francis.

BEN I know what he's thinking: Today's Monday — this must be the Italian equestrian team.

MIRIAM   And what's Father thinking?

FRANK   You'd never guess.

HELEN   Tell us.

MIRIAM   I know — I know: He keeps calling me Corporal — have I been demoted?

FRANK   Wrong — wrong — all wrong.

HELEN   All right — we give up — you tell us.

FRANK   I will not.

MIRIAM   Go. Go on.

SEVERAL TOGETHER   Come on, Father. Tell us. Tell us. We're dying to know.

FRANK   No.

TOM   He can't tell because it's obscene.

FRANK   As a matter of fact —

HELEN   Well?

FRANK   (*To* ANNA) I was looking for you in the crowd.

This is greeted with clapping and with joking 'ohs' and 'ahs'.

That's the truth.

TOM   In that case, and with that set to your jaw, your caption should read: If she's not here, I'll shoot her! (*As he goes off*) Anybody for more coffee? My wonderful coffee?

SEVERAL TOGETHER   No! No! No! No! No! No!

TOM   All right. All right.

FRANK *takes advantage of the chorus to catch* ANNA *by the hand and lead her out to the garden. As he leads her out:*

FRANK   Tom and his silly stories. He can spin them out for hours on end.

He catches both her hands and holds her at arm's length.

Let me look at you. My God, how I missed you. Were they kind to you when I was away? Does the family overwhelm you? Did you miss me? Let me look at you. Let me look at my beautiful, beautiful mascot.

ANNA What do you see?

FRANK What's the serious face for?

ANNA Tell me what you see, Frank.

FRANK I see youth, beauty, directness, simplicity. My wife.

ANNA Anything else?

FRANK An ageing man trembling before her.

ANNA Why is he trembling?

FRANK With intensity. With uncertainty. Because he has never had joy like this. Because he is afraid that somehow he can't cope with so great a joy because he is an ageing man.

ANNA She is trembling too —

He puts his fingers across her lips.

FRANK Because he wants to smother her, wash her in words of love, but he can't because he has no fluency in love words and he's afraid she won't understand that —

Again she tries to speak and again he stops her.

No, no, no. And he's trembling because he's afraid she'll tire of a man so staid, so formal, so ponderous — tire of his earnestness — my God, of *this*! — tire of this solemn, abject display that is the only method he knows. But you'd tell me if I ever began to disgust you, wouldn't you, Anna? Yes, you would. You'd have nothing to say — those eyes would tell me. (*Quick laugh*) I've a confession to make. Let's sit down.

They sit on the summer seat.

There are nine men in this country who know every-thing about you!

ANNA What men?

FRANK The men that I rescued in the desert. Each time I crawled back to base with a man on my back — each trip took about half-an-hour — I told him about you — everything about you — your hair, your neck, your shoulders, the way you laugh — everything. Luckily most of them were too ill to listen. Not that that made any difference — I'd have told them anyway. And one of them — fellow called Driscoll, lost both his legs — I had to carry him like a baby — he kept moaning and crying for his mother and I heard myself shouting to him, 'Shut up, Driscoll! I'm talking to you about my Anna! So shut up! Shut up!' And he did. And he listened. So you probably saved Driscoll's life — just as you have saved mine.

MIRIAM *comes out.*

MIRIAM D'you know what Charlie was saying? You should put down spuds in this garden next year. Great for killing weeds.

ANNA Where's Father Tom?

BEN, HELEN *and* TINA *come out to the garden.*

MIRIAM In the kitchen, I think.

HELEN You don't want more of his coffee, do you?

Laughter.

BEN Every time I hear Uncle Tom mention coffee I think of that famous picnic years ago —

HELEN On Portnoo pier!

BEN That's it.

MIRIAM And the two flasks! Oh, sweet Saviour!

FRANK He'll hear you, Miriam.

TINA What was that? What happened?

FRANK It's a bit unkind to poor Tom.

BEN Poor Tom! I might have been killed.

MIRIAM (*To* ANNA) We all drove out to Portnoo this Sunday —

oh, thirteen — fourteen years ago —

BEN   I was twelve at the time.

FRANK   (*To* ANNA) The place with the lookout post on the hill above it.

HELEN   (*To* ANNA) Haven't you been there?

ANNA   Yes, yes, I know it.

MIRIAM   And Mammy sat with a rug round her knees and the rest of us had a swim and then we spread the cloth out on the pier for the picnic and Uncle Tom had his stuff and we had ours. And it must have been the month of June because I have a distinct memory that it was the first strawberries we'd had that season and Mammy had a carton of cream, fresh cream, and a carton of ice cream, and you know that sensation when you taste the first fresh strawberries of the season — just like the first new spuds — only lighter and —

BEN   Tell the story, will you?

HELEN   We had just begun to eat —

MIRIAM   When suddenly Ben began behaving very strangely.

TINA   Oh, *that* story!

        SIR *enters, listens to the story and reacts to it as the others do. As the narrative unfolds* BEN *acts the part he played.*

BEN   Hic-hup-hic-hic-hic.

MIRIAM   Staggering across the cloth and kicking over the cups and the strawberries and the ice cream; and of course Mammy began to panic —

FRANK   (*To* ANNA) We can laugh at it now.

HELEN   'Epilepsy! My baby boy's got epilepsy!'

TINA   The twelve-year-old baby!

FRANK   It was very frightening.

MIRIAM   And then he fell on his face and started vomiting and Mammy began to cry and Tina started to scream —

TINA   No wonder!

MIRIAM   All into the car — back home like the hammers of hell — and you know those roads along the Gweebarra —

FRANK   She knows them.

HELEN   (*To* BEN) You'd passed out at that stage and Uncle Tom
        was praying in your ear —

MIRIAM   Straight into sick-quarters — frantic phone calls —
        doctors and nurses summoned —

ANNA   What was it? What had happened?

MIRIAM   What had happened was that little Christina here —

TINA   I was six at the time!

MIRIAM   — had switched Uncle Tom's flask and our flask —

BEN   (*To* TINA) Monster!

MIRIAM   — and poor Mammy had given Ben a cup of neat
        whiskey!

ANNA   No!

HELEN   Almost killed him.

BEN   He was never the same since.

ANNA   Oh, poor Tom!

BEN   Oh, poor me!

MIRIAM   And of course he could never own up.

HELEN   Did he know?

MIRIAM   Did he know! Course he knew!

FRANK   The sequel's the best part. Tell her that.

HELEN   That bit's not true, Father.

FRANK   Is it not?

MIRIAM   Doesn't matter if it's true or not — it's part of the
        Butler lore.

ANNA   What's the sequel?

MIRIAM   Ben claims that —

BEN   I do not!

MIRIAM   All right — it is said that when he was lying in sick-
        quarters after he'd had his stomach pumped —

FRANK   Shhh!

MIRIAM   — Uncle Tom came to see him.

BEN   That bit's true.

MIRIAM   — leaned over him, caught him by the throat, and
        said, 'Touch my flask again and I'll break your bloody
        neck!'

> *They all laugh at this. Then continue talking in under-*
> *tones.* CHARLIE *enters and stops beside* SIR *who is*
> *laughing, too.*

CHARLIE What's all the laughing about?
    SIR Sorry?
CHARLIE What are they laughing at?
    SIR They are happy.
CHARLIE *They* are?
    SIR Yes.
CHARLIE They know what's going to happen, don't they?
    SIR They know.
CHARLIE So what are they happy about?
    SIR There's always a gaiety at this stage.
CHARLIE At what stage?

> SIR *is walking towards the family. He is smiling. He*
> *does not look at* CHARLIE.

    SIR Sorry?
CHARLIE What episode is that?
    SIR Look at them — they're so happy.
CHARLIE When is this supposed to have taken place?
    SIR Yes, I'm afraid they've taken a few liberties.
CHARLIE Is this in your book?
    SIR Some of it is, Charlie. And I'm afraid some of it is the
        wishful thinking of lonely people in lonely apart-
        ments. But they're always being true to themselves.
        And even if they've juggled the time a bit they're doing
        no harm. We mustn't be impatient with them.
CHARLIE Cracked, that family. Bloody cracked. Always was.
        And it's the same with my woman every time she gets
        back among them — she's as bad as they are. Look at
        her, for God's sake! I don't see much of that side of her
        when she's at home, I can tell you.

> *He leaves quickly.* SIR *now joins the others.*

   TINA Here's Sir!
    SIR Carry on — carry on — don't let me interrupt.
  FRANK Just recalling a family outing.
    SIR Yes.
 MIRIAM A picnic years ago.

SIR The famous day at Portnoo — I know — I know.

The gaiety ebbs quickly away.

HELEN I don't think we ever went back there, did we?
BEN I didn't.
HELEN Not as a family group.
MIRIAM Not for a picnic.
HELEN Certainly not for a picnic.
TINA I was there one day last Easter. By myself.
FRANK And Anna and I have gone a few times, haven't we?
ANNA Where to?
FRANK Portnoo.
ANNA Yes — once or twice.
FRANK Just for the run. But no picnic, I'm afraid.
SIR It's a pretty place, Portnoo.
FRANK Lovely on a good day.
SIR Beautiful. And across the bay there's an attractive little island.
FRANK Inniskeel — is that what it's called?
SIR That's it.
FRANK Yes.
SIR And when the tide's out, you can walk out to it — out to the island.
FRANK So I believe — I've never done that.
SIR Actually you don't walk out from Portnoo. You go from Narin just over the road.
FRANK I see. No, I've never done that.
SIR Yes. A pretty place, Portnoo. Very pretty place.

Pause.

ANNA Shouldn't we get on with it?
SIR Take your time — I'm in no hurry.
FRANK Perhaps we should.
SIR There's no rush.
MIRIAM Yes, let's start.
FRANK I think we should.
SIR If you would like to make a fresh pot of tea or — ?

ANNA Let's start! Let's start!
SIR Whatever you say . . .
FRANK Yes, the sooner the better.
SIR Very well. (*Opens his ledger*) Where would you like to resume?

Waits — no answers.

Anyone got any preference?

TOM *bursts in from the kitchen.*

TOM I've remembered another use he had for that brass ferrule. You know how people in chapel like to sit spread out in those long pews? Well, he used to go hopping up along the aisle and whatever unfortunate was at the end of the seat he'd prod him — (*Sees* SIR) Oh! You're back!
SIR Only a few minutes — that's all.
TOM (*Looking around*) Are we ready to — to go?
SIR If you are.
TOM Me. Oh, I'm — certainly, certainly. Any time you're ready, I'm — I'm — (*He fades out*)
SIR If no one else has any suggestions may I propose that we do the reasonable thing — in other words carry on almost immediately after we left off, that is to say, just before the return of Frank and Anna and Tom from the reception. Does that suit everybody?

No answer.

And Tom!
TOM Sir?
SIR (*Smiling*) I'll keep watching.
TOM (*Uneasily*) Oh yes, yes, do — do that.

TOM *exits quickly — in his confusion going off left instead of right.*

SIR Not that way, Tom. Over this — (TOM *has gone*) I don't
think we need those things, do we?

He picks up empty coffee mugs, the Enquirer; *adjusts
the chairs.*

MIRIAM I'm not needed, am I?

SIR Not for the time being, thank you. Nor Helen, nor
Tina. (*Looking round the set*) That's more like it, isn't it?

SIR *returns to his stool.* HELEN *and* TINA *and* MIRIAM
move off. Then ANNA. *Finally* FRANK. FRANK *is thinking himself back to the scene that* SIR *has called for. As
he passes* BEN:

BEN Talking about that silly picnic —

FRANK (*To himself*) Let's see. We left the mess. I drove. Anna
was beside me. Tom was in the back —

BEN No, no, the Portnoo picnic — coming home in the car
— you were driving and I was lying across Mother's
lap   I suppose I was drunk, for God's sake

FRANK (*Only now aware of him*) What's that?

BEN And you k-k-k- — and you kept —

SIR 'It is now 3.45 a.m. — '

BEN My head was on your knees — and you had one hand
on the driving wheel — and your other hand kept
s-s-s-s- — your other hand kept —

SIR Frank.

FRANK Sir?

SIR You're off at this point.

FRANK Yes, I know that. (*Irritably to* BEN) What is it? What is
it?

BEN With your other hand, your free hand, all the way
home you kept stroking my face, my face, my cheeks,
my forehead —

SIR Gentlemen, I'm sorry. I must insist.

FRANK (*To* BEN) Not now, later, please —

BEN But what I want to tell you, Father, and what I want
you to know is that I —

243

FRANK   (*Leaving*) Some other time.

SIR   'It is now 3.45 a.m. Tina is sleeping in bed. Helen is getting her case ready. Frank, Anna and Tom are driving home from the reception — Frank and Anna in front, Tom in the back — '

> *He is interrupted by* TOM *who has discovered that he exited the wrong way. He is now crossing in front of* SIR.

TOM   Sorry — sorry — beg your pardon.

SIR   Take your time. No rush.

TOM   Looking for matches.

SIR   And did you get some?

> TOM *taps his jacket pocket.*

Fine — fine. No hurry. We've all the time in the world. (*Calls*) Ready now, Frank?

FRANK   (*Off*) Yes.

SIR   (*Calls*) And Anna?

ANNA   (*Off*) Ready.

SIR   Good. Where was I? Ah — ' — Tom in the back. Ben is alone in the living room. He is moving around.' And that seems to be all the directions I've got. A bit abrupt, isn't it? Could you carry on from there? Thank you.

> *He sits on his stool. The lights change.* BEN *is alone in the living room.*

BEN   There was a fellow in my class at UCD; Sproule — Harry Sproule, from Tipperary. Horsey people. Had a brother doing Arts and another doing Law at the same time. And each had a flat of his own. And the three of them never met during term — not even once. Didn't even travel together. Strange, wasn't it? Harry Sproule. (*He fingers the ornament*)

HELEN   (*Off*) What's that?

BEN   Called his father and mother by their Christian names.

244

Spoke of them warmly — as if they were friends of the family. (*Pause*) Did you ever think what it must have been like for Anna coming into our family?

He circles around the wicker chair, looking at it.

HELEN (*Off*) I can't hear you.

BEN (*Not as loud*) With our bloody boring reminiscences and our bloody awareness and our bloody quivering sensibilities. There must be another way of ordering close relationships, mustn't there? (*Shouts*) Mustn't there?

> HELEN *enters. A cigarette in her mouth. Very brisk. She lifts a book and then goes to the radiator where her tights are spread.*

HELEN Mustn't there what?

BEN I'm saying we're a very closely-knit family.

HELEN I don't know. Are we? I suppose so. Does it matter? Tights drying on a radiator and no heating on!

BEN Maybe I should go now, Helen.

HELEN Go where?

BEN Leave. Before they get back.

HELEN Whatever suits you.

BEN I'd just like to see him for one minute, give him my congratulations and then clear off.

HELEN (*Firmly*) Listen to me. You'll stay where you are. When he comes you'll shake his hand, say your piece, and then leave. Right? Can't wear these tomorrow.

BEN I think I'll take a drink. No, maybe I shouldn't. You'll be here, won't you?

HELEN What do you want me to do, Ben? Stand at your side and hold your hand and stroke it?

She rushes upstairs.

BEN Helen, I've already apologized —

But she is gone. He is wretched.

God! (*Rehearsing*) Congratulations, Sir, I'm really proud of — (*Pause*) Very well done, Frank. Great work. Splendid — (*Pause*) When I heard it on the radio, Father, I was so th-th-th-th-thrill — Oh Christ!

The voice of TOM, *off. Approaching, singing very slowly and very drunkenly.*

TOM   We're here because we're here because we're here because we're here —

> BEN *rushes to the drinks, uncorks a bottle, puts it to his head, corks it again. Then he sits on the armchair right of fireplace.* TOM *arrives at the front door. He knocks loudly on it three times.* BEN *leaps up instinctively, nervously — then sits again.*

Right door — wrong house.

He stands back and examines the façade.

Right house — wrong door.

> *He begins singing again, comes into the garden doing an absurd advancing/retreating dance as he crosses the stage. Finally, very shortly after* ANNA's *entrance, he falls into a deckchair and falls asleep. While* TOM *is dancing* ANNA *enters. She goes straight into the living room. At first she does not see* BEN.

BEN   You're very late.
ANNA   What are you doing here?
BEN   Just to congratulate —
ANNA   Get out! Get out!
BEN   What's wrong?
ANNA   My head's splitting — that's what's wrong! I'm at my wits' end — that's what's wrong!

FRANK *enters the hallway. He is elated, assured, exuding confidence.*

FRANK Helen! Helen!

ANNA Get out, Ben, for God's sake!

Before BEN *can make up his mind* FRANK *enters.*

FRANK I know she won't have gone to bed. She may have —

He stops suddenly when he sees BEN. *They stand looking at one another. Pause.*

BEN I was passing and I just dropped in . . .

FRANK Yes?

Pause.

BEN I heard all about it on the radio and read all the stuff in the papers — and for your sake I was really very — it was just great. (*Holds out his hand*) Congratulations.

FRANK (*Very formally*) Thank you

Then suddenly FRANK *opens his arms and embraces* BEN *warmly.*

Ben! Thank you, son. Thank you.

HELEN *enters from kitchen.*

Do you see who's here?

HELEN Naturally.

FRANK Naturally.

HELEN Well — how did it go? (*To* ANNA) Had you a great night? (*To* FRANK) You have news! I know by your face you have news!

FRANK I had a wonderful night.

HELEN Great.

He catches HELEN *in his arms and swings her round.*

FRANK And I have wonderful news!

HELEN (*To* ANNA) Tell me! (*To* FRANK) Tell me — tell me — tell me —

FRANK Have a guess.

HELEN Guess! How can I guess!

FRANK But first we'll have a celebration drink. (*Looking at* BEN) A double celebration. (*Looking at* ANNA) A treble celebration.

ANNA Where's Father Tom?

FRANK Who cares?

HELEN (*To* ANNA) He's being transferred, isn't he?

FRANK Yes, he's being transferred.

BEN Wonderful.

FRANK Where would you like him to be transferred to?

HELEN Where? Where?

FRANK Guess.

HELEN Ah, Father —

FRANK Take your choice.

HELEN Tell us! Athlone?

FRANK Anywhere you like.

HELEN Ben, where? (*To* FRANK) I know! Cork!

FRANK Cork's for talkers.

BEN You're going to Galway.

FRANK Galway's for ageing men.

HELEN Limerick!

FRANK Good God! Never Limerick!

HELEN Where else? — where else? — it's not! It couldn't be!

FRANK Couldn't be what?

HELEN Dublin?

FRANK Dublin it is.

HELEN Oh, Father!

She kisses him.

FRANK (*To* ANNA) And tell them the rest.

ANNA Better look out for Father Tom.

She goes out to the garden.

FRANK You are in the presence of Lieutenant Colonel Frank Butler —

HELEN Lieutenant — ?

FRANK Administrative Officer, GHQ, Parkgate Street, Dublin City.

HELEN You're taking a hand at us, Father!

FRANK Nothing's official yet. But when the Chief tells the Taoiseach in your presence how highly he considers you and then in the next breath talks about certain vacancies, you know it's in the bag.

HELEN I'm going to waken Tina — phone Miriam —

FRANK Later — later — later. Let's savour it ourselves first.

BEN (*Looking around*) So you'll be leaving here.

FRANK At last, at long last, and without one regret. To Dublin.

HELEN (*Toast*) To the Hero and to Anna.

BEN To you, Father.

FRANK Hold on — where's Anna?

HELEN In the garden.

He goes to the door and looks out to the garden. ANNA *is crouched beside* TOM *trying to waken him.*

FRANK Let him sit there, for God's sake. Come inside and celebrate with the family.

TOM (*Suddenly awake, sings*) We're here because we're here because we're here because we're here —

HELEN So that's the condition.

ANNA (*To* TOM) Come inside and lie down for a while.

FRANK You're a bloody useless slob, Tom. Pull yourself together, man.

HELEN How did Anna enjoy it?

FRANK turns back into the living room. ANNA *gets* TOM *to his feet and they make their way slowly into the room,* TOM *singing intermittently.*

FRANK Anna? Anna was — what's the word? — cynosure of

all eyes. Radiant, that's what Anna was, sitting there beside me, basking in the glory. And the compliments — my God! The Taoiseach called her — incidentally that was by far the best speech of the night. And astonishingly well informed — named every one of the soldiers I had saved and a few personal comments about several of them. And when he was talking about me — well, he was so effusive and so generous that I was almost embarrassed. Talked about 'quiet heroes from quiet places' and 'men whose full development blossomed only in full manhood'. Really eulogistic stuff. Very satisfying.

HELEN And Anna?

BEN Sit over here, Father.

FRANK That's the state he was in after the first course.

HELEN What did he say about Anna?

FRANK Oh, Anna? What's this he called you? — a real tongue-twister — 'the Commandant's comely, composed and curvaceous consort' — at which the men just *howled*. Didn't they?

ANNA Yes.

FRANK Would you like to try that one, Ben?

BEN (*Quickly*) You're OK, Father. You're fine. That's it.

ANNA (*To* BEN) Could I get him something?

FRANK Let him sleep it off. He's beyond sobering.

TOM (*Suddenly awake*) Where's Helen? Want to 'pologize to Helen —

HELEN Hello, Father.

TOM (*Rising*) — 'pologize to Helen — privately — in here, Helen, in here.

TOM *staggers into the kitchen.*

FRANK Ignore him.

HELEN Poor old Tom.

FRANK But the highlight of the evening, Helen — I was presented with an illuminated address by the people of Ballybeg!

TOM (*Off*) Helen!

FRANK The people of Ballybeg — my God! A parchment this
length, all the colours of the rainbow, and a photo of me
stuck crookedly on the top; and read out before everybody by that pompous TD — McLaughlin, McLucas,
what's his name.

HELEN That was nice of them.

FRANK D'you think so? Yes, I suppose the intention was good.
But being publicly addressed by the people of Ballybeg — 'you are our most illustrious citizen' sort of
stuff — my God they don't know me and we don't
know them! But you'll enjoy this — you really will.
Must have left it out in the car. Hold on a second.

TOM (*Off*) Helen!

FRANK I know him in this mood. Ignore him.

FRANK *leaves.*

HELEN Have you ever seen him so elated! I'm delighted for
him. (*She kisses* ANNA) For both of you. Was it exhaust-
ing? Are you falling apart?

TOM (*Off*) Helen!

HELEN Oh my God (*Calls*) Coming! Coming!

She goes into the kitchen. Pause.

ANNA I can take no more of it.

BEN If you just —

ANNA I'm going to clear out in the morning.

BEN Leave him?

ANNA Didn't you hear him? 'I — I — I — I — I — 'And how
they howled — oh, how they howled — after snigger-
ing behind their hands all night.

BEN At him?

ANNA Him — me — what matter? I can stand no more. I've
got to go.

BEN Just walk out?

ANNA I've got to.

BEN Oh, Anna, you can't do that —

ANNA Why not?

BEN That — that would kill him — he'd never understand.
ANNA All right — I'll make him understand. You want him to understand?
BEN What I'm saying is that you just can't walk out without —
ANNA Fine. I'll tell him about us first.
BEN Anna —
ANNA You want him to understand?
BEN Will you please —
ANNA Do you think for one second he's not going to hear?
BEN For Christ's sake —
ANNA That the good people of Ballybeg or his own staff aren't going to let him know somehow?
BEN You won't!
ANNA Make up your mind! Is he not going to understand because he's not told? Or is he going to understand because he'll be told by them or by me — or by you, Ben?
BEN Nobody need say anything. I'll clear out in —
ANNA Yes, you'll clear out — typical Ben! What about me?
BEN I'm warning you, Anna.
ANNA Don't wag your finger at me!
BEN If you tell him —
ANNA Tell him — don't tell him — either way I'm leaving.
BEN I'm saying n-n-n-nothing. I promise you that. Nothing. Nothing. Nothing.
ANNA In that case I'll tell him. He deserves that much from me.
BEN You're a heartless bitch!

Enter HELEN *and* TOM, *arm in arm.*

HELEN Poor Father Tom. D'you know what that was all about? He officiated at all the Butler weddings and all the Butler baptisms but he didn't officiate at Helen's wedding, even though Helen asked him, because Louise disapproved and he hadn't the courage to stand up to Louise and it has been on his conscience ever since and that's why he's drunk tonight — otherwise he'd be cold sober. So.

TOM Am I forgiven, Helen?

HELEN Nothing to forgive, Father.

TOM You know something, Helen?

HELEN What's that, Father?

TOM I'm no damn good, Helen. No damn good at all. I'm
— I'm a washout, Helen.

HELEN Indeed you're not.

TOM You can't fool me, Helen, I know. I *know*.

HELEN You're fine, Father.

TOM And I'm forgiven?

HELEN Completely.

He slumps into a seat.

TOM Thanks be to God.

Almost immediately he is asleep.

HELEN There you are — instant absolution!

FRANK *enters reading in mock heroic style from the
parchment. He begins at the front door.*

FRANK 'We, the people of Ballybeg, learn with great pride and
great delight of the heroic deeds of Commandant
Frank Butler' — Lieutenant Colonel Butler, if you
don't mind, Ballybeg — 'who is an honoured and distinguished member of our parish and whose family
the people of Ballybeg have always held in the highest
esteem.'

HELEN Read it properly, Father. Don't make a mock of it.

FRANK 'We have always known the Hero of Hari' — Who's
that? I beg your pardon — 'to have been an officer of
exemplary habit and behaviour, a citizen of outstanding probity — '

ANNA Frank.

FRANK '— and a father and a family man' — I like this — 'of
noblest Christian integrity and rectitude.'

ANNA Frank.

FRANK Get down on your knees. 'We are confirmed in our estimate, therefore, when the fame of his heroic actions
spread out across the face of — '

ANNA I've something to say to you, Frank.

> *He stops and looks at her.* TINA *comes sleepily down-
> stairs in her dressing gown and is about to enter when
> she hears* ANNA's *voice. She stands outside the living-
> room door.*

I am not going to Dublin with you.

FRANK Nobody's going anywhere, my darling, until official
confirmation comes.

ANNA Then — any time — I'm not going to Dublin — I'm not
going anywhere with you.

> *Pause.*

FRANK What is the matter, my love?

ANNA Are you deaf? Are you stupid? Don't you understand
simple words? (*As he puts out his hand to her*) Don't —
don't — don't touch me! I'm leaving you, Frank —
can't you understand that? Leaving you — leaving
you — is that simple enough?

> *Very long pause during which* FRANK, *puzzled,
> studies her face for clues.*

HELEN I think she's —

FRANK What is wrong, Anna?

HELEN (*To* ANNA) You've had a very tiring —

FRANK (*Firmly*) Please, Helen. (*Quietly to* ANNA) Why are you
leaving me, Anna? Is it something that I have said?

> ANNA *turns away from him because she is crying. She
> shakes her head.*

Is it something that I have done?

ANNA *shakes her head.*

HELEN Anna —
FRANK (*Very sharply*) Helen, please. (*Again, quietly to* ANNA) Is it something that I have not done?

ANNA *shakes her head.*

Then why are you leaving me, Anna?
ANNA You were so long away —
FRANK Five months.
ANNA And we'd been together such a short time —
FRANK Ten days.
ANNA (*Quickly*) And I tried to keep you, to maintain you in my mind — I tried, Frank, I tried. But you kept slipping away from me. I searched Tina for you, and Miriam, but you weren't in them. And then I could remember nothing — only your uniform, the colour of your hair, your footstep in the hall — that's all I could remember — a handsome, courteous, considerate man who had once been kind to me and who wrote me all those simple, passionate letters — too simple, too passionate. And then Ben came. And I found you in him, Frank.
FRANK Found me?
ANNA I was lost.

FRANK *looks at her, then at* BEN, *then back to her.*

FRANK Are you telling me that you and he — ?
ANNA We had an affair! We were lovers, Ben and I! And everybody in the camp knows! Everybody in Ballybeg knows! Everybody except the Butlers! That's what I'm telling you! We had an affair!

TINA *gives a short cry — unheard in the living room — and rushes upstairs.*

HELEN Oh Ben! — you? — Oh God!

255

She turns away from him. FRANK *goes to* TOM *and puts his hand on the chaplain's shoulder.*

FRANK (*Softly*) Chaplain — Chaplain.
TOM Mmmm?
FRANK Help, Chaplain.
TOM (*Wakening*) Wha' — wha' — what's that?
FRANK Advice, counsel, help, Chaplain.
TOM What's the trouble, Frank?
FRANK I need help, Tom.
TOM Terrific, Frank — just terrific — terrific.
FRANK What does a man do, Tom?
TOM Yes, sir — yes, sir — just terrific.
FRANK What should a man do?

> TOM *is asleep again.* FRANK *looks at him. Then very slowly he walks around the room as if he were trying to remember something. Finally, conversationally:*

You know, when I think about it — my God, how she must have suffered. Not that I was insensitive to it — far from it; I used to try to imagine what it was like. I would close my eyes and attempt to invest my body with pain, willing it into my joints, deliberately desiring the experience. But it's not the same thing — not the same thing at all — how could it be? Because it cannot be assumed like that — it has got to be organic, generated from within. And the statistics are fascinating too — well, no, not fascinating — how could they be fascinating; but interesting, interesting. It starts around forty; it's estimated that five to six per cent of the population is affected; and women are three times more susceptible than men. But there you are — she was outside the general pattern. What age was she? Helen was what? — three? — four? — so she can't have been more than twenty-eight or twenty-nine. And she had a very brief introductory period, as they call it. Within six months the hands and feet were swollen and within twelve months the spine was affected. So that within no time at all the fibrous tissues had replaced the normal tissues and when that happens you have at least a partial disorganization of the joints and sometimes complete ankylosis — yes, you'd think I was an authority —

HELEN Father —

FRANK — and of course we attempted everything that was available — physiotherapy, teeth, tonsils, surgery, gold injections, aspirin courses, codeine courses. We even went to a quack in Kerry who promised us that before we'd be halfway home every swelling would have disappeared. And the cortisone era — my God, the miracle era — the cure for everything. And she responded so wonderfully to it at first — absolutely no pain. She was even able to throw away the stick for a couple of weeks. But it was an illusion — an illusion. Back came the pain, worse than ever. Much, much worse. My God, how she suffered. My God, how she suffered.

> *He stops and looks at each person in the room. Then he looks out at* SIR, *whom he now addresses loudly, very deliberately, and with conscious formality. He is very calm and very controlled.*

Sir.

> SIR *speaks quietly and does not raise his eyes from the ledger.*

SIR Frank.

FRANK I wish to protest, Sir. I wish to lodge a formal protest.

SIR Yes, Frank.

FRANK I am quite calm. And I am not bleating. I am not snivelling.

SIR No, Frank.

FRANK But there are certain things that as a soldier — as a man — I wish to state.

SIR Yes, Frank.

FRANK Yes, you did say we could speak our thoughts. That

was established at the outset, wasn't it? Well, I wish to protest against my treatment. I wish to say that I consider I have been treated unfairly.

SIR *(Looking up)* Frank, I —

FRANK No, I'm not addressing you, Sir; I'm not addressing them; I suppose I'm not addressing anybody. And I am fully aware that protesting at this stage is pointless — pointless.

SIR You can —

FRANK No, no, no, of course it is. Absolutely pointless. The ledger's the ledger, isn't it? Nothing can be changed now — not a thing. But an injustice *has* been done to me, Sir, and a protest must be made. I don't claim that I have been blameless. Maybe my faults have been greater than most. But it does seem — well, spiteful that when a point is reached in my life, and late in my life, when certain modest ambitions are about to be realized, when certain happinesses that I never experienced are suddenly about to be attainable, it does seem spiteful that these fulfilments should be snatched away from me — and in a particularly wounding manner. Yes, I think that is unfair. Yes, that is unjust. And that is why I make this formal protest, Sir. Against an injustice done to me. Because I have been treated unfairly, Sir — that is all.

> *He stops and looks around at the others — all isolated, all cocooned in their private thoughts. He opens his mouth as if he is about to address them, but they are so remote from him that he decides against it. He turns slowly and begins to walk upstage.*

SIR Frank!

> FRANK *ignores the call and goes through the door, right, off the fireplace, closing it behind him. This is the only time this door is used. Pause. Suddenly* TOM, *now sober, jumps to his feet. He is very agitated, and when he looks at the others, so contained , so remote, his*

panic increases. He goes to BEN.

TOM You're not going to let him go, are you? You're going
to stop him, aren't you? For God's sake, Ben, you've
got to stop him!

> BEN *remains encased and intact in his privacy.* TOM
> *looks to* HELEN *and goes to her.*

You know what's going to happen! You know what
he's going to do! Stop him. Helen! Stop him! Stop him!

She looks at him as if he were a stranger.

Don't you hear what I'm saying — he has got to be
stopped!

> HELEN *looks away from him.* TOM *now addresses them
> all.*

How can you all sit there! You know what he's going
to do!

No one responds. TOM *now looks to* SIR — *and rushes
to him. He is about to cry with panic and despair.*

You're going to stop him, aren't you, Sir? Yes, you're
the one who can save him. You're not going to let him
do that to himself — no, no, you're not.

SIR The ledger can't be —

TOM What can the ledger not be? — to hell with the ledger
— that's what I say — to hell with that corrupt ledger.

SIR Tom, sit down —

TOM Great — great — 'Tom, sit down' — you know what
Frank's going to do and all you can say is 'Tom, sit
down'.

SIR Sit down and keep quiet.

TOM I will not sit down and I will not keep quiet! My
friend, Frank, has gone into that back room and not

one of you is going to —
SIR Shut up! Now!
TOM I will —
SIR You had your opportunities and you squandered them.
TOM I never had —
SIR Many opportunities, many times. You should have spoken then. We'll have none of your spurious concern now that it's all over. So sit down and shut up!
TOM (*Suddenly deflated*) If I had — sometimes, I — I always tried to — Oh, my Jesus —

For a few seconds his mouth keeps opening and shutting, but no words come. He looks at the others. Pause. Then he shuffles over to ANNA, *sits beside her, puts his arm around her, and rests his face on her shoulder. His body shakes as he cries quietly. Pause. Then suddenly* TINA *comes stumbling down the stairs in a panic and rushes into the living room. She is in a frenzy and looks around wildly.*

TINA (*Shouts*) Daddy-Daddy-Daddy-Daddy!

SIR *leaps to his feet.*

SIR (*Tense whisper*) Not yet! Tina! Not yet!

She freezes. Pause. Then a single revolver shot, off. TINA's *hands go up to her face. She screams. Silence. Pause.* SIR *sits again. Then, very slowly, the others relax and emerge from their cocoons. Cigarettes are lit. A sense of relief. Serenity. The remaining sequence must not be played in a sad, nostalgic mood.* MIRIAM *enters in coat and headscarf.* TOM, *now fully sober, sits with his arms around* ANNA. *From his stool* SIR *watches this slow awakening. Then he rises, stretching his arms, smiling.*

Well — well — well — well — well — well — well.

He goes into the living room.

That wasn't too bad, was it?

No one answers — they are still not quite out of their reveries. He goes to TINA, *catches her chin and wags it.*

And how are you? All right?

She smiles and nods.

(*To all*) That wasn't too bad after all now, was it? No, of course it wasn't. (*To* HELEN) And you with your worries that things were being 'distorted' — (*To* ANNA) — and you afraid that you'd 'messed it all up' — (*To both*) I told you, didn't I? Incidentally, Anna, we made a mistake, you and I — well me, really.

ANNA What was that?

SIR I never introduced you! You're the only person who wasn't introduced. (*Opening ledger*) So let's rectify that — right?

ANNA No, please, Sir —

SIR But I *want* to —

ANNA Please. It doesn't matter now, not in the least. It's of no importance now.

SIR I'm sorry. My mistake.

ANNA It doesn't matter.

SIR As you wish. (*He leafs through the ledger*) I'm sure you're all tired, so what I think we'll do is go straight to the postscript and wind it up with that. 'Not yet, Tina! Not yet! — Single revolver shot — etc, etc — ' We've been through all that —

TOM There was never any doubt in my mind that it was an unfortunate accident. Never. And I said that at the inquest. I mean we were such terrific friends all our lives — no one was going to tell me that Frank Butler took — that it wasn't an accident. And I saw to it that my friend was buried with the full rites of the Church. I saw to that. It was the least I could do for my friend,

Frank Butler — my terrific friend, Frank.

SIR *has been waiting patiently for this to end.*

SIR Yes. A brief enough postscript as it happens. 'Funeral
on Friday afternoon. The following morning Charlie
Donnelly arrived with a van and removed all the
furnishings — ' By the way, where is Charlie? Charlie!

He goes off left to look for him.

MIRIAM I was worried about the children — you know — what
I'd tell them.
TOM Naturally. And how are the kids?
MIRIAM I'd given them cornflakes and a fry for their breakfast
— they're a great crowd for fries — and they were
sitting round the table eating like nobody's business
and I said quietly, 'Your Granda's dead,' I said. 'Your
Granda's gone to heaven to join your Grandma,' I
said. And when they began to cry I said, 'Don't cry for
your Granda,' I said. 'Your Granda was a good man
and a brave man. Ask anybody,' I said, 'and they'll tell
you how good and brave your Granda was.' Wasn't I
right, Father?
TOM God have mercy on his good soul.
MIRIAM And they listened to me. You should have seen them.
They did — they listened — and they stopped crying.
But he was a good man, you know — a good man and
a brave man. No — a great man and a brave man.

She moves slowly off right.

SIR (*Off left*) Charlie! Charlie!
TOM You're going back to London, aren't you?
HELEN Tomorrow afternoon.
TOM Tina's going with you?
HELEN Yes.
TOM You'll look after her well, Helen, won't you? It's a big
city and she's never been away from home and —

TINA Don't worry about me. I'll be all right. I can look after myself.

TOM You'll be in digs with Helen — that's good. And she'll get you fixed up in a job.

TINA I'm not a child, Father. I'm almost nineteen.

TOM All the same, my love —

TINA (*Bitterly*) Why the sudden concern about me? Why all the platitudes? You're the one in trouble, Father — not me.

She goes off quickly.

HELEN She didn't mean that, Father. She's upset. Tina!

She follows TINA *off.* SIR *enters.*

BEN (*Urgently*) Remember just before that last sequence?

SIR (*Consulting ledger*) Mm?

BEN I was going to say something to him and you interrupted.

SIR (*Not listening*) Yes — yes —

TOM *looks around, then drifts aimlessly off.*

BEN Maybe I had some intimation of a moment being missed forever — because there was the sudden necessity to blurt out, to plunge some oversimplification into him before it was too late. And what I was going to say to him was that ever since I was a child I always loved him and always hated her — he was always my hero. And even though it wouldn't have been the truth, it wouldn't have been a lie either: no, no; no lie.

SIR I see.

BEN But I suppose it was just as well it wasn't said like that because he could never receive that kind of directness, and I suppose I could never have said it. But I just hope — I just hope he was able to sense an expression of some k-k-k-k- — of some kind of love for him —

even if it was only in my perfidy —

He goes off slowly.

SIR Yes. (*Back to ledger*) '— removed all the furnishings.' Yes. 'That afternoon Helen and Tina flew to London, where they now live in different flats and seldom meet. Tina works as a waitress in an all-night café and Helen has had to give up her office job because of an acute nervous breakdown. Ben went to Scotland. He came back after seven months. He has been jailed twice for drunk and disorderly behaviour. Father Tom has retired and is living in a nursing home in County Wicklow. He has difficulty walking and spends most of his time in bed.'

CHARLIE*'s brisk entrance interrupts the reading.*

CHARLIE Sorry — sorry — sorry — you were looking for me?
SIR It doesn't matter, Charlie. We're just finishing up.
CHARLIE If I'm here, I'm not wanted. (*Pause*) I mean to say — if I'm wanted, I'm not here. (*Laughs in surprise*) Dammit, they're both right! First time that ever happened! Isn't that a good one! Where's the missus?
SIR She left a few minutes ago.
CHARLIE Oh-ho! Better catch up with her or there'll be hair flying. See you. Good luck — good luck. (*Pauses at exit*) When do I clear out this stuff?
SIR Saturday.
CHARLIE Morning or afternoon?
SIR Morning.
CHARLIE Bang goes the sleep-in. Oh, well, good to get it all out of the road. Luck.

He leaves.

SIR Goodbye, Charlie. Now — ' — spends most of his time in bed. Mrs Butler, Anna, emigrated to America. She lived with an aunt in New Jersey for six months and

264

then went to Los Angeles where she works in the office of a large insurance company — '

He breaks off because he is aware that the place is not empty. Then he sees ANNA.

Oh, you're still here. Heavens, I thought I was alone for a minute. Just the two of us. Not much point in continuing, is there?

ANNA Yes — go on. Please go on.

SIR With this?

ANNA Please.

SIR There's only — what? — two or three lines left.

ANNA Even so.

SIR 'She shares an apartment with an English girl and they go on holidays together. She owns a car and is thinking of buying an apartment of her own. She has never returned to Ireland.' And that's it.

ANNA That's all?

SIR That's all I've got here.

ANNA Are you sure?

SIR Blank pages.

ANNA I see.

She gets up and begins to move off.

SIR Did you expect there'd be something more?

ANNA I just wondered — that's all.

SIR Is there something missing?

ANNA No. Not a thing. Not a single thing.

SIR Ah. Good. Good. All right, Anna?

But she has gone. He shrugs his shoulders and closes the book. He takes a last look round the set and begins to leave. As he leaves, bring down the lights.

ARISTOCRATS

Characters

WILLIE DIVER
TOM HOFFNUNG
UNCLE GEORGE
CASIMIR
ALICE
EAMON
CLAIRE
JUDITH
FATHER
ANNA'S VOICE

Time and Place

Summer, mid-1970s. Ballybeg Hall, the home of District Justice O'Donnell, a large and decaying house overlooking the village of Ballybeg, County Donegal, Ireland.

Set

Most of the action takes place outside the south side of the house. Most recently it was a lawn that has not been cared for in years. Before that it was a grass tennis court and before that a croquet lawn — but no trace of these activities remains.

The lawn stretches right across the full front of stage and up-stage left (left and right from point of view of audience) where it halts at a tall grey gable with uncurtained windows.

Upstage left is a gazebo, with a pagoda roof and badly weather-beaten. A rusty iron seat inside. The gazebo is made of wood and is about to collapse.

A small room — the study — occupies upstage right. One step up into it from the lawn. It is separated from the lawn by two invisible walls. On the third wall, parallel to front of stage, is an early Victorian writing desk. The fourth wall, at right angles to front of stage, has a huge marble fireplace. In front of the fireplace is a chaise longue. In the centre of this study a small table, etc, etc, sufficient furnishings to indicate when the hall flourished and to suggest its present decline.

Downstage right a broken sundial mounted on a stone plinth.

Music

All Chopin piano music.

Scherzo No.2 in B minor, Op.31
Ballade in G minor, Op.23
Waltz in G sharp major, Op.70, No.1
Sonata No.3, Op.58, third movement only: largo
Waltz in E sharp major (Posth)
Waltz in A sharp major (Posth)

ACT TWO

Étude No.3 in E major
Nocturne in F sharp major, Op.15, No.2

ACT THREE

Sonata No.2 in B minor, Op.35, middle section of third movement
Ballade in A flat major, Op.47

Aristocrats was first produced at the Abbey Theatre, Dublin, on 8 March 1979, with the following cast:

WILLIE DIVER	Niall O'Brien
TOM HOFFNUNG	Kevin McHugh
UNCLE GEORGE	Bill Foley
CASIMIR	John Kavanagh
ALICE	Dearbhla Molloy
EAMON	Stephen Rea
CLAIRE	Ingrid Craigie
JUDITH	Kate Flynn
FATHER	Geoff Golden
ANNA'S VOICE	Kathleen Barrington

Directed by	Joe Dowling
Set and costumes by	Wendy Shea
Lighting by	Leslie Scott

for K.H.H.
with affection and gratitude

ACT ONE

Early afternoon on a very warm summer day.

The opening bars of Scherzo No.2 in B minor fill the study and the lawn, then fade to background.

TOM HOFFNUNG *is seated at the table in the study, copying the titles of books into his notebook. He is a quiet, calm, measured American academic in his mid-fifties.*

Inside the door leading out to the hall is WILLIE DIVER. *He is in his mid-thirties and is from the village. He is standing on a chair and attaching a small speaker to the door frame (he is standing on his jacket to protect the seat of the chair).*

Both men work for a few seconds in silence.

Now UNCLE GEORGE *enters from the hall. He is in his late seventies; a brother of* FATHER's. *Panama hat, walking stick, very old and creased off-white linen suit with an enormous red silk handkerchief spilling out of the breast pocket, trousers stopping well above his ankles. His mouth never stops working, vigorously masticating imaginary food. All his gestures are informed with great energy, as if he were involved in some urgent business.*

He is halfway across the study before he realizes that there are other people in the room. Then he stops, stands still and stares at them.

TOM   Hi!

Pause.

WILLIE   Hello, Mister George.

TOM   Come right through. I'm almost finished here.

> GEORGE *hesitates — then turns and exits through the door.*

That's the third time he's attempted to come in here.

Maybe I should go somewhere else.

WILLIE Not at all. He dodges about like that all the time.

TOM Does he never speak?

WILLIE They say he does. I never heard him.

TOM And he's a brother of the District Justice — is that correct?

WILLIE That's it. Fierce man for the booze when he was only a young fellow — drunk himself half crazy. Then all of a sudden packed it in. And stopped speaking.

TOM I wonder why.

WILLIE They say about here that when he wasn't going to be asking for drink he thought it wasn't worth saying anything. But brains — d'you see Mister George? — the smartest of the whole connection, they say.

He gets down from the chair, removes his jacket and carefully rubs the seat with his sleeve.

Could you give us a second, Tom?

TOM How's it going?

WILLIE Nearly finished now.

TOM *joins him at the door.*

TOM Judith's really going to be pleased with this.

WILLIE Do you think so?

TOM Sure she will. What can I do?

WILLIE Show her this when she comes down, will you? There's a volume control at the side here — loud or soft, whatever way she wants it.

TOM Right.

WILLIE And if she wants to turn it off altogether, there's a switch at the bottom here — d'you see?

TOM Got it.

WILLIE I haven't put it up too high for her, have I? What d'you think?

TOM Looks about right to me.

WILLIE An ugly-looking aul' yoke in a room like this, isn't it?

TOM You wouldn't notice it. It's a good job, Willie.

WILLIE Indeed and it's rough enough. But it'll save her running up and down them stairs every turnabout.

TOM Is it on now?

WILLIE I've still to connect it to the lead from the bedroom. Hold on a minute.

> WILLIE *goes out to the hall.* TOM *returns to the table. Just before he sits down* CASIMIR *enters left carrying deckchairs.* CASIMIR *is the only son of the house; in his thirties. Despite the heat he is wearing a knitted V-neck pullover under his sports jacket. One immediately gets a sense that there is something different about him — as he says himself 'peculiar'. But what it is is elusive: partly his shyness, partly his physical movements, particularly the way he walks — rapid, jerky, without ease or grace — partly his erratic enthusiasm, partly his habit of suddenly grinning and giving a mirthless 'hu-hu' at unlikely times, usually when he is distressed. But he is not a buffoon nor is he 'disturbed'. He is a perfectly normal man with distinctive and perhaps slightly exaggerated mannerisms. He now stands at the step just outside the study and talks to* TOM.

CASIMIR Claire.

TOM Yeah.

CASIMIR Playing the piano.

TOM Sure.

CASIMIR My sister Claire.

TOM I know.

CASIMIR Welcome home recital for me.

TOM Some welcome.

CASIMIR Dexterity — simplicity — passion — Claire has everything.

TOM She certainly —

> *But* CASIMIR *has gone and now stands in the middle of the lawn.*

CASIMIR Claire!

CLAIRE   Yes?
CASIMIR   Play the G minor ballade.

The music stops.

CLAIRE   Which?
CASIMIR   The G minor.
CLAIRE   I'm not in the mood for that, Casimir.
CASIMIR   Special request. Please.
CLAIRE   Just a bit of it, then.

> *He stands listening. She begins in the middle of the*
> *G minor ballade, Op.23, just immediately before the*
> *molto crescendo, after three bars.*

CASIMIR   Yes-yes-yes-yes-yes!

> *He sings a few bars with the piano, conducting at*
> *the same time — he is radiant with delight. Then he*
> *returns to the step.*

The G minor. Wonderful, isn't it?
TOM   Yeah.

> CASIMIR *sings a few more bars.*

CASIMIR   When I think of Ballybeg Hall it's always like this: the
sun shining; the doors and windows all open; the
place filled with music.

> *He is suddenly off again — left — for more deck-*
> *chairs. The sound of static from the speaker. Then*
> FATHER's *laboured breathing.* TOM *listens.*

JUDITH   That's the best lunch you've had in days. Let me wipe
your chin.

> FATHER's *incoherent mumbling.*

It's very warm. I don't think you need this quilt, do you?

Incoherent mumbling. TOM *goes to the speaker. He stands listening.*

Oh, Father, you've soiled your pyjamas again! Why didn't you tell me?

FATHER Judith?

JUDITH Come on. Let's get them changed.

FATHER Where's Judith?

JUDITH I'm Judith.

FATHER Where's Judith?

JUDITH I'm here beside you, Father.

FATHER Where's Claire?

JUDITH In the drawing room.

FATHER Where's Claire?

JUDITH Can't you hear her? She's playing the piano for you. Lift your leg, Father.

FATHER Where's Alice?

JUDITH Everybody's here.

FATHER Where's Casimir?

JUDITH Everybody's at home. They're all downstairs.

FATHER Where's Anna?

JUDITH Anna's in Africa — you know that. Now — the other leg. Father, please, I can't get them off unless you help me.

FATHER Where's Judith? Where's Claire? Where's Casimir? Where's Alice? Where's —

JUDITH They're all here. They're all downstairs.

FATHER Let me tell you something in confidence: Judith betrayed the family.

JUDITH Did she?

FATHER I don't want to make an issue of it. But I can tell you confidentially — Judith betrayed us.

JUDITH That's better. Now you're more comfortable.

FATHER Great betrayal; enormous betrayal.

JUDITH Let me feel those tops. Are they wet, too?

FATHER But Anna's praying for her. Did you know that?

JUDITH Yes, I know, Father.

FATHER Anna has the whole convent praying for her.

JUDITH Now let's get these clean ones on. Lift this leg again.

FATHER Where's Judith? Where's Alice? Where's Casimir? Where's Claire?

> WILLIE *returns, carrying a parcel of two bottles of whiskey.* TOM *pretends to consult his notebook.*

WILLIE That's her hooked up. Any sound out of her?

TOM Yeah; something was said a moment ago. Seems to be working fine.

> WILLIE *examines the speaker.*

WILLIE Aye, it should be. She'd need to have this whole house rewired — half of them fittings is dangerous.

TOM Is she aware of that?

WILLIE Sure it would cost her a fortune. Tell her I'll take a run in later and sink them bare wires. And I'll leave this (*parcel*) here for her. A drop of whiskey. I thought maybe, you know, with the family back home and all, she might be a bit short. They come last night, didn't they?

TOM And a late night it was, too. This'll be very welcome. You'll be going to the wedding, won't you?

WILLIE Me? Oh damn the fear.

TOM Will you not?

WILLIE Not at all; that'll be a family affair. What about yourself?

TOM I leave tomorrow.

WILLIE They'll manage without us. (*Leaving*) Well —

TOM OK, Willie. You'll be back later?

WILLIE Aye, sometime. And tell her, too — them groceries she wanted — I left them in the pantry.

TOM I'll tell her.

> FATHER's *voice suddenly very loud and very authoritative.*

FATHER Are you proposing that my time and the time of this court be squandered while the accused goes home and searches for this title which he claims he has in a tin box somewhere?

WILLIE is startled and delighted.

WILLIE Himself by Jaysus!

JUDITH Now this leg — that's it — that's great.

FATHER And that we sit in this freezing court until he comes back? Is that what you propose, Sergeant?

JUDITH Raise your body just a little.

FATHER Because I can tell you I won't have it — I will not have it!

WILLIE Himself by Jaysus, guldering away!

JUDITH That's more comfortable.

FATHER We're all petrified in this place as it is — really petrified. And I will not endure it a second longer. Case dismissed. Court adjourned.

JUDITH Now over on your side and I'll tuck you in and you'll sleep for a while.

A few short mumbling sounds from FATHER; then silence.

WILLIE D'you hear that for a voice, eh? By Jaysus, isn't he a powerful fighting aul' man all the time, eh?

TOM Would you believe it! I've been here four days and I've never seen him yet.

WILLIE Sure he hasn't been down the stairs since the stroke felled him. But before that — haul' your tongue, man — oh be Jaysus he was a sight to behold — oh be Jaysus!

CASIMIR has entered left with more deckchairs which he sets up on the lawn. He now enters the study.

CASIMIR Always Chopin — the great love of her life. She could play all the nocturnes and all the waltzes before she was ten. We thought we had a little Mozart on our hands.

And on her sixteenth birthday she got a scholarship to
go to Paris. But Father — you've met Father?

TOM   Actually I —

CASIMIR   'An itinerant musician? (*Wagging finger*) Ho-ho-ho-ho-
ho.' Wasn't that naughty of him? (*Sees* WILLIE) Ah!

*There is a brief, awkward pause — WILLIE smiling,
expecting to be recognized, CASIMIR staring blankly.
WILLIE finally approaches gauchely.*

WILLIE   How are you, Casimir?

CASIMIR   Yes? Yes? Who have we here?

WILLIE   No, you wouldn't remember me.

CASIMIR   Should I? Should I? Yes, of course I should.

WILLIE   It's —

CASIMIR   Don't — don't tell me — let me guess. I have it — it's
Deegan, the jarvey! Am I right?

WILLIE   Jackie Deegan.

CASIMIR   There you are!

WILLIE   Deegan, the car-man; that's right; he's dead; I'm Diver.

CASIMIR   Diver?

WILLIE   From the back shore.

CASIMIR   Ah.

WILLIE   Willie Diver.

CASIMIR   Ah.

WILLIE   Tony Diver's son — the Slooghter Divers. I used to be
about the gate lodge when my Uncle Johnny was in
it. (*Pause*) Johnny MacLoone and my Auntie Sarah.
(*Pause*) That's going back a fair few years now. My
Uncle Johnny's dead, too — Jaysus, he must be dead
thirty years now. (*Pause*) I seen you this morning from
the upper hill — I've the land all took from Judith.

TOM   And Willie's just rigged up this thing so that your
father can be heard down here now.

CASIMIR   What's that?

TOM   A baby-alarm. Won't that be a help?

CASIMIR   Ah yes; splendid, splendid.

TOM   Save Judith running up and down the stairs.

CASIMIR   Of course; indeed; wonderful; splendid; great idea.

WILLIE I mind one day Casimir and me — we were only cubs this size at the time — the pair of us got into a punt down at the slip and cast off — d'you mind? — and be Jaysus didn't the tide carry us out.

CASIMIR Good Lord! Were we drowned?

WILLIE Damn the bit of us: the wind carried us back in again. Nobody knew a damn thing about us except ourselves.

CASIMIR Well, wasn't that wonderful. Ha-ha. (*Suddenly shakes* WILLIE*'s hand*) Marvellous to see you again. It's so good to be back again. Do you know how long it's been since I was home last? — Eleven years. Now, if you'll pardon me — I'm the chef for today!

WILLIE Surely to God, Casimir.

> CASIMIR *is off again — this time to the gazebo where he finds a few more faded seats which he carries out to the lawn.*

Same aul' Casimir.

TOM Is he?

WILLIE When he'd come home on holidays from the boarding school, sometimes he'd walk down the village street, and we'd all walk in a line behind him, acting the maggot, you know, imitating him. And by Jaysus he never thought of looking round.

TOM That expression — you've taken the land from Judith — what does it mean?

WILLIE She has nobody to work it so she lets it out every year.

TOM How many acres are there?

WILLIE I could hardly tell you. It's all hill and bog.

TOM So you lease it?

WILLIE I sort of take it off her hands — you know.

TOM And you till it?

WILLIE I footer about. I'm no farmer.

TOM But it's profitable land?

WILLIE Profitable? (*Laughs*) If you've a pair of wellingtons, we'll walk it some day.

He goes off towards hall. CASIMIR *is arranging the seats into a wide arc. The music suddenly stops.*

CLAIRE   Casimir!

CASIMIR *stops working.*

CASIMIR   Hello-hello.
CLAIRE   Where are you?
CASIMIR   On the tennis court — just beside the tent.
CLAIRE   Can you hear me?
CASIMIR   Clearly.
CLAIRE   I've a test for you: what's the name of this?

CASIMIR *is suddenly excited, suddenly delighted. He rushes to the step.*

CASIMIR   A test! She's testing me! A game we played all the time when we were children!
CLAIRE   Casimir!

He runs back to the centre of the lawn.

CASIMIR   Go ahead! I'm ready! I'm waiting!

He stands poised, waiting. His eyes are shut tight. His fists clenched on his chest. To himself, as he waits in suspense:

Ha-ha. Good Lord — good Lord — good Lord — good Lord — good Lord —

The music begins: Waltz in G sharp major, Op.70, No.1.

Oh-oh-oh-it's-it's-it's — (*to himself*) — the McCormack Waltz! (*Clapping his hands in relief and delight and now shouting*) The McCormack Waltz! Right, Claire? Full marks? Amn't I right?

CLAIRE Can't hear you.

CASIMIR You can hear me very well. That's it. I know. I *know*.

He runs into the study.

Got it! The McCormack Waltz! It's the G sharp major actually but we call it the McCormack because one night John McCormack, Count John McCormack, you know who I'm talking about? — the tenor? — of course you do! — well, Father had something to do with McCormack getting the papal knighthood — some French cardinal Father knew in the Vatican — and because of that Father and McCormack became great friends.

TOM *begins writing in his notebook.*

TOM Casimir, this is precisely the material I — may I jot down? —

But CASIMIR *is now back at the door and clapping his hands.*

CASIMIR Bravo, Claire darling! Bravo, bravo, bravo!

Now he is back into the centre of the room again.

Anyhow, McCormack was staying here one night and Mother was in one of her down periods and my goodness when she was like that — oh my goodness, poor Mother, for weeks on end how unhappy she'd be.

TOM She was forty-seven when she died?

CASIMIR Forty-six.

TOM Had she been ill for long? Was it sudden?

Pause.

CASIMIR Anyhow, this night Claire played that waltz, the G sharp major, and McCormack asked Mother to dance

283

and she refused but he insisted, he insisted, and finally he got her to the middle of the floor and he put his arm around her and then she began to laugh and he danced her up and down the hall and then in here and then out to the tennis court and you could hear their laughing over the whole house and finally the pair of them collapsed in the gazebo out there. Yes — marvellous! The McCormack Waltz!

TOM   Approximately what year was —

CASIMIR   A great big heavy man — oh, yes, I remember McCormack — I remember his enormous jowls trembling — but Mother said he danced like Nijinsky. (*Suddenly aware*) I'm disturbing your studies, amn't I?

TOM   Actually you're —

CASIMIR   Of course I am. Give me five minutes to make a call and then I'll leave you absolutely in peace.

As he goes to the phone (an old style phone, with a handle at the side) below the fireplace, he picks up a cassette player from the mantelpiece.

Do you know what I did last night even before I unpacked? I made two secret tapes of her to bring back to Helga and the children, just to prove to them how splendid a pianist she really is.

TOM   Have they never been to Ireland?

Momentary pause.

CASIMIR   And I'm going to play them this afternoon while we're having the picnic. And I've another little surprise up my sleeve too: *after* we've eaten. I've got a tape that Anna sent me last Christmas!

TOM   Very nice.

CASIMIR   A really tremendous person, Anna. Actually her name in religion is Sister John Henry and she chose that name because John Henry Newman — you know? — the cardinal? — Cardinal Newman? — of course you do — well, he married Grandfather and Grandmother

O'Donnell — in this very room as a matter of fact — special dispensation from Rome. But of course we think of her as Anna. And the tape she sent me has a message for every member of the family. And it'll be so appropriate now that we're all gathered together again.

As he is saying the last few words he is also turning the handle on the phone.

FATHER Don't touch that!

CASIMIR drops the phone in panic and terror.

CASIMIR Christ! Ha-ha. Oh my God! That — that — that's —
TOM It's only the baby-alarm.
CASIMIR I thought for a moment Father was — was — was —
TOM Maybe I should turn it down a bit.
CASIMIR God, it's eerie — that's what it is — eerie — eerie —

The phone suddenly rings — and his panic is revived. He grabs it.

Hello? Hello? Hello? Yes, I did ring, Mrs Moore. I'm sorry, I'm sorry, I'm very sorry. Could you try that call to Germany for me again? The number is Hamburg — Sorry, sorry, yes of course I gave it to you already; I am sorry — Yes, I'll hold on — (*To* TOM *who is watching him*) Helga, my wife — my wife Helga — to let her know I've arrived safely — she worries herself sick if I don't — Yes, just for the wedding on Thursday, to give Claire away, and then straight off again. Yes, indeed I'll tell her that, Mrs Moore. Thank you, thank you. (*To* TOM) Was always terrified of her, absolutely terrified; postmistress in Ballybeg ever since — Yes, yes, I'll hold on.

TOM fingers the limp servant's bell beside the fireplace.

TOM When did they go out of action?

CASIMIR What's that?

TOM The bells.

CASIMIR Oh I suppose when there was nobody to ring them. Or nobody to obey them. She ought to be at home now.

CLAIRE *begins playing another nocturne.* ALICE *enters. In her mid-thirties. She is hungover after last night. As she enters she touches her cheek which has a bruise mark on it.*

ALICE Morning, everybody.

TOM It's afternoon, Alice.

ALICE Is it?

She blows a kiss to CASIMIR. *He blows one back.*

Am I the last down?

TOM Just about. Is Eamon still asleep?

ALICE He was up and about hours ago. He's gone down to the village to visit his grandmother.

TOM And how are you today?

ALICE I misbehaved very badly last night, did I?

TOM Not at all. You just sat there by yourself, singing nursery rhymes.

ALICE That's all right. Tom, isn't it?

TOM Correct.

ALICE Dr Thomas Hoffnung from Chicago.

TOM You see — you were in great shape.

CASIMIR Hoffnung's the German word for hope. So your name's really Tom Hope. Terrific name, Alice, isn't it? — Tom Hope! Calling Hamburg.

ALICE What?

CASIMIR Helga.

ALICE Give her my love.

CASIMIR She's in terrific form today.

ALICE Is she?

CASIMIR Claire.

ALICE Oh — yes, yes. (*She shades her eyes with her hand and*

286

looks outside) Is it cold?

TOM No, it's a beautiful day.

She sits on the step and holds her head in her hands.
TOM moves back to CASIMIR who is anchored by the
phone.

Perhaps you could confirm a few facts for me, Casimir.
This is where Gerard Manley Hopkins used to sit —
is that correct?

CASIMIR Look at the armrest and you'll see a stain on it.

TOM Where?

CASIMIR The other arm — at the front.

TOM Got it.

CASIMIR He used to recite 'The Wreck of the *Deutschland*' to
Grandmother O'Donnell and he always rested his
teacup just there; and one afternoon he knocked it
over and burned his right hand very severely.

TOM is writing all this information down.

TOM That would have been about — ?

CASIMIR Shhh. Yes, Mrs Moore? Sorry, sorry? Yes-yes-yes —
of course — thank you — thank you. (*He hangs up*)
Something wrong with the lines. Can't even get the
Letterkenny exchange. Poor old Helga'll think I've
deserted her. Tell me again, Tom — I'm ashamed to
say I've forgotten — what's the title of your research?

TOM I can hardly remember it myself.

CASIMIR No, no, please, please.

TOM 'Recurring cultural, political and social modes in the
upper strata of Roman Catholic society in rural Ireland
since the act of Catholic Emancipation.'

CASIMIR Good heavens. Ha-ha.

TOM I know. It's awful. I apologize.

CASIMIR No, no, no, don't apologize. It sounds very — it
sounds — Alice, isn't it very, very? — Right, let's be
systematic. Judith has shown you the family records
and the old estate papers, hasn't she?

TOM Yeah.

CASIMIR And you've seen all the old diaries in the library?

TOM That's all covered.

CASIMIR Splendid, splendid. So what you want now is — well, what?

TOM Family lore, family reminiscences. For example, where did this (*crucifix*) come from?

CASIMIR Cardinal O'Donnell; present from Salamanca. No relation, just a great family friend. And a Donegal man, of course; a neighbour, almost. Remember him, Alice?

ALICE Who?

CASIMIR Cardinal O'Donnell.

ALICE Do I remember him? He must be dead seventy years.

CASIMIR He's not.

ALICE At least.

CASIMIR Is he? Ah. Good heavens. I suppose you're right. In that case. Well, let's see what else we have. Oh, yes, everything has some association. Hopkins you know.

TOM *begins writing.*

TOM Got that.

CASIMIR And this is Chesterton.

TOM Sorry?

CASIMIR G K Chesterton.

TOM The ashtray?

CASIMIR The footstool.

TOM Foot- —

CASIMIR He was giving an imitation of Lloyd George making a speech and he lost his balance and — Kraask! — Bam! — Smaak! — Boom! — down on his back across the fender. And you know the weight of Chesterton — he must be twenty stone! The fender's still dented, isn't it, Alice?

ALICE Yes.

She goes out to the lawn and sits on one of the deck-chairs. CLAIRE begins to play Sonata No.3, Op.58, third movement.

CASIMIR Sprained elbow and bruised ribs.

TOM Great.

CASIMIR Laid up in the nursery for five days.

TOM That could have been when? — doesn't matter — I'll check it out. How often did he visit Ballybeg Hall?

CASIMIR Oh, I've no idea — often, often, often — oh, yes. And Father and Mother spent part of their honeymoon with him in England, (*to* ALICE) didn't they? — (*Sees she is gone*) Oh, they were very close friends. Father wanted me to be christened Gilbert Keith but Mother insisted on Casimir — he was a Polish prince — Mother liked that. And this (*chaise longue*) is Daniel O'Connell, the Liberator — tremendous horseman, O'Connell — see the mark of his riding-boots? And that's the 58 —

TOM The clock?

CASIMIR Chopin sonata — third movement.

TOM Oh.

CASIMIR And this (*candlestick*) is George Moore, the writer — I wonder why that's George Moore — I've no idea — I just know it's George Moore. And this (*book*) is Tom Moore — you know — Byron's friend — (*sings*) 'Believe me if all those endearing young charms / Which I gaze on so fondly today.' And this (*Bible*) is Hilaire Belloc; wedding present to Father and Mother. And this is Yeats. And —

TOM What's Yeats?

CASIMIR This cushion (*on chaise longue*).

TOM Cushion — Yeats —

CASIMIR Oh, he was — he was just tremendous, Yeats, with those cold, cold eyes of his. Oh, yes, I remember Yeats vividly.

TOM That would have been when you were — ?

CASIMIR On one occasion sat up three nights in succession, just there, on Daniel O'Connell, with his head on that cushion and his feet on Chesterton, just because someone had told him we were haunted. Can you imagine! Three full nights! But of course we weren't haunted. There was never a ghost in the Hall. Father wouldn't believe in ghosts. And he was quite peeved about it; oh, quite peeved. 'You betrayed me, Bernard,' he said to Father. 'You betrayed me,' and those cold eyes of his burning with —

He breaks off suddenly because CLAIRE *has switched from the sonata to a waltz — E sharp major (Posth) — 'The Bedtime Waltz'.*

Listen! Listen! 'The Bedtime Waltz'! Oh, that's my favourite — that's easily my favourite.

He joins ALICE *outside.*

Alice, do you know what that is?

ALICE (*Sings*) 'Now off to bed, my darlings,
It's time to say goodnight — '

CASIMIR *and* ALICE *sing together.*

'So up the stairs, my sweethearts,
And soon you'll be sleeping tight.'

TOM *has joined them outside.*

CASIMIR Beautiful, isn't it? Oh, that's easily my favourite; oh, easily, easily. 'The Bedtime Waltz'. It's the E sharp major actually but we call it the Bedtime — don't we, Alice? — because as soon as Mother'd begin to play it, we'd have to dash upstairs — remember? — dash upstairs and wash ourselves and say our night prayers and be in bed before she'd finished. Isn't it so beautiful? (*Sings*) 'Now off to bed, my darlings . . .'

They all listen to the music for a few moments.

My God, isn't she playing well? The impending marriage — that's what it is: the concentration of delight and fear and expectation. And Judith tells me she's been in really bubbling humour for months and months — not one day of depression. Not even one; maybe she's grown out of it. Isn't it marvellous? May I tell you something, Tom? We always said among ourselves, Judith and Alice and I, isn't this true, Alice?

ALICE Isn't what true?

CASIMIR We always said — well, no, it was never quite expressed; but we always, you know, we always suspected — amn't I right, Alice?

ALICE What are you saying, Casimir?

CASIMIR Just that we always thought that perhaps Claire darling was the type of girl, you know, the kind of girl — we always had the idea that our little Claire was one of those highly sensitive, highly intelligent young girls who might choose — who might elect to remain single in life. Ha-ha. That's what we thought. Isn't that true, Alice?

ALICE And we were wrong.

CASIMIR Indeed we were wrong! Thank goodness we were wrong! Not that she isn't an attractive girl, a *very* attractive girl — isn't she attractive, Tom?   don't you find Claire attractive?

ALICE For God's sake, Casimir —

CASIMIR What's wrong with that? Tom finds little Claire attractive or he doesn't find her attractive?

TOM She's a very personable young lady.

CASIMIR Personable — that's the word — an excellent word — personable. Of course she is. And such a sweet nature. And her young man, I gather, is an exceptionally fine type. You've met him, Tom, have you?

TOM Just once — briefly.

CASIMIR I'm really looking forward to meeting him. Aren't you, Alice? A mature man who neither smokes nor drinks and —

ALICE A middle-aged widower with four young children.

CASIMIR That's fine — that's fine. Claire is exceptionally good with children. Judith told me that when she was giving those piano lessons to the children in the village —

ALICE What lessons? What children?

CASIMIR All last winter she went every evening to five or six houses until — you know — poor old Claire — the old trouble — over-anxiety, that's all it is basically, I'm sure that's all it is — and when she had to give it up, I'm sure she missed the pin-money — I mean she must have — what was I talking about? Yes, all those children. Judith wrote and told me they were devoted to her — Judith told me that. And her young man, Jerry, runs a very successful greengrocer's business and he has a great white lorry with an enormous plastic banana on top of the cab and he supplies wonderful fresh vegetables to all the hotels within a twenty-mile radius and he's also an accomplished trumpet player and they play duets together. Good. Good. It all sounds just — just — just so splendid and so — so appropriate. Everything's in hand. Everything's under control. I'm so happy, so happy for her. Ha-ha.

His head rotates between ALICE *and* TOM *in very rapid movements, staring at them with his fixed, anguished smile. Silence. Then suddenly the music changes — a waltz — A sharp major (Posth).*

Dance with me, Alice.
ALICE Casimir.
CASIMIR (*Shouts*) Clever, clever, Claire! Bravo! (*To* ALICE) Please.
ALICE Not now.
CASIMIR In celebration.
ALICE You never could dance.
CASIMIR Try me — come on — come on!
ALICE Please. I'm —

He grabs her hand and pulls her to her feet.

CASIMIR One-two-three
       One-two-three —
ALICE For God's sake —
CASIMIR One-two-three
       One-two-three —

ALICE Casimir!

CASIMIR (*Sings*) 'Alice and Casimir
Alice and Casimir
Alice and Casimir
One-two-three
One-two-three — '

He is now dancing with the reluctant ALICE *and singing so loudly that he does not hear the phone ring.*

TOM Your call, Casimir!

CASIMIR Over and round again
Back and forth, down again —

TOM Casimir!

CASIMIR Isn't she terrific! And an even better ballet dancer, and she has certificates in French to prove it!

TOM Call to Hamburg!

CASIMIR What?

TOM Germany!

CASIMIR stops suddenly. He hears the phone now. The high spirits vanish instantly.

CASIMIR God — Helga — that'll be Helga! Ha-ha.

He runs into the study and grabs the phone.

Halloh? Halloh? Helga? Bist du da, Helga? Halloh? Halloh?

ALICE *flops into a seat.*

TOM I'm sorry, I can't dance.

ALICE Thank God for that. Is that whiskey I saw in there?

TOM Can I get you some?

ALICE Would you, please?

TOM goes into the study and picks up the drinks tray.

CASIMIR Yes, yes, I'm holding, Mrs Moore, I'm holding. (*To* TOM) Terrific!

TOM You're through?

CASIMIR Yes.

TOM Good.

CASIMIR To Letterkenny. (*Into phone*) Very well, thank you, Mrs Moore — they're all very well. And how is Mr Moore keeping? Oh, good Lord, I never heard that — Six years ago? Oh, good heavens, I'm very sorry — (*To* TOM) Ha-ha.

TOM *carries the tray outside.*

ALICE Has he got through?

TOM I think not quite.

ALICE Sometimes when I ring home from London it takes me two hours.

TOM Hey, you've hurt your cheek.

ALICE Have I? Must have bumped into something last night. It's not sore. Have a drink yourself.

TOM I will, thanks. Do you come home often?

ALICE You're not going to interrogate me again, are you?

TOM Would you mind?

ALICE I don't know any answers.

TOM When you were growing up, did you mix at all with the local people?

ALICE We're 'local people'.

TOM Sure; but you're gentry; you're big house.

ALICE Eamon's local — Eamon's from the village.

TOM But as kids did you play with other Ballybeg kids?

ALICE We were sent off to boarding school when we were seven or eight.

TOM Casimir, too?

ALICE He went to the Benedictines when he was six.

TOM Wow. And afterwards?

ALICE After we left boarding school? Judith and Claire and I went to a convent in Carcassonne — a finishing school — and became — young ladies, (*raises glass*) didn't we?

TOM Indeed. And Casimir?

ALICE Began Law in the family tradition but always hated books. So he left home — went to England — worked at various 'genteel' jobs. Then he met Helga and she took him off to Germany. I think he works part-time in a food-processing factory — I don't want to ask him. Helga's the real breadwinner: she's a cashier in a bowling alley. Anything else?

TOM Tell me about Eamon.

She rises and fills her glass again.

ALICE Didn't we talk about that last night?

TOM Briefly.

ALICE What did I tell you?

He consults his notebook.

TOM 'Poised for a brilliant career in the diplomatic service when — '

ALICE 'Poised for a — ' I never said that!

TOM I'm quoting you.

ALICE I *must* have been drunk.

TOM Then the Civil Rights movement began in the North in '68. The Dublin government sent him to Belfast as an observer and after a few months of observing and reporting he joined the movement. Was sacked, of course. Moved to England and is now a probation officer with the Greater London Council. Right?

ALICE Listen — Claire's tired at last.

TOM What was your father's attitude?

ALICE To Eamon?

TOM To the Civil Rights campaign.

ALICE He opposed it. No, that's not accurate. He was in-different: that was across the Border — away in the North.

TOM Only twenty miles away.

ALICE Politics never interested him. Politics are vulgar.

TOM And Judith? What was her attitude? Was she engaged?

ALICE She took part in the Battle of the Bogside. Left Father and Uncle George and Claire alone here and joined the people in the streets fighting the police. That's an attitude, isn't it? That's when Father had his first stroke. And seven months later she had a baby by a Dutch reporter. Does that constitute sufficient engagement?

They are interrupted by the sound of laughter and horseplay from the hall.

CLAIRE Give me that, Eamon!
EAMON Jump for it!
CLAIRE I'm warning you!
CASIMIR Shhhhh — please!
EAMON Jump-jump-jump-jump-jump!
CLAIRE Eamon, I'm telling you!
EAMON Doesn't it suit me?

They burst into the study — EAMON wearing the headdress of Claire's wedding outfit. She is trying to recover it. EAMON is in his thirties. CLAIRE, the youngest daughter, is in her twenties. At this moment she is in one of her high moods: talkative, playful, energetic. On other occasions she is solitary and silent and withdrawn. They are now in the study.

CLAIRE Beautiful on you. Now give it back to me at once!
CASIMIR Please — please.
EAMON Sorry.
CASIMIR Hamburg.
EAMON What?
CASIMIR Helga.
EAMON Ah. (*To* CLAIRE) Behave yourself.
CASIMIR Looking marvellous.
EAMON Me?
CASIMIR Splendid.
EAMON Hungover.
CASIMIR You weren't drunk.
CLAIRE He was full.

EAMON Great cure this morning.
CASIMIR The E sharp major, Claire? The Bedtime — wasn't I right?
CLAIRE Full marks.

> EAMON *suddenly stoops down to the level of the mouth-piece of the phone and speaks rapidly into it.*

EAMON 'Mrs Moore isn't poor — '
CASIMIR Eamon — !
EAMON 'Mrs Moore's a rich aul' hoor!'
CASIMIR Oh, God!
CLAIRE Troublemaker! Come on!
EAMON See you outside, Casimir.
CASIMIR No, nothing, Mrs Moore — I didn't speak — sorry — sorry —

> CLAIRE *has* EAMON *by the arm and drags him outside. As he goes he bumps into the chaise longue, the table, etc. As he does:*

EAMON Begging your pardon, your eminence, your worship, your holiness — sorry, Shakespeare, Lenin, Mickey Mouse, Marilyn Monroe —

> *They are now out on the lawn.*

Like walking through Madame Tussaud's, isn't it, Professor? Or a bloody minefield?

> CLAIRE *grabs her headdress from his head.*

CLAIRE Thank you.
EAMON Won't she be a beautiful bride?
TOM Certainly will.
CLAIRE Lucky for you it's not soiled.
ALICE Let's see it, Claire.
CLAIRE I'm going to shorten that net.
ALICE Very smart. Did you get it in Derry?

CLAIRE Judith made it. And the dress. And her own outfit, too. Economy.

ALICE It's very pretty.

CLAIRE Did you know that on the morning Grandmother O'Donnell got married the whole village was covered with bunting and she gave a gold sovereign to every child under twelve? And the morning Mother got married she distributed roses to everyone in the chapel. I was wondering what I could do — what about a plastic bag of vegetables to every old-age pensioner? I suppose it'll soon be lunchtime, won't it?

TOM That was great music. (*She looks directly at him and does not speak. He feels he has to add something*) Really wonderful. I enjoyed it. Really great.

CLAIRE No, it wasn't.

TOM I thought it was.

CLAIRE I'm only a good pianist. I'm not a great pianist. I thought I was once. But I know I'm not.

EAMON (*To* TOM) So there!

ALICE Is this what you're going to shorten?

CLAIRE Maybe. I don't know. What do you think?

ALICE Let's see it on.

EAMON (*To* ALICE) Granny sends her warmest love. (ALICE *turns away from him*) She was disappointed you weren't with me but I said you had a headache. That wasn't a lie, was it?

ALICE *ignores him. She addresses* CLAIRE.

ALICE Maybe a fraction of an inch; but I like it as it is.

EAMON Down in the village visiting my grandmother, Professor.

TOM So I understand.

EAMON Reared me from a pup, you might say. When I was three the family had to emigrate to Scotland for work and I was left behind with Granny. (*Arms around* CLAIRE) Her very special love to you, she says. And she's sending up a small present tomorrow.

CLAIRE I called in with her the day before yesterday.

EAMON   And brought her yellow roses.

CLAIRE   But I can't persuade her to come to the wedding.

EAMON   All she wanted is to be asked. And you were wearing a white cotton dress and a pale blue headscarf and you looked like an angel. (*He hugs her briefly and releases her*) Over the years, Professor, I've lusted after each of the three O'Donnell girls in turn. (*Sees the drink*) Where was this hidden? I thought we guzzled every drop of booze in the house last night?

TOM   Willie brought it.

EAMON   Willie who?

CLAIRE   Willie who!

TOM   Willie Diver.

EAMON   Of course. Willie Slooghter, the ardent suitor. Sorry I missed him.

TOM   He'll be back later. He was putting up the baby-alarm for Judith. See — on the door frame.

CLAIRE   That's going to be a great help.

EAMON *raises his glass to the speaker.*

EAMON   The judicial presence restored. District Justice O'Donnell, Sir, welcome downstairs again. (*To* CLAIRE) Is it true that Willie practically haunts the place?

CLAIRE   A little bit, I'm afraid. But he's very helpful to Judith; and very generous.

CLAIRE *now sits and begins to sew her headdress.*
ALICE *drifts upstage and sits alone in the gazebo.* TOM
sits close to the sundial and glances through his notes.

EAMON   Always was. One civil and one decent man. (*Drinks*) Your good health, William. D'you know what someone in the pub was telling me this morning? He has five hundred slot machines in amusement arcades all round the county. Can you imagine? He'd be worth a fortune if he looked after them but he never goes near them! I'm sorry — Claire? (*Offering a drink*)

CLAIRE   The doctor doesn't allow me to take alcohol when I'm on sedatives.

EAMON Aren't you a wise and obedient girl. Professor? (*Drink*)

TOM It's Tom. I'm OK.

EAMON That's someone you should meet.

TOM Who's that?

EAMON My grandmother. You'd find her interesting. Worked all her life as a maid here in the Hall.

TOM In the Hall? Here?

EAMON Didn't you know that? Oh, yes, yes. Something like fifty-seven years continuous service with the District Justice and his wife, Lord have mercy on her; and away back to the earlier generation, with his father, the High Court Judge, and his family. Oh, you should meet her before you leave — a fund of stories and information.

TOM She sounds —

EAMON Carriages, balls, receptions, weddings, christenings, feasts, deaths, trips to Rome, musical evenings, tennis — that's the mythology I was nurtured on all my life, day after day, year after year — the life of the 'quality' — that's how she pronounces it, with a flat 'a'. A strange and marvellous education for a wee country boy, wasn't it? No, not an education — a permanent pigmentation. I'll tell you something, Professor: I know more about this place, infinitely more, here and here (*head and heart*) than they know. Sure? (*Drink*) You'll enjoy this. (*Now to* ALICE *up in the gazebo*) Telling the Professor about the night I told Granny you and I were getting married. (*To* TOM) Not a notion in the world we were going out, of course. My God, Miss Alice and her grandson! Anyhow. 'Granny,' I said this night, 'Alice and I are going to get married.' 'Alice? Who's Alice? Alice Devenny? Alice Byrne? Not Alice Smith!' 'Alice O'Donnell.' 'What Alice O'Donnell's that?' 'Alice O'Donnell of the Hall.' A long silence. Then: 'May God and His holy mother forgive you, you dirty-mouthed upstart!' (*Laughs*) Wasn't that an interesting response? As we say about here: Now you're an educated man, Professor — what do you make of that response?

TOM Oh boy.

EAMON 'Oh boy'?

TOM What do *you* make of it?

EAMON Would you like to meet her?

TOM That would be —

EAMON I'm sure I could manage to squeeze an appointment.

TOM Actually I'm leaving to- —

EAMON She'd love to talk to you; I know she would.

TOM Perhaps some other —

EAMON She's crazy about Americans. She has a sister a waitress in the Bronx and a picture of Tom Mix above her bed. Hello, Uncle George. Sit down and give us a bit of your crack.

> *This to* UNCLE GEORGE *who has entered left — his usual entrance, finding himself in the middle of the group before he is aware that they are there. As before, he stands and stares and then retreats the way he came.*

There goes one happy man.

> CASIMIR *has hung up and now stands at the study/lawn door.*

CASIMIR Can't get past Letterkenny. But they'll keep trying.

EAMON Casimir? (*Drink*)

CASIMIR Later, perhaps. Now be patient for another few minutes and I'll bring out a beautiful picnic lunch.

CLAIRE Do you need any help?

CASIMIR Me? Didn't I tell you what the boys call me? The Kindermädchen.

CLAIRE What's that? (*To* TOM) What does that mean?

TOM Is it the — children's maid? The nanny?

CASIMIR Well, yes, I suppose that's the literal translation but in this context it means — it means — well, it's really a kind of comical, affectionate term. They like to pull my leg, you know. Contrary to popular opinion the German temperament is naturally very — very frivolous and very, *very* affectionate. Where's Alice?

ALICE Hello.

CASIMIR What are you hiding there for?

ALICE Getting drunk.

CASIMIR Now you're being frivolous. Right — ten minutes at the outside.

He goes back into the study and off into the hall.

TOM The telephone system here is really unsatisfactory, isn't it?

EAMON All a game.

TOM In what way?

EAMON Casimir pretending he's calling Helga the Hun. All a game. All a fiction.

ALICE Oh shut up!

EAMON No one has ever seen her. We're convinced he's invented her.

TOM *laughs uncertainly.*

TOM Is he serious, Claire?

EAMON And the three boys — Herbert, Hans and Heinrich. And the dachshund bitch called Dietrich. And his job in the sausage factory. It has the authentic ring of phoney fiction, hasn't it?

CLAIRE Don't listen to him, Tom.

ALICE *has come down from the gazebo to fill her glass.*

ALICE What's your phoney fiction?

EAMON That I'm a laughing broth of an Irish boy. (*To* TOM) What was the word you used a few minutes ago — that yoke in there — what did you call it? A baby- —?

TOM Baby-alarm.

EAMON That's it — baby-alarm.

TOM You place a small microphone above a baby's cot so that if it cries —

EAMON I know — I know how it works. No practical experience of course — have we, love? Just that I find the name curious. Good luck. Yes, I suppose baby-alarm has an aptness in the circumstances. But there's another word — what's the name I'm looking for? — What do you call the peep-hole in a prison door? Judas hole! That's it. Would that be more appropriate? But then we'd have to decide who's spying on whom, wouldn't we? No; let's keep baby-alarm. Gentler. (*Laughs*) 'Baby-alarm' — yes, I like baby-alarm. (*To* ALICE) Shouldn't you go easy on that?

ALICE Shut up.

EAMON (*To* TOM) Less than twenty-four hours away from temperate London and already we're reverting to drunken Paddies. Must be the environment, mustn't it? Man-a-dear but that's a powerful aul' lump of a summer's day.

> TOM *is looking at his notes.* ALICE *has gone back to the gazebo.* EAMON *crosses to* CLAIRE *who is sewing and sits beside her. He puts his arm round her.*

I'm talking too much, amn't I? (*Pause*) I always talk too much in this house, don't I? Is it because I'm still intimidated by it? (*Pause*) And this was always a house of reticence, of things unspoken, wasn't it? (*She looks at him and smiles. He touches her chin*) Keep your peace, little wise one. (*He removes his arm from round her*) Judith tells me I'm proposing the toast to the groom's family.

CLAIRE You know Jerry, don't you?

EAMON Not very well. He was that bit older. (*Aware*) Well — a few years — and when you're young it seems a lot. (*She takes his glass and drinks*) Hey! What about those pills?

CLAIRE I haven't taken today's yet.

EAMON Why not?

CLAIRE You know his sister, Ellen?

EAMON Yes.

CLAIRE Do you like her?

EAMON   Ellen has her own ways.

CLAIRE   She'll be living in the house with Jerry and me.

EAMON   For a while, maybe. Ellen'll marry and move out.

CLAIRE   No, she won't move out. And she won't marry now
         — she's almost fifty-four — she's only a year younger
         than Jerry. And the house is hers. And yesterday she
         said to me that she'll carry on as usual — doing the
         cooking and the housework. So I'll have nothing to do.
         A life of leisure. Maybe take the children for walks —
         she suggested that. But that's all. The whole day idle.
         And he's getting me a car next Christmas so that I
         won't even have to walk. Next time you're back I'll
         have put on ten stone!

EAMON   I thought Jerry would want a working wife?

CLAIRE   Oh, yes. He's buying a piano so that I can teach the
         children to play. Maybe one of them will become a
         concert pianist?

         She gets up and moves across the lawn.

EAMON   What the hell's keeping Casimir with the grub?

         He rises and pours himself another drink.

         God bless Willie Diver. Did you know I was his best
         man? My God, *that* was a wedding. I was seventeen,
         Willie was eighteen, and Nora Sheridan, known
         locally as Nora the Nun — for reasons of Irish irony,
         Professor — Nora was thirty if she was a day. And at
         seventeen I thought: My God, lucky aul' Slooghter,
         marrying the village pro, my God he'll be getting it
         morning, noon and night and what more could a man
         want! But of course the marriage lasted five months
         and the brave Nora cleared off with a British soldier
         stationed in Derry and was never seen again and aul'
         Willie was back with the rest of us hoping to get it
         maybe once a year on St Patrick's night with big Tessie
         Mulligan if you promised to take her and her twin
         sister to the pig co-op dance. Isn't life full of tiny frus-

TOM   trations, Professor? And how's the research going?
TOM   Satisfactorily.
EAMON   Are you writing a book?
TOM   Eventually.
EAMON   About?
TOM   I'm not going to bore you with my theories.
EAMON   Please. (*To* ALICE) We're captivated — aren't we, love?
TOM   Alice is not captivated.
EAMON   Alice reveals her passion in oblique ways.
TOM   I'd really rather not —
EAMON   But I'm interested; I'm genuinely interested. Please.
TOM   Well, when we talk about the big house in this country, we usually mean the Protestant big house with its Anglo-Irish tradition and culture; and the distinction is properly made between that tradition and culture and what we might call the native Irish tradition and culture which is Roman Catholic.
EAMON   With reservations — yes. So?
TOM   So what I'm researching is the life and the lifestyle of the Roman Catholic big house — by no means as thick on the ground but still there; what we might call a Roman Catholic aristocracy — for want of a better term.
EAMON   No, no, it's a good term; I like the term. The Professor's talking about you, love!
TOM   And the task I've set myself is to explore its political, cultural and economic influence both on the ascendancy ruling class and on the native peasant tradition. Over the past one-hundred-and-fifty years — in fact since Catholic Emancipation — what political clout did they wield, what economic contribution did they make to the status of their co-religionists, what cultural effect did they have on the local peasantry?
EAMON   The Professor's talking about me, love! And Ballybeg Hall's your prototype?
TOM   No, just one example.
EAMON   And what conclusions have you reached?
TOM   None yet, Eamon. I'm still digging.
EAMON   Ah. Let's see can we help the Professor. What were the

questions again? What political clout did they wield? (*Considers. Then sadly shakes his head*) What economic help were they to their co-religionists? (*Considers. Then sadly shakes his head*) What cultural effect did they have on the local peasantry? Alice? (*Considers. Then sadly shakes his head*) We agree, I'm afraid. Sorry, Professor. Bogus thesis. No book.

TOM OK. So no book.

EAMON But you'll go ahead all the same, won't you?

TOM I may well be so obtuse.

> CASIMIR *enters the study, carrying a large tray. As he crosses the lawn he chants:*

CASIMIR 'What we are about to receive is a magnificent lunch which will be served on the lawn and it has been prepared specially and with meticulous care by — '

> *He is now on the lawn and is about to put the tray on the ground when his chant is interrupted by* FATHER'S *clear and commanding voice.*

FATHER Casimir!

> CASIMIR *jumps to attention; rigid, terrified.*

CASIMIR Yes sir!

FATHER Come to the library at once. I wish to speak to you.

> CASIMIR *now realizes that the voice has come from the speaker.*

CASIMIR Christ — oh-oh-oh my God — Ha-ha. Isn't that a very comical joke — I almost stood to attention — I almost stood —

> *He looks round at the others who are staring at him. He tries to smile. He is totally lost. He looks at the tray; then sinks to the ground with it, ending in a*

kneeling position.

That's the second time I was caught — the second time —

JUDITH enters with the teapot. The eldest of the O'Donnell family: almost forty. She is dressed in old working clothes. Her appearance is of little interest to her.

JUDITH Did you bring the sugar and the sandwiches, Casimir? I've got the tea here.
FATHER At once, Sir. And bring your headmaster's report with you. I intend to get to the bottom of this.
CASIMIR Judith?
JUDITH What is it?
CASIMIR Judith?

She goes quickly outside, gets down beside him and takes him in her arms. He is crying now.

I'm sorry — I'm sorry — I'm very sorry.
JUDITH It's all right.
CASIMIR I'm very sorry, very sorry.
JUDITH Everything's all right — everything's fine.
CASIMIR I don't think it's fair, Judith.
JUDITH Shhhhh.
CASIMIR That's the second time I was caught by it. It's not fair — it's not fair.
JUDITH Shhhhh.
CASIMIR Ha-ha. It's not fair.

She rocks him in her arms as if he were a baby. The others look away. Bring lights down slowly.

ACT TWO

About an hour later. The remains of the lunch are scattered over the lawn: dishes, linen napkins, food, some empty wine bottles.

The sun, the food, the wine have taken their toll: EAMON *is sprawled on the grass, dozing.* JUDITH, *her eyes closed, her face tilted up to the sun, is smoking a cigarette.* WILLIE *is sitting on the step immediately above and behind her.* CLAIRE *is sitting apart from the others, close to the sundial.* TOM *is in the gazebo reading a newspaper but aware of what the others are doing.*

CASIMIR *is crawling around on his hands and knees, moving along very slowly and feeling the ground very carefully with his fingertips. He is totally concentrated on this strange task. He is looking for the holes left by croquet hoops; on the same site as the vanished tennis court.*

Only ALICE *is lively. She has had a little too much to drink and she is pacing about, glass in hand, occasionally making giddy, complicated little steps with her feet.*

ALICE   I know you're paying no attention to me — old Alice is a little tiddly, isn't she? But what I'm suggesting is very sensible. The meal will be over at half-one or two; and the happy couple will drive off into eternal bliss. And what's to become of the rest of us? Sit looking at one another with melancholy faces? Sleep? Talk about old times? Listen to Father on the baby-alarm? (*Short giggle — then remorse. To* CASIMIR) Apologies. Withdraw that. That was unkind. So what do we do? My suggestion is — no, it's a formal proposal, Madam Chairman (*Judith*) — I put it to your worship that we all head off somewhere and have some fun ourselves. You'll drive us, Willie, won't you?

WILLIE   Surely to God. Anywhere you want.

ALICE   All set, then. Where'll we go? Glencolmcille! Who's for —

JUDITH *sits up very quickly and lifts the writing pad at her side (her list of wedding preparations).*

JUDITH Willie isn't free to go anywhere.

ALICE *grimaces extravagantly behind her back.*

ALICE Oooooh. So Willie isn't free. All right, we'll club together and rent a car — no, *I'll* rent a car and you'll all be my guests. Is that a unanimous verdict?

JUDITH Let's get back to these things.

ALICE And we'll bring our court clerk with us and every word we utter will be carefully recorded.

JUDITH Where had we got to? Any word from the photographer?

WILLIE He'll be there at the chapel and then he'll come up here afterwards.

ALICE God help the poor man if he thinks he's heard one word of truth since he came here. Is he in the library?

TOM Careful, Alice: I'm here.

ALICE All you're hearing is lies, my friend — lies, lies, lies.

TOM What's the truth?

ALICE Later in the day and alcoholic Alice'll tell all.

JUDITH I've asked one of the Moloney girls to look after Father while we're at the church. Are you busy that morning?

WILLIE Doing nothing.

JUDITH Could you run her up? About half-nine?

WILLIE No bother.

JUDITH Thanks.

ALICE Well, if none of you want to come with me, as Sister Thérèse used to say — remember her strange English? — 'Boo-gar the whole lot of you!'

She slumps into a chair and closes her eyes.

JUDITH 'Food' — that's all got except for the ham.

CASIMIR Hurrah!

CASIMIR'*s sudden triumphant exclamation startles everybody.* EAMON *wakens suddenly.*

There you are! Knew they were here!

EAMON God.

CASIMIR There! Look — look — look!

He has a finger stuck into the ground.

ALICE Good old Casimir!

CASIMIR Now if there's one there, there must be another somewhere beside it.

He bends over to his search again. EAMON *gets to his
feet.*

EAMON What is he at? Who's missing?

JUDITH What's the position about the flowers, Claire?

CASIMIR Here it is! (*He stands up*) You see — I remember it. Distinctly! (*He marks the spot with a napkin*) That means
that there must be another one — (*he strides across the
lawn*) — somewhere about here. (*He grins at* EAMON)
Amn't I right?

EAMON I'm sure you are.

CASIMIR Seven in all — isn't that it?

EAMON At least.

CASIMIR No, no, just seven; and the peg in the middle.

*He suddenly drops on his hands and knees again and
begins groping.*

EAMON Who is Peg?

JUDITH Claire!

CLAIRE Sorry?

JUDITH The flowers arrive on the last bus tomorrow night?

CLAIRE (*Vague, indifferent*) I think so.

JUDITH And Jerry'll collect them and bring them up here?

CLAIRE Yes — probably — I suppose so.

JUDITH Claire, it's —

WILLIE I'll remind him this evening.

JUDITH Would you?

WILLIE And if he's busy I'll collect them.

EAMON *picks up the cassette player and switches it on — Étude No.3 in E major. He sings with it in a parody of the Crosby style of the late forties.*

EAMON 'So deep is the night — '

CASIMIR, *automatically, without looking up:*

CASIMIR Terrific. The E major étude — right, Claire?
EAMON F major.

CASIMIR *sits up.*

CASIMIR Are you — ? No, it's the — Ah, you're taking a hand at me, Eamon! I know you are. Ha-ha. Very good. Very comical.

He bends to his search again.

EAMON 'No moon tonight; no friendly star to guide me on my way — boo bc doo ba ba dc ba   '

He pours himself a drink.

JUDITH What arrangement have you come to with Miss Quirk, Claire?
CLAIRE No arrangement.
JUDITH Is she going to play or is she not?
CLAIRE I told you all I know. I met her by accident.
JUDITH And what did she say?
CLAIRE All she said was 'I play the harmonium at every wedding in Ballybeg.'
ALICE (*Eyes closed*) Who? Miss Quirk? Oh my God!
CLAIRE I don't care. Let her play if she wants.
JUDITH Did she ask you what music you wanted?
CLAIRE You know very well she can play only two pieces.
ALICE Tom Hoffnung!
TOM Hello?
ALICE Before you leave you should meet Miss Quirk.

TOM Yeah?

ALICE She's the Scott Joplin of Donegal.

JUDITH (*To* WILLIE) I suppose I'll have to pay her something?

WILLIE I'll look after it. You can square with me later.

> EAMON *is wandering around, glass in hand. He sings with the tape again, inventing the words he has forgotten.*

EAMON 'And so am I, lonely and forgotten by the stream — ' (*To* WILLIE) Remember dancing to that in the Corinthian in Derry?

WILLIE Every Friday night.

EAMON The steam rising out of us from getting soaked cycling in on the bikes.

WILLIE And the big silver ball going round and round up on the ceiling. Jaysus.

EAMON Tommy McGee on the sax; Bobby Kyle on piano; Jackie Fogarty on drums; young Turbet on clarinet.

WILLIE And slipping out to the cloakroom for a slug out of the bottle.

EAMON And the long dresses — the New Look — isn't that what it was called?

WILLIE Oh Jaysus.

EAMON (*To* JUDITH) Remembrance of things past.

JUDITH (*To* WILLIE) Is that coffee stone cold?

> WILLIE *rises immediately.*

WILLIE If there's any left in it.

> *He goes to the remains of the picnic.*

EAMON Do you remember the night we sneaked out to the Corinthian on my uncle's motor bike?

JUDITH Yes.

EAMON We were still sitting over there (*gazebo*) when the sun came up.

CASIMIR Here we are! Two more holes! Corner number two!

All agreed?

He stands up, marks the position with a napkin as before, and goes to another part of the lawn.

EAMON You wore your mother's silver tiara in your hair. Do you remember?

JUDITH Yes.

EAMON Everything?

CASIMIR So that number three must be about — here.

He drops on his hands and knees again and begins groping.

ALICE (*Eyes closed*) I have it on very good authority that in the privacy of her digs Miss Quirk plays the ukulele and sings dirty songs.

EAMON There was a hedgehog caught in the tennis net. He had rolled himself up into a ball and his spikes were up against danger. Like me, you said. Do you remember?

JUDITH Yes.

EAMON And I asked you to marry me.

ALICE I'm ashamed to say I like dirty songs, Tom.

EAMON And you said yes.

JUDITH Where had we got to? — Taxis. What about taxis, Willie?

WILLIE You'll need only two. The car that leaves Jerry at the chapel then comes up here for you and Claire; and it waits here until the other car has headed off with the rest of the family and then it follows on. (*He returns with a cup of coffee*) There's a wee drop in it — it's not too bad. They were good times, Eamon, eh?, them nights in the Corinthian.

EAMON They were good times, Professor.

TOM What were?

EAMON Plebeian past times. Before we were educated out of our emotions.

313

He switches up the volume of the cassette while he sings again.

'So deep is the night, ba-ba-dee-boo-ba-ba-ba-ba — '

He reduces the volume again.

JUDITH I think we have enough wine.
ALICE I hope there's plenty wine.
WILLIE (*To* ALICE) I left in two cases — is that enough?

ALICE *now opens her eyes and sits forward.*

ALICE Good ole Willie! (*Sings*) 'Drink to me only with thine eyes — '

Immediately EAMON *begins singing.*

EAMON 'Boo-ba-de-boo-ba-ba — '
ALICE 'And I will pledge with mine.'

CASIMIR, *without interrupting his search, joins* ALICE.

'Or leave a kiss but in the cup
And I'll not look for wine.'

ALICE *sits back, closes her eyes and continues humming.*

EAMON (*To* TOM) Recognize it?
TOM Elizabethan. Is it Ben Jonson?
EAMON The very buck. Used to nip into the scullery and recite it to Granny.
TOM I think perhaps I should check that.
EAMON Would I tell you a lie?
FATHER I have considered very carefully everything I have heard and I must now ask you to — I must request — I must — I — I —

> *The suddenness and authority of* FATHER's *voice create a stillness, almost an unease. Nobody speaks for a few seconds.*

JUDITH He's very restless today.

CASIMIR I wasn't caught that time — no, no! I wasn't caught that time — ha-ha!

FATHER Judith!

> CASIMIR *stiffens.*

Judith? Judith? Where's Judith? Jud-ith!

ALICE Stay where you are. I'll go. (*She rises*)

JUDITH It's all right. He probably wants nothing at all.

> JUDITH *goes off quickly.* ALICE *walks about. She is slightly unsteady.*

ALICE But I would like to go — I would like to help. Why won't ohe let me help? When I went up to see him last night just after I arrived, I got such a shock — he's so altered. Isn't he altered? I mean he was always such a big strong man with such power, such authority; and then to see him lying there, so flat under the clothes, with his mouth open —

> CASIMIR *stands up. He has been listening to* ALICE *and the vigour of his announcement this time is forced.*

CASIMIR The third! There you are! Number three! (*He marks it as before*) Only one more to get.

> *He crosses the lawn to the fourth corner but does not go down on his hands and knees. He stands listening to* ALICE.

ALICE I caught his face between my hands — isn't that right, Casimir? You were there beside me — and I held it like that. And it was such a strange sensation — I must never have touched his face before — is that possible never to have touched my father's face? And it seemed so small between my hands; and it was so cool and his beard so rough and I felt so — so equal to him. (*She begins to cry*) And then he opened his eyes. And he didn't recognize me — isn't that right, Casimir? And that's when I began to cry. He didn't know me. He didn't know you, either, Casimir, did he?

CASIMIR No.

ALICE He didn't know me either. It was so strange — your own father, not knowing you. He didn't know you either, Casimir, did he?

CASIMIR No.

ALICE His own flesh and blood. Did he know you, Willie?

WILLIE Well, you see like, Alice, I'm not his son.

ALICE That's true. And that's when I began to cry. I'm sorry — I'm sorry — I know I'm slightly drunk but I'm still capable of — of — of —

EAMON offers ALICE *Judith's coffee — she brushes past him.*

I want a drink. Who's hidden the drink? Where's the drink all hidden? (*She finds it and helps herself*) Oh dear, dear God.

EAMON 'Boo-ba-de-ba-ba-ba-ba; boom-boom-boom.'

EAMON moves over beside CLAIRE. CASIMIR *gets down on his hands and knees again.* ALICE *drops into a seat and closes her eyes.*

Whatever he's looking for, he deserves to find it.

CLAIRE The remains of an old croquet court.

EAMON Ah. Before my time.

A new tape begins: Nocturne in F sharp major, Op.15 No.2. CLAIRE *is fingering a gold watch.*

Present from Jerry?

CLAIRE For my last birthday.

EAMON Very handsome, isn't it?

JUDITH Is something wrong?

CLAIRE Yes.

FATHER Judith?

JUDITH I'm here beside you.

CLAIRE And I told you, didn't I — he's getting me a car for Christmas.

JUDITH What's the matter?

EAMON Lucky you.

FATHER Judith?

JUDITH What is it?

CLAIRE And he's had the whole house done up from top to bottom. New carpets everywhere — even in the kitchen. I helped Ellen choose them.

JUDITH Are you cold? Do you want the quilt on again?

Without any change in her tone, and smiling as if she were chatting casually, CLAIRE *continues:*

CLAIRE I'm in a mess, Eamon.

JUDITH You're upset today

CLAIRE I don't know if I can go on with it.

JUDITH You got your pills, didn't you?

FATHER Judith betrayed the family — did you know that?

JUDITH Yes. Now that's better.

FATHER Great betrayal; enormous betrayal.

JUDITH Let me feel those tops.

FATHER But Anna's praying for her. Did you know that?

JUDITH Yes, I know that, Father.

CLAIRE Listen to them! (*Short laugh*) It goes on like that all the time, all the time. I don't know how Judith stands it. She's lucky to be so — so strong-minded. Sometimes I think it's driving me mad. Mustn't it have been something trivial like that that finally drove Mother to despair? And then sometimes I think: I'm going to miss it so much. I'm so confused, Eamon.

EAMON Aren't we all confused?

CLAIRE But if you really loved someone the way you're

supposed to love someone you're about to marry, you shouldn't be confused, should you? Everything should be absorbed in that love, shouldn't it? There'd be no reservations, would there? I'd love his children and his sister and his lorry and his vegetables and his carpets and everything, wouldn't I? And I'd love all of him, too, wouldn't I?

EAMON *puts his arm round her.*

That's one of the last nocturnes he wrote.
EAMON Is it?
CLAIRE Why does he not see that I'm in a mess, Eamon?
EAMON You don't have to go on with it, you know.

CASIMIR *is suddenly and triumphantly on his feet again.*

CASIMIR Number four! There you are! The complete croquet court! See, Eamon? Look, Claire! I remember! I knew!

CLAIRE *jumps up. She is suddenly vigorous, buoyant, excited. Her speech is rapid.*

CLAIRE Come on — who's for a game?
CASIMIR Me-me-me!
CLAIRE Give me a mallet.

CASIMIR *mimes giving her one.*

CASIMIR There you are.
CLAIRE Is this the best you have?
CASIMIR It's brand new — never been used.
CLAIRE Where are the hoops?
CASIMIR All in position. Just a second. (*He drops three more napkins in the centre of the court*) That's it. This one (*centre napkin*) is the peg.
CLAIRE And the balls?
CASIMIR At your feet.

CLAIRE Right.
CASIMIR Who goes first?
CLAIRE The bride-to-be — who else?
CASIMIR Wonderful! Off you go. Ladies and gentlemen — please — give the players room. Thank you. Thank you.
CLAIRE First shot of the game.
CASIMIR And a beautiful, beautiful shot it is. Now for the champion.

> *This imaginary game and their exchanges about it continue during the following sequences.* EAMON *rises; switches off the cassette; picks up a bottle of wine and a glass; drifts across the lawn. As he passes* WILLIE:

EAMON 'Ba-ba-de-boo-ba-ba.' Many hedgehogs about now?
WILLIE What?
EAMON Hedgehogs — you know — (*he mimes one*) — many of them about?
WILLIE How the hell would I know about hedgehogs?
EAMON 'Ba-ba-de-boo-ba-ba — Ba-ba-boo — '
WILLIE Hedgehogs! Jaysus!

> WILLIE *goes to the croquet court and watches the game.*

CASIMIR That was good — that was very good.
CLAIRE That was brilliant.
CASIMIR But watch this. This is how it's really done. Aaaaah!

> ALICE *opens her eyes, sits forward, and watches* CLAIRE *and* CASIMIR *in bewilderment.*

CLAIRE That ball hit your leg.
CASIMIR It did not.
CLAIRE I saw it — you winced.
CASIMIR (*To* ALICE) Did the ball hit my leg?
ALICE What?
CASIMIR Did you see me wince?

CLAIRE   You did. I saw you. I saw you.

ALICE   What are you doing?

CASIMIR   Croquet. (*To* CLAIRE) My turn — right?

CLAIRE   I'll let you off this time. (*To* ALICE) Keep an eye on him — he cheats.

ALICE   Where are the — ?

CLAIRE   But he's still not winning. (*To* CASIMIR) And watch where you're swinging that mallet.

ALICE   Oh my God.

> *She closes her eyes and sinks back in her seat. The game continues.* UNCLE GEORGE *enters the study — his usual entrance — and is out on the lawn before he discovers it is occupied. He stops and looks around.*

WILLIE   Hello, Mister George.

> UNCLE GEORGE *goes back into the study — and off.*

EAMON   Hello, Uncle George. Goodbye, Uncle George. Not one of you is aware that on the day of our wedding Uncle George shook my hand and spoke seven words. And the seven words he spoke were: 'There's going to be a great revolution.' And I thought that after all those years of silence and contemplation that must be a profound remark. (EAMON *is now beside* TOM. *He sits very close to him and smiles warmly at him*) Wasn't I a fool?

TOM   Were you?

EAMON   I'm wiser now.

TOM   Good.

EAMON   And I've solved your problem.

TOM   Which one's that, Eamon?

EAMON   Your book.

TOM   Have I a problem?

EAMON   It has to be a fiction — a romantic fiction — like Helga the Hun.

TOM   Yeah?

EAMON   A great big blockbuster of a Gothic novel called *Ballybeg Hall — From Supreme Court to Sausage Factory*; four

generations of a great Irish Catholic legal dynasty; the
gripping saga of a family that lived its life in total
isolation in a gaunt Georgian house on top of a hill
above the remote Donegal village of Ballybeg; a family
without passion, without loyalty, without commitments;
administering the law for anyone who happened to be
in power; above all wars and famines and civil strife and
political upheaval; ignored by its Protestant counterparts, isolated from the mere Irish, existing only in its
own concept of itself, brushing against reality occasionally by its cultivation of artists; but tough — oh, yes,
tough, resilient, tenacious; and with one enormous
talent for — no, a *greed* for survival — that's the family
motto, isn't it? — *Semper Permanemus.* Don't for a second
underestimate them. What do you think?

TOM   It's your fiction.

EAMON   A bit turgid — yes — I can see that. (*Suddenly happy
again*) But the romantic possibilities are there — oh,
yes, by God. Mother, for example. Make Mother central.

ALICE   Leave Mother out of it.

EAMON   Why?

ALICE   You really are a bastard!

EAMON   Because I see Mother as central?

ALICE   For Christ's sake!

EAMON   Trust me — I'm an ex-diplomat.

ALICE   Trust you!

EAMON   Yes, I have pieties, too. (*To* TOM) She was an actress.
Did you know that? No, you didn't — that little detail
was absorbed into the great silence. Yes; travelling
round the country with the Charles Doran Company.
Spotted by the judge in the lounge of the Railway
Hotel and within five days decently wed and en-
sconced in the Hall here and bugger poor aul' Charles
Doran who had to face the rest of rural Ireland without a Colleen Bawn! And a raving beauty by all
accounts. No sooner did Yeats clap eyes on her than a
sonnet burst from him — 'That I may know the beauty
of that form' — Alice'll rattle it off for you there. Oh,
terrific stuff. And O'Casey — haven't they told you

that one? — poor O'Casey out here one day plough-
terin' after tennis balls and spoutin' about the workin'
man when she appeared in the doorway in there and
the poor creatur' made such a ram-stam to get to her
that he tripped over the Pope or Plato or Shirley
Temple or somebody and smashed his bloody glasses!
The more you think of it — all those calamities —
Chesterton's ribs, Hopkins's hand, O'Casey's aul'
specs — the County Council should put up a sign outside that room — Accident Black Spot — shouldn't
they? Between ourselves, it's a very dangerous house,
Professor.

TOM   What have you got against me, Eamon?

EAMON   And of course you'll have chapters on each of the
O'Donnell forebears: Great Grandfather — Lord Chief
Justice; Grandfather — Circuit Court Judge; Father —
simple District Justice; Casimir — failed solicitor. A
fairly rapid descent; but no matter, no matter; good for
the book; failure's more lovable than success. D'you
know, Professor, I've often wondered: if we had had
children and they wanted to be part of the family legal
tradition, the only option open to them would have
been as criminals, wouldn't it? (*Offering the bottle*)
There's enough here for both of us. No? (*He pours a
drink for himself*) After we went upstairs last night,
Alice and I, we had words, as they say. She threw a
book at me. And I struck her. You've noticed her
cheek, haven't you? No one else here would dream of
commenting on it; but you did, didn't you? And she
didn't tell you, did she? Of course she didn't. That's
why she's freezing me. But she'll come round. It'll be
absorbed. Duty'll conquer.

TOM   I don't want to hear about your —

EAMON   What have I got against you?

TOM   Yes. You're the only member of the family who has
been — less than courteous to me since I came here. I
don't know why that is. I guess you resent me for
some reason.

EAMON *considers this. He is not smiling now.*

EAMON Nervous; that's all. In case — you'll forgive me — in case you're not equal to your task. In case you'll loot and run. Nervous that all you'll see is (*indicates the croquet game*) — the make believe.

> JUDITH *enters the study. As she does, the phone rings. She answers it.*

No, I don't resent you, Professor. I'm sure you're an honest recorder. I'm nervous of us; we don't pose to our best advantage.

JUDITH Casimir!

CASIMIR Hello?

CLAIRE I have you on the run now.

CASIMIR You certainly have not.

JUDITH Phone, Casimir!

> *His usual response to this:*

CASIMIR The phone! — Helga — That'll be Helga — sorry — sorry — excuse me — sorry —

> *As he rushes into the study he trips on the step.*

I beg your pardon — forgive me —

> *He rushes on in.*

CLAIRE You play for him until he comes back, Willie.

WILLIE Me?

CLAIRE There's nothing to it.

WILLIE Aw, g'way out of that.

CLAIRE Come on. You start over there.

WILLIE Sure I mean to say —

CLAIRE You aim for that post first and then you drive the ball through the hoop over in that far corner.

CASIMIR Hello? Hello? Hello?

WILLIE *looks round at the others. He is embarrassed and afraid of being laughed at — particularly by* EAMON *— so he laughs foolishly.*

WILLIE Me playing croquet — and nothing to play with! Jaysus! Sure I never even seen the game in my —

CLAIRE You've been watching us, haven't you? (*Thrusts a mallet into his hand*) Go on! All you do is hit the ball. It's very simple.

WILLIE All the same you feel a bit of an eejit — (*To* EAMON) They have me playing croquet now, Eamon! Without balls nor nothin'! Jaysus!

EAMON Go ahead, William. Take the plunge. Submit to baptism. You'll never look back.

WILLIE I couldn't —

CLAIRE If you're going to play, will you play!

CASIMIR Halloh? Halloh? Helga? Wer spricht dort, bitte?

WILLIE *hesitates. Then suddenly flings off his jacket, spits on his hands and rubs them together.*

WILLIE Right — right — I'll play — indeed and I'll play — where's the ball? — Give us a mallet — out of my road — where do I begin? Let me at it.

As before keep up the dialogue during the CLAIRE / WILLIE *game.* JUDITH, *who has been tidying in the study, now comes out.*

EAMON How is he?

JUDITH All right, I think. It might be just the heat. (*He gives her his glass*) What about you?

He looks around — finds another.

EAMON Here we are.

CLAIRE Very good, Willie. You're getting the hang of it.

WILLIE Am I? By Jaysus maybe I am too.

324

EAMON *sits beside* JUDITH. *She is aware he is looking at her.*

JUDITH It's almost warm. (*Pause*) I get sleepy if I take more than one glass. (*Pause*) This must be my third today.

ALICE *moves in her seat.*

ALICE Oh, that's very nice.

JUDITH She's got older looking.

EAMON Yes.

JUDITH Has it become a real problem?

EAMON When is a problem a real problem?

JUDITH I suppose when you can't control it.

EAMON She was fine until November, dry for almost eighteen months. Since then she's been in hospital twice. And I knew this trip would be a disaster.

JUDITH I tried to talk to her last night —

EAMON About her drinking?

JUDITH No, no; about London. I was suggesting she get a job. She said none of us was trained to do anything. And she's right — we're not. Anyhow she cut me off. But she was always closer to Claire; and Casimir, of course.

EAMON We live in a damp basement flat about half the size of the morning room, I'm out all day and a lot of nights. It's a very lonely life for her. You'll miss Claire.

JUDITH Yes.

EAMON She won't be far away.

JUDITH That's true.

EAMON Just you and Father.

JUDITH And Uncle George.

EAMON And Uncle George.

JUDITH Yes.

EAMON It'll be a quiet house.

JUDITH We manage.

WILLIE Go on — go on — go on — go on — go on.

EAMON You said that morning you'd marry me.

JUDITH We manage because we live very frugally. There's Father's pension; and I get some money from letting

the land; and I grow all the vegetables we use; and I
enjoy baking —

EAMON Why did you change your mind?

JUDITH So that apart from doctors' bills the only expenses we
have are fuel and electric and the phone. And I'm
thinking of getting rid of the phone. It's used very
little anyhow.

EAMON You never told me why.

WILLIE You missed it! You missed it!

CLAIRE I did not!

WILLIE You weren't within a bloody mile of it! Ha-ha-ha-ha.

JUDITH And I have Willie. I don't think I could manage without Willie's help. Yes, I probably could. Yes, of course
I would. But he's the most undemanding person I
know. Some intuitive sense he has: he's always there
when I want him. And everything he does is done so
simply, so easily, that I almost take him for granted.

EAMON Judith, I —

*She closes her eyes and her speech becomes tense and
deliberate, almost as if she were talking to herself.*

JUDITH Listen to me, Eamon. I get up every morning at 7.30
and make breakfast. I bring Father his up first. Very
often the bed's soiled so I change him and sponge him
and bring the clothes downstairs and wash them and
hang them out. Then I get Uncle George his breakfast.
Then I let the hens out and dig the potatoes for the
lunch. By that time Claire's usually up so I get her
something to eat and if she's in one of her down times
I invent some light work for her to do, just to jolly her
along, and if she's in one of her high times I've got to
try to stop her from scrubbing down the house from
top to bottom. Then I do out the fire, bring in the turf,
make the beds, wash the dishes. Then it's time to bring
Father up his egg-flip and shave him and maybe
change his clothes again. Then I begin the lunch. And
so it goes on and on, day after day, week after week,
month after month. I'm not complaining, Eamon. I'm

just telling you my routine. I don't even think of it as burdensome. But it occupies every waking moment of every day and every thought of every day. And I know I can carry on — happily almost, yes almost happily — I know I can keep going as long as I'm not diverted from that routine, as long as there are no intrusions on it. Maybe it's an unnatural existence. I don't know. But it's my existence — here — now. And there is no end in sight. So please don't intrude on it. Keep out of it. Now. Altogether. Please.

> *She lights a cigarette. Pause.*

EAMON Whatever the lady wants.

> TOM *joins them.* EAMON *rises and flashes a radiant smile at him.*

> *Semper Permanemus.* (*Almost into* TOM's *face as he shuffles past him*) 'Ba-doo-be-da-da-da-ba-dab — '

> TOM *ignores him. He picks up an empty wine bottle and examines it with excessive interest.*

TOM I've some packing to do. Thank Casimir for lunch, will you?
JUDITH Yes.
TOM I'd be careful of that sun. You should have your head covered.

> *He goes off right.* WILLIE *is down on his hunkers, fanning an imaginary ball through an imaginary hoop.*

WILLIE Come on, my wee darling, come on, come on, come on, another inch, another wee fraction — And it's through! I've won! I've won!

> *He is elated with his triumph. His elation is genuine — not part of the make believe. And his triumph has*

given him a confidence. He reaches for his jacket and
swaggers off the court with great assurance.

CLAIRE It's not over yet.
WILLIE Over! Finished! You're bet! Pack it in! I won, Eamon!
CLAIRE I've one more shot —
WILLIE Bet to the ropes! Your tongue's hanging out! Throw in
the towel! Aul' Slooghter won hands down! Up the
back shore boys!
CLAIRE Watch this, Willie.
WILLIE I'm watching nothing! The game's over! (*To* EAMON)
What do you make of that, lad, eh?
EAMON 'So deep is the n-n-n-n-n-night — '
CLAIRE It's through, Willie.
WILLIE Takes an aul' Diver every time!

ALICE *is awakened by the noise.* WILLIE *pursues* EAMON.

Never had a mallet in my hand before! Never stood
on a croquet court before! Bloody good, eh?
EAMON 'Terrific.' (*He gives one of Casimir's grins*) A real insider
now, Willie.
WILLIE Give us a slug of something there — I'm as dry as a
limekiln. What's in that?

EAMON *hands him the empty wine bottle.*

EAMON Here.
WILLIE Jaysus, that's empty!
EAMON Imagine it's full. Use your peasant talent for fantasy,
man.

CASIMIR *has finished his call. He comes outside. He is*
uneasy but tries to hide it.

CASIMIR Well. That's that job done. Glad to get that off my
mind. What's been happening out here?
JUDITH Did you get through?
CASIMIR Little Heinrich I was speaking to actually — he's the

baby — he's seven — little Heinrich. Helga's out at one of her S. G. meetings. Ha-ha.

ALICE What's her S. G.?

CASIMIR The Spiritualisten Gruppe — she's a spiritualist, Helga — table-rapping, seances, all that stuff — total believer. They meet every fortnight; and they're so passionate about it — oh, my goodness, you've no idea how passionate. I pretend I'm sympathetic — you know — domestic harmony — ha-ha. So that's where she is now — at her S. G. meeting.

JUDITH I'm sure Heinrich misses you.

CASIMIR Oh yes — oh yes. But the line was bad. And the trouble is, you see, the trouble is his English is as bad as my German — if that's possible! No problem, no problem at all when we're together — I mean we can smile and make signs and stagger on; but it's so difficult on the phone. And of course Helga's right — I mean they've got to be a little German family, haven't they? After all they're German, aren't they? So. Yes, they're all fine, thank goodness. Fine. He said to tell you all 'Grusse' — that's the German for — for 'regards' — 'salutations' — oh, he's a very intelligent young man; very independent; very self-contained. I really must make one more big effort with my German.

JUDITH Time we cleared this mess up.

CASIMIR No, no; not yet. I've a great treat for all of you — Anna's tape.

ALICE I forgot about that.

CASIMIR Could you all gather round and I'll play the tape Anna sent me last Christmas. Messages for everybody! A real, real treat!

WILLIE Maybe I should go and leave yous to —

CASIMIR Go? For heaven's sake! I'd be deeply offended if you left. And so would Anna.

He begins to arrange the seats in a wide arc facing out. The others help him and begin picking up the remains of the picnic. As they do this work the following passages overlap:

JUDITH (*To* CLAIRE) What tape is this?

CLAIRE I don't know. Never heard of it.

ALICE (*To* WILLIE) How did it go?

WILLIE What?

ALICE That mad game you were playing.

WILLIE I won.

ALICE How do you know when you lose?

CASIMIR Would you sit here, Eamon?

EAMON Anywhere you like.

CASIMIR Splendid. Where's Tom?

JUDITH Gone to do some packing. He said thank you for the lunch.

CASIMIR I don't suppose he'd be very interested. (*As he switches tapes*) Disposing of you temporarily, Claire. But don't worry — we'll reinstate you.

> *Everyone is in position.* CASIMIR *stands before them, the cassette in his hand. He is happy to be master of ceremonies.*

Good. Fine. Splendid. Are we all settled? Well, before I begin, may I explain to our guest here —

CLAIRE Who's the guest?

ALICE I'm the guest.

CASIMIR Willie's our guest — and a very welcome guest he is, too. (ALICE *claps*) And I just wish to explain to him that little Anna joined the convent twenty years ago, when she was only seventeen —

ALICE Eighteen.

CASIMIR — and that apart from one visit home she's been in Africa ever since; so that her knowledge of our lives is perhaps slightly — hasn't kept pace perhaps with the way —

ALICE For God's sake just play it, Casimir.

CASIMIR Yes. Ah. Yes. Play it. Indeed I —

JUDITH Shhhhh!

CLAIRE What?

JUDITH Listen! (*They all listen for a moment*) Sorry. Thought I heard Father. Go ahead.

CASIMIR Should I get Uncle George out?

ALICE Casimir!

CASIMIR Sorry — sorry — no point at all, is there? Yes. Are we all ready? Splendid. Sister John Henry. Little Anna.

He places the cassette player on the lawn and switches it on. ANNA's voice is a child's voice. She speaks slowly and distinctly as if she were reading from a school book.

ANNA Hello Daddy and Judith and Alice and Casimir and little Claire.

ALICE Hello, Anna.

ANNA This is Anna speaking to you all the way from St Joseph's mission in Kuala in Zambia. I hope you are all together when this is being played because I am imagining you all sitting before a big log fire in the drawing room — Daddy spread out and enjoying his well-earned relaxation after his strenuous day in court and the rest of you sitting on the rug or around the Christmas tree in the north window.

ALICE has been trying to attract CLAIRE's attention — she wants her glass refilled, but CLAIRE does not notice her. Finally, she has to whisper:

ALICE Claire.

CASIMIR Shhh.

ALICE Just a drop.

CLAIRE fills the glass.

ANNA How are you all? May I wish each and every one of you — and you, too, dear Nanny — are you there, Nanny?

ALICE Sorry, Sister.

ANNA — may I wish you all a holy and happy Christmas and all of God's peace and content for the new year.

ALICE Amen.

ANNA Later in the tape Reverend Mother who is here beside me will say a few words to you and after that you will hear my school choir singing some Irish songs that I have taught them —

ALICE God!

ANNA — and some African songs they have taught me.

ALICE Good God!

ANNA I hope you will enjoy them. But first I wish to speak to my own dear Daddy. How are you, Daddy? I ought to be cross with you for never writing to me but I know how busy you always are providing for us, and Judith tells me in her letters that you are in very good health. So thank God for that.

> FATHER *enters the study. An emaciated man; eyes distraught; one arm limp; his mouth pulled down at one corner. A grotesque and frightening figure. He is dressed only in pyjamas. The tops are buttoned wrongly and hang off his shoulders; the bottoms about to slip off his waist. He moves very slowly — one step at a time — through the study. He is trying to locate where* ANNA's *voice is coming from — his distraught eyes are rolling round the room. When he speaks his voice is barely audible.*

FATHER Anna?

ANNA But before I go any further, I'm going to play the violin for you — a little piece you always liked me to play for you: 'The Gartan Mother's Lullaby'. Do you remember it?

FATHER (*Slightly louder*) Anna?

ANNA So this is my Christmas present to you, my dear Daddy. I hope you like it.

> *She plays a few bars of the music — the playing of a child. Now* FATHER *is almost at the study door. He raises his head and emits an almost-animal roar.*

FATHER Annaaaaaaaaaaaa!

The listeners outside do not react for a second. Then
they panic. ALICE *grabs the machine to switch it off —*
and instead turns the volume up so that the tape's
scream and FATHER's *roar overlap for a few seconds.*
They all leap to their feet — chairs are overturned —
but seem to be incapable of action. CASIMIR *is on his*
knees, transfixed, immobile. CLAIRE *is on the point of*
hysteria. FATHER's *roar stops. Saliva is dribbling from*
his mouth. He begins to sink to the ground. EAMON,
who is furthest away from him, is the first to move.
He runs to FATHER *and catches him as he collapses so*
that they both sink to the ground together. Now the
tape is silenced.

    EAMON *screams at the others — screams as if his*
own life depended on it.

EAMON Doctor! Call the doctor! For Christ's sake, will someone
call the doctor!

    Blackout.

ACT THREE

Early afternoon two days later. The seats and deckchairs as before.
EAMON *is sitting on the step.* TOM *is changing the film in his camera.* CASIMIR, *his hands behind his back, is restlessly pacing round the perimeter of the tennis court. All three are dressed in lounge suits — they have recently returned from Father's funeral.*
We can hear CLAIRE *playing the piano — Sonata No.2 in B minor, Op.35, middle section of third movement (i.e. portion between 'Dead March' statements — omit 'Dead March'). It will be necessary to repeat this music which runs up to the entrance of* ALICE *and* JUDITH.

CASIMIR (*Pacing*) He was by no means a skilful tennis player, Father, but oh my goodness he was very consistent and very determined. (*Halts*) Alice and I would be over there and he would be here. And before he served he always went through a long ritual of placing his toe precisely on the edge of the line (*he demonstrates*), moving it and adjusting it for maybe twenty seconds until he had it exactly where he wanted it — as if the whole game depended on the exact placing of his toe. (*Paces again*) And of course this always sent Alice and me into fits of secret giggling, so that when he finally did serve, we were never able to return the ball and so he thought he was a much better player than he really was! Yes. Wonderful, wasn't it? (*Halts*) Oh but God help you if he caught you laughing — oh-ho-ho-ho. (*Paces again*) Just about this time we should all have been sitting down at the wedding reception (*looks at watch*) — yes, just about now. Funny, isn't it? The Minor Sonata — that was Grandfather O'Donnell's favourite. Probably because he actually heard Chopin play it.
TOM Who heard Chopin?

CASIMIR Grandfather. Haven't I told you that story?

TOM No.

CASIMIR *comes downstage.*

CASIMIR Oh, yes. At a party in Vienna — a birthday party for Balzac. Everybody was there: Liszt and George Sand and Turgenev and Mendelssohn and the young Wagner and Berlioz and Delacroix and Verdi — and of course Balzac. Everybody. It went on for days. God knows why Grandfather was there — probably gatecrashed. Anyhow that's what Chopin played.

TOM Your grandfather, Casimir?

CASIMIR Grandfather O'Donnell; a great traveller; Europe every year.

TOM But he wouldn't have been a contemporary of these people, would he?

CASIMIR Would he not?

TOM You must mean your great-grandfather, don't you?

CASIMIR Do I? Great-grandfather O'Donnell then. Yes, you're right: he lived in Europe for six months one time to escape the fever that followed the famine here. A party in Vienna. The expression became part of the family language: anything great and romantic and exciting that had happened in the past or might happen in the future, we called it 'a party in Vienna' — yes. Very beautiful, isn't it? And there was another detail about that party: Chopin was playing that sonata and Balzac began to sing it and Grandfather told Balzac to shut up and Chopin said, 'Bravo, Irishman! Bravo!' Grandfather, of course, was thrilled. Isn't it beautiful, Eamon?

EAMON Yes.

CASIMIR (*Pacing again*) Chopin died in Paris, you know, and when they were burying him they sprinkled Polish soil on his grave. (*Pause*) Because he was Polish. Did you notice how she went straight to the piano the moment we came back? Like a homing instinct; yes. I often wonder how far she might have gone if Father hadn't thwarted her. Oh, I'm afraid he was more than naughty about that; oh, yes. Oh, I'm afraid he was adept at stifling things. I'm grateful to you for staying over, Tom.

TOM Not at all.

CASIMIR I appreciate it very much.

TOM The least I could do.

CASIMIR Is your father dead?

TOM Yeah.

CASIMIR *goes to him and very formally shakes his hand.*

CASIMIR I'm very, very sorry.

TOM Thank you.

CASIMIR It is a great loss.

TOM Indeed.

CASIMIR When did he die?

TOM When I was three months old.

CASIMIR Good Lord.

He begins pacing again.

TOM A few details, Casimir; perhaps you could help me with them?

CASIMIR Yes?

TOM You mentioned that your mother played the piano — (*producing notebook*) — where are we? — Yeah — you talked about her playing a waltz at bedtime.

CASIMIR The E sharp major — oh, yes, that's *my* favourite; that's easily my favourite.

TOM You're sure about that?

CASIMIR That The Bedtime's the E sharp major? Oh, I'm —

TOM No, no; that your mother did play the piano.

CASIMIR *halts.*

Just that I inferred from something Judith said in passing that your mother did not in fact play.

CASIMIR Judith said that?

TOM   What I understood was —

CASIMIR   You must have taken her up wrong, Tom. Oh, yes, Mother was a splendid pianist. By no means as talented as little Claire; but very competent. And a lovely singer. Oh, yes. Her favourite piece was a song called 'Sweet Alice'. And Father hated it — hated it. 'Rubbish,' he called it. 'Vulgar rubbish.' So that she never sang it when he was around. Oh, yes, she had lots of songs like that from her childhood. Do you know that song, Eamon?

EAMON   (*Sings*) 'Do you remember — '

CASIMIR *joins him.*

'— Sweet Alice, Ben Bolt?
Sweet Alice with hair so brown?'

CASIMIR   That's it — that's it! It's not insensitive of us to sing just after Father's funeral, is it? Ha-ha. Anyway. I remember when she'd sing 'Sweet Alice' she seemed to become very, very young again and very, very beautiful, as if the song restored to her something she had lost, something that had withered in her — Oh, yes, she was a very talented pianist.

TOM   I'm sure I misunderstood Judith. It's of no importance. I'll check it again. And the other query was —

He consults his notebook again; hesitates; decides not to pursue the enquiry; closes the book and puts it in his pocket.

Yeah; that's OK; that can wait, too. No more problems.

CASIMIR   What was the other query?

TOM   Question mark after Yeats; that's all.

CASIMIR   What about him?

TOM   Just that you said you remember him sitting in —

CASIMIR   Oh my goodness yes; oh, he was just tremendous, Yeats, with those cold, cold eyes of his. Oh, yes, I remember Yeats vividly.

TOM Sure.

CASIMIR What's the question mark for?

TOM It's of no significance. I think I got myself a little confused here, too. Doesn't matter.

CASIMIR What's the confusion?

The music stops. TOM *produces his notebook again.*

TOM Well, you were born on April 1, 1939.

CASIMIR Good heavens — don't I know! All Fools' Day! Yes?

TOM And Yeats died the same year. Two months earlier. I've double-checked it. (*He looks up from his notes.* CASIMIR *is staring at him. Pause*) I make little mistakes like that all the time myself. My mother worked for the Bell Telephone Company and until I went to High School I thought she worked for a Mr Bell who was my uncle for God's sake — It's a natural misunderstanding, that's all — I mean a man like Yeats is a visitor to your home, a friend of the family, you hear a lot of talk about him, and naturally after a time, naturally you come to think you actually — I've some correspondence to catch up with. Forgive me.

He goes into the study and off. CASIMIR *grimaces at* EAMON.

CASIMIR Ha-ha. It was very kind of Tom to stay over. I appreciate that very much. (*Begins pacing again*) Father would have been so pleased by that funeral today — no, not pleased — gratified, immensely gratified. The packed chapel; the music; that young curate's fine, generous panegyric, and he didn't know Father at all, Judith says. Then down through the village street — his village, his Ballybeg — that's how he thought of it, you know, and in a sense it was his village. Did you know that it used to be called O'Donnellstown? Yes, years and years ago. How simple it all was this time, wasn't it? You remember Mother's funeral, don't you? — all that furtiveness, all that whispering, all those half-

truths. We didn't know until the very last minute
would they allow her a Christian burial at all because
of the circumstances — remember? But today it was
— today was almost — festive by comparison, wasn't
it? Every shop shut and every blind drawn; and men
kneeling on their caps as the hearse passed; and
Nanny sobbing her heart out when the coffin was
being lowered — did you see her? — of course you
did — you were beside her. All that happened, didn't
it, Eamon? All that happened? Oh, yes, he would have
been so gratified.

EAMON There are certain things, certain truths, Casimir, that
are beyond Tom's kind of scrutiny.

The same sonata music begins again.

CASIMIR Oh, there are. Oh, yes, there are — aren't there? Yes —
yes. I discovered a great truth when I was nine. No,
not a great truth; but I made a great discovery when I
was nine — not even a great discovery but an important, a very important discovery for me. I suddenly
realized I was different from other boys. When I say I
was different I don't mean — you know — good Lord
I don't for a second mean I was — you know — as they
say nowadays 'homo sexual' — good heavens I must
admit, if anything, Eamon, if anything I'm — (*looks
around*) — I'm vigorously hetero sexual ha-ha. But of
course I don't mean that either. No, no. But anyway.
What I discovered was that for some reason people
found me — peculiar. Of course I sensed it first from
the boys at boarding school. But it was Father with his
usual — his usual directness and honesty who made
me face it. I remember the day he said to me: 'Had you
been born down there' — we were in the library and
he pointed down to Ballybeg — 'Had you been born
down there, you'd have become the village idiot. For-
tunately for you, you were born here and we can
absorb you.' Ha-ha. So at nine years of age I knew certain things: that certain kinds of people laughed at me;

that the easy relationships that other men enjoy would always elude me; that — that — that I would never succeed in life, whatever — you know — whatever 'succeed' means —

EAMON Casimir —

CASIMIR No, no, please. That was a very important and a very difficult discovery for me, as you can imagine. But it brought certain recognitions, certain compensatory recognitions. Because once I recognized — once I acknowledged that the larger areas were not accessible to me, I discovered — I had to discover smaller, much smaller areas that were. Yes, indeed. And I discovered that if I conduct myself with some circumspection, I find that I can live within these smaller, perhaps very confined territories without exposure to too much hurt. Indeed I find that I can experience some happiness and perhaps give a measure of happiness, too. My great discovery. Isn't it so beautiful? (*Music*) Somehow the Hall doesn't exist without him. (*He begins pacing again*) We must have a talk sometime, Eamon.

EAMON Yes.

CASIMIR I don't think we ever had a talk, you and I, had we?

EAMON I don't think so.

CASIMIR I'd really like to talk to you because I think you — I think you understand — (*he gestures towards the house*) — what it has done to all of us.

EAMON I don't know about that.

CASIMIR Oh, yes, you do. I know you do. And you would tell me about your work and about London and I would tell you about my boys and about Hamburg. Will you, Eamon, please?

EAMON Of course.

CASIMIR Good. Great. Next time we meet. We even have our agenda all ready, haven't we? When I went up to see him the evening I arrived — was it only two days ago? — I stood looking down at him and I remembered a poem called 'My Father, Dying', and the last lines go:
    'But on any one
    of these nights soon,

for you, the dark will not crack with dawn,
and then I will begin
with you that hesitant conversation
going on and on and on.'
Something disquieting about that line 'going on and
on and on', isn't there? Ha-ha.

> JUDITH *and* ALICE *enter.* CASIMIR *resumes pacing.*
> JUDITH *in a dark dress and carrying Alice's case.* ALICE
> *with coat and handbag. They deposit these things in*
> *the study.*

ALICE   Thanks. Just leave it there.
JUDITH   When's your bus?
ALICE   We've another fifteen or twenty minutes yet.
JUDITH   Willie'll be here. He said he'll run you down.
ALICE   That'd be handy.

> *They both come out to the lawn.*

There's tea in there if you want it.
EAMON   None for me.
ALICE   Casimir?
CASIMIR   Not at the moment, thank you.
JUDITH   Did you get your flight fixed up?
CASIMIR   Mrs Moore did all the phoning, made all the arrangements. She was wonderful.
JUDITH   Does Helga know?
CASIMIR   I sent her a telegram. I should be home at midnight.

> EAMON *touches* ALICE*'s cheek with his index finger.*

EAMON   It's healed.
ALICE   Is it?
EAMON   Almost.
ALICE   I heal quickly.
EAMON   Sorry.
ALICE   I've packed your things.
EAMON   Thanks.

ALICE Have you the tickets?

He taps his jacket pocket.

I'll be glad to be home, if it's only to get a sleep. (*Aloud*)
Tom hasn't left yet, has he?
JUDITH He's in the library; some dates he wants to check
again.
EAMON 'Check', 'recheck', 'double-check', 'cross-check'.
JUDITH He's talking about waiting over until the morning.
EAMON Wasn't he lucky to be here for Father's death? I
suppose he'll interpret that as 'the end of an epoch'.
JUDITH Isn't it?
EAMON Is it?
CASIMIR He's from Chicago, he tells me. And I suspect he may
be a very wealthy man: his uncle owns the Bell Tele-
phone Company.
EAMON He should never have been let set foot here.
JUDITH He asked my permission.
EAMON To pry?
JUDITH To chronicle.
EAMON Ah.
JUDITH To record the truth.
EAMON Better still. And you said, 'Go ahead, stranger.'
JUDITH Is there something to hide?

EAMON *spreads his hands.*

Besides — it's my home.

Brief pause. Then quickly:

ALICE It wasn't exactly the biggest funeral ever seen in Ballybeg, was it?
CASIMIR Did you notice — the whole village closed down.
ALICE For the minute it took the hearse to pass through. And
as Sister Thérèse would say: 'The multitude in the
church was a little empty, too.'
CASIMIR I thought the Requiem Mass very moving.

ALICE Until Miss Quirk cut loose. For God's sake, did nobody tell her it wasn't the wedding?

JUDITH She would have played anyway.

ALICE But maybe not 'This Is My Lovely Day'. Or is that one of the two pieces?

JUDITH You might have got 'Bless This House'.

ALICE Father would not have been amused. Casimir, will you please stop prowling around?

CASIMIR Oh. Sorry — sorry.

He sits — as if he were about to take off again.

ALICE Who was the man standing just behind Willie at the graveside? — Glasses, pasty-looking, plump, bald. I noticed him in the chapel, too; in the front pew on the men's side.

EAMON Jerry.

ALICE Who?

EAMON Jerry McLaughlin.

ALICE Who's Jerry Mc — ? Not — !

EAMON *nods.*

For God's sake! But that man could be her father, Judith!

JUDITH Easy.

The music stops suddenly. Silence.

ALICE She couldn't have heard me, could she?

CLAIRE Casimir!

CASIMIR Hello-hello.

CLAIRE What's the name of this?

ALICE (*Relieved*) God.

CASIMIR *leaps up.*

CASIMIR A test! She's testing me again! (*Shouts*) Go ahead! I'm ready! I'm waiting!

He moves upstage and stands poised, waiting. His eyes are shut tight, etc, etc, as before. The music is the Ballade in A flat major, Op.47.

ALICE   You never told me he was like that.

JUDITH   Like what?

ALICE   That's an elderly man. (*To* EAMON) Did you know he was like that?

CASIMIR   Good Lord — good Lord — good Lord — good Lord —

ALICE   She's only — what? — twenty-seven? Twenty-eight?

CASIMIR   I know it — I know it so well — but what is it? — What *is* it? —

ALICE   Thank God the wedding's postponed for three months. Maybe she'll come to her senses in the meantime. How could the poor child marry a man like that, for God's sake?

JUDITH   I've no idea. (*Rises*) There are some things we've got to get settled before you all leave. (*Shouts*) Claire, could you come out for a few minutes?

ALICE   So that's Jerry McLaughlin.

EAMON   He looks older than he is.

JUDITH   Claire!

ALICE   Oh dear, dear, dear, dear, dear.

The music stops. CASIMIR *comes downstage.*

CASIMIR   (*To* EAMON) It's a sonata — a sonata — I know that — either 58 or 59 — but which? Which?

EAMON   Don't ask me.

ALICE   (*To* EAMON) What age is he?

CASIMIR   Oh, Lord, I should know. Alice?

ALICE   What?

CASIMIR   58 or 59?

ALICE   Is he serious?

CASIMIR   59 — that's my guess.

ALICE   He's right.

CASIMIR   Am I?

ALICE   He must be that. Oh, the poor baby!

CLAIRE *enters — she is not wearing mourning clothes.*
ALICE *studies her face with anxious compassion.*

CLAIRE (*To* CASIMIR) Well?
CASIMIR It's a sonata.
CLAIRE Is it?
CASIMIR Isn't it?
ALICE Claire darling, that was just beautiful playing.
CLAIRE Thanks.
CASIMIR Yes; it's a sonata.
CLAIRE So you've said.
CASIMIR Is it not?
ALICE Would you like to sit here, facing the sun?
CLAIRE I'm fine. (*To* CASIMIR) You don't know!
JUDITH Please, everybody —
CASIMIR And it's either — and I'm not absolutely certain —
CLAIRE You don't know!
JUDITH Claire —
CASIMIR It's either the —
JUDITH May I — ?
CASIMIR 58 — right?
JUDITH Please may I speak?
CLAIRE (*Whispers*) Wrong.
CASIMIR (*Whispers*) 59?
JUDITH Could I have a moment now that we're all here?
CASIMIR Sorry — sorry. I beg your pardon, Judith.
CLAIRE (*Whispers*) Completely wrong.
JUDITH We haven't got all that much time. (*To* CASIMIR) Here's a seat.

He sits. CLAIRE *grins at him behind* JUDITH's *back. He signals another answer. She rejects this, too. He is deflated.* ALICE *has not taken her eyes off* CLAIRE. *Now she goes to her.*

ALICE I got a glimpse of you coming down the aisle this morning and I had a sudden memory of you coming down on the morning of your First Communion; and you looked exactly the same as you did then — not one day older — a beautiful little innocent child. Hasn't changed a bit, has she? (*She looks round for confirmation; but everyone is silent and waiting*) What's wrong?

JUDITH I would like to talk about what's to happen now that Father's gone — before you all leave.

ALICE Sorry. Sorry. Of course. Go ahead.

JUDITH I know he has left everything to the four of us — the house, the furnishings, the land. And the question is: what are we going to do?

ALICE Well, as far as I'm concerned, my home's in London, Casimir's is in Hamburg, and this house is yours and Claire's. (*To* CASIMIR) Isn't that right?

CASIMIR Oh, yes; oh, yes, indeed.

ALICE Naturally we'll come back now and again. But the Hall must be your home. So the next time we're here we'll sign over to you whatever our share is — or better still have the papers drawn up and sent to us. The important thing is to have it all formal. (*To* CASIMIR) Don't you agree?

CASIMIR I —

ALICE (*To* JUDITH) I see no problem.

EAMON What has Casimir to say?

CASIMIR Me? Oh, yes, Alice is right, absolutely right. I mean I would hope to bring the boys over sometime for a holiday — a short holiday — if I may. But I would be really happy for you to have it all, Judith — and Claire — oh, yes, very happy. You deserve it. It should be yours. It must be yours. Oh, yes.

ALICE So. We're all agreed.

CASIMIR One small thing: would it be possible — would you mind very much if I took that photo of Mother in the silver frame — a keepsake, you know —

ALICE That's the one on the drawing-room mantelpiece?

CASIMIR Yes. It's really very small. But I would — I would really cherish that. If I may.

ALICE And the sooner the place is in your names the better — before we all have a big row some day! And that's that. All settled. (*To* EAMON) Do we need to keep an eye on the time?

EAMON Judith has other ideas I think.

ALICE Have you? What ideas?

JUDITH Owning the place, going on living here — it's not as simple as it looks. In fact it's impossible.

ALICE Why?

JUDITH We can't afford it. You've forgotten — no, you've never known — the finances of this place. For the past seven years we've lived on Father's pension. That was modest enough. And now that's gone. The only other income is from the land and Willie takes that because no one else would; but that can't continue. So that from now on there's no money coming in. Last October when the storm lifted the whole roof off the back return I tried to get an overdraft from the bank. The manager was very sympathetic but he couldn't help — actually what he said was that the house was a liability.

EAMON That's bloody —

JUDITH Then I got a dealer down from Dublin to evaluate the library and some of the furniture. He offered me seventy pounds for the grandmother clock and ninety pounds for the whole library. So eventually Willie and I put up polythene sheets and nailed them to the rafters. And the floor in the morning room has collapsed with dry rot — haven't you seen it? — and every time there's heavy rain, we have to distribute — (*to* CLAIRE) how many is it? — seventeen buckets in the upstairs rooms to catch the water. And the only fire we had all last winter was in Father's bedroom. And on a day like this it looks so beautiful, doesn't it?

Short pause.

ALICE Judith, God forgive us, we never for a second suspected —

JUDITH That's just one side of the story.

ALICE Oh but we can all help. We must. None of us is wealthy but the very least we can do is —

JUDITH So there's no point in signing the place over to us —

well, over to me. I'm not going to go on living here. Maybe Claire —

CLAIRE I'm getting out, too, amn't I? I'm getting married, amn't I?

ALICE (*To* JUDITH) Where will you go? What will you do?

JUDITH The first thing I'm going to do is take the baby out of the orphanage.

ALICE Of course. Yes.

JUDITH 'The baby' — he's seven now. (*To* CASIMIR) Do you know he's two days younger than your Heinrich? Where I'll go I haven't made up my mind yet. Willie has a mobile home just outside Bundoran. He has a lot of slot-machines around that area and he wants me to go there with him.

ALICE That would be —

JUDITH But he doesn't want the baby. So that settles that. Anyhow I've got to earn a living somehow. But the only reason I brought all this up is — what's to become of Uncle George?

EAMON What you're saying is that after Claire's wedding — if you can wait that length — you're going to turn the key in the door and abandon Ballybeg Hall?

JUDITH I'm asking —

EAMON You know what will happen, don't you? The moment you've left the thugs from the village will move in and loot and ravage the place within a couple of hours. Is that what you're proposing? Oh, your piety is admirable.

JUDITH I'm asking what's to become of Uncle George.

EAMON Judith's like her American friend: the Hall can be assessed in terms of roofs and floors and overdrafts.

ALICE Eamon —

EAMON No, no; that's all it means to her. Well I know its real worth — in this area, in this county, in this country. And Alice knows. And Casimir knows. And Claire knows. And somehow we'll keep it going. Somehow we'll keep it going. Somehow we'll —

ALICE Please, Eamon.

JUDITH *breaks down. Pause.*

EAMON Sorry — sorry — sorry again — Seems to be a day of public contrition. What the hell is it but crumbling masonry. Sorry. (*Short laugh*) Don't you know that all that is fawning and forelock-touching and Paddy and shabby and greasy peasant in the Irish character finds a house like this irresistible? That's why we were ideal for colonizing. Something in us needs this — aspiration. Don't despise us — we're only hedgehogs, Judith. Sorry.

He goes to the gazebo.

ALICE He hates going back to London. He hates the job. (*Pause*) What is there to say? There's nothing to say, is there?

JUDITH No.

Silence. CLAIRE *rises and crosses the lawn. As she passes* CASIMIR:

CLAIRE A ballade.
CASIMIR Sorry?
CLAIRE Ballade A flat major.
CASIMIR (*Indifferently*) Ah. Was it really? No, I'd never have got that. There you are. Never.

He gets up and begins his pacing. Pause.

ALICE So the baby's seven now?
JUDITH Eight next month.
ALICE The woman in the flat above us has a little girl. She comes in to us every evening after school. Eamon buys her sweets. She's devoted to him. He's great with children.
JUDITH Yes?
ALICE Avril. Avril Harper. Lovely affectionate child.
JUDITH What age is she?
ALICE She's just eight.

JUDITH   They say that's a very interesting age.
ALICE   She's a very interesting child. And a very affectionate child.

The conversation dies again. ALICE *rises.*

CASIMIR   (*To* CLAIRE) There's still some clay on your shoes.
CLAIRE   Did you notice a wreath of red and yellow roses at the foot of the grave? That was from the children I taught last winter. There were five of them and they put their pocket money together to buy it. Wasn't that kind of them? And each of them came up to me in turn and shook my hand very formally and said how sorry they were. I asked them to be sure and visit me in my new home. They said they would. I made them promise. They said they would.

Another silence.

ALICE   Are you sure Willie's coming?
JUDITH   Yes; he knows; he'll be here.
ALICE   Time enough anyway.
CASIMIR   There was a telegram from the Bishop, Judith.
JUDITH   Yes.
CASIMIR   Out on the hall table.
JUDITH   I saw it.
ALICE   What did it say?
CASIMIR   Deepest sympathy to you all and to George on your great loss — something like that.
JUDITH   We still haven't reached a decision about Uncle George.

CASIMIR *suddenly stops pacing and exclaims — almost wails — in his panic.*

CASIMIR   Oh my God!
CLAIRE   What?
CASIMIR   Oh good God!

He dashes into the study, as always tripping on the step and apologizing over his shoulder.

Sorry — sorry — I beg your —

He rushes to the phone. His sudden departure shatters the mood. EAMON *comes out of the gazebo. The others come together.*

ALICE What's wrong, Casimir?
EAMON What happened?
JUDITH Is he ill?
ALICE I don't know. He suddenly bolted.
CLAIRE Listen!
EAMON Is he sick?
CLAIRE Listen!
CASIMIR Hello? Hello? Yes, Mrs Moore, it's me again. I'm afraid. I'm a nuisance, amn't I? That telegram I sent to Germany — Yes, yes, indeed the house will be lonely — Very nice sermon, indeed; very moving — I'll tell her that; of course I will; thank you very much —
ALICE I thought he was going to be sick.
CASIMIR That telegram I sent to Germany an hour ago, Mrs Moore — has it gone? Ah. Well. That's that — No, no, I'm not complaining — oh, no — I'm delighted, thank you, absolutely delighted, thank you —

He rings off and comes outside. He is thoroughly wretched. Everybody is staring at him. He manages one of his grins.

CASIMIR Ha-ha. Oh good God.
ALICE Is something wrong?
CLAIRE What's the matter, Casimir?
CASIMIR Sent a telegram to Helga. To let her know I'd be home tonight.
ALICE And so you will.
CASIMIR Yes.
JUDITH What's wrong, Casimir?

CASIMIR Tried to cancel it but it's gone. I told you she's a great believer in that spiritualist stuff — seances, ghosts, things — I told you that, didn't I? Yes, I did. Well, you see, I've only suddenly realized what I said in the telegram. What I said was — FATHER BURIED THIS MORNING ARRIVING HAMBURG MIDNIGHT TONIGHT. Ha-ha. Oh my God.

Their sympathy for his genuine anguish prevents them from laughing outright. But CLAIRE *sniggers first — then* ALICE *— then they all collapse. And finally he joins them. Comments like 'Arriving Hamburg midnight tonight', 'I thought he was sick', 'He said "I'm absolutely delighted, Mrs Moore"', 'Poor Father in Germany'. In the middle of this release* UNCLE GEORGE *enters right in his usual manner.* ALICE *sees him first. She looks at him — then makes a sudden decision. She rushes to* EAMON.

ALICE Do me a favour, Eamon.
EAMON What?
ALICE A big favour — please?
EAMON What is it?
ALICE Uncle George — let us take him.
EAMON To London?
ALICE Please, Eamon.
EAMON He wouldn't come.
ALICE Let me try. Please.
EAMON Would he come?
ALICE (*Calls*) Uncle George!

He stops just as he is about to make his retreat. She goes to him.

I want you to come to London with Eamon and me. You wouldn't have to talk. You wouldn't ever have to say a word. But you'd be great company for me, just being there. I wouldn't be lonely if you were there with me.

ALICE *reaches forward to catch his hand but withdraws again. Long pause.*

GEORGE Haven't been in London since the year nineteen and ten; to be precise the week Edward the Seventh died. Saw it all. That's what *I* call a funeral.

ALICE Will you come? Please.

Short pause.

GEORGE Another visit's about due, I suppose. I'll pack.

He marches off the way he came.

ALICE Thank you, Uncle George — thank you. (*Elated, to* EAMON) He's coming! (*To all*) He's coming with us to London! Do you mind?

EAMON Where will he sleep?

ALICE On the divan — anywhere — he won't mind — he never cared about his comfort. You're sure you don't mind?

EAMON He'll be *my* keepsake.

WILLIE *enters through the study.*

WILLIE Sorry I'm a bit late. Who needs a lift down to the bus?

ALICE Thanks, Willie. I suppose we should start moving.

CASIMIR Time enough yet, aren't we?

JUDITH Anybody feel like something to eat?

WILLIE No time for eating now.

JUDITH (*To* EAMON) A cup of tea?

EAMON No thanks.

JUDITH A drink?

EAMON Nothing.

ALICE How long a delay have you in London before your Hamburg flight?

CASIMIR An hour and a half.

ALICE We'll stay with you at the airport and eat there.

JUDITH (*To* WILLIE) Uncle George is going with Alice and

Eamon.

WILLIE Going where?

JUDITH London.

WILLIE You're joking me. Are you serious?

JUDITH Yes.

WILLIE Jaysus, he'll fair keep London in chat.

> *They are all seated again:* CLAIRE *close to* CASIMIR;
> WILLIE *beside* JUDITH; EAMON *on the ground at* ALICE'S
> *feet, his head resting against her leg; the three couples
> spread across the lawn. There is an unspoken wish to
> protract time, to postpone the final breaking up.*
> CASIMIR *picks up the cassette.*

CASIMIR What'll it be?

CLAIRE Your pleasure.

CASIMIR My pleasure — right.

CLAIRE But not a test.

CASIMIR Not a test; no more tests; just my pleasure.

> *Pause.*

WILLIE They gave him a nice enough wee send off, didn't
they?

JUDITH Yes.

WILLIE I was up in court before him once — did I ever tell you
that one?

JUDITH What was that?

WILLIE First car I ever had. No tax, no insurance, no licence,
no brakes, no nothing — buck all except that the damn
thing kind of went. Jaysus. And I mind I swore a pack
of lies to him.

JUDITH Were you fined?

WILLIE Let me off with a caution! He must have believed me.
No, he didn't. Knew damn well I was a liar. He just
pretended he believed me. Jaysus, he was a strange
bird. How are you?

JUDITH Slight headache. It's nothing.

WILLIE I thought so — I was watching you in the chapel.

354

Here.

JUDITH What's that?

WILLIE Aspirin. Got them on the way up.

JUDITH Thanks. I'll take them later.

'The Bedtime Waltz' on the cassette.

WILLIE I don't want to hustle yous; but if you're getting the 3.30 you'd need to start moving.

Nobody hears him.

CASIMIR You're too young to remember Mother singing that.

CLAIRE Am I?

CASIMIR Oh, yes; much too young.

CLAIRE I think I remember her — I'm not sure. You'll come back again for my wedding, won't you?

CASIMIR Wouldn't miss it for all the world. Three months time, isn't it?

CLAIRE I wish it were tomorrow. I would love it would be tomorrow.

CASIMIR Three months? Oh my goodness three months'll fly — just fly. We'll all be back again before you know. What's three months? Three months is nothing, nothing, nothing.

Brief pause.

ALICE What are you thinking?

EAMON That in a way it's as difficult for me as it is for you.

ALICE What is?

EAMON Leaving; leaving for good. I know it's your home. But in a sense it has always been my home, too, because of Granny and then because of you.

ALICE I don't know what I feel. Maybe a sense of release; of not being pursued; of the possibility of — (*short pause*) — of 'fulfilment'. No. Just emptiness. Perhaps maybe a new start. Yes, I'll manage.

EAMON Because you're of that tradition.

ALICE What tradition?

EAMON Of discipline; of self-discipline — residual aristocratic instincts.

ALICE I'm the alcoholic, remember.

EAMON So was Uncle George — once.

ALICE You and Judith always fight.

EAMON No, we don't. When did you discover that?

ALICE I've always known it. And I think it's because you love her. I think it's because you think you love her; and that's the same thing. No, it's even more disturbing for you. And that's why I'm not unhappy that this is all over — because love is possible only in certain contexts. And now that this is finished you may become less unhappy in time.

EAMON Have we a context?

ALICE Let's wait and see.

WILLIE Does nobody want to catch this bus?

JUDITH Don't worry, Willie. They'll make it.

> CASIMIR *has been humming with the cassette. Now he stops.*

CASIMIR What you must all do — what you must all do very soon — is come to Hamburg for a holiday! Helga and I have some wonderful friends you'll enjoy meeting — novelists, poets, painters, musicians! — marvellous people! — and we'll have a great reunion of the whole family! It will be like old times! Everybody'll come next summer! Next summer in Hamburg!

EAMON A party in Vienna.

CASIMIR Yes, yes, yes indeed, Eamon! Exactly! That's what it'll be — a party in Vienna!

> CLAIRE *switches off the cassette player.*

CLAIRE (*Calmly*) I'm suddenly sick of Chopin — isn't that strange? Just suddenly sick of him. I don't think I'll ever play Chopin again.

356

Silence. Then EAMON *begins to sing softly.*

EAMON 'Oh don't you remember Sweet Alice, Ben Bolt — '
WILLIE I'm telling you, Eamon, that aul' bus isn't going to
wait for you, you know.
ALICE 'Sweet Alice with hair so brown — '

EAMON *and* ALICE *sing together.*

'She wept with delight when you gave her a smile
And trembled with fear at your frown — '

While they are singing the line above:

JUDITH I keep thinking I hear sounds from that speaker.

WILLIE *begins to rise.*

WILLIE I'll take it down now.
JUDITH Don't touch it! (*Softer*) Not just now. Not just at this
moment.

CASIMIR *has walked round to* EAMON *and* ALICE *and
sings with them. All three:*

'In the old church yard in the valley, Ben Bolt
In a corner obscure and alone
They have fitted a slab of granite so grey
And Sweet Alice lies under the stone — '

While they are singing, UNCLE GEORGE *has entered the
study. He puts his small case on the ground and his
coat across a chair and sits with his hands on his lap.
He has all the patience in the world.*

As he sings CASIMIR *glances over the house.* CLAIRE
*begins to hum. One has the impression that this after-
noon — easy, relaxed, relaxing — may go on indefi-
nitely.*

357

WILLIE	I'm telling you — they're going to miss it!
JUDITH	No, they won't.
WILLIE	They're cutting it close then. Jaysus they're cutting it very close.
SINGERS	'They have fitted a slab of granite so grey
	And Sweet Alice lies under the stone — '

Before the song ends bring the lights down slowly to dark.

FAITH
HEALER

Characters

FRANK

GRACE

TEDDY

Note

Stage directions have been kept to a minimum. In all four parts the director will decide when and where the monologuist sits, walks, stands etc.

Faith Healer was first produced at the Longacre Theatre, New York, on 5 April 1979, with the following cast:

FRANK   James Mason
GRACE   Clarissa Kaye
TEDDY   Donal Donnelly

Directed by   Jose Quintero

Faith Healer was first produced at the Abbey Theatre, Dublin, on 28 August 1980, with the following cast:

FRANK   Donal McCann
GRACE   Kate Flynn
TEDDY   John Kavanagh

Directed by   Joe Dowling
Set and costumes by   Wendy Shea

for Anne again

PART ONE

Frank

The stage is in darkness. Brief pause.

Then out of this darkness comes FRANK's *incantation, 'Aberarder, Aberayron . . .' At the end of the second line bring up lights very slowly, first around him and then gradually on the whole set. Throughout this opening incantation he is standing downstage left, feet together, his face tilted upwards, his eyes shut tight, his hands in his overcoat pockets, his shoulders hunched.*

He is middle-aged; grey or greying; pale, lined face. The overcoat is unbuttoned, the collar up at the back; either navy or black, and of heavy nap material; a good coat once but now shabby, stained, slept-in. Underneath he is wearing a dark suit that is polished with use; narrow across the shoulders; sleeves and legs too short. A soiled white shirt. A creased tie. Vivid green socks.

Three rows of chairs — not more than fifteen seats in all — occupy one third of the acting area stage left. These seats are at right angles to the audience.

On the backdrop is a large poster:

THE FANTASTIC FRANCIS HARDY

FAITH HEALER

ONE NIGHT ONLY

This poster is made of some fabric, linen perhaps, and is soiled and abused.

FRANK (*Eyes closed*) Aberarder, Aberayron,
      Llangranog, Llangurig,
      Abergorlech, Abergynolwyn,
      Llandefeilog, Llanerchymedd,
      Aberhosan, Aberporth . . .

All those dying Welsh villages. (*Eyes open*) I'd get so tense before a performance, d'you know what I used to do? As we drove along those narrow, winding roads I'd recite the names to myself just for the mesmerism, the sedation, of the incantation —

Kinlochbervie, Inverbervie,
Inverdruie, Invergordon,
Badachroo, Kinlochewe,
Ballantrae, Inverkeithing,
Cawdor, Kirkconnel,
Plaidy, Kirkinner . . .

Welsh — Scottish — over the years they became indistinguishable. The kirks or meeting houses or schools — all identical, all derelict. Maybe in a corner a withered sheaf of wheat from a harvest thanksgiving of years ago or a fragment of a Christmas decoration across a window — relics of abandoned rituals. Because the people we moved among were beyond that kind of celebration.

Hardly ever cities or towns because the halls were far too dear for us. Seldom England because Teddy and Gracie were English and they believed, God help them, that the Celtic temperament was more receptive to us. And never Ireland because of me —

I beg your pardon — *The Fantastic Francis Hardy, Faith Healer, One Night Only.* (*A slight bow*) The man on the tatty banner.

He takes off his overcoat, selects an end chair from one of the rows, and throws the coat across it. This chair and coat will be in the same position at the opening of Part Four.

When we started out — oh, years and years ago — we used to have *Francis Hardy, Seventh Son of a Seventh Son* across the top. But it made the poster too expensive and Teddy persuaded me to settle for the modest 'fantastic'. It was a favourite word of his and maybe in this case he employed it with accuracy. As for the Seventh Son — that was a lie. I was in fact the only child of elderly parents, Jack and Mary Hardy, born in the village of Kilmeedy in County Limerick where my father was sergeant of the guards. But that's another story . . .

The initials were convenient, weren't they? FH — Faith Healer. Or if you were a believer in fate, you might say my life was deter-

mined the day I was christened. Perhaps if my name had been
Charles Potter I would have been . . . Cardinal Primate; or Patsy
Muldoon, the Fantastic Prime Minister. No, I don't mock those
things. By no means. I'm not respectful but I don't mock.

Faith healer — faith healing. A craft without an apprentice-
ship, a ministry without responsibility, a vocation without a
ministry. How did I get involved? As a young man I chanced
to flirt with it and it possessed me. No, no, no, no, no — that's
rhetoric. No; let's say I did it . . . because I could do it. That's
accurate enough. And occasionally it worked — oh, yes, occasionally it *did* work. Oh, yes. And when it did, when I stood before
a man and placed my hands on him and watched him become
whole in my presence, those were nights of exultation, of con-
summation — no, not that I was doing good, giving relief,
spreading joy — good God, no, nothing at all to do with that;
but because the questions that undermined my life then became
meaningless and because I knew that for those few hours I had
become whole in myself, and perfect in myself, and in a manner
of speaking, an aristocrat, if the term doesn't offend you.

But the questionings, the questionings . . . They began
modestly enough with the pompous struttings of a young man,
Am I endowed with a unique and awesome gift? My God, yes, I'm
afraid so. And I suppose the other extreme was, *Am I a con man?*
— which of course was nonsense, I think. And between those
absurd exaggerations the possibilities were legion. Was it all
chance? — or skill? — or illusion? — or delusion? Precisely
what power did I possess? Could I summon it? When and how?
Was I its servant? Did it reside in my ability to invest someone
with faith in me or did I evoke from him a healing faith in himself? Could my healing be effected without faith? But faith in
what? — in me? — in the possibility? — faith in faith? And is
the power diminishing? You're beginning to masquerade, aren't
you? You're becoming a husk, aren't you? And so it went on
and on and on. Silly, wasn't it? Considering that nine times out
of ten nothing at all happened. But they persisted right to the
end, those nagging, tormenting, maddening questions that
rotted my life. When I refused to confront them they ambushed
me. And when they threatened to submerge me I silenced them
with whiskey. That was efficient for a while. It got me through

the job night after night. And when nothing happened or when something did happen it helped me to accept that. But I can tell you this: there was one thing I did know, one thing I always knew right from the beginning — I always knew, drunk or sober, I always knew when nothing was going to happen.

Teddy. Yes, let me tell you about Teddy, my manager. Cockney. Buoyant. Cheerful. Tiny nimble feet. Dressed in cord jacket, bow-tie, greasy velour hat. I never knew much about his background except that he had been born into show business. And I never understood why he stayed with me because we barely scraped a living. But he had a devotion to me and I think he had a vague sense of being associated with something . . . spiritual, and that gave him satisfaction. If you met him in a bar he'd hold you with those brown eyes of his. 'I've 'andled some of *the* most sensational properties in my day, dear 'eart, believe me. But I've threw 'em all up for Mr 'ardy 'ere, 'cos 'e is just the most fantastic fing you've ever seen.' And listening to him I'd almost forget what indeed he had given up to tour with us — a Miss Mulatto and Her Three Pigeons, and a languid whippet called Rob Roy who took sounds from a set of bagpipes. Humbling precedents, if I were given to pride. And he believed all along and right up to the end that somewhere one day something 'fantastic' was going to happen to us. 'Believe me, dear 'eart,' perhaps when we had barely enough petrol to take us to the next village, 'believe me, we are on the point of making a killing'. He was a romantic man. And when he talked about this killing I had a fairytale image of us being summoned to some royal bedroom and learned doctors being pushed aside and I'd raise the sleeping princess to life and we'd be wined and dined for seven days and seven nights and sent on our way with bags of sovereigns. But he was a man of many disguises. Perhaps he wasn't romantic. Perhaps he knew that's what I'd think. Perhaps he was a much more perceptive man than I knew.

And there was Grace, my mistress. A Yorkshire woman. Controlled, correct, methodical, orderly. Who fed me, washed and ironed for me, nursed me, humoured me. Saved me, I'm sure, from drinking myself to death. Would have attempted to reform me because that was her nature, but didn't because her instincts were wiser than her impulses. Grace Dodsmith from Scarbor-

ough — or was it Knaresborough? I don't remember, they all
sound so alike, it doesn't matter. She never asked for marriage
and for all her tidiness I don't think she wanted marriage —
her loyalty was adequate for her. And it was never a heady
relationship, not even in the early days. But it lasted. A surviving relationship. And yet as we grew older together I thought it
wouldn't. Because that very virtue of hers — that mulish, un-
questioning, indefatigable loyalty — settled on us like a heavy
dust. And nothing I did, neither my bitterness nor my deliberate
neglect nor my blatant unfaithfulness, could disturb it.

We'd arrive in the van, usually in the early evening. Pin up the
poster. Arrange the chairs and benches. Place a table inside the
door for the collection. Maybe sweep the place out. Gracie'd make
tea on the primus stove. Teddy'd try out his amplifying system.
I'd fortify myself with some drink. Then we'd wait. And wait. And
as soon as darkness fell a few would begin to sidle in —

Penllech, Pencader,
Dunvegan, Dunblane,
Ben Lawers, Ben Rinnes,
Kirkliston, Bennane . . .

Teddy and his amplifying system: I fought with him about
it dozens of times and finally gave in to him. Our row was over
what he called 'atmospheric background music'. When the
people would have gathered Teddy would ask them — he held
the microphone up to his lips and assumed a special, reverential
tone — he'd ask them to stay in their seats while I moved among
them. 'Everybody'll be attended to, dear 'eart. Relax. Take it easy.
And when Mr 'ardy gets to you, no need to tell 'im wot's
bovvering you — Mr 'ardy knows. Just trust 'im. Put yourself
in 'is 'ands. And God bless you all. And now, dear 'eart — Mr
'ardy, Faif 'ealer!' At which point I'd emerge — and at the same
moment Teddy'd put on his record.

And as I'd move from seat to seat, among the crippled and
the blind and the disfigured and the deaf and the barren, a voice
in the style of the thirties crooned Jerome Kern's song:

'Lovely, never, never change,
Keep that breathless charm,
Won't you please arrange it,
'Cause I love you

Just the way you look tonight.'
Yes: we were always balanced somewhere between the absurd and the momentous.

(*Moving through seats*) And the people who came — what is there to say about them? They were a despairing people. That they came to me, a mountebank, was a measure of their despair. They seldom spoke. Sometimes didn't even raise their eyes. They just sat there, very still, assuming that I divined their complaints. Abject. Abased. Tight. Longing to open themselves and at the same time fearfully herding the anguish they contained against disturbance. And they hated me — oh, yes, yes, yes, they hated me. Because by coming to me they exposed, publicly acknowledged, their desperation. And even though they told themselves they were here because of the remote possibility of a cure, they knew in their hearts they had come not to be cured but for confirmation that they were incurable; not in hope but for the elimination of hope; for the removal of that final, impossible chance — that's why they came — to seal their anguish, for the content of a finality.

And they knew that I knew. And so they defied me to endow them with hopelessness. But I couldn't do even that for them. And they knew I couldn't. A peculiar situation, wasn't it? No, not peculiar — eerie. Because occasionally, just occasionally, the miracle would happen. And then — panic — panic — panic! Their ripping apart! The explosion of their careful calculations! The sudden flooding of dreadful, hopeless hope! I often thought it would have been a kindness to them not to go near them.

And there was another thing about them. When Teddy was introducing me I would look at them and sometimes I got a strange sense that they weren't there on their own behalf at all but as delegates, *legati*, chosen because of their audacity; and that outside, poised, mute, waiting in the half-light, were hundreds of people who held their breath while we were in the locality. And I sometimes got the impression, too, that if we hadn't come to them they would have sought us out.

We were in the north of Scotland when I got word that my mother had had a heart attack. In a village called Kinlochbervie, in Sutherland, about as far north as you can go in Scotland. A picturesque little place, very quiet, very beautiful, looking

across to the Isle of Lewis in the Outer Hebrides; and we were
enjoying a few days rest there. Anyhow, when the news came
Teddy drove me down to Glasgow. Gracie wanted to come with
me and couldn't understand when I wouldn't take her. But she
used her incomprehension as fuel for her loyalty and sent me
off with a patient smile.

It was my first time home in twenty years. My father had
retired and was living in a housing estate outside Dublin. When
he opened the door he didn't recognize me — I had to tell him
who I was. Then he shook my hand as if I were an acquaintance
and led me up to the bedroom.

She was exactly as I remembered her — illness hadn't rav-
aged her. Sleeping silently. Her skin smooth and girlish, her chin
raised as if in expectation. Jesus, I thought, Oh my Jesus, what
am I going to do?

'She looks nice,' he said.

'Yes,' I said. 'She looks great.'

He cleared his throat.

'She passed away quietly. You missed her by approximately
one hour and ten minutes,' as if he were giving evidence. And
then he cried.

And I felt such overwhelming relief that when he cried I cried
easily with him.

Twelve years later I was back in Ireland again; with Teddy
and Gracie. Things had been lean for a long time. Or as Teddy
put it, 'If we want to eat, we've got to open up new territory, dear
'eart. You've cured 'em all 'ere. Come on — let's go to the lush
pickings of Ireland.' And I agreed because I was as heartsick
of Wales and Scotland as they were. And the whiskey wasn't as
efficient with the questions as it had been. And my father had
died in the meantime. And I suppose because I always knew
we would end up there. So on the last day of August we crossed
from Stranraer to Larne and drove through the night to County
Donegal. And there we got lodgings in a pub, a lounge bar really,
outside a village called Ballybeg, not far from Donegal Town.

There was no sense of homecoming. I tried to simulate it but
nothing stirred. Only a few memories, wan and neutral. One
of my father watching me through the bars of the dayroom
window as I left for school — we lived in a rented house across

the street. One of playing with handcuffs, slipping my hands in and out through the rings. One of my mother making bread and singing a hymn to herself: 'Yes, heaven, yes, heaven, yes, heaven is the prize.' And one of a group of men being shown over the barracks — I think they were inspectors from Dublin — and my father saying, 'Certainly, gentlemen, by all means, gentlemen, anything you say, gentlemen.' Maybe one or two other memories. They evoked nothing.

When we came downstairs to the lounge in the pub we got caught up in the remnants of a wedding party — four young men, locals, small farmers, whose friend had just gone off on his honeymoon a few hours earlier. Good suits. White carnations. Dark, angular faces. Thick fingers and black nails. For a while they pretended to ignore us. Then Ned, the biggest of them, asked bluntly who we were and what we were. Teddy told them. 'Dear 'eart . . . the . . . most . . . sensational . . . fantastic.' And either at the extravagance of the introduction or because of an unease, they suddenly exploded with laughter and we were embraced. We formed a big circle and drank and chatted. Gracie sang — 'Ilkley Moor'? — something like that. Teddy entertained them with tales of our tours ranging from the outrageous to the maudlin and ended with his brown eyes moist with tears: 'Dear 'earts, the insights it 'as given me into tortured 'umanity.' And I told myself that I was indeed experiencing a homecoming. All irony was suspended.

Then suddenly a man called Donal who had scarcely spoken up to this thrust a bent finger in front of my face and challenged, 'Straighten that, Mr Hardy.' And the bar went still.

I caught the finger between the palms of my hands and held it there and looked into his face. Already he was uneasy — he wanted to withdraw the challenge. He began to stammer how the accident happened — something about a tractor, a gearbox, a faulty setting. And as he spoke I massaged the finger. And when he stopped talking I opened my hands and released him. The finger was whole . . .

Badrallach, Kilmore,
Llanfaethlu, Llanfechell,
Kincardine, Kinros,
Loughcarron, Loughgelly . . .

We caroused right through the night. Toasts to the landlord who claimed he met my father once and as the night went on that they were close friends. Toasts to Teddy and Gracie. Toasts to my return. To Donal's finger. Toasts to the departed groom and his prowess. To the bride and her fertility. To the rich harvest — the corn, the wheat, the barley. Toasts to all Septembers and all harvests and to all things ripe and eager for the reaper. A Dionysian night. A Bacchanalian night. A frenzied, excessive Irish night when ritual was consciously and relentlessly debauched.

Then sometime before dawn McGarvey was remembered. Their greatest, their closest friend McGarvey who in his time had danced with them and drunk with them and built roads with them and cut turf with them. McGarvey who ought to have been best man that day — my God, who else? — and who wasn't even at the wedding reception. And as they created him I saw McGarvey in my mind, saw his strained face and his mauve hands and his burning eyes, crouched in his wheelchair and sick with bitterness. Saw him and knew him before Teddy in his English innocence asked why he wasn't there; before Ned told us of the fall from the scaffolding and the paralysis. Saw him and recognized our meeting: an open place, a walled yard, trees, orange skies, warm wind. And knew, knew with cold certainty that nothing was going to happen. Nothing at all.

I stood at the window and watched them set off to fetch McGarvey. Four of them getting into a battered car; now serious and busy with good deeds; now being polite to one another, holding doors open, you sit in front, no you, no you. Then they were gone, the car sluggish under their weight.

Teddy lay slumped in a stupor in a corner. Gracie went round the tables, emptying ashtrays, gathering glasses and leaving them on the counter, straightening chairs. No intimation whatever of danger. I suggested she should go to bed and she went off. Why wouldn't she? — the housework was finished.

He comes right down, walking very slowly, until he is as close as he can be to the audience. Pause.

The first Irish tour! The great homecoming! The new beginning! It was all going to be so fantastic! And there I am, pretending to subscribe to the charade. (*He laughs*) Yes; the restoration of Francis Hardy. (*Laughs again*)

But we'll come to that presently. Or as Teddy would have put it: why don't we leave that until later, dear 'eart? Why don't we do that? Why not?

Indeed.

He looks at the audience for about three seconds. Then quick black.

PART TWO

Grace

We discover GRACE HARDY *on stage, the same set as Part One, with the rows of seats removed. She is sitting on a wooden chair beside a small table on which are ashtrays, packets of cigarettes, the remains of a bottle of whiskey, a glass.*

She is in early middle age. Indifferent to her appearance and barely concealing her distraught mental state. Smoking a lot — sometimes lighting one cigarette from the other.

GRACE (*Eyes closed*) Aberarder, Aberayron,
      Llangranog, Llangurig,
      Abergorlech, Abergynolwyn,
      Penllech, Pencader,
      Llandefeilog, Llanerchymedd . . .
That most persistent of all the memories, (*eyes open*) that most persistent and most agonizing —
    But I *am* getting stronger, I *am* becoming more controlled — I'm sure I am. I measure my progress — a silly index, I know, and he would certainly have scoffed at it — but I can almost measure my progress by the number of hours I sleep and the amount I drink and the number of cigarettes I smoke. And, as they say, I've a lot to be thankful for; I know I have. And I like living in London. And the bedsitter's small but it's warm and comfortable. And it's a pleasant walk to the library in Paddington where I work four hours every morning. And on my way home, if the day's fine, I usually go through the park. And at night I listen to the radio or I read — oh, I read a lot — fiction, romance, history, biography, whatever I take home with me, whatever's handy; and I've begun to make a rug for the hearth

— I'll do a bit at that or maybe I'll try a new recipe or read the paper or knit or — or — And on Thursday afternoons I go to the doctor to get my pills renewed. He said to me last week, he said to me, 'Of course you've had a traumatic experience, Mrs Hardy; absolutely horrific. But it's over — finished with. And you've really got to be stern with yourself. You were a solicitor once, weren't you? Well, what you must do now is bring the same mental rigour, the same discipline to your recovery that you once brought to a legal case.' And he looked so pleased with his analogy and so clean and so pleasant and so efficient and, yes, so innocent, sitting there behind his desk with his grey suit and his college tie and his clear eyes and his gold pen poised, and he meant so well and he was so patient and it was all so simple for him; and I found myself nodding yes, yes, yes to him, yes, yes; and I thought: that's how you used to nod to Frank, too, especially in that last year — yes, yes, yes, Frank, you know you can, Frank, I swear you can — but he's watching me warily — nothing was simple for him — he's watching me and testing me with his sly questions and making his own devious deductions, probing my affirmations for the hair crack, tuned for the least hint of excess or uncertainty, but all the same, all the same drawing sustenance from me — oh, yes, I'm sure of that — finding some kind of sustenance in me — I'm absolutely sure of that, because finally he drained me, finally I was exhausted.

But I *am* making progress. And I suppose what I really mean by that is that there are certain restricted memories that I can invite now, that I can open myself fully to, like a patient going back to solids. I can think about the night the old farmer outside Cardiff gave him £200 for curing his limp — just handed him his wallet — and we booked into the Royal Abercorn and for four nights we lived like kings. And the weekend we spent one Easter walking in the Grampian mountains. I can think about that; yes, memories like that I can receive and respond to them. Because they *were* part of our lives together. But then as soon as I begin to open under them, just as soon as it seems that I'm beginning to come together again —

(*Eyes closed tight*) Abergorlech, Abergynolwyn,
    Llandefeilog, Llanerchymedd,
    Aberhosan, Aberporth . . .

It's winter, it's night, it's raining, the Welsh roads are narrow, we're on our way to a performance. (*Eyes open*) He always called it a performance, teasing the word with that mocking voice of his — 'Where do I perform tonight?' 'Do you expect a performance in a place like this?' — as if it were a game he might take part in only if he felt like it, maybe because that was the only way he could talk about it. Anyhow, Teddy's driving as usual, and I'm in the passenger seat, and he's immediately behind us, the Fantastic Francis Hardy, Faith Healer, with his back to us and the whiskey bottle between his legs, and he's squatting on the floor of the van — no, not squatting — crouched, wound up, concentrated, and happy — no, not happy, certainly not happy, I don't think he ever knew what happiness was — but always before a performance he'd be . . . in complete mastery — yes, that's close to it — in such complete mastery that everything is harmonized for him, in such mastery that anything is possible. And when you speak to him he turns his head and looks beyond you with those damn benign eyes of his, looking past you out of his completion, out of that private power, out of that certainty that was accessible only to him. God, how I resented that privacy! And he's reciting the names of all those dying Welsh villages — Aberarder, Aberayron, Llangranog, Llangurig — releasing them from his mouth in that special voice he used only then, as if he were blessing them or consecrating himself. And then, for him, I didn't exist. Many, many, many times I didn't exist for him. But before a performance this exclusion — no, it wasn't an exclusion, it was an erasure — this erasure was absolute: he obliterated me. Me who tended him, humoured him, nursed him, sustained him — who debauched myself for him. Yes. That's the most persistent memory. Yes. And when I remember him like that in the back of the van, God how I hate him again —

Kinlochbervie, Inverbervie,
Inverdruie, Invergordon,
Badachroo, Kinlockewe,
Ballantrae, Inverkeithing,
Cawdor, Kirkconnel,
Plaidy, Kirkinner . . .

(*Quietly, almost dreamily*) Kinlochbervie's where the baby's buried, two miles south of the village, in a field on the left hand side of the road as you go north. Funny, isn't it, but I've never met anybody who's been to Kinlochbervie, not even Scottish people. But it *is* a very small village and very remote, right away up in the north of Sutherland, about as far north as you can go in Scotland. And the people there told me that in good weather it is very beautiful and that you can see right across the sea to the Isle of Lewis in the Outer Hebrides. We just happened to be there and we were never back there again and the week that we were there it rained all the time, not really rained but a heavy wet mist so that you could scarcely see across the road. But I'm sure it is a beautiful place in good weather. Anyhow, that's where the baby's buried, in Kinlochbervie, in Sutherland, in the north of Scotland. Frank made a wooden cross to mark the grave and painted it white and wrote across it *Infant Child of Francis and Grace Hardy* — no name, of course, because it was stillborn — just *Infant Child*. And I'm sure that cross is gone by now because it was a fragile thing and there were cows in the field and it wasn't a real cemetery anyway. And I had the baby in the back of the van and there was no nurse or doctor so no one knew anything about it except Frank and Teddy and me. And there was no clergyman at the graveside — Frank just said a few prayers that he made up. So there is no record of any kind. And he never talked about it afterwards; never once mentioned it again; and because he didn't, neither did I. So that was it. Over and done with. A finished thing. Yes. But I think it's a nice name, Kinlochbervie — a complete sound — a name you wouldn't forget easily . . . (*Tense again*) God, he was such a twisted man! With such a talent for hurting. One of his mean tricks was to humiliate me by always changing my surname. It became Dodsmith or Elliot or O'Connell or McPherson — whatever came into his head; and I came from Yorkshire or Kerry or London or Scarborough or Belfast; and he had cured me of a blood disease; and we weren't married — I was his mistress — always that — that was the one constant: 'You haven't met Gracie McClure, have you? She's my mistress,' knowing so well that that would wound me and it always did; it shouldn't have; I should have become so used to it; but it always did. And Teddy — Teddy wasn't just a fit-up man who was always in trouble with the police for pilfering but a devoted servant, dedicated acolyte to the holy man. It wasn't that he was simply a liar — I never understood it — yes, I knew that he wanted to hurt me, but it was much more complex than that; it was some compulsion he had to adjust, to re-fashion, to re-create everything around him. Even the people who came to him — they weren't just sick people who were confused and frightened and wanted to be cured; no, no; to him they were . . . yes, they were real enough, but not real as persons, real as fictions, his fictions, extensions of himself that came into being only because of him. And if he cured a man that man became for him a successful fiction and therefore actually real, and he'd say to me afterwards, 'Quite an interesting character that, wasn't he? I knew that would work.' But if he didn't cure him the man was forgotten immediately, allowed to dissolve and vanish as if he had never existed. Even his father, and if he loved anyone he loved his father, even he was constantly re-created, even after his death. He was in fact a storeman in a factory in Limerick — I met him once, a nice old man; but Frank wasn't content with that — he made him a stonemason and a gardener and a bus driver and a guard and a musician. It was as if — and I'm groping at this   but it seemed to me that he kept re-making people according to some private standard of excellence of his own, and as his standards changed, so did the person. But I'm sure it was always an excellence, a perfection, that was the cause of his restlessness and the focus of it.

We were in Wales when he got word of his father's death. He went home alone. And when he came back he spoke of the death as if it had been his mother's. 'She passed away quietly,' he said. 'I don't know how father'll manage without her.' And the point was his mother had been dead for years when I first met him. Oh, he was a convoluted man.

The first day I went to the doctor he was taking down all the particulars and he said to me, 'And what was your late husband's occupation, Mrs Hardy?' 'He was an artist,' I said — quickly — casually — but with complete conviction — just the way he might have said it. Wasn't that curious? Because the thought had never occurred to me before. And then because I said it and the doctor wrote it down, I knew it was true . . .

I left him once. Yes; I left *him*! Up and left. God, when I think of it! We'd been married seven years at the time, and within that twelve months I'd had a pleurisy and then two miscarriages in quick succession and I suppose I was feeling very sorry for myself. And we'd been living that winter in a derelict cottage in Norfolk miles from anyone — it was really a converted byre. I remember kneeling before a tiny grate and crying because the timber was so wet the fire wouldn't light, and trying to get to sleep on a damp mattress on the floor. Anyway we'd had a fight about something silly; and I must have been very depressed or suddenly worked myself up into a stupid panic because on some mad impulse I tore a page off an old calendar and wrote on the back of it, 'Dear Frank I'm leaving you because I cannot endure the depravity of our lives any longer do not follow me I love you deeply Grace.' Wasn't it awful! 'I love you deeply' — to a man like that. And 'Do not follow me' — do not follow me! — God, I had some kind of innocence then!

Anyhow, I went home. For the first time and the last time. I got the night-crossing from Glasgow and then the bus to Omagh and walked the three miles out to Knockmoyle. I remember I stood at the gates for a while and looked up the long straight avenue flanked with tall straight poplars, across the lawn, beyond the formal Japanese garden and into the chaotic vegetable plot where my mother messed about and devoted her disturbed life to. It was Bridie, the housekeeper, who reared me; and Mother in her headscarf and wellingtons was a strange woman who went in and out of the mental hospital.

Father was in the breakfast room, in a wicker chair beside a huge fire, with a rug around his knees and his head slightly forward and staring straight in front of him just as he did when he was on the bench and hectoring a defendant. The stroke had spared his features and he looked so distinguished with his patrician face and his white hair perfectly groomed and his immaculate grey suit.

And I knocked on the table so that I wouldn't startle him and I said, 'It's me, Father. It's Grace.'

'What's that? Speak up!'

And I could hear old Bridie moving about the kitchen and I was afraid she'd hear me and come up and throw her arms around me before I'd have a chance to kiss him over and over

again and say sorry and tell him how often I thought about him.
I moved round so that I was directly in front of him.
'It's Grace, Father.'
'Yes? Yes?'
'Grace — Gracie.'
'Raise your voice. You're mumbling.'
'Timmikins,' I said — that's what he used to call me when I
was a child.
'Who?'
'Timmikins,' I said again.
'I know who it is,' he said.
'I came home to see you,' I said.
He gazed at me for a long, long time. And his mouth opened
and shut but no sound came. And then finally and suddenly the
words and the remembrance came together for him.
'You ran off with the mountebank.' And he wasn't accusing
— all he wanted was corroboration.
'Frank and I got married,' I said.
'Yes, you ran off with the mountebank just after you qualified.
And you killed your mother — you know that. But I told her
you'd be back. Six months, I said; give her six months and she'll
come crawling back.'
I was crouching in front of him and holding his cold hands
and our faces were so close that I could smell his breath.
'Father,' I said, 'Father, listen — '
But words were now spilling out of him, not angry words but
the tired formula words of the judge sentencing me to nine
months in jail but suspending the sentence because he understood I came from a professional family with a long and worthy
record of public service and hoping that I would soon regret
and atone for the blemish I had brought on that family and on
my own profession and threatening that if I ever appeared before him again he would have no option but to send me to jail
and impose the maximum penalty et cetera, et cetera, et cetera.
And as I watched him and listened to him and felt the darts
of his spittle on my face I had an impulse — and I thank God I
resisted it — a calm, momentary impulse to do an ugly, shame-
ful thing: I wanted to curse him — no, not curse him — assault
and defile him with obscenities and to articulate them slowly

and distinctly and brutally into his patrician face; words he never used; a language he didn't speak; a language never heard in that house. But even in his confusion he'd understand it and recognize it as the final rejection of his tall straight poplars and the family profession and his formal Japanese gardens. But more important, much, much more important, recognize it as my proud testament to my mountebank and the van and the wet timber and the primus stove and the dirty halls and everything he'd call squalor. But thank God I didn't do that. Instead — and he was still sentencing me — I just walked away. And I never saw him again. And he died before the year was over. And the next night I was back in the Norfolk byre, back on the damp mattress and kissing Frank's face and shoulders and chest and telling him how sorry I was; and he's drunk and giving me his sly smile and saying little. And then I was pregnant again and this time I held on to it for the full time. And that was the black-faced, macerated baby that's buried in a field in Kinlochbervie in Sutherland in the north of Scotland —

Badrallach, Kilmore,
Llanfaethlu, Llanfechell,
Kincardine, Kinross,
Loughcarron, Loughgelly . . .

(*At banner*) Faith healer — faith healing — I never understood it, never. I tried to. In the beginning I tried diligently — as the doctor might say I brought all my mental rigour to bear on it. But I couldn't even begin to apprehend it — this gift, this craft, this talent, this art, this magic — whatever it was he possessed, that defined him, that was, I suppose, essentially him. And because it was his essence and because it eluded me I suppose I was wary of it. Yes, of course I was. And he knew it. Indeed, if by some miracle Frank could have been the same Frank without it, I would happily have robbed him of it. And he knew that, too — how well he knew that; and in his twisted way read into it the ultimate treachery on my part. So what I did was, I schooled myself — I tried to school myself — to leave it to him and him with it and be content to be outside them. And for a time that seemed to work for both of us: we observed the neutrality of the ground between us. But as time went on and particularly in the last few years when he became more frantic and more

382

truculent, he began to interpret my remove as resentment, even as hostility, or he pretended he did — you could never be sure with him — and he insisted on dragging me into the feud between himself and his talent. And then we would snarl and lunge and grapple at one another and things were said that should never have been said and that lay afterwards on our lives like slow poison. When his talent was working for him the aggression wasn't quite so bitter — after he'd cured someone he'd be satisfied just to flaunt himself, to taunt me: 'And what does the legal mind make of all that? Just a con, isn't it? Just an illusion, isn't it?' And I'd busy myself putting away the chairs or taking down the banner. But when he couldn't perform — and in those last two years that became more and more frequent, the more desperate he became — then he'd go for me with bared teeth as if I were responsible and he'd scream at me, 'You were at your very best tonight, Miss O'Dwyer, weren't you? A great night for the law, wasn't it? You vengeful, spiteful bitch.' And I'd defend myself. And we'd tear one another apart.

As soon as we'd open the doors that's where I'd take my seat, at a table if there was one, or if there wasn't, with a tray on my knee; because sometimes they'd pay on their way in, now and again far more than they could afford, I suppose in the hope that somehow it would sweeten Frank to them. And that's where I'd sit all through the performance and collect whatever they'd leave on the way out.

And when they'd all be seated — 'all'! Many a time we were lucky to have half-a-dozen — then Teddy'd put on the record, a worn-out hissing version of a song called 'The Way You Look Tonight'. I begged Frank to get something else, anything else. But he wouldn't. It had to be that. 'I like it,' he'd say, 'and it confuses them.'

Then Teddy'd come out and make his announcement. And then Frank would appear.

I wish you could have seen him. It wasn't that he was a handsome man. He wasn't really. But when he came out before those people and moved among them and touched them — even though he was often half drunk — he had a special . . . magnificence. And I'd sit there and watch him and I'd often find myself saying to myself, 'Oh you lucky woman'. Oh, yes, oh, indeed, yes.

She sits and pours a drink.

I didn't want to come back to Ireland. Neither did Teddy. But he insisted. He had been in bad shape for months and although he didn't say it — he would never have said it — I knew he had some sense that Ireland might somehow recharge him, maybe even restore him. Because in that last year he seemed to have lost touch with his gift. And of course he was drinking too much and missing performances and picking fights with strangers — cornering someone in a pub and boasting that he could perform miracles and having people laugh at him; or else lying in the back of the van — we lived in it most of the time now — lying in the van and not speaking or eating for days.

But the real trouble was the faith healing. It wasn't that he didn't try — I suppose trying hadn't much to do with it anyway — but he tried too hard, he tried desperately, and usually nothing happened, nothing at all. I remember, just a few weeks before we came back, he met an old woman in an off-licence in Kilmarnock and he told her he could cure her arthritis. And he tried. And he failed. In the old days he wouldn't have given her another thought; but he became obsessed with that old woman, found out where she lived, went to her house again and again until finally her son-in-law threw him out and threatened to get the police for him.

So on the last day of August we crossed from Stranraer to Larne and drove through the night to County Donegal. And there we got lodgings in a pub, a lounge bar really, outside a village called Ballybeg, not far from Donegal Town. (*She moves again*) And the strange thing was that night began so well. I remember watching him and thinking: yes, his sense was true, he *is* going to be restored here — he was so easy and so relaxed and so charming, and there was nobody more charming than him when he wanted to be. I could tell even by the way he was drinking — not gulping down the first three or four drinks as if they were only preliminaries. And he chatted to the landlord and they talked about the harvest and about fishing and about the tourist trade. He even introduced me as his wife — God, I suppose that ought to have alerted me.

And there was a group of young men in the lounge, five of

them, local men on their way home from their friend's wedding; and one of them, the youngest of them, was in a wheelchair. And they were sitting in a corner by themselves and you could tell they wanted to be left alone. And when I saw him go over to them I had a second of unease. But whatever it was he said to them, they smiled and shook hands with him and moved into the centre of the lounge and he called me over and we all sat round in a big circle and one of them ordered a drink and the landlord joined us and we just sat there and chatted and laughed and told stories and sang songs. Where was Teddy? (*Remembering*) Yes, he was there, too, just outside the circle, slightly drunk and looking a bit bewildered. And it began as such a happy night — yes, happy, happy, happy! The young men were happy. I was happy. And Frank — yes, yes, I know he was happy too. And then out of the blue — we were talking about gambling — Frank suddenly leaned across to one of the wedding guests, a young man called Donal, and said, 'I can cure that finger of yours'. And it was dropped as lightly, as casually, as naturally into the conversation as if he had said, 'This is my round'. So naturally that the others didn't even hear it and went on talking. And he caught the twisted finger between his palms and massaged it gently and then released it and the finger was straight and he turned immediately to me and gave me an icy, exultant, theatrical smile and said, 'That's the curtain-raiser'.

And I knew at once — I knew it instinctively — that before the night was out he was going to measure himself against the cripple in the wheelchair.

And he did. Yes. Outside in the yard. I watched from an upstairs window. But that was hours later, just after daybreak. And throughout the night the others had become crazed with drink and he had gone very still and sat with his eyes half closed but never for a second taking them off the invalid.

Before they all went out to the yard — it was almost dawn — I gripped him by the elbow. 'For Christ's sake, Frank, please, for my sake,' and he looked at me, no, not at me, not at me, past me, beyond me, out of those damn benign eyes of his; and I wasn't there for him . . .

Aberarder, Kinlochbervie,
Aberayron, Kinlochbervie,

Invergordon, Kinlochbervie . . . in Sutherland, in the north of Scotland . . .

(*By rote*) But I *am* getting stronger. I *am* becoming more controlled. I can measure my progress by the number of hours I sleep and the amount I drink and — and —

Oh my God I'm in such a mess — I'm really in such a mess — how I want that door to open — how I want that man to come across that floor and put his white hands on my face and still this tumult inside me — Oh my God I'm one of his fictions too, but I need him to sustain me in that existence — Oh my God I don't know if I can go on without his sustenance.

Fade to black.

PART THREE

Teddy

We discover TEDDY *on stage. He is probably in his fifties but it would be difficult to pinpoint his age accurately because he has a showman's verve and perkiness that make him appear younger than that.*

He is wearing a bow tie, checked shirt, smoking-jacket/dressing gown (short), house slippers.

We discover him sitting beside the table — the same small table as in Part Two; but Teddy's chair is more comfortable than Grace's. He is listening to a recording of Fred Astaire singing 'The Way You Look Tonight' — an old record player and a very abused record.

Occasionally during his monologue he goes to a small locker — like a hospital locker — where he keeps his bottles of beer. Beside this locker is an empty dog basket.

The poster is in the same position as in Part One and Part Two.

(No attempt has been made to write this monologue in the phonetic equivalent of Cockney/London English. But the piece must be played in that dialect.)

TEDDY *is sitting with his eyes closed, his head back, listening to the music.*

> 'Some day when I'm awf'ly low
> When the world is cold,
> I will feel a glow just thinking of you
> And the way you look tonight . . . '

At the end of the first verse he opens his eyes, sees that his glass is empty, goes to the locker, gets a bottle of beer and comes back to his seat. Omit all the middle verses — go from the first verse to the last. As TEDDY *gets his drink he sings odd lines with the record:*

> 'Lovely, never, never change,
> Keep that breathless charm,
> Won't you please arrange it
> 'Cause I love you

Just the way you look tonight.
Mm, mm, mm, mm,
Just the way you look tonight.'

TEDDY What about that then, eh? Fred Astaire. Fantastic, isn't
it? One of the greats, Freddy. Just fantastic. I could listen
to that all day — (*Sings*) 'Just the way you look . . .' It
was Gracie insisted on that for our theme music. And
do you know why, dear heart? She wouldn't admit it to
him but she told me. Because that was the big hit the
year she and Frank was married. Can you imagine! But
of course as time goes by she forgets that. And of course
he never knows why it's our theme — probably thinks
I've got some sort of a twisted mind. So that the two of
them end up blaming *me* for picking it! But by that time
I really like the tune, you know; and anyway it's the
only record we have. So I keep it. And old Teddy he's
the only one of the three of us that knows its romantic
significance. I'll tell you something, dear heart: spend
your life in showbusiness and you become a philosopher.

But it is a fantastic tune, isn't it? Did you ever look
back over all the great artists — old Freddy here, Lillie
Langtry, Sir Laurence Olivier, Houdini, Charlie Chaplin,
Gracie Fields — and did you ever ask yourself what
makes them all top-liners, what have they all got in
common? OK, I'll tell you. Three things. Number one:
they've got ambition this size. OK? Number two:
they've got a talent that is sensational and unique —
there's only one Sir Laurence — right? Number three:
not one of them has two brains to rub together. You
think I'm joking? I promise you. They know they have
something fantastic, sure, they're not that stupid. But
what it is they have, how they do it, how it works, what
that sensational talent is, what it all means — believe
me, they don't know and they don't care and even if
they did care they haven't the brains to analyze it.

Let me tell you about two dogs I had once. OK? One
was a white poodle and she was so brilliant — I mean,
that dog she knew what you were thinking about

388

before you even thought about it yourself. Before I'd come home at night, d'you know what that dog would do? She'd switch on the electric fire, pull the curtains, and leave my slippers and a bottle of beer sitting there beside my chair. But put her in front of an audience — fell apart — couldn't do nothing. Right. Now the other dog he was a whippet. Maybe you remember him, Rob Roy, the Piping Dog? (*Brief pause*) Well, it was quite a few years ago. Anyway, you see that whippet, he was fantastic. I mean to say, just tell me how many times in your life has it been your privilege to hear a three-year-old male whippet dog play 'Come into the Garden, Maud' on the bagpipes and follow for his encore with 'Plaisir d'Amour'. OK? Agreed. Sensational talent. Ambition? I couldn't stop him rehearsing. Morning, noon and night he'd sit there blowin' the bloody thing and working them bellows with his back leg — all night long if I'd let him. That's all he lived for, being on top of the heap. And brains? Had he brains, that whippet? Let me tell you. I had that dog four and a half years until he expired from pulmonary exhaustion. And in all that time that whippet couldn't even learn his name! I mean it. I mean apart from his musical genius that whippet in human terms was educationally subnormal. A retarded whippet, in fact. I'd stub my toe against something, and I'd say 'God!', and who'd come running to me, wagging his tail? I tell you: a philosopher that's what you become.

I'll give you another example. One of the best acts I ever handled — Miss Mulatto and Her Pigeons. You see that kid? D'you know what the kid could do? I swear to God this is no lie, that kid talked pigeon! I swear. Fluent. That kid could plant her pigeons all over the house — some here, some there, some down there; and then she'd stand in the centre of the stage and she'd speak to them in a great flood of pigeon, you know — I can't do it, I can't even speak English — but this flood of pigeon would come out of her. And suddenly all those birds — a hundred and twenty of them, I should know, six to a box, twenty boxes, that's when I had to buy the van — all those birds would rise up from all over the house and come flying in like a bloody massive snowstorm and smother her on the stage. Fantastic. Can you imagine it? Her being able to talk to every one of them hundred and twenty birds and for all I know maybe them all speaking different languages! I said to her once, 'Mary Brigid,' I said, that was her name, Mary Brigid O'Donnell, I said, 'What do you say to them?' And she tossed her head and she said, 'Say to them? How would I know what I say to them, Teddy? I just make sounds at them.' See? (*He touches his head*) Nothing. Empty. But what a talent! What an artist! And another thing, when those birds all died that winter of '47 — all of them, just like that, within twenty-four hours, we were in Crewe at the time, the vet said it was galloping shingles — after those birds died Mary Brigid never worked again. I suppose it'd be like as if . . . as if someone sat on Yehudi Menuhin's fiddle and smashed it. God! Bloody artists!

TEDDY *disposes of the empty bottle and sings as he does:*

'Oh, but you're lovely
With your smile so warm,
And your cheek so soft
There is nothing for me but to love you — '
I'll tell you something: if you're thinking of going into the promotion business, let me tell you something — I'll give you this for nothing — it's the best advice you'll ever get — and it has been the one ruling principle in all my years as a professional man: if you're going to handle great artists you must handle them — believe me, I know what I'm talking about — you must handle them on the basis of a relationship that is strictly business only. Personally, in the privacy of your heart, you may love them or you may hate them. But that has nothing to do with it. Your client he has his job to do. You have your job to do. On that basis you complement each other. But let that relationship between you spill over into friendship or affection and believe me, dear heart, the coupon's torn. The one rule I've always lived by: friends is friends and work is work, and as the poet says, never the twain shall meet. OK? OK. (*Indicating poster*) Him? No, he was no great artist. Course he was no great artist. Never anything more than a mediocre artist. At best. Believe me. I should know, shouldn't I? Sure he had talent. Talent? He had more talent — listen to me — he had more talent than — and brains? — brains! — that's all the stupid bastard had was brains!

For Christ's sake, brains! And what did they do for him, I ask you, all those bloody brains? They bloody castrated him — that's what they done for him — bloody knackered him! So what do you end up handling? A bloody fantastic talent that hasn't one ounce of ambition because his bloody brains has him bloody castrated! Tell me — go ahead — you tell me — you tell me — I genuinely want to know — what sort of act is that to work with, to spend your life with? How do you handle an act like that? You tell *me*. I never knew! I never learned! Oh, for God's sake, no wonder I have ulcers!

(*Pause. Then softly*) But when his brain left him alone. When he was in form.

There was one night in particular. Wales it was. Village called Llanblethian. An old Methodist church that I get for ten bob. A week before Christmas.

And we're flat broke. And Frank, he's on two bottles of whiskey a day at this stage. And Gracie and him they've been fighting something terrible and she's disappeared off somewhere. And I've a pocketful of bills to pay.

OK. Eight o'clock. I open the doors. I'm not exactly knocked down in the stampede. As a matter of fact, dear heart — nobody, God. And now it's snowing. I close the doors. Frank he's looking like he's about to die, and his hands and his shoulders they're shaking like this. 'Get me a drink,' he says. I pretend I don't hear him. The door's flung open. The stampede? (*He shakes his head*) Gracie. 'Where's the genius?' she shouts. 'I came to see the great Irish genius. Where is he?' And he hears her and he screams, 'Get that bitch out! Get rid of that bitch!' 'Oh, he's here, is he?' she says. 'Physician, heal thyself!' she says with this great, mad, mocking voice. 'Out! Out!' he shouts. 'The genius!' she screams. 'Out! Out!' 'Genius!' And their voices they're echoing up through those dirty big oak rafters of the church so that it goes on and on and on . . . Oh, God, I mean to say, dear heart . . .

Finally — it must be near nine o'clock now — we're about to pack up and the door opens and in come ten people. I don't remember all the details now. There's two kids, I know; one of them has this great big lump on his cheek. And there's a woman with crutches. And there's another young woman with a crying baby in her arms. And there's a young man with dark glasses and one of those white sticks for blind people. Five or six others — I can't remember — I mean I didn't know then the kind of night it was going to be, did I? Oh, yes, and an old man, a farmer — he's lame — he's helped in by his daughter. And they all sit down. And I goes through my paces: Ladies and Gentlemen and et cetera and so on. And then I goes to Frank and I says, 'OK, Frank?' And very slowly he straightens up and when I see his face I'm sure he's going to be sick and he doesn't answer me at all but sort of — you know — drifts past me and down to them and among them.

He slowly pours the remains of a bottle into his glass, then takes a drink.

All I can say now is that it was . . . I mean I don't ask you to believe what happened. Quite honestly — and I don't say this with no belligerence — it makes no difference to me whether you believe me or not. But what happened that night in that old Methodist hall in the village of Llanblethian in Glamorganshire in Wales is that every single person in that church was cured. Ten people. All made right again. I'd seen him do fantastic things before but I'd never seen him do anything on that scale. Never. And I'll tell you a funny thing: there was no shouting or cheering or dancing with joy, nothing at all like that. Hardly a word was spoken. It was like as if not only had he taken away whatever it was was wrong with them, but like he had given them some great content in themselves as well. That sounds silly, doesn't it? But that's the way it seemed.

And when he had finished they all got to their feet and shook his hand, one after the other, very formal like. And the old farmer, the one who'd been lame and had been helped in by his daughter, he made a little speech. He said, in that lilting Welsh accent — I can't do that neither — he said, 'Mr Hardy, as long as men live in Glamorganshire, you'll be remembered here.' And whatever way he said it, you knew it was true; and whatever way he said Glamorganshire, it sounded like the whole world. And then he took out his wallet and placed it on the table and he said, 'I hope I'm not insulting you, sir.' And they all went out.

(*Short pause*) That was one of the big nights, that was. I mean we were stunned — Gracie — me — Frank himself; we just stood looking at one another. I mean to say — ten people — all in a few minutes. And then he suddenly went crazy with delight. And he threw his arms around me and kissed me on both cheeks. And then he ran down to Gracie and caught her in his arms and lifted her up into the air and danced her up and down the aisle of that old church and the two of them sang at the top of their voices, 'Lovely, never, never change', trying to sing and dance and at the same time breaking their sides laughing. And then he flung the doors open and they ran outside and sang and danced in the snow. What a pair! Oh my dear, what a pair! Like kids they were. Just like kids. Then I heard the van starting up. But by the time I got out they were gone. Just like that. Didn't see them again for four days — what happened was they went off to some posh hotel in Cardiff and lived it up until the wallet was empty. Just like kids, you know. Thoughtless; no thought for tomorrow. And no cruelty intended — oh no, no cruelty. But at a time like that a bit thoughtless. And that's understandable, too, after a night like that, isn't it? Just a little bit thoughtless — that's all.

He goes to the locker for another bottle. As he goes:

What a funny couple they were, though. Oh dear, what a funny couple. I mean, to spend the greater part of their lives together, fighting as they did; and when I say fighting, I mean really sticking the old knife in and turning it as hard as they could. I never understood it — job for the headshrink, isn't it? — why two people should burn themselves out in that way. Sure they could have split. Why didn't they then? Don't ask me. For God's sake why didn't I leave them and get myself something nice and simple and easy like — like — like a whistling dolphin? And what was the fighting all about in the end? All right you could say it was because the only thing that finally mattered to him was his work — and that would be true. Or you could say it was because the only thing that finally mattered to her was him — and I suppose that would be true, too. But when you put the two propositions together like that — I don't know — somehow they both become only half-truths, you know.

Or maybe you could say that no artist should ever be married. I've heard that theory, too; and after a lifetime in the profession I would incline to the conclusion that that theory has quite a bit of validity in it. I mean look at Rob Roy, the Piping Dog. Just consider for one minute the fortune I could have made in stud fees when that dog was a household name. Queuing up with their bitches they were; queuing bloody up. Twenty nicker a throw they were offering me. I thought I was sitting on a gold-mine. Do you know what I did in anticipation of the fortune that was going to come pouring in? I got a fifteen-foot black Carrara marble headstone with gold lettering put up over my mother's grave. Set me back £214, that did. OK — and what happened? — what happened every single time? I'll tell you. I come into the room here with a very beautiful and very sexy whippet bitch. He's just been rehearsing and he's lying there in that basket, gasping for breath. I say to him, 'Look at this then, old Rob. Who's good to you then, eh?' But he's temperamental — he won't look up. And the bitch, she's rolling her eyes and waggling all over and laughing like a bloody gypsy. 'Come on, boy,' I say, 'come on, come on. You've got a nice friend here.' And what does he do every time, every single time? He gets to his feet. He gives this great yawn. And then suddenly — just like that — goes for her throat! For her bloody *throat* for God's sake! Tries to tear her limb from bloody limb! Course he's stupid but he's not that stupid! I mean he knows what it's all about! My God, he knows! My God, there's days he's so randy, that whippet, there's days I daren't strap the bloody bagpipes to him! And yet look what he does when it's bloody handed to him on a plate — some of the most beautiful whippet bitches in the country and every one of them crying out for it! Goes for her throat and tries to desecrate my mother's memory at the same time! Oh my God — artists! I ask you!

He gathers the empty bottles on the table and drops them into a waste-paper basket. As he does:

Ups and downs — losses and gains — roundabouts and swings

— isn't that it?

And if that night in Llanblethian was one of the high spots, I suppose the week we spent in that village in Sutherland was about as bad a patch as we ever struck. For Gracie it was. Certainly for Gracie. And for me, too, I think. Oh, that's going back a fair few years. About the time he really began to lose control of the drinking. Anyway, there we were away up in Sutherland — what *was* the name of that village? Inverbuie? Inverbervie? Kinlochbervie? — that's it! — Kinlochbervie! — very small, very remote, right away up in the north of Sutherland, about as far north as you can go in Scotland, and looking across at the Isle of Lewis in the Outer Hebrides.

I'll always remember our first sight of that village. We climb up this long steep hill through this misty fog and when we get to the top we stop; and away down below us in the valley — there's Kinlochbervie; and it is just bathed in sunshine. First time we've seen the sun in about a month. And now here's this fantastic little village sitting on the edge of the sea, all blue and white and golden, and all lit up and all sparkling and all just heavenly. And Gracie she turns to me and she says, 'Teddy,' she says, 'this is where my baby'll be born.' Even though she wasn't due for three more weeks. But she was right. That's where the baby was born.

OK. We head down into the valley and just about two miles out of the village the front axle goes *thrackk!* Terrific. Frank, he's out cold in the back. So I leave Gracie sunbathing herself on a stone wall and I hikes it into Kinlochbervie to get help.

That was a Tuesday morning. The following Friday we're still there, still waiting for a local fisherman called Campbell who's out in his trawler to come back 'cause he's the only local who owns a tractor and we're depending on his mother who happens to be deaf as a post to persuade him when he comes back to tow us the thirty-five miles to the nearest village where there's a blacksmith but there's a chance, too, that this blacksmith might not be at home when we get there because his sister, Annie, she's getting married to a postman in Glasgow and the blacksmith may be the best man. One of those situations — you know.

(*Shouts*) 'Are you sure this blacksmith can fix axles, dear heart?' 'Och, Annie, she's a beautiful big strong girl with brown eyes.'

Right. We hang about. And since funds are low — as usual — Gracie and Frank they sleep in the van and I'm kipping in a nearby field. I don't mind; the weather's beautiful. Saturday passes — no Campbell. Sunday passes — no Campbell. And then on Sunday evening . . . the baby's born.

Very slowly he goes for another beer, opens it, pours it. As he does this he whistles a few lines of 'The Way You Look Tonight' through his teeth. Then, with sudden anger:

Christ, you've got to admit he really was a bastard in many ways! I know he was drinking heavy — I know — I know all that! But for Christ's sake to walk away deliberately when your wife's going to have your baby in the middle of bloody nowhere — I mean to say, to do that deliberately, that's some kind of bloody-mindedness, isn't it? And make no mistake, dear heart: it was deliberate, it was bloody-minded. 'Cause as soon as she starts having the pains I go looking for him, and there he is heading up the hill, and I call after him, and I know he hears me, but he doesn't answer me. Oh, Christ, there really was a killer instinct deep down in that man!

Pause. He takes a drink, puts the glass down on the table and looks at it.

I don't know . . . I don't know how we managed. God, when I think of it. Her lying on my old raincoat in the back of the van . . . shouting for him, screaming for him . . . all that blood . . . her bare feet pushing, kicking against my shoulders . . . 'Frank!' she's screaming, 'Frank! Frank!' and I'm saying, 'My darling, he's coming — he's coming, my darling — he's on his way — he'll be here any minute' . . . and then that — that little wet thing with the black face and the black body, a tiny little thing, no size at all . . . a boy it was . . .

(*Pause*) And afterwards she was so fantastic — I mean she was so bloody fantastic. She held it in her arms, just sitting there on the roadside with her back leaning against the stone wall and her legs stretched out in front of her, just sitting there in the sun and looking down at it in her arms. And then after about half-an-hour she said, 'It's time to bury it now, Teddy.' And we went into a nearby field and I had to chase the cows away 'cause they kept following us and I dug the hole and I put it in the hole and I covered it up again. And then she asked me was I not going to say no prayers over it and I said sure, why not, my darling, I said; but not being much of a praying man I didn't know right what to say; so I just said this was the infant child of Francis Hardy, Faith Healer, and his wife, Grace Hardy, both citizens of Ireland, and this was where their infant child lies, in Kin-lochbervie, in Sutherland; and God have mercy on all of us, I said.

And all the time she was very quiet and calm. And when the little ceremony was concluded she put her two white hands on my face and brought me to her and kissed me on the forehead. Just once. On the forehead.

And later that evening I made a cross and painted it white and placed it on top of the grave. Maybe it's still there. You never know. About two miles south of the village of Kinlochbervie. In a field on the left-hand side of the road as you go north. Maybe it's still there. Could still well be. Why not? Who's to say?

(*Pause*) Oh, he came back all right; just before it was dark. Oh, sure. Sober as a judge, all spruced up, healthy-looking, sun-burned, altogether very cocky; and full of old chat to me about should we have a go in the Outer Hebrides or maybe we should cross over to the east coast or should we plan a journey even further north now that the weather was so good — you know, all business, things he never gave a damn about. And he seemed so — you know — so on top of things, I thought for a while, I thought: My God, he doesn't know! He genuinely doesn't know! But then suddenly in the middle of all this great burst of interest I see him glancing into the van with the corner of the eye — not that there was anything to see; I had it all washed out by then — but it was the way he done it and the way he kept on talking at the same time that I *knew* that *he* knew; and not only that he knew but that he knew it all right down to the last detail. And even though the old chatter never faltered for a minute, whatever way he kept talking straight into my face, I knew too that — oh, I don't know how to put it — but I got this feeling that in a kind of way — being the kind of man he was — well somehow I got the feeling, I *knew* that he *had* to keep talking because he had suffered all that she had suffered and that now he was . . . about to collapse. Yeah. Funny, wasn't it? And many a time since then I get a picture of him going up that hill that Sunday afternoon, like there's some very important appointment he's got to keep, walking fast with his head down and pretending he doesn't hear me calling him. And I've thought maybe — course it was bloody-minded of him! I'm not denying that! — but maybe being the kind of man he was, you know, with that strange gift he had, I've thought maybe — well, maybe he had to have his own way of facing things . . .

Oh, I don't know. None of my business, was it? None of my concern, thank the Lord, except in so far as it might affect the performance of my client. Listen to me, dear heart, I'll give you this for nothing, the best advice you'll ever get — the *one* rule I've always lived by: friends is friends and work is work and never the twain shall meet as the poet says. OK? OK.

With a glass in his hand he goes slowly upstage until he is standing beneath the poster. As he goes he hums the lines 'Some day when I'm awf'ly low, When the world is cold'. He reads:

The Fantastic Francis Hardy, Faith Healer: One Night Only. Nice poster though, isn't it? A lifetime in the business and that's the only memento I've kept. That's a fact. See some people in our profession? — they hoard everything: press-clippings, posters, notices, photographs, interviews — they keep them all. Never believed in that though. I mean the way I look at it, you've got to be a realist, you know, live in the present. Look at Sir Laurence — you think he spends his days poring over old albums? No, we don't have time for that. And believe me I've had my share of triumphs and my share of glory over the years; and I'm grateful for that. But I mean it doesn't butter no parsnips for me today, does it?

And do you know, dear heart, it was almost thrown out! Well, I mean it *was* thrown out — I just happened to spot it in this pile of stuff that Gracie's landlord had dumped outside for the dustmen. I'd come straight from the morgue in Paddington, and the copper there he'd given me her address; and there I was, walking along the street, looking for number 27; and there it is, lying on the footpath where her landlord had dumped it. I mean, if it had been raining it would have been destroyed, wouldn't it? But there it was, neat as you like. And just as I was picking it up, this city gent he's walking past and he says, 'How dare you steal private property, Sir!' (*In a fury*) And I caught him by the neck and I put my fist up to his face and I said to him; I said to him, 'You open your fucking mouth once more, mate, just once fucking more, and I'll fucking well make fucking sausage meat of you!'

(*Pause while he controls himself again*) If you'll pardon the language, dear heart. But I just went berserk. I mean half-an-hour before, this copper he'd brought me to Paddington and I'm still in a state of shock after that. And besides it's only — what? — twelve months since the whole County Donegal thing: that night in the Ballybeg pub and then hanging about waiting for the trial of those bloody Irish Apaches and nobody in the courtroom understands a word I'm saying — they had to get an interpreter to explain to the judge in English what the only proper Englishman in the place was saying! God!

And I'm still only getting over all that when this copper comes up here one morning while I'm shaving and I opens the door and he asks me my name and I tell him and then he says I'm to go to Paddington with him right away to . . .

He stops suddenly and stares for a long time at the audience.

Tell you what — why don't I go back twelve months and tell you first about that night in Ballybeg? Why don't I do that? Why not? (*He gets another bottle, opens it, pours it*) It was the last day of August and we crossed from Stranraer to Larne and drove through the night to County Donegal. And there we got lodgings in a pub, a lounge bar really, outside a village called Ballybeg, not far from Donegal Town.

He takes a drink and leaves the glass down. Pause.

You see that night in that pub in Ballybeg? You know how I spent that night? I spent the whole of that night just watching them. Mr and Mrs Frank Hardy. Side by side. Together in Ireland. At home in Ireland. Easy; relaxed; chatting; laughing. And it was like as if I was seeing them for the first time in years and years — no! not seeing them but *remembering* them. Funny thing that, wasn't it? I'm not saying they were strangers to me — strangers? I mean, Frank and Gracie, how could they be strangers to *me*! — but it was like as if I was seeing them as they were once, as they might have been all the time — like if there was never none of the bitterness and the fighting and the wettings and the bloody van and the smell of the primus stove and the bills and the booze and the dirty halls and that hassle that we never seemed to be able to rise above. Like away from all that, all that stuff cut out, this is what they could be.

And there they were, the centre of that big circle round that big lounge, everybody wanting to talk to them, them talking to everybody, now and then exchanging an odd private word between themselves, now and then even touching each other very easy and very casual.

And she was sitting forward in this armchair. And she was all animation and having a word with everybody and laughing all the time. And she was wearing this red dress. And her hair it was tied back with a black ribbon. And how can I tell you how fantastic she looked?

And then sometime around midnight someone said, 'Why don't you sing us a song, Gracie?' And as natural as you like, as if she done it every day of the week, she stood up and sang an Irish song called 'Believe me if all those endearing young charms / Which I gaze on so fondly today' — Christ, I don't mean that's the title; that's the whole first verse for Christ's sake. And it wasn't that she was a sensational singer — no, no, she wasn't. I mean she had this kind of very light, wavery kind of voice — you know, like the voice of a kid of ten or eleven. But she stands up there in that Irish pub, in that red dress and with her hair all back from her face; and she's looking at him as she's singing; and we're all looking at her; and the song — it sort of comes out of her very simple and very sweet, like in a way not as if she's performing but as if the song's just sort of rising out of her by itself. And I'm sitting there just outside the circle, sitting there very quiet, very still. And I'm saying to myself. 'Oh Jesus, Teddy boy . . . Oh my Jesus . . . What are you going to do?'

And then I looks over at Frank — I mean I just happen to look over, you know the way you do — and there he is, gazing across at me. And the way he's gazing at me and the look he has on his face is exactly the way he looks into somebody he knows he's going to cure. I don't know — it's a hard thing to explain if you've never seen it. It's a very serious look and it's a very compassionate look. It's a look that says two things. It says: no need to speak — I know exactly what the trouble is. And at the same time it says: I am now going to cure you of that trouble. That's the look he gave me. He held me in that look for — what? — thirty seconds. And then he turned away from me and looked at her — sort of directed his look towards her so that I had to look at her too. And suddenly she is this terrific woman that of course I love very much, married to this man that I love very much — love maybe even more. But that's all. Nothing more. That's all. And that's enough.

And for the first time in twenty years I was so content — so content, dear heart, do you know what I done? I got drunk in celebration — slowly, deliberately, happily slewed! And someone must have carried me upstairs to bed because the next thing I know Gracie's hammering on my chest and shouting and sobbing, 'Get up, Teddy! Get up! Something terrible has happened! Something horrible!'

Long pause as he goes and gets another beer.

But I was telling you about the poster and how it's lying on the street outside Gracie's digs. That's it. How I've just come from Paddington and how the copper he's given me her address. That's right — I've told you all that. Or to go back to the morning of that same day — twelve months exactly after that night in Ballybeg.

OK. I'm shaving. Knock at the door. This copper. Asks me my name. I tell him. Asks me to come with him to the morgue in Paddington to identify a body. What body? Body of a lady. And

I say what lady? And he says a Mrs Grace Hardy. And I say come off it, she's in Ireland, that's where I left her. And he says you must be mistaken, she's been in London for the past four months, living in digs in number 27 Limewood Avenue. Limewood Avenue! I mean this here is Limewood Grove! Limewood Avenue's just four streets away. And I say she's there now, is she? And he says no, she's dead, she's in the morgue. And I say you must be wrong, copper. And he says no mistake, she's dead, from an overdose of sleeping tablets, and would I come with him please and make a formal identification.

So the copper he brought me in a van to Paddington — you know, just like our van; only his van I'm sure it's taxed and insured. But it's the same inside: two seats in the front, me driving, her beside me, and Frank in the back all hunched up with the bottle between his legs. And there she was. Gracie all right. Looking very beautiful. Oh my dear, I can't tell you how beautiful she looked.

And the copper he said, 'Is that Grace Hardy?' 'It is,' I said. 'Did you know her well?' 'Oh yes,' I said, 'a professional relationship going back twenty-odd years.' 'Cause that's what it was, wasn't it, a professional relationship? Well it certainly wasn't nothing more than that, I mean, was it?

He stands for some seconds just looking at the audience. Then he does not see them anymore. He sits on his chair and puts on the record. After the first few lines fade rapidly to black.

PART FOUR

Frank

The poster is gone. The set is empty except for the single chair across which lies Frank's coat exactly as he left it in Part One.

We discover FRANK *standing downstage left, where we left him.*

In this final section FRANK *is slightly less aloof, not quite as detached as in Part One. To describe him now as agitated would be a gross exaggeration. But there should be tenuous evidence of a slightly heightened pulse rate, of something approximating to excitement in him, perhaps in the way his mind leaps without apparent connection from thought to thought; and his physical movements are just a shade sharper.*

FRANK   (*Eyes shut*) Aberarder, Kinlochbervie,
Aberayron, Kinlochbervie,
Invergordon, Kinlochbervie . . . in Sutherland, in the north of Scotland . . .
(*He opens his eyes. A very brief pause. Then recovering quickly*) But I've told you all that, haven't I? — how we were holidaying in Kinlochbervie when I got word that my mother had died? Yes, of course I have. I've told you all that. (*Begins moving*) A picturesque little place, very quiet, very beautiful, looking across to the Isle of Lewis . . . about as far north as you can go in . . . in Scotland . . .

He keeps moving. As he does he searches his pockets. Produces a newspaper clipping, very tattered, very faded.

I carried this around with me for years. A clipping from the *West Glamorgan Chronicle*. 'A truly remarkable

403

event took place in the old Methodist church in Llanblethian on the night of December 21st last when an itinerant Irish faith healer called Francis Harding . . .' For some reason they never seem to — (*he shrugs in dismissal*) '. . . cured ten local people of a variety of complaints ranging from blindness to polio. Whether these very astonishing cures were effected by auto-suggestion or whether Mr Harding is indeed the possessor of some extra-terrestrial power . . . ' Nice word that. '. . . we are not as yet in a position to adjudicate. But our preliminary investigations would indicate that something of highly unusual proportions took place that night in Llanblethian.'

'Unusual proportions' . . . (*Short laugh*)

Never knew why I kept it for so long. Its testimony? I don't think so. Its reassurance? No, not that. Maybe, I think . . . maybe just as an identification. Yes, I think that's why I kept it. It identified me — even though it got my name wrong.

Yes, that *was* a strange night. One of those rare nights when I could — when I could have moved mountains. Ten people — one after the other. And only one of them came back to thank me — an old farmer who was lame. I remember saying to Gracie the next day, 'Where are the other nine?' — in fun, of course; of course in fun. But she chose to misunderstand me and that led to another row.

Yes; carried it for years; until we came back to Ireland. And that night in that pub in Ballybeg I crumpled it up (*he does this now*) and threw it away.

I never met her father, the judge. Shortly after Gracie and I ran off together he wrote me a letter; but I never met him. He said in it — the only part I remember — he used the phrase 'implicating my only child in your career of chicanery'. And I remember being angry and throwing the letter to her; and I remember her reading that line aloud and collapsing on the bed with laughing and kicking her heels in the air and repeating the phrase over and over again — I suppose to demonstrate her absolute loyalty to me. And I remember thinking how young she *did* look and how cruel her laughter at him was. Because by then my anger against him had died and I had some envy of the man who could use the word 'chicanery' with such confidence.

I would have liked to have had a child. But she was barren.

And anyhow the life we led wouldn't have been suitable. And he might have had the gift. And he might have handled it better than I did. I wouldn't have asked for anything from him — love, affection, respect — nothing like that. But I would have got pleasure just in looking at him. Yes. A child would have been something. What is a piece of paper? Or those odd moments of awe, of gratitude, of adoration? Nothing, nothing, nothing . . .

(*Looking around*) It was always like this — shabby, shabby, bleak, derelict. We never got that summons to Teddy's royal palace; not even to a suburban drawing room. And it would have been interesting to have been just once — not for the pretensions, no, no, but to discover was it possible in conditions other than these, just for the confirmation that this despair, this surrender wasn't its own healing. Yes, that would have been interesting.

And yet . . . and yet . . .

(*Suddenly, rapidly*) Not for a second, not for a single second was I disarmed by the warmth and the camaraderie and the deference and the joviality and the joy and the effusion of that homecoming welcome that night in that pub in Ballybeg. No, not for a second. Of course I responded to it. Naturally I responded to it. And yes, the thought did cross my mind that at long last is there going to be — what? — a fulfilment, an integration, a full blossoming? Yes, that thought occurred to me. But the moment that boy Donal threatened me with his damned twisted finger that illusion quickly vanished. And I knew, I knew instinctively why I was being hosted.

Aberarder, Kinlochbervie,
Aberayron, Kinlochbervie,
Invergordon, Kinlochbervie . . .

Where had we got to? Ah, yes — Teddy had been put to bed and Gracie had finished her housekeeping — I could hear her moving about upstairs; and the wedding guests had gone to get McGarvey. Only the landlord and myself in that huge, garish lounge.

I walked around it for a time.

I thought of Teddy asleep upstairs, at peace and reconciled at last. And I wondered had I held on to him out of selfishness, should I have attempted to release him years ago. But I thought

— no; his passion was a sustaining one. And maybe, indeed, maybe I had impoverished him now.

And I thought of Gracie's mother and the one time we met, in Dublin, on her way back to hospital. We were in a restaurant together, the three of us, Gracie and she and I; and she never spoke until Gracie had gone off to pay the bill and then she said, 'I suffer from nerves, you know,' her face slightly averted from me but looking directly at me at the same time and smiling at me. I said I knew. I was afraid she was going to ask me for help. 'What do you make of that?' I said I was sure she would get better this time. 'You know, there are worse things,' she said. I said I knew that. 'Much, much worse,' she went on and she was almost happy-looking now. 'Look at her father — he is obsessed with order. That's worse.' 'I suppose so,' I said. 'And Grace — she wants devotion, and that's worse still.' 'Is it?' I asked. 'And what do you want?' And before I could answer, Gracie came back, and the smile vanished, and the head dropped. And that was all. No request for help. And I never heard her voice again.

And I remembered — suddenly, for no reason at all — the day my father took me with him to the horse fair in Ballinasloe. And the only incident I remembered was that afternoon, in a pub. And a friend of my father's, Eamon Boyle, was with us; and the two men were slightly drunk. And Boyle put his hand on my head and said to my father, 'And what's this young man going to be, Frank?' And my father opened his mouth and laughed and said, 'Be Jaysus, Boyle, it'll be hard for him to beat his aul' fella!' And for the first time I saw his mouth was filled with rotten teeth. And I remember being ashamed in case Boyle had seen them too. Just a haphazard memory. Silly. Nothing to it. But for some reason it came back to me that night.

And I thought of the first big row Grace and I had. I don't know what it was about. But I know we were in Norfolk at the time, living in a converted byre. And she was kneeling in front of the grate, trying to kindle some wet timber; and I can't remember what I said but I remembered her reply; and what she said was: 'If you leave me, Frank, I'll kill myself.' And it wasn't that she was demented — in fact she was almost calm, and smiling. But whatever way she looked straight at me, without fully facing me, I recognized then for the first time that there was more of her mother than her father in her; and I realized that I would have to be with her until the very end.

He walks upstage. Pause.

I must have walked that floor for a couple of hours. And all the time the landlord never moved from behind the bar. He hadn't spoken since the wedding guests left. He wouldn't even look at me. I think he hated me. I know he did. I asked him for a last drink. Then he spoke in a rush: 'Get to hell out of here before they come back, Mister! I know them fellas — savage bloody men. And there's nothing you can do for McGarvey — nothing nobody can do for McGarvey. You know that.' 'I know that,' I said. 'But if you do nothing for him, Mister, they'll kill you. I know them. They'll kill you.' 'I know that, too,' I said. But he rushed into a back room.

I poured a drink for myself. A small Irish with an equal amount of water. The thought occurred to me to get drunk but I dismissed it as . . . inappropriate. Then I heard the car return and stop outside. A silence. Then Donal's head round the door.

'McGarvey's here. But he's shy about coming in. Come you out. They're waiting for you out there in the yard.'

'Coming,' I said.

He puts on the hat and overcoat and buttons it slowly. When that is done he continues:

There were two yards in fact. The first one I went into — it was immediately behind the lounge — it was a tiny area, partially covered, dark, cluttered with barrels and boxes of empties and smelling of stale beer and toilets. I knew that wasn't it.

Then I found a wooden door. I passed through that and there was the other, the large yard. And I knew it at once.

I would like to describe that yard to you.

It was a September morning, just after dawn. The sky was orange and everything glowed with a soft radiance — as if each detail of the scene had its own self-awareness and was satisfied with itself.

The yard was a perfect square enclosed by the back of the

building and three high walls. And the wall facing me as I walked out was breached by an arched entrance.

Almost in the centre of the square but a little to my left was a tractor and a trailer. In the back of the trailer were four implements: there was an axe and there was a crowbar and there was a mallet and there was a hay fork. They were resting against the side of the trailer.

In the corners facing me and within the walls were two mature birch trees and the wind was sufficient to move them.

The ground was cobbled but pleasant to walk on because the cobbles were smooth with use.

And I walked across that yard, over those worn cobbles, towards the arched entrance because, framed in it, you would think posed symmetrically, were the four wedding guests; and in front of them, in his wheelchair, McGarvey.

The four looked . . . diminished in that dawn light; their faces whiter; their carnations chaste against the black suits. Ned was on the left of the line, Donal on the right, and the other two, whose names I never knew, between them.

And McGarvey. Of course, McGarvey. More shrunken than I had thought. And younger. His hands folded patiently on his knees; his feet turned in, his head slightly to the side. A figure of infinite patience, of profound resignation, you would imagine. Not a hint of savagery. And Ned's left hand protectively on his shoulder.

And although I knew that nothing was going to happen, nothing at all, I walked across the yard towards them. And as I walked I became possessed of a strange and trembling intimation: that the whole corporeal world — the cobbles, the trees, the sky, those four malign implements — somehow they had shed their physical reality and had become mere imaginings, and that in all existence there was only myself and the wedding guests. And that intimation in turn gave way to a stronger sense: that even we had ceased to be physical and existed only in spirit, only in the need we had for each other.

He takes off his hat as if he were entering a church and holds it at his chest. He is both awed and elated. As he speaks the remaining lines he moves very slowly downstage.

And as I moved across that yard towards them and offered myself to them, then for the first time I had a simple and genuine sense of homecoming. Then for the first time there was no atrophying terror; and the maddening questions were silent.

At long last I was renouncing chance.

Pause for about four seconds. Then quick black.

TRANSLATIONS

Characters

MANUS
SARAH
JIMMY JACK
MAIRE
DOALTY
BRIDGET
HUGH
OWEN
CAPTAIN LANCEY
LIEUTENANT YOLLAND

Time and Place

The action takes place in a hedge school in the townland of Baile Beag/Ballybeg, an Irish-speaking community in County Donegal.

Act One: An afternoon in late August 1833.
Act Two: A few days later.
Act Three: The evening of the following day.

One interval — between the two scenes in Act Two.

Note

For the convenience of readers and performers unfamiliar with the language, roman letters have been used for the Greek words and quotations in the text. The originals, together with the Latin and literal translations, appear on pp. 494-5.

Translations was first produced by Field Day Theatre Company at the Guildhall, Derry, on 23 September 1980, with the following cast:

MANUS	Mick Lally
SARAH	Ann Hasson
JIMMY JACK	Roy Hanlon
MAIRE	Nuala Hayes
DOALTY	Liam Neeson
BRIDGET	Brenda Scallon
HUGH	Ray McAnally
OWEN	Stephen Rea
CAPTAIN LANCEY	David Heap
LIEUTENANT YOLLAND	Shaun Scott

Directed by	Art O Briain
Designed by	Consolata Boyle
Design assistance	Magdalena Rubalcava
	Mary Friel
Lighting by	Rupert Murray

Field Day Theatre Company was formed by Brian Friel and Stephen Rea. *Translations* was their first production.

for Stephen Rea

ACT ONE

The hedge school is held in a disused barn or hay shed or byre. Along the back wall are the remains of five or six stalls — wooden posts and chains — where cows were once milked and bedded. A double door left, large enough to allow a cart to enter. A window right. A wooden stairway without a banister leads to the upstairs living quarters, off, of the schoolmaster and his son. Around the room are broken and forgotten implements: a cartwheel, some lobster pots, farming tools, a battle of hay, a churn, etc. There are also the stools and bench-seats which the pupils use and a table and chair for the master. At the door a pail of water and a soiled towel. The room is comfortless and dusty and functional — there is no trace of a woman's hand.

When the play opens MANUS *is teaching* SARAH *to speak. He kneels beside her. She is sitting on a low stool, her head down, very tense, clutching a slate on her knees. He is coaxing her gently and firmly and — as with everything he does — with a kind of zeal.*

MANUS *is in his late twenties/early thirties; the master's older son. He is pale faced, lightly built, intense, and works as an unpaid assistant — a monitor — to his father. His clothes are shabby; and when he moves we see that he is lame.* SARAH'S *speech defect is so bad that all her life she has been considered locally to be dumb and she has accepted this: when she wishes to communicate she grunts and makes unintelligible nasal sounds. She has a waiflike appearance and could be any age from seventeen to thirty-five.*

JIMMY JACK CASSIE — *known as the Infant Prodigy — sits by himself, contentedly reading Homer in Greek and smiling to himself. He is a bachelor in his sixties, lives alone, and comes to these evening classes partly for the company and partly for the intellectual stimulation. He is fluent in Latin and Greek but is in no way pedantic — to him it is perfectly normal to speak these tongues. He never washes. His clothes — heavy top coat, hat, mittens, which he wears now — are filthy and he lives in them summer and winter, day and night. He now reads in a quiet voice and smiles in profound satisfaction. For*

JIMMY *the world of the gods and the ancient myths is as real and as immediate as everyday life in the townland of Baile Beag.*

MANUS *holds* SARAH's *hands in his and he articulates slowly and distinctly into her face.*

MANUS   We're doing very well. And we're going to try it once more — just once more. Now — relax and breathe in . . . deep . . . and out . . . in . . . and out . . .

> SARAH *shakes her head vigorously and stubbornly.*

Come on, Sarah. This is our secret.

> *Again vigorous and stubborn shaking of* SARAH's *head.*

Nobody's listening. Nobody hears you.

JIMMY   *'Ton d'emeibet epeita thea glaukopis Athene . . .'*

MANUS   Get your tongue and your lips working. 'My name —' Come on. One more try. 'My name is —' Good girl.

SARAH   My . . .

MANUS   Great. 'My name —'

SARAH   My . . . my . . .

MANUS   Raise your head. Shout it out. Nobody's listening.

JIMMY   *'. . . alla hekelos estai en Atreidao domois . . .'*

MANUS   Jimmy, please! Once more — just once more — 'My name —' Good girl. Come on now. Head up. Mouth open.

SARAH   My . . .

MANUS   Good.

SARAH   My . . .

MANUS   Great.

SARAH   My name . . .

MANUS   Yes?

SARAH   My name is . . .

MANUS   Yes?

> SARAH *pauses. Then in a rush:*

SARAH My name is Sarah.
MANUS Marvellous! Bloody marvellous!

> MANUS *hugs* SARAH. *She smiles in shy, embarrassed*
> *pleasure.*

Did you hear that, Jimmy? — 'My name is Sarah' —
clear as a bell. (*To* SARAH) The Infant Prodigy doesn't
know what we're at.

> SARAH *laughs at this.* MANUS *hugs her again and*
> *stands up.*

Now we're really started! Nothing'll stop us now!
Nothing in the wide world!

> JIMMY, *chuckling at his text, comes over to them.*

JIMMY Listen to this, Manus.
MANUS Soon you'll be telling me all the secrets that have been
in that head of yours all these years. Certainly, James
— what is it? (*To* SARAH) Maybe you'd set out the
stools?

> MANUS *runs up the stairs.*

JIMMY Wait till you hear this, Manus.
MANUS Go ahead. I'll be straight down.
JIMMY '*Hos ara min phamene rabdo epemassat Athene* — ' 'After
Athene had said this, she touched Ulysses with her
wand. She withered the fair skin of his supple limbs
and destroyed the flaxen hair from off his head and
about his limbs she put the skin of an old man . . . '!
The divil! The divil!

> MANUS *has emerged again with a bowl of milk and a*
> *piece of bread.* JIMMY *continues:*

And wait till you hear! She's not finished with him yet!

As MANUS *descends the stairs he toasts* SARAH *with his bowl.*

JIMMY '*Knuzosen de oi osse* — ' 'She dimmed his two eyes that were so beautiful and clothed him in a vile ragged cloak begrimed with filthy smoke . . . '! D'you see! Smoke! Smoke! D'you see! Sure look at what the same turf smoke has done to myself! (*He rapidly removes his hat to display his bald head*) Would you call that flaxen hair?

MANUS Of course I would.

JIMMY 'And about him she cast the great skin of a filthy hind, stripped of the hair, and into his hand she thrust a staff and a wallet'! Ha-ha-ha! Athene did that to Ulysses! Made him into a tramp! Isn't she the tight one?

MANUS You couldn't watch her, Jimmy.

JIMMY You know what they call her?

MANUS '*Glaukopis Athene.*'

JIMMY That's it! The flashing-eyed Athene! By God, Manus, sir, if you had a woman like that about the house it's not stripping a turf bank you'd be thinking about — eh?

MANUS She was a goddess, Jimmy.

JIMMY Better still. Sure isn't our own Grania a class of a goddess and —

MANUS Who?

JIMMY Grania — Grania — Diarmuid's Grania.

MANUS Ah.

JIMMY And sure she can't get her fill of men.

MANUS Jimmy, you're impossible.

JIMMY I was just thinking to myself last night: if you had the choosing between Athene and Artemis and Helen of Troy — all three of them Zeus's girls — imagine three powerful-looking daughters like that all in the one parish of Athens! — now, if you had the picking between them, which would you take?

MANUS (*To* SARAH) Which should I take, Sarah?

JIMMY No harm to Helen; and no harm to Artemis; and in-

deed no harm to our own Grania, Manus. But I think
I've no choice but to go bull-straight for Athene. By
God, sir, them flashing eyes would fair keep a man
jigged up constant!

Suddenly and momentarily, as if in spasm, JIMMY
*stands to attention and salutes, his face raised in
pained ecstasy.* MANUS *laughs. So does* SARAH. JIMMY
goes back to his seat and his reading.

MANUS You're a dangerous bloody man, Jimmy Jack.

JIMMY 'Flashing-eyed'! Hah! Sure Homer knows it all, boy.
Homer knows it all.

MANUS *goes to the window and looks out.*

MANUS Where the hell has he got to?

SARAH *goes to* MANUS *and touches his elbow. She
mimes rocking a baby.*

Yes, I know he's at the christening; but it doesn't take
them all day to put a name on a baby, does it?

SARAH *mimes pouring drinks and tossing them back
quickly.*

You may be sure. Which pub?

SARAH *indicates.*

Gracie's?

No. Further away.

Con Connie Tim's?

No. To the right of there.

Anna na mBréag's?

Yes. That's it.

Great. She'll fill him up. I suppose I may take the class
then.

> MANUS *begins to distribute some books, slates and
> chalk, texts, etc, beside the seats.* SARAH *goes over to
> the straw and produces a bunch of flowers she has
> hidden there. During this:*

JIMMY '*Autar o ek limenos prosebe* — ' 'But Ulysses went forth
from the harbour and through the woodland to the
place where Athene had shown him he could find the
good swineherd who — '*o oi biotoio malista kedeto*' —
what's that, Manus?
MANUS 'Who cared most for his substance.'
JIMMY That's it! 'The good swineherd who cared most for
his substance above all the slaves that Ulysses possessed . . . '

> SARAH *presents the flowers to* MANUS.

MANUS Those are lovely, Sarah.

> *But* SARAH *has fled in embarrassment to her seat and
> has her head buried in a book.* MANUS *goes to her.*

Flow-ers.

> *Pause.* SARAH *does not look up.*

Say the word: flow-ers. Come on — flow-ers.
SARAH Flowers.
MANUS You see? — you're off!

> MANUS *leans down and kisses the top of* SARAH'*s head.*

And they're beautiful flowers. Thank you.

> MAIRE *enters, a strong-minded, strong-bodied woman in her twenties with a head of curly hair. She is carrying a small can of milk.*

MAIRE Is this all's here? Is there no school this evening?
MANUS If my father's not back I'll take it.

> MANUS *stands awkwardly, having been caught kissing* SARAH *and with the flowers almost formally at his chest.*

MAIRE Well now, isn't that a pretty sight. There's your milk. How's Sarah?

> SARAH *grunts a reply.*

MANUS I saw you out at the hay.

> MAIRE *ignores this and goes to* JIMMY.

MAIRE And how's Jimmy Jack Cassie?
JIMMY Sit down beside me, Maire.
MAIRE Would I be safe?
JIMMY No safer man in Donegal.

> MAIRE *flops on a stool beside* JIMMY.

MAIRE Ooooh. The best harvest in living memory, they say; but I don't want to see another like it. (*Showing* JIMMY *her hands*) Look at the blisters.
JIMMY *Esne fatigata?*
MAIRE *Sum fatigatissima.*
JIMMY *Bene! Optime!*
MAIRE That's the height of my Latin. Fit me better if I had even that much English.
JIMMY English? I thought you had some English?
MAIRE Three words. Wait — there was a spake I used to have

off by heart. What's this it was? (*Her accent is strange because she is speaking a foreign language and because she does not understand what she is saying*) 'In Norfolk we besport ourselves around the maypoll.' What about that!

MANUS Maypole. (*Again* MAIRE *ignores* MANUS)

MAIRE God have mercy on my Aunt Mary — she taught me that when I was about four, whatever it means. Do you know what it means, Jimmy?

JIMMY Sure you know I have only Irish like yourself.

MAIRE And Latin. And Greek.

JIMMY I'm telling you a lie: I know one English word.

MAIRE What?

JIMMY Bo-som.

MAIRE What's a bo-som?

JIMMY You know — (*he illustrates with his hands*) — bo-som — bo-som — you know — Diana, the huntress, she has two powerful bosom.

MAIRE You may be sure that's the one English word you would know. (*Rises*) Is there a drop of water about?

MANUS *gives* MAIRE *his bowl of milk.*

MANUS I'm sorry I couldn't get up last night.

MAIRE Doesn't matter.

MANUS Biddy Hanna sent for me to write a letter to her sister in Nova Scotia. All the gossip of the parish. 'I brought the cow to the bull three times last week but no good. There's nothing for it now but Big Ned Frank.'

MAIRE (*Drinking*) That's better.

MANUS And she got so engrossed in it that she forgot who she was dictating to: 'The aul' drunken schoolmaster and that lame son of his are still footering about in the hedge school, wasting people's good time and money.'

MAIRE (*She has to laugh at this*) She did not!

MANUS And me taking it all down. 'Thank God one of them new national schools is being built above at Poll na gCaorach.' It was after midnight by the time I got back.

MAIRE Great to be a busy man.

MAIRE *moves away.* MANUS *follows.*

MANUS I could hear music on my way past but I thought it
was too late to call.

MAIRE (*To* SARAH) Wasn't your father in great voice last night?

SARAH *nods and smiles.*

It must have been near three o'clock by the time you
got home?

SARAH *holds up four fingers.*

Was it four? No wonder we're in pieces.

MANUS I can give you a hand at the hay tomorrow.

MAIRE That's the name of a hornpipe, isn't it? — 'The Scholar
in the Hayfield' — or is it a reel?

MANUS If the day's good.

MAIRE Suit yourself. The English soldiers below in the tents,
them sapper fellas, they're coming up to give us a
hand. I don't know a word they're saying, nor they
me; but sure that doesn't matter, does it?

MANUS What the hell are you so crabbed about?!

DOALTY *and* BRIDGET *enter noisily. Both are in their
twenties.* DOALTY *is brandishing a surveyor's pole.
He is an open-minded, open-hearted, generous and
slightly thick young man.* BRIDGET *is a plump, fresh
young girl, ready to laugh, vain, and with a country-
woman's instinctive cunning. As* DOALTY *enters he
does his imitation of the master.*

DOALTY Vesperal salutations to you all.

BRIDGET He's coming down past Carraig na Rí and he's as full
as a pig!

DOALTY *Ignari, stulti, rustici* — pot-boys and peasant whelps
— semi-literates and illegitimates.

BRIDGET He's been on the batter since this morning; he sent the
wee ones home at eleven o'clock.

DOALTY   Three questions. Question A — Am I drunk? Question
         B — Am I sober? (*Into* MAIRE's *face*) *Responde — responde!*
BRIDGET Question C, Master — When were you last sober?
MAIRE   What's the weapon, Doalty?
BRIDGET I warned him. He'll be arrested one of these days.
DOALTY   Up in the bog with Bridget and her aul' fella, and the
         Red Coats were just across at the foot of Cnoc na Móna,
         dragging them aul' chains and peeping through that
         big machine they lug about everywhere with them —
         you know the name of it, Manus?
MAIRE   Theodolite.
BRIDGET How do you know?
MAIRE   They leave it in our byre at night sometimes if it's
         raining.
JIMMY   Theodolite — what's the etymology of that word,
         Manus?
MANUS   No idea.
BRIDGET Get on with the story.
JIMMY   *Theo — theos* — something to do with a god. Maybe
         thea — a goddess! What shape's the yoke?
DOALTY   'Shape'! Will you shut up, you aul' eejit you! Anyway,
         every time they'd stick one of these poles into the
         ground and move across the bog I'd creep up and
         shift it twenty or thirty paces to the side.
BRIDGET God!
DOALTY   Then they'd come back and stare at it and look at their
         calculations and stare at it again and scratch their
         heads. And cripes, d'you know what they ended up
         doing?
BRIDGET Wait till you hear!
DOALTY   They took the bloody machine apart!

         And immediately he speaks in gibberish — an imita-
         tion of two very agitated and confused sappers in
         rapid conversation.

BRIDGET That's the image of them!
MAIRE   You must be proud of yourself, Doalty.
DOALTY   What d'you mean?

MAIRE That was a very clever piece of work.

MANUS It was a gesture.

MAIRE What sort of gesture?

MANUS Just to indicate . . . a presence.

MAIRE Hah!

BRIDGET I'm telling you — you'll be arrested.

> *When* DOALTY *is embarrassed — or pleased — he reacts physically. He now grabs* BRIDGET *around the waist.*

DOALTY What d'you make of that for an implement, Bridget? Wouldn't that make a great aul' shaft for your churn?

BRIDGET Let go of me, you dirty brute! I've a headline to do before Big Hughie comes.

MANUS I don't think we'll wait for him. Let's get started.

> *Slowly, reluctantly, they begin to move to their seats and specific tasks.* DOALTY *goes to the bucket of water at the door and washes his hands.* BRIDGET *sets up a hand mirror and combs her hair.*

BRIDGET Nellie Ruadh's baby was to be christened this morning. Did any of yous hear what she called it? Did you, Sarah?

> SARAH *grunts: No.*

Did you, Maire?

MAIRE No.

BRIDGET Our Seamus says she was threatening she was going to call it after its father.

DOALTY Who's the father?

BRIDGET That's the point, you donkey you!

DOALTY Ah.

BRIDGET So there's a lot of uneasy bucks about Baile Beag this day.

DOALTY She told me last Sunday she was going to call it Jimmy.

BRIDGET You're a liar, Doalty.

DOALTY Would I tell you a lie? Hi, Jimmy, Nellie Ruadh's aul' fella's looking for you.

JIMMY For me?

MAIRE Come on, Doalty.

DOALTY Someone told him . . .

MAIRE Doalty!

DOALTY He heard you know the first book of the Satires of Horace off by heart . . .

JIMMY That's true.

DOALTY . . . and he wants you to recite it for him.

JIMMY I'll do that for him certainly, certainly.

DOALTY He's busting to hear it.

JIMMY *fumbles in his pockets.*

JIMMY I came across this last night — this'll interest you — in Book Two of Virgil's *Georgics.*

DOALTY Be God, that's my territory all right.

BRIDGET You clown you! (*To* SARAH) Hold this for me, would you (*her mirror*)?

JIMMY Listen to this, Manus. '*Nigra fere et presso pinguis sub vomere terra . . .*'

DOALTY Steady on now — easy, boys, easy — don't rush me, boys — (*He mimes great concentration*)

JIMMY Manus?

MANUS 'Land that is black and rich beneath the pressure of the plough . . .'

DOALTY Give *me* a chance!

JIMMY 'And with *cui putre* — with crumbly soil — is in the main best for corn.' There you are!

DOALTY There you are.

JIMMY 'From no other land will you see more wagons wending homeward behind slow bullocks.' Virgil! There!

DOALTY 'Slow bullocks'!

JIMMY Isn't that what I'm always telling you? Black soil for corn. *That's* what you should have in that upper field of yours — corn, not spuds.

DOALTY Would you listen to that fella! Too lazy be Jaysus to wash himself and he's lecturing me on agriculture! Would you go and take a running race at yourself,

Jimmy Jack Cassie! (*Grabs* SARAH) Come away out of
this with me, Sarah, and we'll plant some corn together.
MANUS All right — all right. Let's settle down and get some
work done. I know Sean Beag isn't coming — he's at
the salmon. What about the Donnelly twins? (*To* DOALTY)
Are the Donnelly twins not coming anymore?

DOALTY *shrugs and turns away.*

Did you ask them?
DOALTY Haven't seen them. Not about these days.

DOALTY *begins whistling through his teeth. Suddenly
the atmosphere is silent and alert.*

MANUS Aren't they at home?
DOALTY No.
MANUS Where are they then?
DOALTY How would I know?
BRIDGET Our Seamus says two of the soldiers' horses were
found last night at the foot of the cliffs at Machaire
Buidhe and . . .

*She stops suddenly and begins writing with chalk on
her slate.*

D'you hear the whistles of this aul' slate? Sure no-
body could write on an aul' slippery thing like that.
MANUS What headline did my father set you?
BRIDGET 'It's easier to stamp out learning than to recall it.'
JIMMY Book Three, the *Agricola* of Tacitus.
BRIDGET God but you're a dose.
MANUS Can you do it?
BRIDGET There. Is it bad? Will he ate me?
MANUS It's very good. Keep your elbow in closer to your side.
Doalty?
DOALTY I'm at the seven-times table. I'm perfect, skipper.

MANUS *moves to* SARAH.

MANUS Do you understand those sums?

SARAH *nods: Yes.* MANUS *leans down to her ear.*

My name is Sarah.

MANUS *goes to* MAIRE. *While he is talking to her the others swop books, talk quietly, etc.*

Can I help you? What are you at?

MAIRE Map of America. (*Pause*) The passage money came last Friday.

MANUS You never told me that.

MAIRE Because I haven't seen you since, have I?

MANUS You don't want to go. You said that yourself.

MAIRE There's ten below me to be raised and no man in the house. What do you suggest?

MANUS Do you want to go?

MAIRE Did you apply for that job in the new national school?

MANUS No.

MAIRE You said you would.

MANUS I said I might.

MAIRE When it opens this is finished: nobody's going to pay to go to a hedge school.

MANUS I know that and I . . .

He breaks off because he sees SARAH, *obviously listening, at his shoulder. She moves away again.*

I was thinking that maybe I could . . .

MAIRE It's £56 a year you're throwing away.

MANUS I can't apply for it.

MAIRE You *promised* me you would.

MANUS My father has applied for it.

MAIRE He has not!

MANUS Day before yesterday.

MAIRE For God's sake, sure you know he'd never —

MANUS I couldn't — I can't go in against him.

MAIRE *looks at him for a second.*

MAIRE Suit yourself. (*To* BRIDGET) I saw your Seamus heading off to the Port fair early this morning.

BRIDGET And wait till you hear this — I forgot to tell you this. He said that as soon as he crossed over the gap at Cnoc na Móna — just beyond where the soldiers are making the maps — the sweet smell was everywhere.

DOALTY You never told me that.

BRIDGET It went out of my head.

DOALTY He saw the crops in Port?

BRIDGET Some.

MANUS How did the tops look?

BRIDGET Fine — I think.

DOALTY In flower?

BRIDGET I don't know. I think so. He didn't say.

MANUS Just the sweet smell — that's all?

BRIDGET They say that's the way it snakes in, don't they? First the smell; and then one morning the stalks are all black and limp.

DOALTY Are you stupid? It's the rotting stalks makes the sweet smell for God's sake. That's what the smell is — rotting stalks.

MAIRE Sweet smell! Sweet smell! Every year at this time somebody comes back with stories of the sweet smell. Sweet God, did the potatoes ever fail in Baile Beag? Well, did they ever — ever? Never! There was never blight here. Never. Never. But we're always sniffing about for it, aren't we? — looking for disaster. The rents are going to go up again — the harvest's going to be lost — the herring have gone away for ever — there's going to be evictions. Honest to God, some of you people aren't happy unless you're miserable and you'll not be right content until you're dead!

DOALTY Bloody right, Maire. And sure St Colmcille prophesied there'd never be blight here. He said:

'The spuds will bloom in Baile Beag
Till rabbits grow an extra lug.'

And sure that'll never be. So we're all right. Seven

threes are twenty-one; seven fours are twenty-eight; seven fives are forty-nine — Hi, Jimmy, do you fancy my chances as boss of the new national school?

JIMMY What's that? — what's that?

DOALTY Agh, g'way back home to Greece, son.

MAIRE You ought to apply, Doalty.

DOALTY D'you think so? Cripes, maybe I will. Hah!

BRIDGET Did you know that you start at the age of six and you have to stick at it until you're twelve at least — no matter how smart you are or how much you know.

DOALTY Who told you that yarn?

BRIDGET And every child from every house has to go all day, every day, summer or winter. That's the law.

DOALTY I'll tell you something — nobody's going to go near them — they're not going to take on — law or no law.

BRIDGET And everything's free in them. You pay for nothing except the books you use; that's what our Seamus says.

DOALTY 'Our Seamus.' Sure your Seamus wouldn't pay anyway. She's making this all up.

BRIDGET Isn't that right, Manus?

MANUS I think so.

BRIDGET And from the very first day you go you'll not hear one word of Irish spoken. You'll be taught to speak English and every subject will be taught through English and everyone'll end up as cute as the Buncrana people.

> SARAH *suddenly grunts and mimes a warning that the master is coming. The atmosphere changes. Sudden business. Heads down.*

DOALTY He's here, boys. Cripes, he'll make yella meal out of me for those bloody tables.

BRIDGET Have you any extra chalk, Manus?

MAIRE And the atlas for me.

> DOALTY *goes to* MAIRE *who is sitting on a stool at the back.*

DOALTY Swop you seats.

MAIRE Why?

DOALTY There's an empty one beside the Infant Prodigy.

MAIRE I'm fine here.

DOALTY Please, Maire. I want to jouk in the back here.

> MAIRE *rises.*

God love you. (*Aloud*) Anyone got a bloody table-book? Cripes, I'm wrecked. (SARAH *gives him one*) God, I'm dying about you.

> *In his haste to get to the back seat* DOALTY *bumps into* BRIDGET *who is kneeling on the floor and writing laboriously on a slate resting on top of a bench-seat.*

BRIDGET Watch where you're going, Doalty!

> DOALTY *gooses* BRIDGET. *She squeals. Now the quiet hum of work:* JIMMY *reading Homer in a low voice;* BRIDGET *copying her headline;* MAIRE *studying the atlas;* DOALTY, *his eyes shut tight, mouthing his tables;* SARAH *doing sums. After a few seconds:*

BRIDGET Is this 'g' right, Manus? How do you put a tail on it?

DOALTY Will you shut up! I can't concentrate!

> *A few more seconds of work. Then* DOALTY *opens his eyes and looks around.*

False alarm, boys. The bugger's not coming at all. Sure the bugger's hardly fit to walk.

> *And immediately* HUGH *enters. A large man, with residual dignity, shabbily dressed, carrying a stick. He has, as always, a large quantity of drink taken, but he is by no means drunk. He is in his early sixties.*

HUGH *Adsum*, Doalty, *adsum*. Perhaps not in *sobrietate perfecta* but adequately *sobrius* to overhear your quip. Vesperal salutations to you all. (*Various responses*)

JIMMY *Ave*, Hugh.

HUGH James.

He removes his hat and coat and hands them and his stick to MANUS, *as if to a footman.*

Apologies for my late arrival: we were celebrating the baptism of Nellie Ruadh's baby.

BRIDGET (*Innocently*) What name did she put on it, Master?

HUGH Was it Eamon? Yes, it was Eamon.

BRIDGET Eamon Donal from Tor! Cripes!

HUGH And after the *caerimonia nominationis* — Maire?

MAIRE The ritual of naming.

HUGH Indeed — we then had a few libations to mark the occasion. Altogether very pleasant. The derivation of the word 'baptize'? — where are my Greek scholars? Doalty?

DOALTY Would it be — ah — ah —

HUGH Too slow. James?

JIMMY '*Baptizein*' — to dip or immerse.

HUGH Indeed — our friend Pliny Minor speaks of the '*baptisterium*' — the cold bath.

DOALTY Master.

HUGH Doalty?

DOALTY I suppose you could talk then about baptizing a sheep at sheep-dipping, could you?

Laughter. Comments.

HUGH Indeed — the precedent is there — the day you were appropriately named Doalty — seven nines?

DOALTY What's that, Master?

HUGH Seven times nine?

DOALTY Seven nines — seven nines — seven times nine — seven times nine are — cripes, it's on the tip of my tongue, Master — I knew it for sure this morning — funny that's the only one that foxes me —

BRIDGET (*Prompt*) Sixty-three.

DOALTY What's wrong with me: sure seven nines are fifty-three, Master.

HUGH Sophocles from Colonus would agree with Doalty Dan Doalty from Tulach Álainn: 'To know nothing is the sweetest life.' Where's Sean Beag?

MANUS He's at the salmon.

HUGH And Nora Dan?

MAIRE She says she's not coming back anymore.

HUGH Ah. Nora Dan can now write her name — Nora Dan's education is complete. And the Donnelly twins?

Brief pause.

BRIDGET They're probably at the turf. (*She goes to* HUGH) There's the one-and-eight I owe you for last quarter's arithmetic and there's my one-and-six for this quarter's writing.

HUGH *Gratias tibi ago.* (*He sits at his table*) Before we commence our *studia* I have three items of information to impart to you — (*To* MANUS) A bowl of tea, strong tea, black —

MANUS *leaves.*

Item A: on my perambulations today — Bridget? Too slow. Maire?

MAIRE *Perambulare* — to walk about.

HUGH Indeed — I encountered Captain Lancey of the Royal Engineers who is engaged in the ordnance survey of this area. He tells me that in the past few days two of his horses have strayed and some of his equipment seems to be mislaid. I expressed my regret and suggested he address you himself on these matters. He then explained that he does not speak Irish. Latin? I asked. None. Greek? Not a syllable. He speaks — on his own admission — only English; and to his credit he seemed suitably verecund — James?

JIMMY *Verecundus* — humble.

HUGH Indeed — he voiced some surprise that we did not speak his language. I explained that a few of us did, on occasion — outside the parish of course — and then usually for the purposes of commerce, a use to which his tongue seemed particularly suited — (*Shouts*) and a slice of soda bread — and I went on to propose that our own culture and the classical tongues made a happier conjugation — Doalty?

DOALTY *Conjugo* — I join together. (DOALTY *is so pleased with himself that he prods and winks at* BRIDGET)

HUGH Indeed — English, I suggested, couldn't really express us. And again to his credit he acquiesced to my logic. Acquiesced — Maire? (MAIRE *turns away impatiently.* HUGH *is unaware of the gesture*) Too slow. Bridget?

BRIDGET *Acquiesco.*

HUGH *Procede.*

BRIDGET *Acquiesco, acquiescere, acquievi, acquietum.*

HUGH Indeed — and Item B . . .

MAIRE Master.

HUGH Yes?

MAIRE *gets to her feet uneasily but determinedly. Pause.*

Well, girl?

MAIRE We should all be learning to speak English. That's what my mother says. That's what I say. That's what Dan O'Connell said last month in Ennis. He said the sooner we all learn to speak English the better.

Suddenly several speak together.

JIMMY What's she saying? What? What?

DOALTY It's Irish he uses when he's travelling around scrounging votes.

BRIDGET And sleeping with married women. Sure no woman's safe from that fella.

JIMMY Who-who-who? Who's this? Who's this?

HUGH *Silentium!* (*Pause*) Who is she talking about?

MAIRE I'm talking about Daniel O'Connell.

HUGH Does she mean that little Kerry politician?

MAIRE I'm talking about the Liberator, Master, as you well know. And what he said was this: 'The old language is a barrier to modern progress.' He said that last month. And he's right. I don't want Greek. I don't want Latin. I want English.

MANUS *reappears on the platform above.*

I want to be able to speak English because I'm going to America as soon as the harvest's all saved.

MAIRE *remains standing.* HUGH *puts his hand into his pocket and produces a flask of whiskey. He removes the cap, pours a drink into it, tosses it back, replaces the cap, puts the flask back into his pocket.*

HUGH We have been diverted — *diverto* — *divertere* — Where were we?

DOALTY Three items of information, Master. You're at Item B.

HUGH Indeed — Item B — Item B — yes — On my way to the christening this morning I chanced to meet Mr George Alexander, Justice of the Peace. We discussed the new national school. Mr Alexander invited me to take charge of it when it opens. I thanked him and explained that I could do that only if I were free to run it as I have run this hedge school for the past thirty-five years — filling what our friend Euripides calls the '*aplestos pithos*' — James?

JIMMY 'The cask that cannot be filled.'

HUGH Indeed — and Mr Alexander retorted courteously and emphatically that he hopes that is how it will be run.

MAIRE *now sits.*

Indeed. I have had a strenuous day and I am weary

437

of you all. (*He rises*) Manus will take care of you.

> HUGH *goes towards the steps.* OWEN *enters.* OWEN *is the younger son, a handsome, attractive young man in his twenties. He is dressed smartly — a city man. His manner is easy and charming: everything he does is invested with consideration and enthusiasm. He now stands framed in the doorway, a travelling bag across his shoulder.*

OWEN Could anybody tell me is this where Hugh Mór O'Donnell holds his hedge school?

DOALTY It's Owen — Owen Hugh! Look, boys — it's Owen Hugh!

> OWEN *enters. As he crosses the room he touches and has a word for each person.*

OWEN Doalty! (*Playful punch*) How are you, boy? *Jacobe, quid agis?* Are you well?

DOALTY Fine. Fine.

OWEN And Bridget! Give us a kiss. Aaaaaah!

BRIDGET You're welcome, Owen.

OWEN It's not — ? Yes, it *is* Maire Chatach! God! A young woman!

MAIRE How are you, Owen?

> OWEN *is now in front of* HUGH. *He puts his two hands on his father's shoulders.*

OWEN And how's the old man himself?

HUGH Fair — fair.

OWEN Fair? For God's sake you never looked better! Come here to me.

> *He embraces* HUGH *warmly and genuinely.*

Great to see you, Father. Great to be back. (HUGH's *eyes are moist — partly joy, partly the drink*)

HUGH I — I'm — I'm — pay no attention to —

OWEN Come on — come on — come on — (*He gives* HUGH *his handkerchief*) Do you know what you and I are going to do tonight? We are going to go up to Anna na mBréag's . . .

DOALTY Not there, Owen.

OWEN Why not?

DOALTY Her poteen's worse than ever.

BRIDGET They say she puts frogs in it!

OWEN All the better. (*To* HUGH) And you and I are going to get footless drunk. That's arranged.

> OWEN *sees* MANUS *coming down the steps with tea and soda bread. They meet at the bottom.*

And Manus!

MANUS You're welcome, Owen.

OWEN I know I am. And it's great to be here. (*He turns round, arms outstretched*) I can't believe it. I come back after six years and everything's just as it was! Nothing's changed! Not a thing! (*Sniffs*) Even that smell — that's the same smell this place always had. What is it anyway? Is it the straw?

DOALTY Jimmy Jack's feet.

> *General laughter. It opens little pockets of conversation round the room.*

OWEN And Doalty Dan Doalty hasn't changed either!

DOALTY Bloody right, Owen.

OWEN Jimmy, are you well?

JIMMY Dodging about.

OWEN Any word of the big day? (*This is greeted with 'ohs' and 'ahs'*) Time enough, Jimmy. Homer's easier to live with, isn't he?

MAIRE We heard stories that you own ten big shops in Dublin — is it true?

OWEN Only nine.

BRIDGET And you've twelve horses and six servants.

OWEN Yes — that's true. God Almighty, would you listen to
      them — taking a hand at me!

MANUS When did you arrive?

OWEN We left Dublin yesterday morning, spent last night in
      Omagh and got here half-an-hour ago.

MANUS You're hungry then.

HUGH Indeed — get him food — get him a drink.

OWEN Not now, thanks; later. Listen — am I interrupting you
      all?

HUGH By no means. We're finished for the day.

OWEN Wonderful. I'll tell you why. Two friends of mine are
      waiting outside the door. They'd like to meet you and
      I'd like you to meet them. May I bring them in?

HUGH Certainly. You'll all eat and have . . .

OWEN Not just yet, Father. You've seen the sappers working
      in this area for the past fortnight, haven't you? Well,
      the older man is Captain Lancey . . .

HUGH I've met Captain Lancey.

OWEN Great. He's the cartographer in charge of this whole
      area. Cartographer — James? (OWEN *begins to play this
      game — his father's game — partly to involve his class-
      room audience, partly to show he has not forgotten it, and
      indeed partly because he enjoys it*)

JIMMY A maker of maps.

OWEN Indeed — and the younger man that I travelled with
      from Dublin, his name is Lieutenant Yolland and he
      is attached to the toponymic department — Father?
      — *Responde — responde!*

HUGH He gives names to places.

OWEN Indeed — although he is in fact an orthographer —
      Doalty? — too slow — Manus?

MANUS The correct spelling of those names.

OWEN Indeed — indeed! (OWEN *laughs and claps his hands.
      Some of the others join in*) Beautiful! Beautiful! Honest
      to God, it's such a delight to be back here with you all
      again — 'civilized' people. Anyhow — may I bring
      them in?

HUGH Your friends are our friends.

OWEN I'll be straight back.

There is general talk as OWEN *goes towards the door.*
He stops beside SARAH.

That's a new face. Who are you?

A very brief hesitation.

SARAH My name is Sarah.
OWEN Sarah who?
SARAH Sarah Johnny Sally.
OWEN Of course! From Bun na hAbhann! I'm Owen —
Owen Hugh Mór. From Baile Beag. Good to see you.

During this OWEN-SARAH *exchange:*

HUGH Come on now. Let's tidy this place up. (*He rubs the top*
of his table with his sleeve) Move, Doalty — lift those
books off the floor.
DOALTY Right, Master; certainly, Master; I'm doing my best,
Master.

OWEN *stops at the door.*

OWEN One small thing, Father.
HUGH *Silentium!*
OWEN I'm on their payroll.

SARAH, *very elated at her success, is beside* MANUS.

SARAH I said it, Manus!

MANUS *ignores* SARAH. *He is much more interested*
in OWEN *now.*

MANUS You haven't enlisted, have you?!

SARAH *moves away.*

OWEN Me, a soldier? I'm employed as a part-time, underpaid, civilian interpreter. My job is to translate the quaint, archaic tongue you people persist in speaking into the King's good English.

He goes out.

HUGH Move — move — move! Put some order on things! Come on, Sarah — hide that bucket. Whose are these slates? Somebody take these dishes away. *Festinate! — Festinate!*

MANUS *goes to* MAIRE *who is busy tidying.*

MANUS You didn't tell me you were definitely leaving.
MAIRE Not now.
HUGH Good girl, Bridget. That's the style.
MANUS You might at least have told me.
HUGH Are these your books, James?
JIMMY Thank you.
MANUS Fine! Fine! Go ahead! Go ahead!
MAIRE You talk to me about getting married — with neither a roof over your head nor a sod of ground under your foot. I suggest you go for the new school; but no — 'My father's in for that.' Well now he's got it and now this is finished and now you've nothing.
MANUS I can always . . .
MAIRE What? Teach Classics to the cows? Agh —

MAIRE *moves away from* MANUS. OWEN *enters with* LANCEY *and* YOLLAND. CAPTAIN LANCEY *is middle-aged; a small, crisp officer, expert in his field as cartographer but uneasy with people — especially civilians, especially these foreign civilians. His skill is with deeds, not words.* LIEUTENANT YOLLAND *is in his late twenties/ early thirties. He is tall and thin and gangling, blond hair, a shy, awkward manner. A soldier by accident.*

OWEN Here we are. Captain Lancey — my father.
LANCEY Good evening.

HUGH *becomes expansive, almost courtly, with his visitors.*

HUGH You and I have already met, sir.

LANCEY Yes.

OWEN And Lieutenant Yolland — both Royal Engineers — my father.

HUGH You're very welcome, gentlemen.

YOLLAND How do you do.

HUGH *Gaudeo vos hic adesse.*

OWEN And I'll make no other introductions except that these are some of the people of Baile Beag and — what? — well you're among the best people in Ireland now.

He pauses to allow LANCEY *to speak.* LANCEY *does not.*

Would you like to say a few words, Captain?

HUGH What about a drop, sir?

LANCEY A what?

HUGH Perhaps a modest refreshment? A little sampling of our *aqua vitae*?

LANCEY No, no.

HUGH Later perhaps when —

LANCEY I'll say what I have to say, if I may, and as briefly as possible. Do they speak *any* English, Roland?

OWEN Don't worry. I'll translate.

LANCEY I see. (*He clears his throat. He speaks as if he were addressing children — a shade too loudly and enunciating excessively*) You may have seen me — seen me — working in this section — section? — working. We are here — here — in this place — you understand? — to make a map — a map — a map and —

JIMMY *Nonne Latine loquitur?*

HUGH *holds up a restraining hand.*

HUGH James.

LANCEY (*To* JIMMY) I do not speak Gaelic, sir. (*He looks at* OWEN)

OWEN Carry on.

LANCEY A map is a representation on paper — a picture — you understand picture? — a paper picture — showing, representing this country — yes? — showing your country in miniature — a scaled drawing on paper of — of — of —

Suddenly DOALTY *sniggers. Then* BRIDGET. *Then* SARAH. OWEN *leaps in quickly.*

OWEN It might be better if you *assume* they understand you —

LANCEY Yes?

OWEN And I'll translate as you go along.

LANCEY I see. Yes. Very well. Perhaps you're right. Well. What we are doing is this. (*He looks at* OWEN. OWEN *nods reassuringly*) His Majesty's government has ordered the first ever comprehensive survey of this entire country — a general triangulation which will embrace detailed hydrographic and topographic information and which will be executed to a scale of six inches to the English mile.

HUGH (*Pouring a drink*) Excellent — excellent.

LANCEY *looks at* OWEN.

OWEN A new map is being made of the whole country.

LANCEY *looks to* OWEN: *Is that all?* OWEN *smiles reassuringly and indicates to proceed.*

LANCEY This enormous task has been embarked on so that the military authorities will be equipped with up-to-date and accurate information on every corner of this part of the Empire.

OWEN The job is being done by soldiers because they are skilled in this work.

LANCEY And also so that the entire basis of land valuation can be reassessed for purposes of more equitable taxation.

OWEN This new map will take the place of the estate agent's

444

map so that from now on you will know exactly what
is yours in law.

LANCEY In conclusion I wish to quote two brief extracts from the
white paper which is our governing charter: (*Reads*) 'All
former surveys of Ireland originated in forfeiture and
violent transfer of property; the present survey has
for its object the relief which can be afforded to the pro-
prietors and occupiers of land from unequal taxation.'

OWEN The captain hopes that the public will cooperate with
the sappers and that the new map will mean that
taxes are reduced.

HUGH A worthy enterprise — *opus honestum!* And Extract B?

LANCEY 'Ireland is privileged. No such survey is being under-
taken in England. So this survey cannot but be re-
ceived as proof of the disposition of this government
to advance the interests of Ireland.' My sentiments, too.

OWEN This survey demonstrates the government's interest
in Ireland and the captain thanks you for listening so
attentively to him.

HUGH Our pleasure, Captain.

LANCEY Lieutenant Yolland?

YOLLAND I — I — I've nothing to say — really —

OWEN The captain is the man who actually makes the new
map. George's task is to see that the place-names on
this map are . . . correct. (*To* YOLLAND) Just a few words
— they'd like to hear you. (*To class*) Don't you want
to hear George, too?

MAIRE Has he anything to say?

YOLLAND (*To* MAIRE) Sorry-sorry?

OWEN She says she's dying to hear you.

YOLLAND (*To* MAIRE) Very kind of you — thank you . . . (*To class*)
I can only say that I feel — I feel very foolish to —
to — to be working here and not to speak your language. But I intend to rectify that — with Roland's
help — indeed I do.

OWEN He wants me to teach him Irish!

HUGH You are doubly welcome, sir.

YOLLAND I think your countryside is — is — is — is very beautiful. I've fallen in love with it already. I hope we're

not too — too crude an intrusion on your lives. And I know that I'm going to be happy, very happy, here.

OWEN He is already a committed Hibernophile —

JIMMY He loves —

OWEN All right, Jimmy — we know — he loves Baile Beag; and he loves you all.

HUGH Please . . . May I . . . ?

HUGH is now drunk. He holds on to the edge of the table.

OWEN Go ahead, Father. (*Hands up for quiet*) Please — please.

HUGH And we, gentlemen, we in turn are happy to offer you our friendship, our hospitality, and every assistance that you may require. Gentlemen — welcome!

A few desultory claps. The formalities are over. General conversation. The soldiers meet the locals. MANUS and OWEN meet downstage.

OWEN Lancey's a bloody ramrod but George's all right. How are you anyway?

MANUS What sort of a translation was that, Owen?

OWEN Did I make a mess of it?

MANUS You weren't saying what Lancey was saying!

OWEN 'Uncertainty in meaning is incipient poetry' — who said that?

MANUS There was nothing uncertain about what Lancey said: it's a bloody military operation, Owen! And what's Yolland's function? What's 'incorrect' about the place-names we have here?

OWEN Nothing at all. They're just going to be standardized.

MANUS You mean changed into English?

OWEN Where there's ambiguity, they'll be anglicized.

MANUS And they call you Roland! They both call you Roland!

OWEN Shhhhh. Isn't it ridiculous? They seemed to get it wrong from the very beginning — or else they can't pronounce Owen. I was afraid some of you bastards would laugh.

MANUS Aren't you going to tell them?

OWEN Yes — yes — soon — soon.

MANUS But they . . .

OWEN Easy, man, easy. Owen — Roland — what the hell. It's only a name. It's the same me, isn't it? Well, isn't it?

MANUS Indeed it is. It's the same Owen.

OWEN And the same Manus. And in a way we complement each other.

He punches MANUS *lightly, playfully, and turns to join the others. As he goes:*

All right — who has met whom? Isn't this a job for the go-between?

MANUS *watches* OWEN *move confidently across the floor, taking* MAIRE *by the hand and introducing her to* YOLLAND. HUGH *is trying to negotiate the steps.* JIMMY *is lost in a text.* DOALTY *and* BRIDGET *are reliving their giggling.* SARAH *is staring at* MANUS.

ACT TWO

Scene One

The sappers have already mapped most of the area. YOLLAND's *official task, which* OWEN *is now doing, is to take each of the Gaelic names — every hill, stream, rock, even every patch of ground which possessed its own distinctive Irish name — and anglicize it, either by changing it into its approximate English sound or by translating it into English words. For example, a Gaelic name like Cnoc Bán could become Knockban or — directly translated — Fair Hill. These new standardized names were entered into the Name Book, and when the new maps appeared they contained all these new anglicized names. Owen's official function as translator is to pronounce each name in Irish and then provide the English translation.*

The hot weather continues. It is late afternoon some days later. Stage right: an improvised clothes line strung between the shafts of the cart and a nail in the wall; on it are some shirts and socks.

A large map — one of the new blank maps — is spread out on the floor. OWEN *is on his hands and knees consulting it. He is totally engrossed in his task which he pursues with great energy and efficiency.*

YOLLAND's *hesitancy has vanished — he is at home here now. He is sitting on the floor, his long legs stretched out before him, his back resting against a creel, his eyes closed. His mind is elsewhere. One of the reference books — a church registry — lies open on his lap.*

Around them are various reference books, the Name Book, a bottle of poteen, some cups, etc.

OWEN *completes an entry in the Name Book and returns to the map on the floor.*

OWEN   Now. Where have we got to? Yes — the point where that stream enters the sea — that tiny little beach there. George!

YOLLAND   Yes. I'm listening. What do you call it? Say the Irish name again?

OWEN Bun na hAbhann.

YOLLAND Again.

OWEN Bun na hAbhann.

YOLLAND Bun na hAbhann.

OWEN That's terrible, George.

YOLLAND I know. I'm sorry. Say it again.

OWEN Bun na hAbhann.

YOLLAND Bun na hAbhann.

OWEN That's better. Bun is the Irish word for bottom. And Abha means river. So it's literally the mouth of the river.

YOLLAND Let's leave it alone. There's no English equivalent for a sound like that.

OWEN What is it called in the church registry?

Only now does YOLLAND *open his eyes.*

YOLLAND Let's see . . . Banowen.

OWEN That's wrong. (*Consults text*) The list of freeholders calls it Owenmore — that's completely wrong; Owenmore's the big river at the west end of the parish. (*Another text*) And in the grand jury lists it's called — God! — Binhone! — wherever they got that. I suppose we could anglicize it to Bunowen; but somehow that's neither fish nor flesh.

YOLLAND *closes his eyes again.*

YOLLAND I give up.

OWEN (*At map*) Back to first principles. What are we trying to do?

YOLLAND Good question.

OWEN We are trying to denominate and at the same time describe that tiny area of soggy, rocky, sandy ground where that little stream enters the sea, an area known locally as Bun na hAbhann . . . Burnfoot! What about Burnfoot?

YOLLAND (*Indifferently*) Good, Roland, Burnfoot's good.

OWEN George, my name isn't . . .

YOLLAND B-u-r-n-f-o-o-t?

OWEN Are you happy with that?

YOLLAND Yes.

OWEN Burnfoot it is then. (*He makes the entry into the Name Book*) Bun na hAbhann — B-u-r-n-

YOLLAND You're becoming very skilled at this.

OWEN We're not moving fast enough.

YOLLAND (*Opens eyes again*) Lancey lectured me again last night.

OWEN When does he finish here?

YOLLAND The sappers are pulling out at the end of the week. The trouble is, the maps they've completed can't be printed without these names. So London screams at Lancey and Lancey screams at me. But I wasn't intimidated.

MANUS *emerges from upstairs and descends.*

'I'm sorry, sir,' I said, 'but certain tasks demand their own tempo. You cannot rename a whole country overnight.' Your Irish air has made me bold. (*To* MANUS) Do you want us to leave?

MANUS Time enough. Class won't begin for another half-hour.

YOLLAND Sorry — sorry?

OWEN Can't you speak English?

MANUS *gathers the things off the clothes line.* OWEN *returns to the map.*

We now come across that beach . . .

YOLLAND Trá — that's the Irish for beach. (*To* MANUS) I'm picking up the odd word, Manus.

MANUS So.

OWEN . . . on past Burnfoot; and there's nothing around here that has any name that I know of until we come down here to the south end, just about here . . . and there should be a ridge of rocks there . . . Have the sappers marked it? They have. Look, George.

YOLLAND Where are we?

OWEN There.

YOLLAND I'm lost.

OWEN Here. And the name of that ridge is Druim Dubh. Put English on that, Lieutenant.

YOLLAND Say it again.

OWEN Druim Dubh.

YOLLAND Dubh means black.

OWEN Yes.

YOLLAND And Druim means . . . what? a fort?

OWEN We met it yesterday in Druim Luachra.

YOLLAND A ridge! The Black Ridge! (*To* MANUS) You see, Manus?

OWEN We'll have you fluent at the Irish before the summer's over.

YOLLAND Oh, I wish I were. (*To* MANUS *as he crosses to go back upstairs*) We got a crate of oranges from Dublin today. I'll send some up to you.

MANUS Thanks. (*To* OWEN) Better hide that bottle. Father's just up and he'd be better without it.

OWEN Can't you speak English before your man?

MANUS Why?

OWEN Out of courtesy.

MANUS Doesn't he want to learn Irish? (*To* YOLLAND) Don't you want to learn Irish?

YOLLAND Sorry — sorry? I — I —

MANUS I understand the Lanceys perfectly but people like you puzzle me.

OWEN Manus, for God's sake!

MANUS (*Still to* YOLLAND) How's the work going?

YOLLAND The work? — the work? Oh, it's — it's staggering along — I think — (*To* OWEN) — isn't it? But we'd be lost without Roland.

MANUS (*Leaving*) I'm sure. But there are always the Rolands, aren't there?

He goes upstairs and exits.

YOLLAND What was that he said? — something about Lancey, was it?

OWEN He said we should hide that bottle before Father gets

his hands on it.

YOLLAND Ah.

OWEN He's always trying to protect him.

YOLLAND Was he lame from birth?

OWEN An accident when he was a baby: Father fell across his cradle. That's why Manus feels so responsible for him.

YOLLAND Why doesn't he marry?

OWEN Can't afford to, I suppose.

YOLLAND Hasn't he a salary?

OWEN What salary? All he gets is the odd shilling Father throws him — and that's seldom enough. I got out in time, didn't I? (YOLLAND *is pouring a drink*) Easy with that stuff — it'll hit you suddenly.

YOLLAND I like it.

OWEN Let's get back to the job. Druim Dubh — what's it called in the jury lists? (*Consults texts*)

YOLLAND Some people here resent us.

OWEN Dramduff — wrong as usual.

YOLLAND I was passing a little girl yesterday and she spat at me.

OWEN And it's Drimdoo here. What's it called in the registry?

YOLLAND Do you know the Donnelly twins?

OWEN Who?

YOLLAND The Donnelly twins.

OWEN Yes. Best fishermen about here. What about them?

YOLLAND Lancey's looking for them.

OWEN What for?

YOLLAND He wants them for questioning.

OWEN Probably stolen somebody's nets. Dramduffy! Nobody ever called it Dramduffy. Take your pick of those three.

YOLLAND My head's addled. Let's take a rest. Do you want a drink?

OWEN Thanks. Now, every Dubh we've come across we've changed to Duff. So if we're to be consistent I suppose Druim Dubh has to become Dromduff. (YOLLAND *is now looking out the window*) You can see the end of the ridge from where you're standing. But D-r-u-m- or D-r-o-m- ? (*Name Book*) Do you remember — which did we agree on for Druim Luachra?

YOLLAND That house immediately above where we're camped —

OWEN Mm?

YOLLAND The house where Maire lives.

OWEN Maire? Oh, Maire Chatach.

YOLLAND What does that mean?

OWEN Curly-haired; the whole family are called the Catachs. What about it?

YOLLAND I hear music coming from that house almost every night.

OWEN Why don't you drop in?

YOLLAND Could I?

OWEN Why not? We used D-r-o-m then. So we've got to call it D-r-o-m-d-u-f-f — all right?

YOLLAND Go back up to where the new school is being built and just say the names again for me, would you?

OWEN That's a good idea. Poolkerry, Ballybeg —

YOLLAND No, no; as they still are in your own language.

OWEN Poll na gCaorach, (YOLLAND *repeats the names silently after him*) Baile Beag, Ceann Balor, Lios Maol, Machaire Buidhe, Baile na gGall, Carraig na Rí, Mullach Dearg —

YOLLAND Do you think I could live here?

OWEN What are you talking about?

YOLLAND Settle down here — live here.

OWEN Come on, George.

YOLLAND I mean it.

OWEN Live on what? Potatoes? Buttermilk?

YOLLAND It's really heavenly.

OWEN For God's sake! The first hot summer in fifty years and you think it's Eden. Don't be such a bloody romantic. You wouldn't survive a mild winter here.

YOLLAND Do you think not? Maybe you're right.

DOALTY *enters in a rush.*

DOALTY Hi, boys, is Manus about?

OWEN He's upstairs. Give him a shout.

DOALTY Manus! The cattle's going mad in that heat — Cripes, running wild all over the place. (*To* YOLLAND) How are you doing, skipper?

MANUS *appears.*

YOLLAND Thank you for — I — I'm very grateful to you for —
DOALTY Wasting your time. I don't know a word you're saying. Hi, Manus, there's two bucks down the road there
asking for you.
MANUS (*Descending*) Who are they?
DOALTY Never clapped eyes on them. They want to talk to
you.
MANUS What about?
DOALTY They wouldn't say. Come on. The bloody beasts'll end
up in Loch an Iubhair if they're not capped. Good
luck, boys!

DOALTY *rushes off.* MANUS *follows him.*

OWEN Good luck! What were you thanking Doalty for?
YOLLAND I was washing outside my tent this morning and he
was passing with a scythe across his shoulder and he
came up to me and pointed to the long grass and then
cut a pathway round my tent and from the tent down
to the road — so that my feet won't get wet with the
dew. Wasn't that kind of him? And I have no words
to thank him . . . I suppose you're right: I suppose I
couldn't live here . . . Just before Doalty came up to
me this morning I was thinking that at that moment
I might have been in Bombay instead of Ballybeg. You
see, my father was at his wits' end with me and finally
he got me a job with the East India Company — some
kind of a clerkship. This was ten, eleven months ago.
So I set off for London. Unfortunately I — I — I missed
the boat. Literally. And since I couldn't face Father
and hadn't enough money to hang about until the
next sailing, I joined the army. And they stuck me into
the Engineers and posted me to Dublin. And Dublin
sent me here. And while I was washing this morning
and looking across the Trá Bhán I was thinking how

very, very lucky I am to be here and not in Bombay.

OWEN Do you believe in fate?

YOLLAND Lancey's so like my father. I was watching him last night. He met every group of sappers as they reported in. He checked the field kitchens. He examined the horses. He inspected every single report — even examining the texture of the paper and commenting on the neatness of the handwriting. The perfect colonial servant: not only must the job be done — it must be done with excellence. Father has that drive, too; that dedication; that indefatigable energy. He builds roads — hopping from one end of the Empire to the other. Can't sit still for five minutes. He says himself the longest time he ever sat still was the night before Waterloo when they were waiting for Wellington to make up his mind to attack.

OWEN What age is he?

YOLLAND Born in 1789 — the very day the Bastille fell. I've often thought maybe that gave his whole life its character. Do you think it could? He inherited a new world the day he was born — The Year One. Ancient time was at an end. The world had cast off its old skin. There were no longer any frontiers to man's potential. Possibilities were endless and exciting. He still believes that. The Apocalypse is just about to happen . . . I'm afraid I'm a great disappointment to him. I've neither his energy, nor his coherence, nor his belief. Do I believe in fate? The day I arrived in Ballybeg — no, Baile Beag — the moment you brought me in here I had a curious sensation. It's difficult to describe. It was a momentary sense of discovery; no — not quite a sense of discovery — a sense of recognition, of confirmation of something I half knew instinctively; as if I had stepped . . .

OWEN Back into ancient time?

YOLLAND No, no. It wasn't an awareness of *direction* being changed but of experience being of a totally different order. I had moved into a consciousness that wasn't striving nor agitated, but at its ease and with its own conviction and assurance. And when I heard Jimmy

Jack and your father swapping stories about Apollo and Cuchulainn and Paris and Ferdia — as if they lived down the road — it was then that I thought — I knew — perhaps I could live here . . . (*Now embarrassed*) Where's the pot-een?

OWEN Poteen.

YOLLAND Poteen — poteen — poteen. Even if I did speak Irish I'd always be an outsider here, wouldn't I? I may learn the password but the language of the tribe will always elude me, won't it? The private core will always be . . . hermetic, won't it?

OWEN You can learn to decode us.

> HUGH *emerges from upstairs and descends. He is dressed for the road. Today he is physically and mentally jaunty and alert — almost self-consciously jaunty and alert. Indeed, as the scene progresses, one has the sense that he is deliberately parodying himself. The moment* HUGH *gets to the bottom of the steps* YOLLAND *leaps respectfully to his feet.*

HUGH (*As he descends*) *Quantumvis cursum longum fessumque moratur*
Sol, sacro tandem carmine vesper adest.
I dabble in verse, Lieutenant, after the style of Ovid. (*To* OWEN) A drop of that to fortify me.

YOLLAND You'll have to translate it for me.

HUGH Let's see — No matter how long the sun may linger on his long and weary journey
At length evening comes with its sacred song.

YOLLAND Very nice, sir.

HUGH English succeeds in making it sound . . . plebeian.

OWEN Where are you off to, Father?

HUGH An *expeditio* with three purposes. Purpose A: to acquire a testimonial from our parish priest — (*To* YOLLAND) a worthy man but barely literate; and since he'll ask me to write it myself, how in all modesty can I do myself justice? (*To* OWEN) Where did this (*drink*) come from?

OWEN Anna na mBréag's.

HUGH (*To* YOLLAND) In that case address yourself to it with circumspection. (*And* HUGH *instantly tosses the drink back in one gulp and grimaces*) Aaaaaaagh! (*Holds out his glass for a refill*) Anna na mBréag means Anna of the Lies. And Purpose B: to talk to the builders of the new school about the kind of living accommodation I will require there. I have lived too long like a journeyman tailor.

YOLLAND Some years ago we lived fairly close to a poet — well, about three miles away.

HUGH His name?

YOLLAND Wordsworth — William Wordsworth.

HUGH Did he speak of me to you?

YOLLAND Actually I never talked to him. I just saw him out walking — in the distance.

HUGH Wordsworth? . . . No. I'm afraid we're not familiar with your literature, Lieutenant. We feel closer to the warm Mediterranean. We tend to overlook your island.

YOLLAND I'm learning to speak Irish, sir.

HUGH Good.

YOLLAND Roland's teaching me.

HUGH Splendid.

YOLLAND I mean — I feel so cut off from the people here. And I was trying to explain a few minutes ago how remarkable a community this is. To meet people like yourself and Jimmy Jack who actually converse in Greek and Latin. And your place-names — what was the one we came across this morning? — Termon, from Terminus, the god of boundaries. It — it — it's really astonishing.

HUGH We like to think we endure around truths immemorially posited.

YOLLAND And your Gaelic literature — you're a poet yourself —

HUGH Only in Latin, I'm afraid.

YOLLAND I understand it's enormously rich and ornate.

HUGH Indeed, Lieutenant. A rich language. A rich literature. You'll find, sir, that certain cultures expend on their vocabularies and syntax acquisitive energies and ostentations entirely lacking in their material lives. I suppose you could call us a spiritual people.

OWEN (*Not unkindly, more out of embarrassment before* YOLLAND) Will you stop that nonsense, Father.

HUGH Nonsense? What nonsense?

OWEN Do you know where the priest lives?

HUGH At Lios na Muc, over near . . .

OWEN No, he doesn't. Lios na Muc, the Fort of the Pigs, has become Swinefort. (*Now turning the pages of the Name Book — a page per name*) And to get to Swinefort you pass through Greencastle and Fair Head and Strandhill and Gort and Whiteplains. And the new school isn't at Poll na gCaorach — it's at Sheepsrock. Will you be able to find your way?

HUGH *pours himself another drink.*

HUGH Yes, it is a rich language, Lieutenant, full of the mythologies of fantasy and hope and self-deception — a syntax opulent with tomorrows. It is our response to mud cabins and a diet of potatoes; our only method of replying to . . . inevitabilities. (*To* OWEN) Can you give me the loan of half-a-crown? I'll repay you out of the subscriptions I'm collecting for the publication of my new book. (*To* YOLLAND) It is entitled: 'The Pentaglot Preceptor or Elementary Institute of the English, Greek, Hebrew, Latin and Irish Languages; Particularly Calculated for the Instruction of Such Ladies and Gentlemen as may Wish to Learn without the Help of a Master.'

YOLLAND (*Laughs*) That's a wonderful title!

HUGH Between ourselves — the best part of the enterprise. Nor do I, in fact, speak Hebrew. And that last phrase — 'without the Help of a Master' — that was written before the new national school was thrust upon me — do you think I ought to drop it now? After all you don't dispose of the cow just because it has produced a magnificent calf, do you?

YOLLAND You certainly do not.

HUGH The phrase goes. And I'm interrupting work of moment.

He goes to the door and stops there.

To return briefly to that other matter, Lieutenant. I understand your sense of exclusion, of being cut off from a life here; and I trust you will find access to us with my son's help. But remember that words are signals, counters. They are not immortal. And it can happen — to use an image you'll understand — it can happen that a civilization can be imprisoned in a linguistic contour which no longer matches the landscape of . . . fact. Gentlemen.

He leaves.

OWEN 'An *expeditio* with three purposes'— the children laugh at him: he always promises three points and he never gets beyond A and B.

YOLLAND He's an astute man.

OWEN He's bloody pompous.

YOLLAND But so astute.

OWEN And he drinks too much. Is it astute not to be able to adjust for survival? Enduring around truths immemorially posited — hah!

YOLLAND He knows what's happening.

OWEN What is happening?

YOLLAND I'm not sure. But I'm concerned about my part in it. It's an eviction of sorts.

OWEN We're making a six-inch map of the country. Is there something sinister in that?

YOLLAND Not in —

OWEN And we're taking place-names that are riddled with confusion and —

YOLLAND Who's confused? Are the people confused?

OWEN — and we're standardizing those names as accurately and as sensitively as we can.

YOLLAND Something is being eroded.

OWEN Back to the romance again. All right! Fine! Fine! Look where we've got to.

He drops on his hands and knees and stabs a finger at the map.

We've come to this crossroads. Come here and look at it, man! Look at it! And we call that crossroads Tobair Vree. And why do we call it Tobair Vree? I'll tell you why. Tobair means a well. But what does Vree mean? It's a corruption of Brian — (*Gaelic pronunciation*) Brian — an erosion of Tobair Bhriain. Because a hundred-and-fifty years ago there used to be a well there, not at the crossroads, mind you — that would be too simple — but in a field close to the crossroads. And an old man called Brian, whose face was disfigured by an enormous growth, got it into his head that the water in that well was blessed; and every day for seven months he went there and bathed his face in it. But the growth didn't go away; and one morning Brian was found drowned in that well. And ever since that crossroads is known as Tobair Vree — even though that well has long since dried up. I know the story because my grandfather told it to me. But ask Doalty — or Maire — or Bridget — even my father — even Manus — why it's called Tobair Vree; and do you think they'll know? I know they don't know. So the question I put to you, Lieutenant, is this: what do we do with a name like that? Do we scrap Tobair Vree altogether and call it — what? — The Cross? Crossroads? Or do we keep piety with a man long dead, long forgotten, his name 'eroded' beyond recognition, whose trivial little story nobody in the parish remembers?

YOLLAND Except you.

OWEN I've left here.

YOLLAND You remember it.

OWEN I'm asking you: what do we write in the Name Book?

YOLLAND Tobair Vree.

OWEN Even though the well is a hundred yards from the actual — crossroads — and there's no well anyway — and what the hell does Vree mean?

YOLLAND Tobair Vree.

OWEN That's what you want?

YOLLAND Yes.

OWEN You're certain?

YOLLAND Yes.

OWEN Fine. Fine. That's what you'll get.

YOLLAND That's what you want, too, Roland. (*Pause*)

OWEN (*Explodes*) George! For God's sake! *My name is not Roland!*

YOLLAND What?

OWEN (*Softly*) My name is Owen. (*Pause*)

YOLLAND Not Roland?

OWEN Owen.

YOLLAND You mean to say — ?

OWEN Owen.

YOLLAND But I've been —

OWEN O-w-e-n.

YOLLAND Where did Roland come from?

OWEN I don't know.

YOLLAND It was never Roland?

OWEN Never.

YOLLAND Oh my God!

> *Pause. They stare at one another. Then the absurdity of the situation strikes them suddenly. They explode with laughter.* OWEN *pours drinks. As they roll about their lines overlap.*

YOLLAND Why didn't you tell me?

OWEN Do I look like a Roland?

YOLLAND Spell Owen again.

OWEN I was getting fond of Roland.

YOLLAND Oh my God!

OWEN O-w-e-n.

YOLLAND What'll we write —

OWEN — in the Name Book?!

YOLLAND R-o-w-e-n!

OWEN Or what about Ol-

YOLLAND Ol- what?

OWEN Oland! (*And again they explode*)

MANUS *enters. He is very elated.*

MANUS What's the celebration?

OWEN A christening!

YOLLAND A baptism!

OWEN A hundred christenings!

YOLLAND A thousand baptisms! Welcome to Eden!

OWEN Eden's right! We name a thing and — bang! — it leaps into existence!

YOLLAND Each name a perfect equation with its roots.

OWEN A perfect congruence with its reality. (*To* MANUS) Take a drink.

YOLLAND Poteen — beautiful.

OWEN Lying Anna's poteen.

YOLLAND Anna na mBréag's poteen.

OWEN Excellent, George.

YOLLAND I'll decode you yet.

OWEN (*Offers drink*) Manus?

MANUS Not if that's what it does to you.

OWEN You're right. Steady — steady — sober up — sober up.

YOLLAND Sober as a judge, Owen.

MANUS *moves beside* OWEN.

MANUS I've got good news! Where's Father?

OWEN He's gone out. What's the good news?

MANUS I've been offered a job.

OWEN Where? (*Now aware of* YOLLAND) Come on, man — speak in English.

MANUS For the benefit of the colonist?

OWEN He's a decent man.

MANUS Aren't they all at some level?

OWEN Please. (MANUS *shrugs*) He's been offered a job.

YOLLAND Where?

OWEN Well — tell us!

MANUS I've just had a meeting with two men from Inis Meadhon. They want me to go there and start a hedge school. They're giving me a free house, free turf, and free milk; a rood of standing corn; twelve drills of potatoes; and — (*he stops*)

OWEN And what?

MANUS A salary of £42 a year!

OWEN Manus, that's wonderful!

MANUS You're talking to a man of substance.

OWEN I'm delighted.

YOLLAND Where's Inis Meadhon?

OWEN An island south of here. And they came looking for you?

MANUS Well, I mean to say . . . (OWEN *punches* MANUS)

OWEN Aaaaagh! This calls for a real celebration.

YOLLAND Congratulations.

MANUS Thank you.

OWEN Where are you, Anna?

YOLLAND When do you start?

MANUS Next Monday

OWEN We'll stay with you when we're there. (*To* YOLLAND) How long will it be before we reach Inis Meadhon?

YOLLAND How far south is it?

MANUS About fifty miles.

YOLLAND Could we make it by December?

OWEN We'll have Christmas together. (*Sings*) 'Christmas Day on Inis Meadhon . . . '

YOLLAND (*Toast*) I hope you're very content there, Manus.

MANUS Thank you.

YOLLAND *holds out his hand.* MANUS *takes it. They shake warmly.*

OWEN (*Toast*) Manus.

MANUS (*Toast*) To Inis Meadhon.

He drinks quickly and turns to leave.

OWEN Hold on — hold on — refills coming up.

MANUS I've got to go.

OWEN Come on, man; this is an occasion. Where are you rushing to?

MANUS I've got to tell Maire.

MAIRE *enters with her can of milk.*

MAIRE You've got to tell Maire what?

OWEN He's got a job!

MAIRE Manus?

OWEN He's been invited to start a hedge school in Inis Meadhon.

MAIRE Where?

MANUS Inis Meadhon — the island! They're giving me £42 a year and . . .

OWEN A house, fuel, milk, potatoes, corn, pupils, what-not!

MANUS I start on Monday.

OWEN You'll take a drink. Isn't it great?

MANUS I want to talk to you for —

MAIRE There's your milk. I need the can back.

MANUS *takes the can and runs up the steps.*

MANUS (*As he goes*) How will you like living on an island?

OWEN You know George, don't you?

MAIRE We wave to each other across the fields.

YOLLAND Sorry-sorry?

OWEN She says you wave to each other across the fields.

YOLLAND Yes, we do; oh, yes; indeed we do.

MAIRE What's he saying?

OWEN He says you wave to each other across the fields.

MAIRE That's right. So we do.

YOLLAND What's she saying?

OWEN Nothing — nothing — nothing. (*To* MAIRE) What's the news?

MAIRE *moves away, touching the text books with her toe.*

MAIRE   Not a thing. You're busy, the two of you.

OWEN   We think we are.

MAIRE   I hear the Fiddler O'Shea's about. There's some talk
of a dance tomorrow night.

OWEN   Where will it be?

MAIRE   Maybe over the road. Maybe at Tobair Vree.

YOLLAND   Tobair Vree!

MAIRE   Yes.

YOLLAND   Tobair Vree! Tobair Vree!

MAIRE   Does he know what I'm saying?

OWEN   Not a word.

MAIRE   Tell him then.

OWEN   Tell him what?

MAIRE   About the dance.

OWEN   Maire says there may be a dance tomorrow night.

YOLLAND   (*To* OWEN) Yes? May I come? (*To* MAIRE) Would anybody object if I came?

MAIRE   (*To* OWEN) What's he saying?

OWEN   (*To* YOLLAND) Who would object?

MAIRE   (*To* OWEN) Did you tell him?

YOLLAND   (*To* MAIRE) Sorry-sorry?

OWEN   (*To* MAIRE) He says may he come?

MAIRE   (*To* YOLLAND) That's up to you.

YOLLAND   (*To* OWEN) What does she say?

OWEN   (*To* YOLLAND) She says —

YOLLAND   (*To* MAIRE) What-what?

MAIRE   (*To* OWEN) Well?

YOLLAND   (*To* OWEN) Sorry-sorry?

OWEN   (*To* YOLLAND) Will you go?

YOLLAND   (*To* MAIRE) Yes, yes, if I may.

MAIRE   (*To* OWEN) What does he say?

YOLLAND   (*To* OWEN) What is she saying?

OWEN   Oh for God's sake!

To MANUS *who is descending with the empty can.*

You take on this job, Manus.

MANUS   I'll walk you up to the house. Is your mother at home?
I want to talk to her.

MAIRE What's the rush? (*To* OWEN) Didn't you offer me a drink?
OWEN Will you risk Anna na mBréag?
MAIRE Why not.

> YOLLAND *is suddenly intoxicated. He leaps up on a*
> *stool, raises his glass and shouts:*

YOLLAND Anna na mBréag! Baile Beag! Inis Meadhon! Bombay!
Tobair Vree! Eden! And poteen — correct, Owen?
OWEN Perfect.
YOLLAND And bloody marvellous stuff it is, too. I love it! Bloody,
bloody, bloody marvellous!

> *Simultaneously with his final 'bloody marvellous' bring*
> *up very loud the introductory music of the reel. Then*
> *immediately go to black. Retain the music throughout*
> *the very brief interval.*

ACT TWO

Scene Two

The following night.

This scene may be played in the schoolroom, but it would be preferable to lose — by lighting — as much of the schoolroom as possible, and to play the scene down front in a vaguely 'outside' area.

The music rises to a crescendo. Then in the distance we hear MAIRE *and* YOLLAND *approach — laughing and running. They run on, hand-in-hand. They have just left the dance. Fade the music to distant background. Then after a time it is lost and replaced by guitar music.* MAIRE *and* YOLLAND *are now down front, still holding hands and excited by their sudden and impetuous escape from the dance.*

MAIRE   Oh my God, that leap across the ditch nearly killed me.

YOLLAND   I could scarcely keep up with you.

MAIRE   Wait till I get my breath back.

YOLLAND   We must have looked as if we were being chased.

> *They now realize they are alone and holding hands — the beginnings of embarrassment. The hands disengage. They begin to drift apart. Pause.*

MAIRE   Manus'll wonder where I've got to.

YOLLAND   I wonder did anyone notice us leave.

> *Pause. Slightly further apart.*

MAIRE   The grass must be wet. My feet are soaking.

YOLLAND   Your feet must be wet. The grass is soaking.

> *Another pause. Another few paces apart. They are now a long distance from one another.*

YOLLAND (*Indicating himself*) George.

MAIRE *nods: Yes-yes.*

MAIRE Lieutenant George.
YOLLAND Don't call me that. I never think of myself as Lieutenant.
MAIRE What-what?
YOLLAND Sorry-sorry? (*He points to himself again*) George.

MAIRE *nods: Yes-yes. Then points to herself.*

MAIRE Maire.
YOLLAND Yes, I know you're Maire. Of course I know you're Maire. I mean I've been watching you night and day for the past —
MAIRE (*Eagerly*) What-what?
YOLLAND (*Points*) Maire. (*Points*) George. (*Points both*) Maire and George.

MAIRE *nods: Yes-yes-yes.*

I — I — I —
MAIRE Say anything at all. I love the sound of your speech.
YOLLAND (*Eagerly*) Sorry-sorry?

> *In acute frustration he looks around, hoping for some inspiration that will provide him with communicative means. Now he has a thought: he tries raising his voice and articulating in a staccato style and with equal and absurd emphasis on each word.*

Every-morning-I-see-you-feeding-brown-hens-and-giving-meal-to-black-calf — (*The futility of it*) — Oh my God.

> MAIRE *smiles. She moves towards him. She will try to communicate in Latin.*

468

MAIRE   *Tu es centurio in — in — in exercitu Britannico —*
YOLLAND   Yes-yes? Go on — go on — say anything at all — I
love the sound of your speech.
MAIRE   *— et es in castris quae — quae — quae sunt in agro —*
(The futility of it) — Oh my God.

> YOLLAND *smiles. He moves towards her. Now for her*
> *English words:*

George — water.
YOLLAND   'Water'? Water! Oh yes — water — water — very
good — water — good — good.
MAIRE   Fire.
YOLLAND   Fire — indeed — wonderful — fire, fire, fire — splen-
did — splendid!
MAIRE   Ah . . . ah . . .
YOLLAND   Yes? Go on.
MAIRE   Earth.
YOLLAND   'Earth'?
MAIRE   Earth. Earth.

> YOLLAND *still does not understand.* MAIRE *stoops*
> *down and picks up a handful of clay. Holding it out:*

Earth.
YOLLAND   Earth! Of course — earth! Earth. Earth. Good Lord,
Maire, your English is perfect!
MAIRE   *(Eagerly)* What-what?
YOLLAND   Perfect English. English perfect.
MAIRE   George —
YOLLAND   That's beautiful — oh, that's really beautiful.
MAIRE   George —
YOLLAND   Say it again — say it again —
MAIRE   Shhh.

> *She holds her hand up for silence — she is trying to*
> *remember her one line of English. Now she remem-*
> *bers it and she delivers the line as if English were her*
> *language — easily, fluidly, conversationally.*

George, 'In Norfolk we besport ourselves around the maypoll.'

YOLLAND Good God, do you? That's where my mother comes from — Norfolk. Norwich actually. Not exactly Norwich town but a small village called Little Walsingham close beside it. But in our own village of Winfarthing we have a maypole too and every year on the first of May —

He stops abruptly, only now realizing. He stares at her. She in turn misunderstands his excitement.

MAIRE (*To herself*) Mother of God, my Aunt Mary wouldn't have taught me something dirty, would she?

Pause. YOLLAND *extends his hand to* MAIRE. *She turns away from him and moves slowly across the stage.*

YOLLAND Maire. (*She still moves away*) Maire Chatach. (*She still moves away*) Bun na hAbhann? (*He says the name softly, almost privately, very tentatively, as if he were searching for a sound she might respond to. He tries again*) Druim Dubh?

MAIRE *stops. She is listening.* YOLLAND *is encouraged.*

Poll na gCaorach. Lios Maol. (MAIRE *turns towards him*) Lios na nGall.

MAIRE Lios na nGrádh.

They are now facing each other and begin moving — almost imperceptibly — towards one another.

Carraig an Phoill.

YOLLAND Carraig na Rí. Loch na nÉan.

MAIRE Loch an Iubhair. Machaire Buidhe.

YOLLAND Machaire Mór. Cnoc na Móna.

MAIRE Cnoc na nGabhar.
YOLLAND Mullach.
MAIRE Port.
YOLLAND Tor.
MAIRE Lag.

She holds out her hands to YOLLAND. *He takes them.*
Each now speaks almost to himself/herself.

YOLLAND I wish to God you could understand me.
MAIRE Soft hands; a gentleman's hands.
YOLLAND Because if you could understand me I could tell you
how I spend my days either thinking of you or gazing
up at your house in the hope that you'll appear even
for a second.
MAIRE Every evening you walk by yourself along the Trá
Bhán and every morning you wash yourself in front
of your tent.
YOLLAND I would tell you how beautiful you are, curly-headed
Maire. I would so like to tell you how beautiful you
are.
MAIRE Your arms are long and thin and the skin on your
shoulders is very white.
YOLLAND I would tell you . . .
MAIRE Don't stop — I know what you're saying.
YOLLAND I would tell you how I want to be here — to live here
— always — with you — always, always.
MAIRE 'Always'? What is that word — 'always'?
YOLLAND Yes-yes; always.
MAIRE You're trembling.
YOLLAND Yes, I'm trembling because of you.
MAIRE I'm trembling, too. (*She holds his face in her hand*)
YOLLAND I've made up my mind . . .
MAIRE Shhhh.
YOLLAND I'm not going to leave here . . .
MAIRE Shhh — listen to me. I want you, too, soldier.
YOLLAND Don't stop — I know what you're saying.
MAIRE I want to live with you — anywhere — anywhere at
all — always — always.

YOLLAND 'Always'? What is that word — 'always'?

MAIRE Take me away with you, George.

> *Pause. Suddenly they kiss.* SARAH *enters. She sees them. She stands shocked, staring at them. Her mouth works. Then almost to herself:*

SARAH Manus . . . Manus!

> SARAH *runs off. Music to crescendo.*

ACT THREE

The following evening. It is raining.

SARAH and OWEN alone in the schoolroom. SARAH, more waiflike than ever, is sitting very still on a stool, an open book across her knee. She is pretending to read but her eyes keep going up to the room upstairs. OWEN is working on the floor as before, surrounded by his reference books, map, Name Book, etc. But he has neither concentration nor interest; and like SARAH he glances up at the upstairs room. After a few seconds MANUS emerges and descends carrying a large paper bag which already contains his clothes. His movements are determined and urgent. He moves around the classroom, picking up books, examining each title carefully, and choosing about six of them which he puts into his bag. As he selects these books:

OWEN   You know that old limekiln beyond Con Connie Tim's pub, the place we call The Murren? — Do you know why it's called The Murren?

> *MANUS does not answer.*

I've only just discovered: it's a corruption of Saint Muranus. It seems Saint Muranus had a monastery somewhere about there at the beginning of the seventh century. And over the years the name became shortened to The Murren. Very unattractive name, isn't it? I think we should go back to the original — Saint Muranus. What do you think? The original's Saint Muranus. Don't you think we should go back to that?

> *No response. OWEN begins writing the name into the Name Book. MANUS is now rooting about among the forgotten implements for a piece of rope. He finds a piece. He begins to tie the mouth of the flimsy, over-*

*loaded bag — and it bursts, the contents spilling out
on the floor.*

MANUS Bloody, bloody, bloody hell!

*His voice breaks in exasperation: he is about to cry.
OWEN leaps to his feet.*

OWEN Hold on. I've a bag upstairs.

He runs upstairs. SARAH waits until OWEN is off.

SARAH Manus . . . Manus, I . . .

*MANUS hears SARAH but makes no acknowledgement.
He gathers up his belongings. OWEN reappears with
the bag he had on his arrival.*

OWEN Take this one — I'm finished with it anyway. And it's
supposed to keep out the rain.

*MANUS transfers his few belongings. OWEN drifts back
to his task. The packing is now complete.*

MANUS You'll be here for a while? For a week or two anyhow?
OWEN Yes.
MANUS You're not leaving with the army?
OWEN I haven't made up my mind. Why?
MANUS Those Inis Meadhon men will be back to see why I
haven't turned up. Tell them — tell them I'll write to
them as soon as I can. Tell them I still want the job but
that it might be three or four months before I'm free
to go.
OWEN You're being damned stupid, Manus.
MANUS Will you do that for me?
OWEN Clear out now and Lancey'll think you're involved
somehow.
MANUS Will you do that for me?
OWEN Wait a couple of days even. You know George — he's

a bloody romantic — maybe he's gone out to one of the islands and he'll suddenly reappear tomorrow morning. Or maybe the search party'll find him this evening, lying drunk somewhere in the sandhills. You've seen him drinking that poteen — doesn't know how to handle it. Had he drink on him last night at the dance?

MANUS   I had a stone in my hand when I went out looking for him — I was going to fell him. The lame scholar turned violent.

OWEN   Did anybody see you?

MANUS   (*Again close to tears*) But when I saw him standing there at the side of the road — smiling — and her face buried in his shoulder — I couldn't even go close to them. I just shouted something stupid — something like, 'You're a bastard, Yolland.' If I'd even said it in English . . . 'cause he kept saying 'Sorry-sorry?' The wrong gesture in the wrong language.

OWEN   And you didn't see him again?

MANUS   'Sorry?'

OWEN   Before you leave tell Lancey that — just to clear yourself.

MANUS   What have I to say to Lancey? You'll give that message to the islandmen?

OWEN   I'm warning you: run away now and you're bound to be —

MANUS   (*To* SARAH) Will you give that message to the Inis Meadhon men?

SARAH   I will.

MANUS *picks up an old sack and throws it across his shoulders.*

OWEN   Have you any idea where you're going?

MANUS   Mayo, maybe. I remember Mother saying she had cousins somewhere away out in the Erris Peninsula. (*He picks up his bag*) Tell Father I took only the Virgil and the Caesar and the Aeschylus because they're mine anyway — I bought them with the money I got for that pet lamb I reared — do you remember that pet lamb? And tell him that Nora Dan never returned the dictionary and that she still owes him two-and-six for last quarter's reading — he always forgets those things.

OWEN Yes.

MANUS And his good shirt's ironed and hanging up in the press and his clean socks are in the butter box under the bed.

OWEN All right.

MANUS And tell him I'll write.

OWEN If Maire asks where you've gone. . . ?

MANUS He'll need only half the amount of milk now, won't he? Even less than half — he usually takes his tea black. (*Pause*) And when he comes in at night — you'll hear him; he makes a lot of noise — I usually come down and give him a hand up. Those stairs are dangerous without a banister. Maybe before you leave you'd get Big Ned Frank to put up some sort of a handrail. (*Pause*) And if you can bake he's very fond of soda bread.

OWEN I can give you money. I'm wealthy. Do you know what they pay me? Two shillings a day for this — this — this —

MANUS *rejects the offer by holding out his hand.*

Goodbye, Manus.

MANUS *and* OWEN *shake hands. Then* MANUS *picks up his bag briskly and goes towards the door. He stops a few paces beyond* SARAH, *turns, comes back to her. He addresses her as he did in Act One but now without warmth or concern for her.*

MANUS What is your name? (*Pause*) Come on. What is your name?

SARAH My name is Sarah.

MANUS Just Sarah? Sarah what? (*Pause*) Well?

SARAH Sarah Johnny Sally.

MANUS And where do you live? Come on.

SARAH I live in Bun na hAbhann. (*She is now crying quietly*)

MANUS Very good, Sarah Johnny Sally. There's nothing to stop you now — nothing in the wide world. (*Pause. He looks down at her*) It's all right — it's all right — you did no harm — you did no harm at all.

He stoops over her and kisses the top of her head — as if in absolution. Then briskly to the door and off.

OWEN Good luck, Manus!

SARAH (*Quietly*) I'm sorry . . . I'm sorry . . . I'm so sorry, Manus . . .

OWEN *tries to work but cannot concentrate. He begins folding up the map. As he does:*

OWEN Is there a class this evening? (SARAH *nods: yes*) I suppose Father knows. Where is he anyhow? (SARAH *points*) Where? (SARAH *mimes rocking a baby*) I don't understand — where? (SARAH *repeats the mime and wipes away tears*. OWEN *is still puzzled*) It doesn't matter. He'll probably turn up.

BRIDGET *and* DOALTY *enter, sacks over their heads against the rain. They are self-consciously noisier, more ebullient, more garrulous than ever — brimming over with excitement and gossip and brio.*

DOALTY You're missing the crack, boys! Cripes, you're missing the crack! Fifty more soldiers arrived an hour ago!

BRIDGET And they're spread out in a big line from Sean Neal's over to Lag and they're moving straight across the fields towards Cnoc na nGabhar!

DOALTY Prodding every inch of the ground in front of them with their bayonets and scattering animals and hens in all directions!

BRIDGET And tumbling everything before them — fences,

ditches, haystacks, turf-stacks!

DOALTY They came to Barney Petey's field of corn — straight through it be God as if it was heather!

BRIDGET Not a blade of it left standing!

DOALTY And Barney Petey just out of his bed and running after them in his drawers: 'You hoors you! Get out of my corn, you hoors you!'

BRIDGET First time he ever ran in his life.

DOALTY Too lazy, the wee get, to cut it when the weather was good.

SARAH *begins putting out the seats.*

BRIDGET Tell them about Big Hughie.

DOALTY Cripes, if you'd seen your aul' fella, Owen.

BRIDGET They were all inside in Anna na mBréag's pub — all the crowd from the wake —

DOALTY And they hear the commotion and they all come out to the street —

BRIDGET Your father in front; the Infant Prodigy footless behind him!

DOALTY And your aul' fella, he sees the army stretched across the countryside —

BRIDGET Oh my God!

DOALTY And Cripes, he starts roaring at them!

BRIDGET 'Visigoths! Huns! Vandals!'

DOALTY *'Ignari! Stulti! Rustici!'*

BRIDGET And wee Jimmy Jack jumping up and down and shouting, 'Thermopylae! Thermopylae!'

DOALTY You never saw crack like it in your life, boys. Come away on out with me, Sarah, and you'll see it all.

BRIDGET Big Hughie's fit to take no class. Is Manus about?

OWEN Manus is gone.

BRIDGET Gone where?

OWEN He's left — gone away.

DOALTY Where to?

OWEN He doesn't know. Mayo, maybe.

DOALTY What's on in Mayo?

OWEN (*To* BRIDGET) Did you see George and Maire Chatach

leave the dance last night?

BRIDGET We did. Didn't we, Doalty?

OWEN Did you see Manus following them out?

BRIDGET I didn't see him going out but I saw him coming in by himself later.

OWEN Did George and Maire come back to the dance?

BRIDGET No.

OWEN Did you see them again?

BRIDGET He left her home. We passed them going up the back road — didn't we, Doalty?

OWEN And Manus stayed till the end of the dance?

DOALTY We know nothing. What are you asking us for?

OWEN Because Lancey'll question me when he hears Manus's gone. (*Back to* BRIDGET) That's the way George went home? By the back road? That's where you saw him?

BRIDGET Leave me alone, Owen. I know nothing about Yolland. If you want to know about Yolland, ask the Donnelly twins.

Silence. DOALTY *moves over to the window.*

(*To* SARAH) He's a powerful fiddler, O'Shea, isn't he? He told our Seamus he'll come back for a night at Hallowe'en.

OWEN *goes to* DOALTY *who looks resolutely out the window.*

OWEN What's this about the Donnellys? (*Pause*) Were they about last night?

DOALTY Didn't see them if they were. (*Begins whistling through his teeth*)

OWEN George is a friend of mine.

DOALTY So.

OWEN I want to know what's happened to him.

DOALTY Couldn't tell you.

OWEN What have the Donnelly twins to do with it? (*Pause*) Doalty!

DOALTY I know nothing, Owen — nothing at all — I swear to

God. All I know is this: on my way to the dance I saw their boat beached at Port. It wasn't there on my way home after I left Bridget. And that's all I know. As God's my judge. The half-dozen times I met him I didn't know a word he said to me; but he seemed a right enough sort . . . (*With sudden excessive interest in the scene outside*) Cripes, they're crawling all over the place! Cripes, there's millions of them! Cripes, they're levelling the whole land!

> OWEN *moves away.* MAIRE *enters. She is bareheaded and wet from the rain; her hair in disarray. She attempts to appear normal but she is in acute distress, on the verge of being distraught. She is carrying the milk can.*

MAIRE Honest to God, I must be going off my head. I'm half-way here and I think to myself, 'Isn't this can very light?' and I look into it and isn't it empty.

OWEN It doesn't matter.

MAIRE How will you manage for tonight?

OWEN We have enough.

MAIRE Are you sure?

OWEN Plenty, thanks.

MAIRE It'll take me no time at all to go back up for some.

OWEN Honestly, Maire.

MAIRE Sure it's better you have it than that black calf that's . . . that . . . (*She looks around*) Have you heard anything?

OWEN Nothing.

MAIRE What does Lancey say?

OWEN I haven't seen him since this morning.

MAIRE What does he *think*?

OWEN We really didn't talk. He was here for only a few seconds.

MAIRE He left me home, Owen. And the last thing he said to me — he tried to speak in Irish — he said, 'I'll see you yesterday' — he meant to say 'I'll see you tomorrow'. And I laughed that much he pretended to get cross

and he said 'Maypoll! Maypoll!' because I said that
word wrong. And off he went, laughing — laughing,
Owen! Do you think he's all right? What do *you* think?

OWEN I'm sure he'll turn up, Maire.

MAIRE He comes from a tiny wee place called Winfarthing.

She suddenly drops on her hands and knees on the floor
— where OWEN *had his map a few minutes ago — and*
with her finger traces out an outline map.

Come here till you see. Look. There's Winfarthing. And
there's two other wee villages right beside it; one of
them's called Barton Bendish — it's there; and the
other's called Saxingham Nethergate — it's about
there. And there's Little Walsingham — that's his
mother's townland. Aren't they odd names? Sure
they make no sense to me at all. And Winfarthing's
near a big town called Norwich. And Norwich is in a
county called Norfolk. And Norfolk is in the east of
England. He drew a map for me on the wet strand
and wrote the names on it. I have it all in my head
now: Winfarthing — Barton Bendish — Saxingham
Nethergate — Little Walsingham — Norwich — Norfolk. Strange sounds, aren't they? But nice sounds;
like Jimmy Jack reciting his Homer.

She gets to her feet and looks around; she is almost
serene now.

(*To* SARAH) You were looking lovely last night, Sarah.
Is that the dress you got from Boston? Green suits
you. (*To* OWEN) Something very bad's happened to
him, Owen. I know. He wouldn't go away without
telling me. Where is he, Owen? You're his friend —
where is he?

Again she looks around the room; then sits on a stool.

I didn't get a chance to do my geography last night.

The master'll be angry with me. (*She rises again*) I think I'll go home now. The wee ones have to be washed and put to bed and that black calf has to be fed . . . My hands are that rough; they're still blistered from the hay. I'm ashamed of them. I hope to God there's no hay to be saved in Brooklyn. (*She stops at the door*) Did you hear? Nellie Ruadh's baby died in the middle of the night. I must go up to the wake. It didn't last long, did it?

> MAIRE *leaves. Silence.*

OWEN I don't think there'll be any class. Maybe you should . . .

> OWEN *begins picking up his texts.* DOALTY *goes to him.*

DOALTY Is he long gone? — Manus.
OWEN Half-an-hour.
DOALTY Stupid bloody fool.
OWEN I told him that.
DOALTY Do they know he's gone?
OWEN Who?
DOALTY The army.
OWEN Not yet.
DOALTY They'll be after him like bloody beagles. Bloody, bloody fool, limping along the coast. They'll overtake him before night for Christ's sake.

> DOALTY *returns to the window.* LANCEY *enters — now the commanding officer.*

OWEN Any news? Any word?

> LANCEY *moves into the centre of the room, looking around as he does.*

LANCEY I understood there was a class. Where are the others?

OWEN   There was to be a class but my father —
LANCEY This will suffice. I will address them and it will be
their responsibility to pass on what I have to say to
every family in this section.

> LANCEY *indicates to* OWEN *to translate.* OWEN *hesitates,
> trying to assess the change in* LANCEY's *manner and
> attitude.*

I'm in a hurry, O'Donnell.
OWEN   The captain has an announcement to make.
LANCEY Lieutenant Yolland is missing. We are searching for
him. If we don't find him, or if we receive no information as to where he is to be found, I will pursue the
following course of action. (*He indicates to* OWEN *to
translate*)
OWEN   They are searching for George. If they don't find him —
LANCEY Commencing twenty-four hours from now we will
shoot all livestock in Ballybeg. (OWEN *stares at* LANCEY)
At once.
OWEN   Beginning this time tomorrow they'll kill every animal
in Baile Beag — unless they're told where George is.
LANCEY If that doesn't bear results, commencing forty-eight
hours from now we will embark on a series of evictions
and levelling of every abode in the following selected
areas —
OWEN   You're not — !
LANCEY Do your job. Translate.
OWEN   If they still haven't found him in two days' time they'll
begin evicting and levelling every house starting with
these townlands.

> LANCEY *reads from his list.*

LANCEY Swinefort.
OWEN   Lios na Muc.
LANCEY Burnfoot.
OWEN   Bun na hAbhann.
LANCEY Dromduff.

OWEN Druim Dubh.

LANCEY Whiteplains.

OWEN Machaire Bán.

LANCEY Kings Head.

OWEN Cnoc na Rí.

LANCEY If by then the lieutenant hasn't been found we will proceed until a complete clearance is made of this entire section.

OWEN If Yolland hasn't been got by then they will ravish the whole parish.

LANCEY I trust they know exactly what they've got to do. (*Pointing to* BRIDGET) I know you. I know where you live. (*Pointing to* SARAH) Who are you? Name! (SARAH's *mouth opens and shuts, opens and shuts. Her face becomes contorted*) What's your name? (*Again* SARAH *tries frantically*)

OWEN Go on, Sarah. You can tell him.

> But SARAH *cannot. And she knows she cannot. She closes her mouth. Her head goes down.*

OWEN Her name is Sarah Johnny Sally.

LANCEY Where does she live?

OWEN Bun na hAbhann.

LANCEY Where?

OWEN Burnfoot.

LANCEY I want to talk to your brother — is he here?

OWEN Not at the moment.

LANCEY Where is he?

OWEN He's at a wake.

LANCEY What wake?

> DOALTY, *who has been looking out the window all through Lancey's announcements, now speaks — calmly, almost casually.*

DOALTY Tell him his whole camp's on fire.

LANCEY What's your name? (*To* OWEN) Who's that lout?

OWEN Doalty Dan Doalty.

LANCEY Where does he live?

OWEN Tulach Álainn.

LANCEY What do we call it?

OWEN Fair Hill. He says your whole camp is on fire.

> LANCEY *rushes to the window and looks out. Then he wheels on* DOALTY.

LANCEY I'll remember you, Mr Doalty. (*To* OWEN) You carry a big responsibility in all this.

> *He goes off.*

BRIDGET Mother of God, does he mean it, Owen?

OWEN Yes, he does.

BRIDGET We'll have to hide the beasts somewhere — our Seamus'll know where. Maybe at the back of Lios na nGrádh — or in the caves at the far end of the Trá Bhán. Come on, Doalty! Come on! Don't be standing about there!

> DOALTY *does not move.* BRIDGET *runs to the door and stops suddenly. She sniffs the air. Panic.*

The sweet smell! Smell it! It's the sweet smell! Jesus, it's the potato blight!

DOALTY It's the army tents burning, Bridget.

BRIDGET Is it? Are you sure? Is that what it is? God, I thought we were destroyed altogether. Come on! Come on!

> *She runs off.* OWEN *goes to* SARAH *who is preparing to leave.*

OWEN How are you? Are you all right?

> SARAH *nods: Yes.*

Don't worry. It will come back to you again.

SARAH *shakes her head.*

It will. You're upset now. He frightened you. That's all's wrong.

Again SARAH *shakes her head, slowly, emphatically, and smiles at* OWEN. *Then she leaves.* OWEN *busies himself gathering his belongings.* DOALTY *leaves the window and goes to him.*

DOALTY He'll do it, too.
OWEN Unless Yolland's found.
DOALTY Hah!
OWEN Then he'll certainly do it.
DOALTY When my grandfather was a boy they did the same thing. (*Simply, altogether without irony*) And after all the trouble you went to, mapping the place and thinking up new names for it.

OWEN *busies himself. Pause.* DOALTY, *almost dreamily:*

I've damned little to defend but he'll not put me out without a fight. And there'll be others who think the same as me.
OWEN That's a matter for you.
DOALTY If we'd all stick together. If we knew how to defend ourselves.
OWEN Against a trained army.
DOALTY The Donnelly twins know how.
OWEN If they could be found.
DOALTY If they could be found. (*He goes to the door*) Give me a shout after you've finished with Lancey. I might know something then.

He leaves. OWEN *picks up the Name Book. He looks at it momentarily, then puts it on top of the pile he is carrying. It falls to the floor. He stoops to pick it up — hesitates — leaves it. He goes upstairs. As* OWEN *ascends,* HUGH *and* JIMMY JACK *enter. Both wet and*

486

> *drunk.* JIMMY *is very unsteady. He is trotting behind*
> HUGH, *trying to break in on* HUGH'*s declamation.*
> HUGH *is equally drunk but more experienced in*
> *drunkenness: there is a portion of his mind which*
> *retains its clarity.*

HUGH There I was, appropriately dispositioned to proffer
my condolences to the bereaved mother . . .

JIMMY Hugh —

HUGH . . . and about to enter the *domus lugubris* — Maire
Chatach?

JIMMY The wake house.

HUGH Indeed — when I experience a plucking at my elbow:
Mister George Alexander, Justice of the Peace. 'My
tidings are infelicitous,' said he — Bridget? Too slow.
Doalty?

JIMMY *Infelix* — unhappy.

HUGH Unhappy indeed. 'Master Bartley Timlin has been
appointed to the new national school.' 'Timlin? Who
is Timlin?' 'A schoolmaster from Cork. And he will be
a major asset to the community. He is also a very
skilled bacon curer!'

JIMMY Hugh —

HUGH Ha-ha-ha-ha-ha! The Cork bacon curer! *Barbarus hic
ego sum quia non intelligor ulli* — James?

JIMMY Ovid.

HUGH *Procede.*

JIMMY 'I am a barbarian in this place because I am not
understood by anyone.'

HUGH Indeed — (*Shouts*) Manus! Tea! I will compose a satire
on Master Bartley Timlin, schoolmaster and bacon
curer. But it will be too easy, won't it? (*Shouts*) Strong
tea! Black!

> *The only way* JIMMY *can get* HUGH'*s attention is by*
> *standing in front of him and holding his arms.*

JIMMY Will you listen to me, Hugh!

HUGH James. (*Shouts*) And a slice of soda bread.

JIMMY I'm going to get married.
HUGH Well!
JIMMY At Christmas.
HUGH Splendid.
JIMMY To Athene.
HUGH Who?
JIMMY Pallas Athene.
HUGH *Glaukopis Athene?*
JIMMY Flashing-eyed, Hugh, flashing-eyed!

> *He attempts the gesture he has made before: standing
> to attention, the momentary spasm, the salute, the
> face raised in pained ecstasy — but the body does not
> respond efficiently this time. The gesture is grotesque.*

HUGH The lady has assented?
JIMMY She asked *me* — I assented.
HUGH Ah. When was this?
JIMMY Last night.
HUGH What does her mother say?
JIMMY Metis from Hellespont? Decent people — good stock.
HUGH And her father?
JIMMY I'm meeting Zeus tomorrow. Hugh, will you be my best man?
HUGH Honoured, James; profoundly honoured.
JIMMY You know what I'm looking for, Hugh, don't you? I mean to say — you know — I — I — I joke like the rest of them — you know? — (*Again he attempts the pathetic routine but abandons it instantly*) You know yourself, Hugh — don't you? — you know all that. But what I'm really looking for, Hugh — what I really want — companionship, Hugh — at my time of life, companionship, company, someone to talk to. Away up in Beann na Gaoithe — you've no idea how lonely it is. Companionship — correct, Hugh? Correct?
HUGH Correct.
JIMMY And I always liked her, Hugh. Correct?
HUGH Correct, James.
JIMMY Someone to talk to.

HUGH Indeed.

JIMMY That's all, Hugh. The whole story. You know it all now, Hugh. You know it all.

As JIMMY *says those last lines he is crying, shaking his head, trying to keep his balance, and holding a finger up to his lips in absurd gestures of secrecy and intimacy. Now he staggers away, tries to sit on a stool, misses it, slides to the floor, his feet in front of him, his back against the broken cart. Almost at once he is asleep.* HUGH *watches all of this. Then he produces his flask and is about to pour a drink when he sees the Name Book on the floor. He picks it up and leafs through it, pronouncing the strange names as he does. Just as he begins* OWEN *emerges and descends with two bowls of tea.*

HUGH Ballybeg. Burnfoot. King's Head. Whiteplains. Fair Hill. Dunboy. Green Bank.

OWEN *snatches the book from* HUGH.

OWEN I'll take that. (*In apology*) It's only a catalogue of names.

HUGH I know what it is.

OWEN A mistake — my mistake — nothing to do with us. I hope that's strong enough (*tea*).

He throws the book on the table and crosses over to JIMMY.

Jimmy. Wake up, Jimmy. Wake up, man.

JIMMY What — what-what?

OWEN Here. Drink this. Then go on away home. There may be trouble. Do you hear me, Jimmy? There may be trouble.

HUGH (*Indicating Name Book*) We must learn those new names.

OWEN (*Searching around*) Did you see a sack lying about?

HUGH We must learn where we live. We must learn to make them our own. We must make them our new home.

OWEN *finds a sack and throws it across his shoulders.*

OWEN   I know where I live.

HUGH   James thinks he knows, too. I look at James and three thoughts occur to me: A — that it is not the literal past, the 'facts' of history, that shape us, but images of the past embodied in language. James has ceased to make that discrimination.

OWEN   Don't lecture me, Father.

HUGH   B — we must never cease renewing those images; because once we do, we fossilize. Is there no soda bread?

OWEN   And C, Father — one single, unalterable 'fact': if Yolland is not found, we are all going to be evicted. Lancey has issued the order.

HUGH   Ah. *Edictum imperatoris.*

OWEN   You should change out of those wet clothes. I've got to go. I've got to see Doalty Dan Doalty.

HUGH   What about?

OWEN   I'll be back soon.

As OWEN *exits:*

HUGH   Take care, Owen. To remember everything is a form of madness.

He looks around the room, carefully, as if he were about to leave it forever. Then he looks at JIMMY, *asleep again.*

The road to Sligo. A spring morning. 1798. Going into battle. Do you remember, James? Two young gallants with pikes across their shoulders and the *Aeneid* in their pockets. Everything seemed to find definition that spring — a congruence, a miraculous matching of hope and past and present and possibility. Striding across the fresh, green land. The rhythms of perception heightened. The whole enterprise of consciousness accelerated. We were gods that morning, James; and I had recently married *my* goddess, Caitlin Dubh Nic

Reactainn, may she rest in peace. And to leave her and my infant son in his cradle — that was heroic, too. By God, sir, we were magnificent. We marched as far as — where was it? — Glenties! All of twenty-three miles in one day. And it was there, in Phelan's pub, that we got homesick for Athens, just like Ulysses. The *desiderium nostrorum* — the need for our own. Our *pietas*, James, was for older, quieter things. And that was the longest twenty-three miles back I ever made. (*Toasts* JIMMY) My friend, confusion is not an ignoble condition.

MAIRE *enters.*

MAIRE I'm back again. I set out for somewhere but I couldn't remember where. So I came back here.
HUGH Yes, I will teach you English, Maire Chatach.
MAIRE Will you, Master? I must learn it. I need to learn it.
HUGH Indeed you may well be my only pupil.

He goes towards the steps and begins to ascend.

MAIRE When can we start?
HUGH Not today. Tomorrow, perhaps. After the funeral. We'll begin tomorrow. (*Ascending*) But don't expect too much. I will provide you with the available words and the available grammar. But will that help you to interpret between privacies? I have no idea. But it's all we have. I have no idea at all. (*He is now at the top*)
MAIRE Master, what does the English word 'always' mean?
HUGH *Semper — per omnia saecula.* The Greeks called it 'aei'. It's not a word I'd start with. It's a silly word, girl.

He sits. JIMMY *is awake. He gets to his feet.* MAIRE *sees the Name Book, picks it up, and sits with it on her knee.*

MAIRE When he comes back this is where he'll come to. He told me this is where he was happiest.

JIMMY *sits beside* MAIRE.

JIMMY   Do you know the Greek word *endogamein*? It means to marry within the tribe. And the word *exogamein* means to marry outside the tribe. And you don't cross those borders casually — both sides get very angry. Now, the problem is this: is Athene sufficiently mortal or am I sufficiently godlike for the marriage to be acceptable to her people and to my people? You think about that.

HUGH   *Urbs antiqua fuit* — there was an ancient city which, 'tis said, Juno loved above all the lands. And it was the goddess's aim and cherished hope that here should be the capital of all nations — should the fates perchance allow that. Yet in truth she discovered that a race was springing from Trojan blood to overthrow some day these Tyrian towers — a people *late regem belloque superbum* — kings of broad realms and proud in war who would come forth for Lybia's downfall — such was — such was the course — such was the course ordained — ordained by fate . . . What the hell's wrong with me? Sure I know it backwards. I'll begin again. *Urbs antiqua fuit* — there was an ancient city which, 'tis said, Juno loved above all the lands.

  Begin to bring down the lights.

And it was the goddess's aim and cherished hope that here should be the capital of all nations — should the fates perchance allow that. Yet in truth she discovered that a race was springing from Trojan blood to overthrow some day these Tyrian towers — a people kings of broad realms and proud in war who would come forth for Lybia's downfall . . .

  Black.

Greek and Latin Used in the Text

page 418 τὸν δ' ἠμείβετ' ἔπειτα θεὰ γλαυκῶπις Ἀθήνη (Homer,
Odyssey, XIII, 420): (Lit.) 'But the grey-eyed goddess
Athene then replied to him'
ἀλλὰ ἔκηλος / ἧσται ἐν Ἀτρεΐδαο δόμοις (Odyssey,
XIII, 423-4): (Lit.) 'but he sits at ease in the halls of the
Sons of Athens'

419 ὡς ἄρα μιν φαμένη ῥάβδῳ ἐπεμάσσατ' Ἀθήνη (Odyssey,
XIII, 429): (Lit.) 'As she spoke Athene touched him with
her wand'

420 κνύζωσεν δέ οἱ ὄσσε (Odyssey, XIII, 433): (Lit.) 'She
dimmed his eyes'

420/488 γλαυκῶπις Ἀθήνη (Odyssey, XIII, 329): (Lit.) flashing-
eyed Athene

422 αὐτὰρ ὁ ἐκ λιμένος προσέβη (Odyssey, XIV, 1): (Lit.)
'But he went forth from the harbour'
ὅ οἱ βιότοιο μάλιστα (Odyssey, XIV, 3): (Lit.) 'he cared
very much for his substance'

423 Esne fatigata?: Are you tired?
Sum fatigatissima: I am very tired
Bene! Optime!: Good! Excellent!

425 Ignari, stulti, rustici: Ignoramuses, fools, peasants

426 Responde — responde!: Answer — answer!
θέος: a god
θεὰ: a goddess

428 Nigra fere et presso pinguis sub vomere terra: Land that
is black and rich beneath the pressure of the plough
cui putre: crumbly soil

433 Adsum: I am present
sobrietate perfecta: with complete sobriety

434 sobrius: sober
Ave: hail
caerimonia nominationis: ceremony of naming
βχπτίζειν: to dip or immerse
baptisterium: a cold bath, swimming-pool

435 Gratias tibi ago: I thank you
studia: studies
Perambulare: to walk through

494

435 *Verecundus*: shame-faced, modest

436 *Conjugo*: I join together
acquiescere: to rest, to find comfort in
Procede: proceed

437 *Silentium!* : Silence!
divertere: to turn away
ἄπληστος πίθος: unfillable cask

438 *Jacobe, quid agis?*: James, how are you?

442 *Festinate!*: Hurry!

443 *Gaudeo vos hic adesse*: Welcome
Nonne Latine loquitur?: Does he not speak Latin?

445 *opus honestum!*: an honourable task

456 *Quantumvis cursum longum fessumque moratur
Sol, sacro tandem carmine vesper adest*:
No matter how long the sun delays on his long weary
course
At length evening comes with its sacred song
expeditio: an expedition

469 *Tu es centurio in exercitu Britannico*: You are a centurion
in the British Army
et es in castris quae sunt in agro: And you are in the
camp in the field

478 *Ignari! Stulti! Rustici!* Ignoramuses! Fools! Peasants!

487 *domus lugubris*: house of mourning
Infelix: unlucky, unhappy
Barbarus hic ego sum quia non intelligor ulli: I am a bar-
barian here because I am not understood by anyone
Procede: proceed

490 *Edictum imperatoris*: the decree of the commander

491 *desiderium nostrorum*: longing / need for our things /
people
pietas: piety
Semper — per omnia saecula: Always — for all time
ἀεί: always

492 ἐνδογαμεῖν to marry within the tribe
ἐξογαμεῖν: to marry outside the tribe
Urbs antiqua fuit: There was an ancient city
late regem belloque superbum: kings of broad realms and
proud in war

Acknowledgements

The editor thanks Jean Fallon and Suella Holland for their invaluable contributions to the preparation of this edition. Acknowledgements are also due to Anne Friel and family, Leah Schmidt and Dinah Wood.

The Freedom of the City was published first by Faber and Faber Limited in 1974 and published by The Gallery Press in 1992.

Volunteers was published first by Faber and Faber Limited in 1979 and published by The Gallery Press in 1989.

Living Quarters was published first by Faber and Faber Limited in 1978 and published by The Gallery Press in 1992.

Faith Healer was published first by Faber and Faber Limited in 1980 and published by The Gallery Press in 1991.

Aristocrats was published first by The Gallery Press in 1980.

Translations was published first by Faber and Faber Limited in 1981.

The Freedom of the City: Quotations from 'Lily of Laguna', 'The Man who Broke the Bank at Monte Carlo' and 'Where Did You Get That Hat?', reproduced by permission of Francis Day and Hunter Ltd.

Faith Healer: 'The Way You Look Tonight' from the film *Swingtime* with music by Jerome Kern, words by Dorothy Fields © 1936, T B Harms Co, British publishers Chappell Music Ltd is reproduced by kind permission.

Aristocrats: Quotations from the poem entitled 'My Father, Dying' by Alastair Reid from his book *Weathering* (Canongate, Edinburgh) used by kind permission of the author.

The song 'Sweet Alice' was written by J Kneass, © 1933, Amsco Music Sales Co, NYC. All rights reserved.

Collected Plays

Volume One
The Enemy Within · *Philadelphia, Here I Come!* ·
The Loves of Cass McGuire · *Lovers: Winners* and *Losers* ·
Crystal and Fox · *The Gentle Island*

Volume Two
The Freedom of the City · *Volunteers* · *Living Quarters* ·
Aristocrats · *Faith Healer* · *Translations*

Volume Three
Three Sisters (after Chekhov) · *The Communication Cord* ·
Fathers and Sons (after Turgenev) · *Making History* ·
Dancing at Lughnasa

Volume Four
The London Vertigo (after Macklin) · *A Month in the Country*
(after Turgenev) · *Wonderful Tennessee* · *Molly Sweeney* ·
Give Me Your Answer, Do!

Volume Five
Uncle Vanya (after Chekhov) · *The Yalta Game* (after Chekhov) ·
The Bear (after Chekhov) · *Afterplay* · *Performances* ·
The Home Place · *Hedda Gabler* (after Ibsen)